The Counties of
BRITAIN

A Tudor Atlas by John Speed

A BRITAINE

A ROMANE

A SAXON

BRITANNIA

A DANE

A NORMAN

THEATRUM
IMPERII MAGNÆ
BRITANNIÆ;

Exactam Regnorum Angliæ,
Scotiæ, Hiberniæ et Insularum
adiacentium Geographiã ob oculos ponens:

una cum

Comitatibus, Centurijs, Urbibus et pri-
marijs Comitatũm oppidis, intra Regnum
Angliæ, divisis et descriptis.

OPUS,

Nuper quidem à IOHANNE SPEDO
cive Londinensi, Anglicè conscriptum:
Nunc verò,
à PHILEMONE HOLLANDO, apud
Coventrianos Medicinæ Doctore,
Latinitate donatum.

IMPRINTED AT LONDON

Excusum apud
Ioann. Sudbury

a Georg. Humble

Anno
Cum Privilegio
1616

And are to be solde by Iohn Sudbury & Georg
Humble, in Popes-head alley at ý signe of ý white Horse.

The Counties of
BRITAIN
A Tudor Atlas by John Speed

Introduction by Nigel Nicolson

County Commentaries by Alasdair Hawkyard

Published in association with The British Library

PAVILION

First published in Great Britain in 1988 by
PAVILION BOOKS LIMITED
196 Shaftesbury Avenue, London WC2H 8JL

Designed by Tom Sawyer

A CIP catalogue record for this book is available
from the British Library

ISBN 1-85145-131-5

Typeset in Garamond Original by Tradespools Limited, Frome
Colour orgination by Adroit PhotoLitho Limited, Birmingham
Printed and bound in West Germany by Mohndruck, Gütersloh

3   5   7   9   10   8   6   4

PUBLISHERS' NOTE

The author and publishers wish to thank Dave Way
of The British Library, Tony Campbell and the staff
of The British Library's Map Library, and the staff of
the Institute of Historical Research, University of
London for their generous help in the making of this
book. Photography was carried out by Andrew Ogilvie,
of the British Library's photographic section.

Maps: The maps reproduced here have been
photographed from the 1616 Latin Edition of John
Speed's *Theatrum Imperii Magnae Britanniae* (*Theatre
of the Empire of Great Britain*), published in London
by John Sudbury and George Humble as the Latin text
edition of the work which had first appeared in 1611–12.
British Library press-mark is Maps C.7.c.20. The
original maps measure on average 15 × 20 inches
(38 × 51 cm) and run in geographical sequence; in this
book the sequence is alphabetical.

Text: Quotations from John Speed are taken from the
original English edition of his commentary printed
on the reverse of each map. Spellings and book titles
have been modernized and New Style dates adopted
throughout.

Contents

Romane Emprours · Heathē Britaines · Chrishā Britaines · Kentish Saxons · Heathē west Saxons · Chrishā west Saxons · First Saxon Monarks

South Saxons

East Saxons

East Angles

Mercian Kings

Northumberland

Later Saxon Monarks

Norman Kings

Andegavion Kings

Kings of France

Kings of Scotland

HONI SOIT QVI MALY PENSE

DIEV ET MON DROIT

THE ACHIEVEMENT OF
OUR SOVERAIGNE KING IAMES
AS HE NOWE BEARETH
With the ARMES of the Severall kings
that have aunciently raigned within
his nowe Dominions

Jodocus Hondius Flander celavit
Anno Domini 1614

Danish Kings · King of Man · Cornish Kings · First Kings of Wales · Later Kings of Wales · Welsh Princes · Kings of Ireland

Introduction
by Nigel Nicolson

L ook at any of Speed's maps in this volume—say Middlesex, one of the smallest counties in England but in a sense its bull's-eye—and notice how carefully he squared it off with pieces of the neighbouring counties and filled in the margins with text and illustrations to widen his display, since every double-page in an atlas must be uniform in size. There are separate plans of London and Westminster, drawings of old St Paul's and of Westminster Abbey (which he calls St Peter's), and on two open books he annotates them with historical information of doubtful veracity. At the foot a small label credits the map to John Norden 'augmented by I Speed', and adds the information that the map could be bought in George Humble's shop near the Exchange. In the bottom left-hand corner appear the words '*Jodocus Hondius celavit*', acknowledging the master-craftsman who engraved the sheet in Amsterdam. The map is not dated, but it is copied from Norden's of 1593.

Already 'Middlesex' tells us a great deal about Speed's methods and purpose. He wished to produce a map which was descriptive, useful, and a pleasure to look at. It could be a traveller's guide, or used for administrative purposes in an office—the boundaries of the hundreds, the units of local government, deer-parks and estates, are all carefully marked—or it could be kept in a private library, where it was a way of travelling in imagination without expense or fatigue. To enhance the pictorial effect, the lettering is elaborate and varied, items like the scale-bar are embellished, and in an empty corner of Surrey, Speed has included a medallion supported by two exotic birds.

As for the body of the map, Speed makes little claim to originality for his Middlesex. He has taken his topographical information from Norden's earlier map, and amended it by personal enquiry and observation. His rivers are emphatically designated, but he shows few bridges and no roads. Relief is indicated by scattered mole-hills that give only a general idea of where the country begins to roll and swell. The towns are marked by groups of buildings, the villages by symbols, the woods by little trees. In short, it is a serviceable map showing the location of all inhabited places and their relative importance, and how they are distributed between the chief features of any stretch of countryside, its rivers, forests and hills. In a study or on the ground anyone could have discovered from a Speed map the essential facts about a tract of thickly settled land. For us it has an additional value that he could hardly have foreseen: it is an historical document that clearly presents us with a picture of

Elizabethan and Jacobean Britain that could be conveyed in no other way.

England then presented a panorama of exceptional loveliness. In 1613 the Venetian Ambassador Foscarini wrote of his journey north to Scotland:

> I have seen a country of great beauty and fertility and very populous. Four things in particular have struck me as being specially worthy of notice. First, that in the 420 miles that I have traversed in my journey from London to the frontiers of this realm, I have not seen a single palm of unfertile land. Second, that every 8 or 10 miles I have found a city or at least a town comparable to the good ones of Italy. Third, a number of navigable rivers including the Thames, the Trent and the Severn, which in their long courses to the sea widen a mile or more. Fourthly, I might have said first, a quantity of most beautiful churches so numerous as to pass belief. The kingdom is most rich in the fertility of the soil and by its extensive commerce with all parts of the world.

The habitations of the urban and rural poor were mean and squalid, and the countryside was littered with the ruins of monasteries which only a few men like William Camden and Speed himself yet regarded as interesting monuments. Castles, although often neglected as fortifications remained in use as homes until being systematically slighted in the Civil War. For all that, England's was a smiling landscape, fecundly rural, busily urban, and the surprise of Foscarini's tribute is that he made no mention of the splendid country-houses that newly adorned the land. The pattern of the open countryside would not have surprised us, apart from more extensive woodland and tracts of open fields, particularly in Dorset and in the North, which had still not been enclosed. Villages had been regularly deserted for two centuries before the Tudors, but by 1600 the pattern of settlement had ceased to alter significantly, and comparing a Speed map with the modern Ordnance Survey of the same area, it is rare to find a village added or abandoned, though a few larger towns like Bournemouth and Tunbridge Wells did not then exist. Speed, of course, cannot show us on his small-scale maps the nature of the country between the settlements, and we have to turn to contemporary plans, like those of the Buckhurst estates on the borders of Kent and Sussex in 1595, to see that the very shapes of the woods and fields have remained remarkably unchanged. He does, however, show us how a population of little more than four million made use of the whole country, mostly in nucleated villages as densely scattered in Northumberland as in Dorset. Contemporaries believed that the land was full to bursting and could not sustain a further increase in population.

The towns were already straggling in ribbon development beyond their medieval walls. London had a population of 200,000, ten times larger than that of any other city, and Norwich, York, Bristol, Exeter, Manchester, Liverpool and Newcastle were already important towns. But England was essentially rural. The fast-growing textile industries of the Cotswolds and the

West Riding, the mining of coal and iron, were still village-based, and the towns were mainly convenient centres for administration, crafts and marketing. Apart from the capital, there were no conurbations. Speed's plotting of Tyneside is a good illustration of the clear separation of town from countryside.

It is surprising that he does not show the main roads, for which he had ample space and many precedents in maps like Symonson's of Kent (1596), and even the famous Gough map of 1360. Did he omit them because they would have snaked unpleasingly across his neat designs? Because their inclusion would have added intolerably to his labours where he had no surveys to copy? Because he thought the information needless when the routes from place to place were self-evident and local guides plentiful? Or because he expected the main users of his maps to be administrators like Pepys, who as late as 1662 turned to Speed's map of the Forest of Dean when looking for new sources of timber for the Navy, 'and there showed me how it lies'?

The road system was in fact well developed. The lanes wound like vermicelli to every part of England. Though carriages were rare, carts were universal, and heavy loads of minerals and building materials were transported great distances as much by land as by water. Nor were the unmetalled roads, except when crossing bog or clay-lands, in as poor a condition as travellers' tales might suggest (then, as now, they exaggerated their hardships), and the medieval bridges were frequent and sturdy enough to make an Elizabethan or Stuart bridge a rarity. Travellers on horseback could reach Chester, Exeter or York from London within four days, an achievement barely equalled when in 1637 scheduled coach services were introduced. The rivers, to which Speed gives much prominence, were highways too. In his day the Thames was navigable by barges as far as Reading, the Severn to Shrewsbury, the Trent beyond Nottingham, and there were constant protests when traffic was impeded by mills and fish-weirs. Equally important for trade and communications was the extensive shipping that plied the coasts of the British Isles.

Travel for recreation was in its infancy, but spas like Bath, Leamington, Buxton and Matlock had become fashionable during Elizabeth's reign, and the owners of distant estates no longer felt themselves confined to them. This is one reason why from the mid-sixteenth century onwards a proper survey of Britain was in urgent demand. Wales, Scotland and Ireland could no longer be left *terra incognita*: geography must be made articulate. Also, as control over the regions was regularized, the Crown became more powerful, and private landowners were now managing the old monastic estates, there was an increasing need for careful cartography and a key to the boundaries of the hundreds. Military and naval tacticians were no longer satisfied with sketches of the main garrison-towns and ports. They must be shown in relation to each other. A commander in the Wars of the Roses had little more to guide him cross-country than Harold in finding his way to Senlac, and before printing was invented, every copy of a rough sketch-map was made by hand. Now they were easily duplicated. But there was a more fundamental reason for the surging interest in cartography. England under the Tudors had become acutely aware of its past and its destiny. A note of national pride permeates Speed's maps. A country so rich in visible reminders of its history, with so promising a future, must proclaim its inheritance and the lavish distribution of its people.

John Speed considered himself primarily an historian. His maps were produced as supplements to his *History of Great Britain* from Julius Caesar to James I. His *History* was a work of modest originality, replete with errors copied from John Barkham and Camden's *Britannia*, but to him it was his *chef-d'oeuvre*, not his atlas. Later generations have reversed this priority.

We know as little about his personal life as we do of Shakespeare's. He was born about 1552 in Cheshire, the son of a tailor who brought him up to the same trade, and in 1582 we find him in London, at Moorfields, where he built a house and married. He became a Freeman of the Merchant Taylors Company, like his father, and devoted his leisure to map-making. In 1598 he gained a patron in Sir Fulke Greville, first Lord Brooke, the poet and statesman, who recognized his cartographic skill, relieved him from tailoring, found him a post in the Customs, and with Queen Elizabeth's support subsidized his map-making, giving him 'full liberty thus to express the inclination of my mind', as Speed recorded his gratitude. Thereafter he devoted himself to history and cartography, but mainly history. He became a member of the Society of Antiquaries, where he met scholars like William Camden, Robert Cotton and William Smith who helped him with his researches, and he drew for local knowledge on antiquarians like William Lambarde for Kent, Richard Carew for Cornwall and George Owen for Pembrokeshire. Later in life he turned to genealogy and religious history, publishing several books with forbidding titles like *Genealogies Recorded in Sacred Scripture* (1611) and *A Cloud of Witnesses* (1616), a work of theology. He died in London in 1629, aged about 77, leaving twelve sons and six daughters.

The portrait of him reproduced in this book is proof of his alert intelligence. He was an ambitious, energetic man, no great scholar, more a compiler who drew together, both in his histories and his maps, the researches and surveys of others. 'Plagiarist' would be too belittling and offensive a term to apply to him, for he added valuable commentaries to his histories, and innovations to his maps, and every creative work is in part a plagiarism of one's predecessors, particularly in history and cartography.

In his youth Speed was credited with 'a very rare and ingenious capacity in drawing and setting forth of maps'. To what extent is this tribute justified? We have very few of his early efforts which first attracted Fulke Greville's interest, and can judge only by his famous atlas. He compiled his maps individually between 1596 and 1610, and published them in a single bound volume divided into four Books under the title *The Theatre of the Empire of Great Britain*. Although bearing the date 1611 on its main title-page, Speed's *Theatre* could not have been published until the following year, since the subsidiary titles for Scotland and Ireland are dated 1612. The word 'Theatre'

IOH. SPEED.

was taken from Abraham Ortelius's *Theatre Orbis Terrarum* (Antwerp, 1570), of which the English edition, *The Theatre of the World*, was published in 1606; and 'Empire' was a long established term, made popular by John Dee, the astrologer and mathematician, in *The British Empire* (1575), before Britain had any empire outside its own islands and not even Scotland within them.

Speed's *Theatre* or atlas consisted in nine pages of preliminary matter, including a decorative title-page and an Address to the Reader, 67 engraved maps of England, Scotland, Wales and Ireland, and an index. There were three general maps: one of the British Isles as a group, one of England and Wales alone, and another of Anglo-Saxon Britain. Then followed 44 maps of the

11

English counties and islands, a map of Wales and thirteen of its individual counties, a single map of Scotland, and a map of Ireland, with four more of its separate provinces.

On the back of each map he printed a page of topographical, administrative and historical comment (not reproduced in this edition), summarizing the main monuments of the county and its chief assets, its climate, agricultural merits and its towns, making the most of all favourable fact, as if drawing up the prospectus for an American colony. For example, in writing of Dorset's small estuaries, he says, 'Vessels of burden [here] discharge their rich treasures, and herself with open hand distributeth her gifts all along the south of this shore'; of the Cambridge colleges, 'For building, beauty, endowments and store of students so replenished that unless it be her other sister Oxford, the like are not found in all Europe'; and of Warwickshire, 'The husbandman smileth in beholding his pains, and the meadowing pastures with their green mantles so embroidered with flowers that from Edgehill we might behold another Eden'. Further praise is lavished on the towns. His plan of Bristol, for example, is annotated, 'There is no dunghill in all the City nor any sink that cometh from any house into the streets but all is conveyed underground'; and Dublin, which he perhaps visited, is described as 'the royal seat of Ireland, strong in her munitions, beautiful in her buildings'. He could be critical, too, for instance of Henry VIII, 'whose hand lay with such weight upon the fair buildings [of the abbeys] that he crushed the juice thereof into his own coffers', and in writing of ecclesiastical power in Durham, he adds the stinging remark, 'the bishops . . . have had the royalties of princes'. But his main purpose was to celebrate: his *Theatre* was a stage on which the glory of Britain's past and present could be re-enacted. No period was too remote for him. Stonehenge ('erected by Aurelius, King of the Britons, in 475 AD') and the Picts' Wall (Hadrian's) are given respectful prominence, and he is keen on battles, illustrating them with armies *en bloc* like phalanxes, with champions in single combat outside. He can hazard the amazing guess that 67,974 men were killed at Hastings, when the total number actually engaged was about 5,000 on each side, and in the sea off Caernarfonshire he depicts a wholly imaginary fight between three ships. Like Herodotus, he was captivated by marvels, but his history, which is written in a racy style, is a considerable feat of compilation and research.

His maps are records of ascertained fact, though they contain several errors. They are county maps, a system which British cartographers originated because the shire was the local unit of government, and to which they clung until the Ordnance Survey straddled county boundaries early in the nineteenth century. Speed took as his models existing maps. Five he credited to Christopher Saxton (Norfolk, Hertfordshire, Worcestershire, Radnorshire and Montgomeryshire), five to John Norden (Sussex, Surrey, Cornwall, Middlesex and Essex), two to William Smith (Cheshire and Lancashire) and Kent to Philip Symonson. Rutland he took from John Harington, the Isle of Wight from William White, the Isle of Man from Thomas Durham, and Holy Island from James Burrell.

His maps of Wales were based on Saxton's which in turn owed much to Humphrey Lhuyd, the Welsh antiquary, who contributed a good map of Wales to Ortelius's atlas. Speed's map of Scotland was closely derived from Gerardus Mercator's two sheets of 1595, and although he again labels this map 'Performed by I Speed', it is fairly obvious from the distortion of Skye and other islands that he had never been there. Ireland is a different matter. Saxton had omitted it entirely, and it was Speed who produced the first detailed maps of the provinces, basing his survey on the pioneering work of Robert Lythe and Francis Jobson, who had mapped different parts of the island for military and civic purposes late in the sixteenth century. However, his general map of Ireland suffers from the distortion of the west coast, which Speed, like his predecessors, considered to run almost due north and south.

For the majority of his maps he did not bother to acknowledge his sources, because there was no law of copyright, or because he considered that he had 'augmented' them sufficiently to claim his work as original. In his Address to the Reader he admits, 'I have put my sickle into other men's corn', but excuses himself by 'my many additions, and dimensions of the Shire-towns and Cities', and by 'mine own travels through every province of England', and, one must add to his credit, of Wales and perhaps of Ireland too. This leaves in doubt how much he actually originated. Probably not much. His Somerset, for example, is almost an exact copy of Saxton's, though unacknowledged. But as an indication of the care he took in revising and checking Saxton's original, he named a village in Wiltshire, North Burcombe, as 'Quaere' (Query), intending, according to David Smith in his *Antique Maps of the British Isles*, to check the name later, forgot, and it was engraved as Quaere in successive issues of the map until corrected 145 years later. One finds the spelling of some names altered from Saxton's and Norden's versions, a village added here and there, and the hundred boundaries inserted, which he obtained from Parliamentary Rolls, but it does not amount to much more than a careful revision. R. A. Skelton, our foremost authority on Speed, concluded: 'Little of his cartographic work on the county maps seems to have been original; the phrase "Performed by John Speed", which occurs on most of the maps not explicitly ascribed to any cartographer, may be taken to mean that he copied, adapted or compiled from the work of others.'

It is therefore relevant to examine the contribution to the *Theatre* of his great predecessor, Christopher Saxton, who is thought to have died about two years before its publication. Saxton's achievement was extraordinary. In 1579 he published an atlas of 34 county maps and one general map of England and Wales which was unprecedented in its astonishing accuracy. It contains only one major error—the Land's End peninsula points west instead of south-west—and minor misplacings, for instance of some coastal villages in Norfolk which are shown slightly inland. For seven years (1573–9) he travelled the country, completing his original survey of Wales in little more than two. He had Government backing, and carried an official letter authorizing him to call on mayors and justices of the peace to conduct him 'unto any tower, castle, high place or hill to view that country', and in detail he was guided by men who could tell him the names of towns and villages, especially in Wales where language added another impediment.

How did he achieve such accuracy in so short a time? Nobody knows. Perhaps he employed a primitive form of triangulation, using plane-table and compass and measuring distances by eye, and where they existed he drew on earlier maps. As he completed each sheet, he had it engraved in London, mostly by Flemish refugees, and combined them into his atlas when he had finished. All his maps were of uniform size, but not to uniform scale. Some counties he combined on one sheet, like Kent-Sussex-Surrey-Middlesex and Oxfordshire-Buckinghamshire-Berkshire, and to Yorkshire alone, his own county and the largest, he devoted a larger fold-out map. He omitted the islands (Wight, Man and the Channel Islands), and there was no map of Scotland or Ireland. On only five maps did he show the division into hundreds.

Saxton's maps were not only accurate, but beautiful works of art. Ships and dolphins patrol the seas, cartouches and coats-of-arms (always including those of Queen Elizabeth and his immediate patron, Thomas Seckford) ornament the borders, and where he had room, he had the county names engraved in lovely

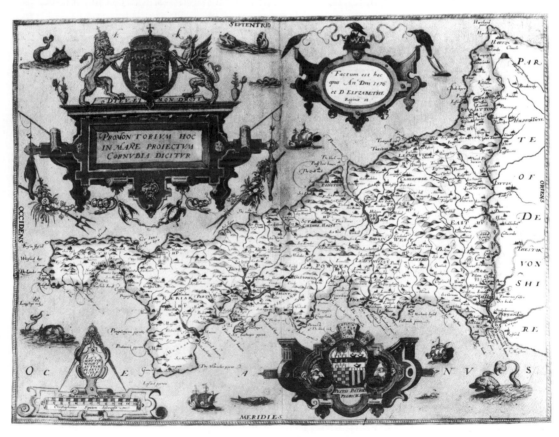

Map of Cornwall by Christopher Saxton, 1579

swash-calligraphy, minisculed to the easily legible names of smaller places.

There is no doubt that Speed drew upon Saxton for his style as well as his information. But wishing with justifiable pride to make his atlas distinctive, he separated Saxton's joined counties, devoting a page to each, included Scotland, Ireland and the offshore islands, and added many more coats-of-arms, the architectural drawings, and, above all, the town-plans. His drawings were not of his own design. He had them copied from originals owned, or published, by Camden, Cotton and others. His Windsor Castle, for example, is taken direct from Hogenberg (1572). But they look as if they had been redrawn by a single hand, probably not Speed's, and then engraved. Some of them, of famous buildings which have been demolished, like Richmond and Nonsuch Palaces in Surrey, are of great historical interest. The rich heraldry he owed mainly to William Smith, incorporating it for decorative effect (the most striking examples are his twenty-four shields of Cambridge), and to flatter the noblemen whom he hoped to attract as customers. He inserted figures too, either allegorical to support his swags and cartouches, like the putti each side of his Orkneys, or representational, like A Roman, A Saxon, A Dane, A Norman, A Briton, on his title-page, the scholars on his map of Cambridgeshire, and the six figures in national costume on his Ireland. In other places he depicted coins and medallions to demonstrate his patriotism and concern for antiquity, like the seven monarchs on his Lancashire. His cartouches demonstrate the exuberance typical of his age. The whole country, in fact, appeared to him an unending pageant.

His town-plans are in most cases the first information we have of their early appearance, and are counted by Skelton as Speed's most important contribution to British topography. There had been a few Tudor town-views, like William Cuningham's of Norwich (1558) and Richard Lyne's of Cambridge (1574), and the five-volume *Civitates Orbis Terrarum* by George Braun and Frans Hogenberg (Cologne, 1572) included bird's-eye views of eleven British cities. Speed did not hesitate to redraw, without acknowledgement, his Bristol and Norwich plans from William Smith (1588), took Westminster and London from Norden's Middlesex, and Chichester from his Sussex. He obtained his views of Carlisle and Berwick from the Cotton MSS, and Newcastle from William Mathew.

But fifty of his seventy-three towns he mapped for the first time. Although he claims specifically as his own surveys only Pembroke, St David's and Caernarfon, they all follow a uniform style, and Skelton thought it probable that he drew them himself. They can best be described as 'map-views', a combination of ground-plan with bird's-eye perspective, showing the buildings in elevation, but the street pattern is clarified by widening them disproportionately. The smaller houses are drawn conventionally like rows of bathing huts, but the grander buildings, like Durham's castle and cathedral, are given such full treatment that the plans become virtual perspectives. No people or vehicles appear in the streets, but in the surrounding country we see men in boats or busy in the fields, in addition to crosses, wind and water mills, maypoles, stocks and even gallows. It is not certain how Speed obtained his information. Skelton believed that after consulting the leading men of a town, he first drew a perspective from an eminence and then measured distances to key points by pacing (as he indicates on his scales), afterwards transforming his sketches into a plan seen from immediately above. His York and Salisbury, for example, are so accurate that they can only be the result of a careful survey. The views set out deliberately to charm. They represent the towns and cities as havens of peace and industry, neat and speckless, freed from the confinement of ancient walls, and illustrate once again his 'zeal of my country's glory', for among the chief manifestations of that glory was the rapid expansion of civic pride.

Like his predecessors, Speed made use of conventional symbols. A town was marked by a cluster of buildings, a village by a church tower, all deliberately out of scale. Woods and parks were indicated by little trees, spaced haphazardly, and he followed Saxton in ringing deer-parks with miniature palings to suggest their importance and flatter his noble customers. The sea was distinguished from the land by hatchering, a variant on Saxton's stippling, or by picturing cliffs in semi-elevation, and to emphasize the friendliness of one and the dangers of the other, he furnished the sea with monsters and shipwrecks, as well as ships in full sail, updating their rigging from Saxton's. For the open water he adopted the Flemish innovation of moiré or watered-silk patterning.

His greatest problem, not satisfactorily solved until the invention of contour-lines by the Dutch chart-maker Cruquius in 1730 (but then only for water-depths in estuaries), was how to indicate relief. The medieval convention, adopted by both Saxton and Speed, was to scatter 'mole-hills', shaded on the east side, to represent high ground. They stand sometimes singly but more often in stylized chains of overlapping sugar-loafs, and rise directly from flat ground without any attempt to portray gently rolling country. The mole-hill was a clumsy device, inconsistent with a true map because it is a profile, not a plan, and equalizes differing gradients, but Speed did contrive some sort of vertical scale by varying the height of his mole-hills in rough proportion to the reality. Snowdonia, for instance, is quite a dinosaur, obliterating much local detail.

Then there was the problem of scale. As some counties are four or five times the size of others, and all had to fit the uniform page-size of the *Theatre*, the scale sometimes changes (but not as frequently as Saxton's), and Speed compensated for this irregularity by including as a decorative feature a scale-bar measured off in miles, often surmounting it by a pair of open dividers, held in his Cambridge map by a scholar in academic robes and in his Cornwall by an allegorical boy. A further difficulty was that the length of a mile varied from county to county. The statute mile of eight furlongs or 1,760 yards was established by Parliament in 1593, but for a century afterwards local wayfarers clung to their 'old' miles, which in Saxton's maps could fluctuate from 1,925 to 2,728 yards, and as late as 1677 Oxfordshire tolerated three variants, the greater, the lesser and the middle mile. To contemporaries one disadvantage

A brass Theodolite dating from 1547

of Speed's maps was that he did not indicate which length of mile he was using.

We must imagine (for his procedural methods are lost to us) that he assembled all these elements—the earlier printed maps with his corrections in manuscript, drawings, portraits, coins, town-plans, scales, texts—and despatched them to the Netherlands to be engraved. The art of engraving maps on copper plates was first developed by the Italians in the late fifteenth century to replace the cruder method of printing from woodcuts, and it made for far greater precision and elegance in lettering, ornament and small details. The engraver, copying his originals or perhaps tracing them, worked on the soft copper with a penlike scalpel called a burin, and his skill was all the greater because everything had to be drawn in reverse so that when printed its mirror-image could be read normally. Alteration, and subsequent amendment, was simple— by rubbing the plate with a burnisher or hammering it from the back—but one drawback was that the plates would wear quickly, sometimes after as few as 300 impressions. However, they could still be used, touched-up or with diminishing sharpness, perhaps up to 4,000 times. Speed's plates were still in use as late as 1770.

His engraver was Jodocus Hondius of Amsterdam, his printer William Hall and John Beale of London, and his map-seller John Sudbury and George

17

Humble. Hondius was one of the foremost map-engravers of his times, and for the beauty and clarity of Speed's maps he deserves the greater share of credit, since the materials reached him in a jumble, perhaps with a layout of each sheet showing how the various elements should be disposed. The elegant lettering, part Roman, part cursive script in the Italian manner, was all his own. As the maps came from the presses, Speed's commentaries were printed on the reverse, and they were bound into the atlas. This was usually plain but sometimes coloured. The colouring was done by hand according to convention—hills brown, woods green, rivers blue, towns and villages red, the sea a pale-blue wash, and the county boundaries outlined differently on each side.

The *Theatre* was published in conjunction with his *History*. The 1627 edition of the atlas alone cost 40 shillings. The price limited its circulation to richer customers and libraries, where many survive, like Pepys's copy, in good condition till this day. The single uncoloured maps, temporarily eclipsing Saxton's, remained in great demand, particularly by the armies of both sides in the Civil War, and the last printing from the original plates was in the 1770s by C. Dicey & Co, who then owned them.

Speed's *Theatre* was a supreme achievement in British map-making. John Ogilby's strip-maps of the English and Welsh roads (1675) were done with greater accuracy to the uniform scale of one inch to the mile, showing a little of the surrounding country, and much of Britain was resurveyed for county-histories like Hasted's of Kent, but Speed's maps remained the basis of British cartography for a century and a half. Today they are of great antiquarian interest, and their popularity among the general public has long survived their usefulness. This new edition, supplemented by Alasdair Hawkyard's descriptions, map by map, is the latest tribute to the tailor from Cheshire who preserved for posterity so much that would otherwise be unknown, and presented it in a manner so intelligible and attractive.

Tracing the Magnetic Pole, Johannes Stradanus c. 1600

John Speed, cartographer

The British Isles

The map of 'The Kingdom of Great Britain and Ireland' serves as general introduction to the series of regional and county maps in Speed's *Theatre of the Empire of Great Britain*. Apart from being the only map to show all three kingdoms together, it is unique also in showing the British Isles' geographical relationship to the Continent. The upper part of the map is flanked by two views, of London and of Edinburgh; the view of London showing the Thames, London Bridge, and Old St Paul's was based on a recent drawing, but the view of Edinburgh was an adaptation of one done sixty years earlier. Beneath the two views are two medallions, one featuring Britannia and the other depicting Cunobelinus. The royal coat of arms is shown top left, and a panel on the right extends the north coast of Scotland to the Isles of Orkney. Of the various parts of the kingdom ruled over by James I only the Shetlands in the north and the Channel Islands in the south are omitted, and of these two only the Shetlands received no coverage in the *Theatre*.

21

THE KINGDOME OF GREAT BRITAINE AND IRELAND

THE ILES OF ORKNAY

EDYNBURGH

CVNO BILIN

THE GER MAN OCEAN

THE BRITISH SEA

Graven by I. Hondius and are to be solde by I. Sudbury and George Humble in Popes head Alley in London. Cum privilegio Regis 1610.

England

The map for 'The Kingdom of England' is based on the earlier map drawn by Christopher Saxton for his *Atlas* published in 1579, but Speed's map is a slight improvement upon his precursor's work. It shows the main topographical features, such as rivers, uplands, lakes, woods and towns, with county boundaries marked and some features named. Apart from its general purpose in showing the basic relationship of one area to another, the map is interesting for its inclusion of the Scilly Isles off Land's End (which are omitted in the map for Cornwall), for its exclusion of the Channel Islands (which were treated under Islands in the *Theatre*), for its borders of costumed figures ranging from the nobility to country folk, and for its numerical table of cities, bishoprics, market towns, castles, parish churches, rivers, bridges, chases, forests and parks listed by county.

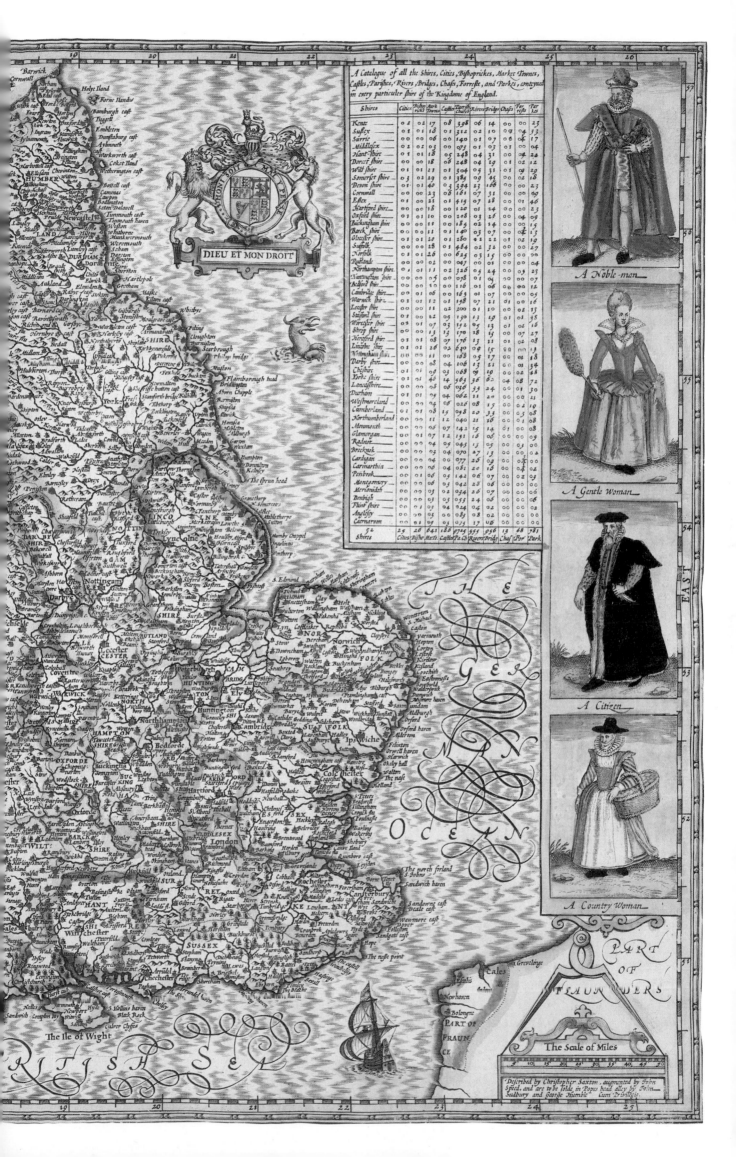

DIEU ET MON DROIT

A Catalogue of all the Shires, Cities, Bishoprickes, Market Townes, Castles, Parishes, Rivers, Bridges, Chases, Forrests, and Parks, contynual in every particuler shire of the Kingdome of England.

Shires	Cities	Bishoprick Townes	Market Townes	Castles	Parishes	Rivers	Bridges	Chases	Forrests	Parks
Kent	02	02	17	08	398	06	14	00	00	25
Sussex	01	01	18	01	312	02	10	00	04	13
Surrie	00	00	06	00	140	01	07	00	04	17
Middlesex	02	02	03	00	073	01	03	00	01	04
Hant-shire	01	01	18	05	248	04	21	00	04	22
Dorset shire	00	00	18	05	248	04	29	00	02	12
Wiltshire	01	01	21	01	304	05	31	01	03	29
Somerset shire	03	02	29	01	385	09	45	00	02	18
Devonshire	01	01	40	01	394	23	166	00	00	23
Cornwall	00	00	23	05	161	07	31	00	00	09
Essex	01	00	21	01	415	07	28	00	01	46
Hartford shire	00	00	18	00	120	01	24	00	00	23
Oxford shire	01	01	10	00	208	03	05	00	04	09
Buckingam shire	00	00	11	01	185	02	14	00	00	13
Barck shire	01	00	11	01	140	03	07	00	02	13
Glocester shire	01	01	26	01	280	04	21	01	02	19
Suffolk	00	00	28	01	464	02	32	00	00	27
Norfolk	01	01	26	00	625	03	15	00	00	09
Rutland	00	00	02	01	047	00	05	00	00	04
Northampton shire	00	01	11	02	326	05	24	00	03	23
Huntington shire	00	00	05	00	078	01	02	00	00	07
Bedford shire	00	00	10	00	116	01	06	00	00	12
Cambridge shire	01	01	06	00	163	01	07	00	00	12
Warwick shire	01	01	12	01	158	07	21	01	00	16
Leicester shire	00	00	11	02	200	01	10	00	02	13
Stafford shire	00	01	12	05	130	13	13	01	01	38
Worcester shire	01	01	07	03	152	05	13	01	01	16
Shrop shire	00	01	13	13	170	18	15	00	07	27
Hereford shire	01	01	08	07	176	13	11	01	02	18
Lincolne shire	01	01	26	02	630	09	15	00	00	18
Nottingham shire	00	00	09	00	168	03	17	00	02	18
Darby	00	00	08	04	106	13	24	00	03	34
Cheshire	01	01	09	03	068	13	10	00	02	48
Yorke shire	01	01	46	14	563	36	62	04	08	72
Lancashire	00	01	27	06	036	23	24	00	01	30
Durham	01	01	05	04	062	11	20	00	00	21
Westmorland	00	00	04	02	026	08	15	00	02	19
Cumberland	01	01	08	15	098	22	03	00	03	08
Northumberland	00	00	11	12	040	21	16	00	00	10
Monmouth	00	00	06	07	142	15	14	01	00	08
Glamorgan	00	01	07	12	151	16	06	01	00	08
Radnor	00	00	04	05	045	13	05	00	00	03
Brecknok	00	00	03	04	070	27	13	00	00	02
Cardigan	00	00	04	00	077	26	05	00	04	00
Carmarthin	00	00	04	03	081	20	16	00	00	00
Penbrok	01	01	06	05	142	06	07	00	00	00
Montgomery	00	00	06	03	047	23	08	00	00	00
Merionidh	00	00	03	02	034	26	07	00	00	00
Denbigh	00	00	05	03	053	24	06	00	00	08
Flint shire	00	01	03	04	024	04	02	00	00	00
Anglesey	00	00	05	00	083	08	02	00	00	00
Carnarvon	00	00	05	03	078	17	06	00	00	00
52 Shires	**29 Cities**	**26 Bisho**	**641 Marts**	**188 Castles**	**9725 Pa:Ch**	**555 Rivers**	**956 Bridg**	**13 Chaf**	**68 For**	**781 Park**

THE GERMAN OCEAN

BRITISH SEA

The Ile of Wight

PART OF FLAUNDERS

PART OF FRAUNCE

The Scale of Miles

Described by Christopher Saxton, augmented by John Speed, and are to be solde in Popes head alley by John Sudbury and George Humble. Cum Privilegio.

A Noble-man

A Gentle Woman

A Citizen

A Country Woman

A Gentle Woman

A Citizen

The Saxon Heptarchy

Although Speed's maps were published in an atlas issued as a separate volume, the project had been conceived as part of a larger scheme of writing a *History of Great Britain* from the Roman Conquest to the accession of James I. This was dedicated to the King and published simultaneously with the *Theatre*, the paging in the two works being continuous. The individual plates for each county had printed on their backs concise summaries of their settlement and historical development, and Speed's map of the Heptarchy showing the seven original Anglo-Saxon kingdoms was meant to draw all these threads of information together with the main body of his *History*. The map also reflected the great interest in the early history of these islands provoked by the Reformation and stimulated by John Foxe's *Book of Martyrs* and other works. Despite the extensive scholarship of men like William Camden, Speed's map of the Heptarchy did not achieve the same high quality as his other maps—perhaps because it had no earlier model to rely on, and thus was entirely Speed's own work—and today it is best remembered for its embellishment, with two borders depicting the original Anglo-Saxon kings and their descendants' conversion to Christianity, and for its being the ancestor to the more scholarly historical and archaeological maps produced by the Ordnance Survey.

KENT — HENGIST — ANNO 456

SOUTH SAXON — ELLA — ANNO 478

WEST SAXON — CHERDIK — ANNO 512

EAST SAXON — ERKEN WIN — ANNO 527

NORTH UMBER LAND — IDA — ANNO 582

EAST ANGLE — UFFA — ANNO 546

MERCIAN — CREDA — ANNO 575

THE IRELAND

IRISH SEA

THE SEA OF THE SCOTS

THE Suderland KINGDOME

KINGDOM. OF

BRITAIN
As it was devided
in the tyme of the Englishe:
Saxons especially during
their Heptarchy

Performed by Iohn Speede & are
to be sold by Iohn Sudbury & Georg
Humble in Popes head alley at London.

THE GER MAYN SEA

THE BRITISH OCEAN

ETHELBERT — ANNO 595 — SEBERT — ANNO 604 — ERPEN WALD — ANNO 624 — EDWIN — ANNO 627 — KENGILS — ANNO 635 — PEADA — ANNO 650 — ETHEL WOLFE — ANNO 662

KENT — EAST SAXON — EAST ANGLE — NORTH UMBER LAND — WEST SAXON — MERCIA — SOUTH SAXON

ERPEN
WALD

EAST
ANGLE

ANNO
624

EDWIN

NORTH
UMBER
LAND

ANNO
627

Bedfordshire

For clarity and simplicity the map for Bedfordshire is one of Speed's finest achievements. The county's landscape is undoubtedly pleasant, but equally undeniably it lacks excitement, being dominated by the river Ouse and its many tributaries. The absence of high ground, or hills of any kind—except in the north of the county and near its boundaries with adjoining shires—and its shortage of woodland made Bedfordshire a difficult county to represent cartographically. Speed and Hondius, appreciating this problem, kept the map's decoration strictly under control so the various elements complement and do not overwhelm the map itself.

Predominantly agricultural, Bedfordshire was ideal for producing barley and for pasture. Its produce was available for sale in ten market towns distributed throughout the county. The chief of these, the town of Bedford, was depicted in an aerial view of its own in the top right-hand corner, with its fortified stone bridge and the remnants of the castle destroyed in 1224. What woods existed were largely confined to parks where deer were kept. Of the twelve parks in the county, all but three were in the neighbourhood of Ampthill. The sumptuous castle at Ampthill had been built by Lord Fanhope, 'a man of great renown in the early fifteenth century out of such spoils as it is said that he won in France'; it contained '4 or 5 fair towers of stone in the inner ward, beside the base court' and was acquired by Henry VIII in 1524. With its well-wooded park, Ampthill remained a favourite residence for the rest of the King's reign, and during 1536 served as an assembly point for the army restoring order in Lincolnshire and Yorkshire. About the time of the compilation of the *Theatre*, Houghton Conquest in the neighbourhood of Ampthill belonged to Mary, Countess of Pembroke (sister to Sir Philip Sidney), and its design—adhering to a popular Jacobean type, but finished with Italianate loggias—could well reflect her diversity of interests and patronage of the arts.

More typical of most houses in Bedfordshire were Bletsoe Castle, the home of the St John family and birthplace of Lady Margaret Beaufort, and Willington, where Sir John Gostwick, treasurer of the court of first fruits and tenths, rebuilt in more suitable style both the house and church. Lavish funerary chapels and tombs (such as those erected for William Wenlock at Luton in the late Middle Ages) continued to be a feature of Bedfordshire after the Reformation, as can be seen from the monuments to the St Johns at Bletsoe and to Gabriel Fowler at Tilsworth, which mirror changes in fashion throughout the

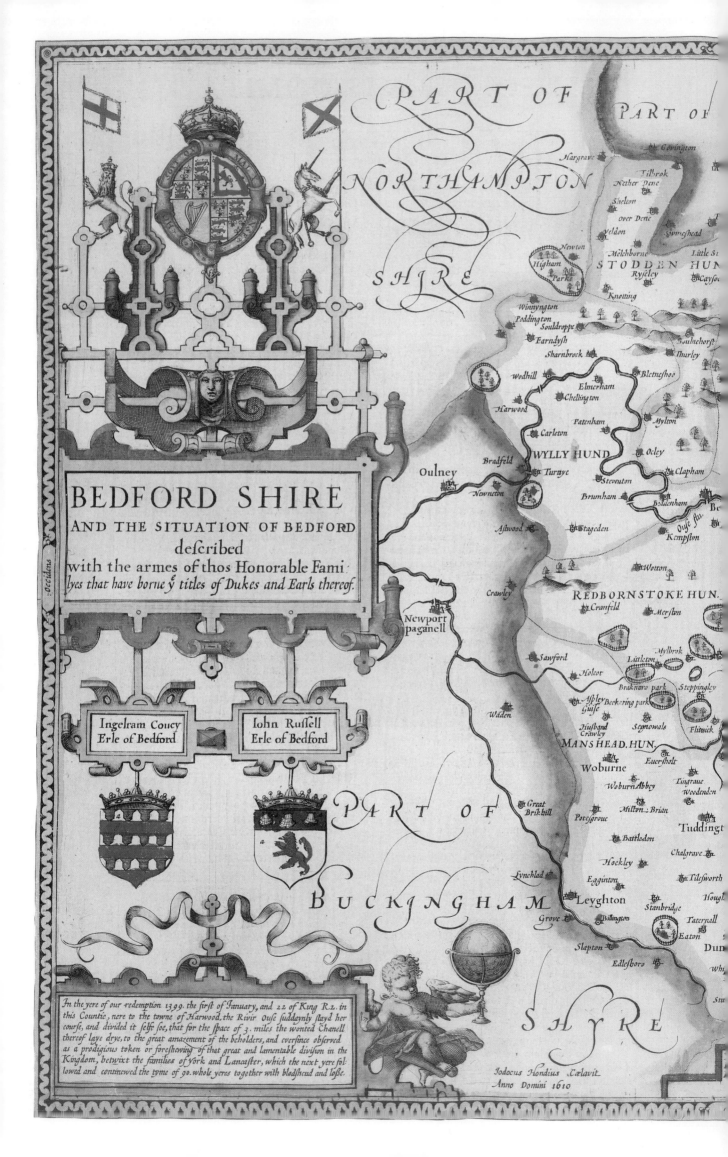

PART OF

PART OF

NORTHAMPTON

SHIRE

BEDFORD SHIRE
AND THE SITUATION OF BEDFORD
described
with the armes of thos Honorable Fami
lyes that have borne ỹ titles of Dukes and Earls thereof.

Ingelram Coucy
Erle of Bedford

Iohn Ruſſell
Erle of Bedford

Occidens

Oulney

Newport
paganell

PART OF

BUCKINGHAM

SHYRE

In the yere of our redemption 1399. the firſt of January, and 22 of King R.2. in
this Countie, nere to the towne of Harwood, the Rivir Ouſe ſuddaynly ſtayd her
courſe, and divided it ſelſe ſoe, that for the ſpace of 3. miles the wonted Chanell
thereof laye drye, to the great amazement of the beholders, and everſince obſerved
as a prodigious token or foreſhewing of that great and lamentable diviſion in the
Kingdom, betwixt the families of York and Lancaſter, which the next yere followed and continewed the tyme of 90. whole yeres together with bloſhed and loſſe.

Iodocus Hondius Cælavit.
Anno Domini 1610

Govington

Hargrave

Tilbrok
Nether Dene
Shelton
over Dene
Yeldon
Swineshead
Little St
STODDEN HUN
Newton
Higham
Parke
Ryſeley
Cayſoe
Knotting
Winnyngton
Poddington
Souldroppe
Earndyſh
Boulnehorſt
Sharnbrook
Thurley
Wodhill
Bletneſhoo
Elmerham
Chellington
Harwood
Patenham
Mylton
Carleton
Ocley
Bradfeld
Turnye
WYLLY HUND
Clapham
Newneton
Steventon
Brunham
Boulenham
Aſhwood
Stageden
Ouſe flu.
Kempſton
Wotton
Crawley
REDBORNSTOKE HUN.
Cranfeld
Merſton
Myllbrok
Sawford
Littleton
Steppingley
Holcot
Braknow park
Aſpley
Guiſe
Beckering park
Semowals
Flitwick
Waden
Huſband
Crawley
MANSHEAD. HUN.
Woburne
Euerſholt
Woburn Abbey
Tingraue
Woodenden
Milton Brian
Tuddingt
Poteſgroue
Battledon
Chalgrave
Hockley
Tileſworth
Egginton
Hougl
Great
Brikhill
Lynchlad
Leyghton
Stanbridge
Grove
Billington
Taternall
Eaton
Slapton
Dun
Edleſboro
Whi
Stu

late sixteenth century and reveal the county to have been no cultural backwater. The principal buildings—castles, churches and houses—tended to be constructed of limestone or flint, but with beds of clay suitable for brick-production. Bricks and roof-tiles were common building materials in the county long before they became popular elsewhere.

Bedfordshire had played an incidental but not unimportant part in the procurement of Henry VIII's divorce from Catherine of Aragon. In 1533 the Queen had been ordered to live at Ampthill while the divorce court under Thomas Cranmer met at Dunstable. At the Dissolution the site of Woburn Abbey was granted to Sir Francis Bryan, Henry VIII's favourite, the master of the henchmen and often called 'Vicar of Hell'; it passed to the Russell family not long after, but its conversion into a major county residence did not begin until the 1630s. Against such events the impact of the Reformation on Bedfordshire was unsensational: if Anglicanism seems to have been easily enforced, there was evidence of an avid interest in sermons and preaching among the less well off, which was to be met so well by John Bunyan in the mid-seventeenth century.

Speed with his interest in freakish occurrences recorded that in 1399 the river Ouse at Harrold 'stood sudden still and refrained to pass further so that forward men passed three miles together on foot in the very depth of her channel'. What happened when the waters upstream, swollen to 'a great height', resumed their normal course he did not say.

Berkshire

Separated from Oxfordshire and Buckinghamshire by the river Thames on its north side and from Wiltshire and Hampshire by the Downs on its east and south sides, Berkshire was—as it still is—a predominantly agricultural and wealthy county with twelve small market towns, smaller villages and many isolated farms and country seats. The Vale of White Horse was unusual in being given over almost in its entirety to corn production: the rest of the county was more mixed in its economy—corn, cattle and wood playing equal shares. As with the other midland counties adjoining it, Berkshire had witnessed considerable enclosure during the sixteenth century, and with that a certain amount of social unrest and occasional rioting.

The river Thames and its tributaries were well stocked with freshwater fish, which played a significant part in the diet of the area. Speed's map is dominated by a magnificent depiction of Windsor Castle as seen from across the Thames. With its keep, towers, turrets and battlemented walls, the castle seems a medieval military stronghold—an impression belied by the numerous windows, the series of galleries and lodgings, the chapels, and the extensive gardens with pavilions, arbours and trellises. These features leave no doubt that Windsor had long since served as a most commodious palace, within easy access of London. Successive monarchs had in turn modified and improved it. Even the parsimonious Elizabeth I had spent some money restoring one of the chapels and having a new gallery, banqueting house and terrace built. Notwithstanding these improvements and alterations, the castle inherited by James I was an old-fashioned place, neglected and much in need of repair. Speed noted that St George's Chapel with its adjoining lodgings in the lower bailey of the castle was the burial place of Henry VI (whom his successor and namesake Henry VII had sought to be canonized), as well as of other later kings, and was the headquarters of the Order of the Garter, the kingdom's prime order of chivalry. On either side of the view of the castle, Speed had engraved the names of the original members and a picture of James I in the robes and insignia of the Order.

Both Elizabeth I and James I often stayed at Windsor for the hunting available in the Great Park and during their progresses through the southern and midland counties. Until the Dissolution of the Monasteries the great Benedictine abbey at Reading had always served as a stopping place in the itineraries of medieval monarchs, and the Crown retained its site and outlying buildings for that purpose after 1539. Although the outer buildings had been kept in repair by

Anno 1350.

The names of them which first received the honorable order of the Garter

of

Saint.
Edward. III.
Edward prince
Hen. D. of Lancast.
Tho. E. of Warwik
Captaine de Bouch
Raph E. Stafford
W. Montacut E. Sales.
Rog. Mert. E of mar.
Iohn de Lisle Knight
Tho. Burwash K.
Ioh. Beauchamp K.
Ioh. de Mohun. K.
Hugh Courtney K.

George.
Tho. Holland K.
Iohn Grey Knight
Rich. fitz. Simon K.
Miles Stapleton K.
Thomas Walle K.
Hugh Wrothsley K.
Nele Loring K.
Iohn Chandos K.
Iames de Audley K.
Otho Holland K.
Henry Eme-King.
Zanchet Dabridg.
Wil Paganell K.

At Radcott-bridge. Thomas Duke of Glocester, the Earles of Arundel, Warwick. Darbye, and Nottingham, encountred with Robert Vere. Duke of Ireland. mantayned against them. by King Richard 2. Where the saide Duke, was putt to flight; and in swymming the Thamesis, hardly escaped, drowning there in his behalfe Sir Tho. Molineux constable of Chester, with many others were slayne. Anno Dom. 1587. R. 2. 11.

Oxford

Cassenton
Wightham
Staunton Haulin-court
Botley
Laurence Hinksey
South Hinksey
Witney
Nort More
Cumnor
HORMER
Kennyngton
Sanforde
Newbridge
Appleton
Wotton HUND.
Rodley
Longworth
Besilslighe
Sunnyngwell
Nuncham
Eysfelde
Sandford Shipton
Abbington
Tames flu
Hynton
Marcham
Clifton
KingstonBagpust
Lang Whittenham
Buckland
GANFELD
Garsforde
Draton
Apleford
Radcot Bridge
Wadley
Pusay
HUNDRED.
Lysford
OKE
HUND.
Myston
Littlew
Lachlad
Part of Bark Shire
nGratton
Kemscot
Stanford
Henny
Steunton
Sutton Curtney
Harwell
Brightw
GLOCESTER
SHIRE
Faringdon
Inglesham EARINGTON
HUND.
Wallington
West Hendrey
Dudcot
North Morton
Kemesford
Colleshul
Lit. Coxwel
South Dnchworth
Ardrington
East Hendred Part
South Morton
Great Coxwel
WANTING HUND
WHITHOR'SE
Locking
PART of Rea ding Hun.
Haghoorne
THE VALE OF
Chilrey
Wantage
COMPTON
Blubery
Hyworthe
SHRIVENHAM
Vffington
Ock flud
Kings Letcombe
Chilton
Spers
holt
Letcomb Basset
Cuckhamsley hill
Kingston lyle
West Ilsley HUNDR
Shriuenham
HUNDR.
Comton
Whithorse hill
KENTBURY
Farnborowe
EastIlsley
Ashbury
Cumpton
Mafton
Hinton
Great Falley
Brightwalton
Biddon
Hamsted
Asha
LAMBORNE
Chaddleworth peysmere
Baydon
LAMBORNE
HUND.
East Garston
Owre chapell
Frilsham
Aubury
Isbury
Little shelford
Cheuley
PART OF
Bucklebur
READIN
Great Shelford
Welforde
HUND
Winter borne
Raniburye
Kennet flud
Chilton
Wickham
Boxford
FAIRCROSSE
Froxfeld
Auington
Spene
east
HUND.
Wolhamph
Thatsham
Hugerford
Hansted
Kinburye
Enborne
Newberye HUNDR
Mershall
Knight bridge
Kennet flud
Bryston
Shauborn
Westwodhey
Newton
Aborn flud
Inkpen

The Scale of Miles

1 2 3 4 5 6 7 8 9 10

Performed by I. Speede and are to be solde in Popes head Alley by I. Sud. and Georg Humble
Cum Privilegio

PART OF
PART
OF
WILT
SHIRE
Tamesis flud

SHIRE
RIBED

PART OF

BVCKINGHAM SHIRE

PART OF
MID:
DLE
SEX

Ewelme

PART OF
OXFORD

Henley

ington
llingford
unnerflie
ngwell
Ipfden
h Stoke
ote
Goring
Whitchurch
Mapledoreham
angborne
erfhe
Sutham
Tileherft
Redding
READING

Little Merlowe
Great Merlowe
Medneham
Greneland
Remenham
Hurley
Bysham
Topley
Madenhead
Colbrok
BERNERSH
HUNDRED
HUND
WARGROVE
Braye
Dorney
Eaton
Upton
Datchet
Horfpenden
Wargrave
Twifort Lawrence
Waltham
Withwaltham
Shatsbrok
Chauorth
RIPPLESMORE
Windfor
Oldwin
for
Waifbury
Shiplake
Ruscombe
Winfor forest
Cauerfham
Sunyng
Hurft
Billmagfhere
HUND
Winkfeld
Winfor par
ke
Egham
Thamefis flud
SONNINGE
Loddon Bridge
Binfeld
Warfeld
PART

Purley
Thele
Witley park
Arberfelde
Part of
Rip: HUNDR
CHARL
TONShinfelde
Swallofelde
Okingham
Eafthamfted
more Hud
ple
Sunnynghill
COOKHAM
Burfelde
Stedes
Silham
Vfton
DRED
Padworth
Barkham
Bagfhot
OF
Stratfeld
Mortimere
PART OF WILT
Shir
Finchamfted HUNDRED
Sandherft
HUNDR
PART
OF WILT
SHIR
Yateley
Silchefter
Hekfelde
Turges
Euerfley
Blackwater

HAM SHIRE SURREY

Thamefis flud
BRAYE
Braye
Stanes
Thamefis flud
Stanes

NORTH
WEST
EAST
SOUTH

Henry VIII and Elizabeth I, the church (which had been built by their ancestor, Henry I, and which contained his tomb) was systematically quarried as a source of flint for building material to be used elsewhere. Abingdon Abbey suffered a fate similar to Reading, but the other religious houses were more fortunate in being converted into domestic dwellings. Bisham Abbey, which had successively been a Templar preceptory, an Augustinian priory and a Benedictine nunnery, passed to the courtier and ambassador Sir Philip Hoby (d. 1558) and his brother Sir Thomas (d. 1566)—the translator of Castiglione's *Courtier* into English—who turned it into a compact courtyard house reflecting something of their diverse Continental experiences.

Dissolution had been greeted with some relief by the inhabitants of the towns which had grown up in the shadow of the great Berkshire abbeys to cater for many of their needs, but the families such as Hoby and Mason who acquired the former interests and estates of the suppressed monasteries also inherited the age-old quarrels, and were themselves soon locked in bitter and protracted disputes over rights with town-dwellers increasingly angered by the perpetuation of issues which they felt should have ended with the suppression of their former seigneurial lords. These unresolved local issues were to lie behind many of the divisions which led eventually to the Civil War, and Berkshire is of considerable interest for providing so many illustrations of the pent-up tensions within a small county community. Moreover, the small manor house at Cumnor figured prominently in international gossip when in 1566 Amy Robsart died as a result of her fall down the stairs there: at the time it was generally believed that her husband the Earl of Leicester wanted his wife out of the way so that he could be free to marry Queen Elizabeth.

What towns there were in Berkshire owed their prosperity largely to weaving and leather production. Of these only Reading was of importance, having areas set aside for specific trades, such as that of shoemaker, and more significantly a separate butter and cheese market to cater for local dairy produce. At the Dissolution the corporation bought the site of the Greyfriars for use as a town hall and an almshouse, and it also maintained a free school for the children of townsmen. Reading also showed municipal enterprise in promoting one of the earliest prestigious town developments in the seventeenth century, that of Blagraves Piazza in 1620. Unfortunately Speed's aerial view of Reading had to be inserted in the top right-hand corner of the plate for Buckinghamshire.

If Speed was impressed by Reading, he was confused by Wallingford, a parliamentary borough with 'a large circuit and strong fortifications' and a bridge across the Thames, but little else: erroneously he accepted the contemporary belief ascribing its defences to the Romans rather than the Anglo-Saxons, yet although mistaken there he was correct in attributing the erection of Windsor Castle to William the Conqueror.

There were three outliers of the county across the Thames, and in Berkshire itself—towards Windsor—there were several detached liberties belonging to Wiltshire: recent attempts to end these anomalies had come to nothing.

Buckinghamshire

Buckinghamshire, a long, narrow county orientated from north to south, is divided into two almost equal parts by the Chiltern Hills which run across it from east to west. The Chilterns had once been entirely covered with beech trees but by 1600 vast tracts of these had been cut down. The reason for this felling was that the beechwoods had become extremely hazardous to the drovers bringing their cattle, sheep, pigs and geese from Wales for sale in London, since they concealed thieves who were able to take refuge with the stolen animals among the trees. To prevent such losses the abbots of St Albans, who owned much of the Chilterns, had first cut clearways through the woods during the thirteenth century, and later felled the remaining trees. Two substantial royal forests remained at Barnwood and Whittlewood, but even these were subject to some clearing as part of the programme inaugurated in 1609 to improve James I's finances. By comparison with other counties, Buckinghamshire had few deer-parks, partly because the woodland had previously been so extensive.

Much of the county's agriculture was geared to feeding or fattening the livestock from Wales before it left for the last stage of the journey to London. Meadow and pasture predominated. The clay soil was also good for ploughing, and in addition to the grass and hay for the drovers' animals, much corn was grown. The terrain was also well suited to grazing sheep, of which in Speed's own phrase there was 'an infinite number' producing a fine-quality wool much in demand throughout Europe. Such were the profits to be gained from being a grazier that in the sixteenth century many Buckinghamshire property owners had converted from arable farming to sheep-grazing, and as a result much land had been enclosed, almost inevitably causing suffering to small farmers, farm-tenants and agricultural labourers who periodically rioted against enclosure. Although successive governments had tried to stem the rate of enclosure, and enclosure commissioners had met with some success in executing their brief, by 1600 Buckinghamshire was one of several midland counties largely enclosed and lacking the field-system which had predominated in the Middle Ages. To meet local needs Buckinghamshire had eleven market towns, but a quick glance at Speed's plan of the most important of these, Buckingham, shows that none of these was large or prosperous, a point well made by contrasting it with the plan of Reading, actually across the river Thames in Berkshire (where Speed had been unable to include that particular town).

BUCKINGHAM

A Scale of Paces

A Podds Lane
B Naſt ende
C Hyghe Strete
D The Chappell
E West Stret
F Caſtell Strete
G Well Strete
K Water Lane
L Cutterne Elme
M Caſtell Hill
N Sheriſes Bridge
P S. Rumbalds Lan
Q Caſtell Bridge
R Præbend House
S Prebend End
T The Lords Bridg
V S Rumbalds well
W Prebend Ende
   beyond the water

BUCKINGHAM
Both
Shyre, and Shire:
towne deſcrib.

Part of

Northampton Shire

POSUI DEUM
ADIUTOREM
MEUM

SEMPER EADEM

UNION

ANNO

WEST

PART

OF

OXFORD

SHIRE

SCALE OF MILES

Laundo
Oulney
Weston
Underwood
Rauinston
Stoke Golding
Thurringham
Aunslop
Gotcherst
Loſhborg
Little Linford
Castlethorp
Haversham
Newp
Great Linford
Staunton
Wuluerton
Pernsham
Stony Stretford
NEUPORT
Culverton
Shenley
Luffeld
Lillingstons
Lekhamsted
Beachampton
Whaddon
Chase
Whaddon
Tottenho
Biddlesden
Whitfeld
BUCKINGHAM
Foſcot
Thornton
Nen
Brakley
Tinueston
Westhury
Shaulston
Mades morton
water streetford
Boreton
Naſhe
Little Haru
Rafley
Fulwell
Buckingham
Thorboro
Berton
Tingwick
HUND
Padbury
Great Harwood
Preston
Addington
Mursley
Chitwood
Hillesden
Winsl
Winston
Steple Claydon
Garnhoro
Goddenton
Twnford
Garnhoro
Hoggeſtoe
Poundon
Middle Claydon
East Claydon
Andley
North Merston
Vuing
Mershe Gibben
Edgcot
Hogshawe
Fulbrok
Pichcot
Quaynton
Shipton Lee
ASHENDEN
Littl
Piddlington
Grendon underwood
Westcote
don
Litherſhall
Waddeſdo
Arncote
Wodsham
Eydrop
Upper Winchington
Bernwood Forest
Wotton
underwood
Aſhendē
Nether W
chington
Hartwe
Boſtall
Dorton
Bryll
Chilton
Cuddenton
Dynt
Ockley
Chersley
Hadnam
Cold Aſton
HUND.
Crandon
Notley
Ilm
Wormenall
Saobinton
Kingſey
Oulſwic
Tame Touſey
Hor
Emmington
Ht
Crowell
Bl
Stoken Church
Ipſton
Turfeld
Pusill
Ha
Aſſenton
R

Thames flu.
Ouse flu.
Tame flu.
Iſe flu.

1 2 3 4 5 6 7 8 9 10

REDDING

A The Priorye
B Gutter lane
C The Free Schole
D St Laurence
E Forbery
F Queens stables
G The Abbey
H Schomakers Row
I Fishe strete
K Buchers Rowe
L Brode strete
M Parishorne lane
N Hosier lane
O Casell Strete
P S. Maryes
Q Minster strete
R Chayne lane
S George lane
T London strete
V Mill Lane
W Olde Strete
X Olde Brūg
1 S Giles church
2 Towne Mills
3 High Bridge
4 S. Giles strete
5 Crowne lane

6 Jone lane
11 Old Streete
12 Dukes stret

50 100 150 200

Cranfeld
Sawford
Halcot
Aspley

PART OF
BEDFORD
SHIRE

Woburne

Brickhill
Little Brickhill
Great Brickhill

Linchlad
Leighton
Grove
Winge
Ascot
Slapton
Mentnore Edlesboro
Cheddington
HUND.
Ivinge
Long Merson
Pitston
Mersworth
Puttinham
Buckland
Tring
Aston Clinton Beacham
Dreyton
Wigginton
Haulton Cholesbury
S. Leonards
ALESBURY HUND.
The Lee

Eaton
Whipsnade
Stadham
Gaddesden
Asbridge
Nettleden

PART
OF HARTFORD
SHIRE

Barkhamsted
Horidge
Bouinden
Latimers
Starret
Cheyney
Rickmansworth

Great Mißenden
Chesham
Little Mißenden
Chesham Boics
Agmundesham
Bradnam
Hitchinden
Part of
Colshull
Hardford
Shire
Chalsunt
S. Gyles
The Feathe
More park
Part
of
Midle
sex

Pen
Highe Wickham
DESBURROUGH
Uburne
Little Merlow
Hedsor
BURNHAM HUND.
Beaconfeld
Chalsunt S. Peters
Hedgeley
Fulmere
STOCKE
Denham
Uxbridge
Ivet
HUND
Mednam HUND.
Great Merlow
Fernham
Wexham
Hurley
Bysham
Thames flu
Burnham
Topley
Stokepoges
Langley
Colbroke
Madenhead
Dorney
Eaton
Upton
Datchet
Horton

PART OF
Windsore
Waisbury
Stanes
SHYRE
Egham

EAST

THE ARMES
of those Honorable
Families which have born
y Titles of Buckinghā.

Walter Gifford Earle

Richard Stranbowe E.

Thomas of Wodstoke E.

Humfr. Stafforde Duke

Performed by Iohn Speed, and are to be sold
in Popes head alley by G. Hubell. Cum Privilegio

1610

Until the Reformation the college at Ashridge had a phial alleged to contain Christ's blood but on the college's suppression this was shown to be no more than clarified honey, a fact which brought down Speed's contempt. After 1539 the Crown kept Ashridge for its own purpose, and its generally healthy situation led to its being chosen as the place where both Prince Edward and Princess Elizabeth were brought up. Ashridge has since been transferred to Hertfordshire, and an outlier of Hertfordshire at Colshill incorporated in Buckinghamshire. Apart from its occasional use by royalty, the county's proximity to Windsor made it an attractive domicile for a number of families prominent in court and national affairs, the most eminent being the Russells at Chenies, the Peckhams at Denham, and the Lees at Quarrendon. The Russells not only remodelled the house at Chenies but set a fashion in funerary chapels in the parish church, the imitation of their example by the Dormers at Wing and others making Buckinghamshire particularly rich in Elizabethan and Jacobean monuments. Closeness to court and recurrent changes in religion in the sixteenth century also account for an unusual diversity of faith in the county, where against the Protestantism of the Russells and the Lees could be set the Catholicism of the Peckhams and the Dormers.

The most important institution in Buckinghamshire was almost certainly the royal foundation of Eton. Established by Henry VI in 1440 under a provost, ten fellows, four clerks, six choristers, a schoolmaster, twenty-four scholars and twenty-four poor and elderly men, the college had undergone various modifications in the later Middle Ages and had survived the Reformation. With its continuing royal patronage and its link with King's College at Cambridge, Eton was unusual in attracting pupils from a distance at a time when few went to school outside their immediate locality. Although Buckinghamshire had no good building stone of its own, high-grade stone was available from adjoining counties to the north. Lack of timber in the county was a more serious construction problem. During the Middle Ages this was overcome by the extensive use of unbaked earth or clay which, when mixed with water, stones and straw, set on a plinth of wood or stone and whitewashed, formed cob or wichert. After the introduction of brick, this was used for the better buildings such as Eton College or Chenies, but cob remained the material favoured by the less well off, and many houses built from it survive in the county today.

Walter Gifford Earle

44

Cambridgeshire

With its heraldic borders, ground-plan of Cambridge, royal arms and four figures in academic dress, one holding a pair of open dividers indicating the scale, the map of Cambridgeshire is one of the most elaborately produced in the *Theatre*. The map affords an important clue as to the length of time involved in the project's realization, as the arms of all the colleges in the University are depicted up to and including Emanuel College established by Sir Walter Mildmay (the Chancellor of the Exchequer) in 1584, but excluding the Countess of Sussex's foundation of Sidney Sussex ten years later, although the map itself is dated 1610: a blank shield and cartouche were perhaps reserved for the new college's arms, but if this was so, the engraver seems not to have been provided with details of the arms to be added.

A quick glance at the map reveals how Cambridgeshire fell into two distinct parts—the Isle of Ely with its surrounding fens in the north, and the rest of the county a chalky hinterland divided by the river Cam in the south. Intersected by numerous broad rivers and man-made dikes, and with extensive areas permanently flooded, virtually the whole Isle could be waterlogged month in, month out. This general predicament had several interesting results: to meet its particular problems the Isle was administered separately from the rest of the county by the Bishop of Ely, whose authority was paramount and roughly analogous to that enjoyed by the Bishop of Durham in the County Palatine of Durham. Its insalubrity and unrelieved dankness meant there were few habitations there, Ely itself comprising little beyond its cathedral, episcopal palace, diocesan administrative offices and parish church. There was, however, an abundance of fish and fowl.

In the immediate aftermath of the Dissolution of the Monasteries, the pioneering work of Ely and Ramsey Abbeys in draining the Fens lapsed, until in 1600 Parliament passed an Act for the recovery of many hundred thousand acres of marsh. Nothing had come of this by 1621, when James I accepted personal responsibility for reclaiming the Fen. Other commitments prevented the King from pressing ahead with the matter before his death in 1625, but in 1630 the determination of the Earl of Bedford started to bring the long-delayed schemes for drainage to realization.

By contrast, the southern part was populous, with extensive woodland, meadow and arable land, which was 'both pleasant and profitable'. Timber was the favourite building material throughout the county, but brick manufac-

45

CAMBRIDGE

P:thagoras house

Kinges colledge backesides

Kinges coll: chas

Pembrok Hall Orchard

S. Thomas lees

Iesus killd walkes and grene

Chcife places in the Citie obferued by Alphabeticall letters.
A. Trinitye Colledge.
B. Kinges Colledge.
C. Clare Hall.
D. Caius Colledge.
E. Sainct Iohns Colledge.
F. Sainct Sepulchre.
G. All holowes in § Iury.
H. Sainct Michael.
I. Trinitye Church.
K. Sainct Edward.
L. Sainct Benets.
M. Corpus Chrifti Coll.
N. Sainct Peters.
O. Sainct Gyles.
P. Magdalen Colledge.
Q. Emanuell Colledge.
R. Chriftes Colledge.
S. Sainct Andrew.
T. Iefus Colledge.
V. Quenes Colledge.
W. Sainct Botolphe
X. Pembrok Hall.
Y. Peter houfe.
Z. Sainct Clement.
1. Litle Sainct Maries.
2. The Caftle

The armes of K. Sigebert founder of the Vniuerfit

St Peters House. 1280.

Pembroke Hall. 1343.

Trinitie Hall. 1347.

Kings Colledge. 1441.

St Katherins Hall. 1475.

Chrifts Colledge. 1505.

Magdalen Colledge. 1519.

EMANVEL

Emanuel Colledge 1584.

WEST

Performed by IOHN SPEEDE. And are to be folde in popes head alley, by John Sudbury and G. Humbell.

ANNO.

William brother to Ranulph E. of Chester

Iohn of Henaud vncle to Phillip Q. to Edward 3.

William Marques of Iuliers,

PART
LINCOLN
SHIRE

Spalding
Coubet
Crowland
Dowfdale
WISBICH
Trokenbo
Thorney
The new Leam
Eldernall
GIRVII.
Peter burgh
Whittlefey
Whittlefey Dike
THE ILE C
Whittlefey Mere
Va Mere
Raley Mere
Yaxley
Tokeworth
Stilton
Holme
Cunnyngton
Ramfey
Bury
PART OF
Sutto
Wiftow
Somerfham
Bluntfham
HVNTING.
Woodhurft
Erith
Huntingdon
St Ives
Holywel
Willingham
Godmanchefter
Heminasfordes
Fenny raton
TON
Swalye
Begars buffie
Cunnyngto
Lowlwe
Offoras
SHIRE
Grauley
Papworth annes
Papworth euered Knapwell
Tofeland
Yelding
Wintering ham
St Neot
Elfworth
Boxworth
Madin
Childe
Hard faw
Croxton
STOW.
Tofte
Gransle ma
Caxton
HV.
Cafcote
PARTE
Waresley
Tetworth
Buene
Stow
Kingfton
Eucrden
Euerfden
OF
Gramfden pua
Wimple
Gamlingay
WETHERL
HVL
BEDFORD
Great Eaft
Arrington
Wali
Potton
Harley
S.George
Cokinghatley
Clopton
Crawden
Wendye
Tadlow
Wladdon
Shenay
ARNINGF
Bafinxborne
Bigleswade
Gilden morden
Abbington
Dunton
Henxworth
Steple
mordc
HVN
Lylyngton
SHIRE
PARE
HARTFORD

PART OF NOR: FOLK

DIEV ET MON DROIT

CAMBRIDGSHIRE described with the deuision of the hundreds, the Townes situation, with the Armes of the Colleges of that famous Vniuersiti:

And also the Armes of all such Princes and noble-men as haue heer: tofore borne the honor: able tytles & dignities of the Earldome of Cambridg.

Walton
Newton
Walsoken
Wisbich.
Emuerth
The Old Podik
Outwell
Elme
Vpwell
Salters lode
Downham
The New Podik
Helgey
Southrey
Welney
maden lode
Presthowses
LY
Littleport
S'heyye
Copthall
ELY
Chetsham
Prickwillow
Mildnall
Downham
Turbilly
Quaney
Thorney
Newbernes
HVN Norney
Istam
Wormleighton
Ely
Brame
Stanney
Soham
Bedelhey
Harimere chap
STAPELHOW
Fordham
Thetforde
Wiken
Snalewell
Badlingham
Stretham
Oye flu
Vpware
Lanworthe
HV: Chipnham
Kennet
Denny
Burwells
Rechet
Exnyng
Kenford
Swasham prior
Newmarket
Moulton
Swasham bulbek
Newmarket heathe
Saxum
Ashley
Horwyngseye
Stowqu
Ditton
Cheueley
Ditton
STANE
Stachworth
Teuershm
Wilborham parua
Burrough
Catilidge
Wilborham mag.
Dullyngham
HV:
FLEDISHE
Westley
Brinklow
Fulburne
RADDESLEY
Cambridge
Willingham
Thirlow
Chery hynton
Carleton
HVN:
Weston
Couell
Gogmagog hills
W: Wratting
HV:
Trumpington
Balsham
Wickham
Witherfeld
Shelford mag
Stapleford
Badburham
CHILFORD
Shelford
Abbingtons
Horseheathe
Pampsford
Hildersham
Haue:
Sawsten
Shedy Campes
rill
Witlesford
Castle Camps
WITLESFORD
LYNTON
HV:
Hinkeston
Chesterford Ma:
Ickleton
PARTE
Strethall
Chesterford parua
Elmeden
Creshall
Great Chishall
Little Chishall
OF ESSEX

PARTE
OF
SVFFOSKE
EAST

Cum Priuilegio.
1610.

Edward Duke of York.
Richard Earle of Cambridge.
Richard Duke of York.

The Armes of the Vniuersitie

Clare Hall 1326.

Corpus Christi Colledge. 1344.

Gonuile & Caius College. 1348.

Queenes Colledge 1448.

Iesus Colledge 1502.

St Iohns Colledge 1508.

Trinitie Colledge. 1546.

tured from the county's large clay deposit had replaced wood as the preferred material for houses among gentle families during the sixteenth century, Kirtling and Sawston being built with it by the North and Huddleston families. Although there was no good building stone there, stone of quality was easily transported in flat-bottomed boats across the Fens from Northamptonshire and elsewhere. Reeds, which were plentiful in the wetlands, supplied the thatch for the roofs of virtually all buildings in Cambridgeshire.

The town of Cambridge owed its origin to the conjunction of four major Roman roads, and from the Anglo-Saxon period it was a busy commercial county town with a number of religious foundations. Scholars attracted by its thriving community moved there from Oxford in 1209, and another batch came from Paris in 1229. From these two migrations, which seem originally only to have been temporary expedients, there emerged during the course of the thirteenth century the University, the first college, Peterhouse, being founded in 1280. By the Reformation there were fifteen colleges: Henry VIII continued a long royal tradition in supporting colleges there by establishing Trinity College in 1547, and the sites of the Franciscan and Dominican priories were used for Emanuel and Sidney Sussex later in the century. Dr Caius re-established Gonville College in 1557. The colleges provided accommodation only for the teachers, and in the absence of hostels students found lodgings for themselves in the town: extortionate rates for these lodgings bred ill-will, and relations between town and gown were not good. Protestantism infected the University at Cambridge later than at Oxford, but for a variety of reasons it became firmly lodged there, the University being something of a Protestant powerhouse by the accession of James I.

As with other counties in East Anglia, Cambridgeshire played a significant part in the succession crisis of 1553. Princess Mary, who was at Royston when Edward VI died, withdrew into the county before travelling on to Kenninghall. The force that the Duke of Northumberland brought to capture Mary, and to defeat her supporters, burnt Sawston Hall because Mary had briefly sheltered there. However, there was an upsurge in popular support for the fleeing princess and Northumberland had to declare for Mary at Cambridge; nonetheless he was arrested there in her name before being taken to the Tower of London to await his own trial and execution.

Cheshire

'If affection to my natural producer blind not the judgement of this my survey,' began John Speed, who had been born in Cheshire in the early 1550s, 'for air and soil ... equals the best', but he went on: 'The climate be cold' even though the county was warmed by its proximity to the Irish Sea, snow and ice not lasting as long as in Shropshire. He considered Cheshire 'wholesome for life', its inhabitants 'generally' attaining to many years.

With outcrops of rock, hills and uplands mainly situated at its peripheries, Cheshire is a surprisingly flat county. At the beginning of the seventeenth century it was still heavily wooded, and the forests at Delamere and Macclesfield were in royal ownership. The banks of the Dee and Vale Royal in the centre of the county were areas more disafforested than most, being given over to arable, meadow and pasture. Cattle were grazed profitably throughout Cheshire, and the butter and cheese produced there were shipped to Ireland and Scotland or transported south to London for sale. There was some sheep-farming towards Derbyshire, but the weavers in Cheshire towns and villages were dependent for their yarn more upon the wool brought into the county in exchange for its grain and dairy products. Fish and birds were also important sources of income and of diet. Cheshire was not, however, wholly dependent upon farming: at Northwich, Middlewich and Nantwich, there were brine springs producing salt; the county's salt came second in quality and quantity only to that from Droitwich in Worcestershire. Leland's keen eye noticed that the prettiness of the salt-producing towns was spoiled by the filth emitted from the furnaces used to boil the brine in making salt.

Chester, situated on the River Dee and linked directly with London by Watling Street, was the county town and a port with a virtual monopoly on trade with Ireland. The silting of the Dee had begun to threaten that monopoly, and to prevent an overall decline in the county's Irish business a new outlet with purpose-built quays had recently been constructed at Neston, lower down the Dee estuary on the Wirral. As a result of the needs of shipowners, of Cheshire merchants and of the Crown's requirements in sending troops, munitions and victuals to Ireland, the marine approaches to the county with their navigational hazards had been repeatedly surveyed, and thus the littoral edges of the Wirral were more accurately delineated in Speed's map than other stretches of coastline elsewhere. The many changes in the shoreline can be readily seen by comparison with a more modern map. Despite problems with

despatching its goods, Chester remained the main port and commercial centre in the north-west until long after the publication of the *Theatre*, and its relative prosperity was somewhat envied by strangers, who also remarked on the 'rows', or galleried streets with shops and merchants' houses situated over cellars or warehouses. Not merely a port and county town, Chester was also the administrative headquarters of the County Palatine and the Earldom of Chester, a feudal honour held by the heir-apparent, and in 1612 enjoyed by Prince Henry; and since 1541 it had also been the seat of a bishopric, carved out of the enormous medieval diocese of Coventry and Lichfield.

From the Middle Ages the favourite building material in Cheshire had been wood, and its timber-framed houses for farmers and gentle families and its cruck-framed cottages for peasants, infilled with lath and lime-plaster and painted black and white, are features of the county. Somewhat unusually, some of its parish churches, like those at Marton and Lower Peover, were timber-framed. The majority of the churches, the former religious houses, the castles and their related defensive systems, were stone-built, using the red sandstone of the area which lends its colour to the soil of the county. Under Queen Elizabeth I the leading families started to use stone for their new houses, Lyme Park and Brereton being constructed in stone during the 1570s and 1580s. These new houses, displaying an awareness of trends in artistic life at court and in the capital, broke with the conservatism that had recently characterized taste in Cheshire. The Reformation had removed the religious houses, which had done so much to stimulate cultural and artistic life in the county during the Middle Ages, and had brought to an end the mystery plays performed at Chester; and with an inadequate income the new bishops had been unable to achieve much as patrons in their stead, preferring to spend their resources in enforcing the Anglican Settlement, in which they had a modest success in Cheshire.

As published in the *Theatre*, the map for Cheshire was engraved by Hondius, but the first proof bore the arms and portrait of Queen Elizabeth and was the work of William Rogers, who died in 1604. A fellow Cheshireman of Speed's, Rogers had engraved coins from Speed's own collection for the edition of William Camden's *Britannia* of 1600, and shortly before his death other prints by Rogers were issued by John Sudbury and George Humble, who went on to become publishers of the *Theatre*. These circumstances suggest that Rogers may have been the original choice as engraver for the project. Roman coins, perhaps from the same collection, figure in the map of Chester placed so prominently and centrally in the revised plate for the county map, as do the arms of James I and of his son and heir Prince Henry, and in the left-hand margin the arms of medieval holders of the Earldom of Chester.

Cornwall

The deep valley of the Tamar gives Cornwall a sense of remoteness and separation. The map reveals a county of innumerable ports and havens and many small rivers. The sea either dominates or permeates every aspect of the peninsula. 'Touching the temperature,' Speed remarked, 'the air thereof is cleansed with bellows, by the billows that ever work from off her environing seas, where through it cometh pure and subtle, and is made thereby very healthy, but withall so piercing and sharp, that it is apter to preserve than recover life.'

The soil was as infertile as the landscape was bleak. Attempts by the inhabitants to improve fertility by spreading seaweed and fine sand and ploughing them in to the soil paid small dividends: cereal production remained low and did not improve in quality. Livestock did not thrive either: sheep in the county were small and produced a coarse wool not suited to fine weaving, Cornish clothiers and weavers having to seek government protection repeatedly to preserve and protect their livelihoods. Only fruits cropping in late summer harvested well. The unsuitability of the county to extensive and profitable farming had two interesting consequences: the landscape of Cornwall remains one of small hamlets and scattered farmsteads rather than of the nucleated villages found elsewhere in England, and the open-field system of small strips was brought to an end gradually during the course of the sixteenth century by enclosure agreed upon beforehand by both the landowner and the tenant farmer, neither of whom had benefited under the old system and neither of whom was to benefit to the disadvantage of the other under the new. The absence of agrarian discontent as the result of the reforming process of enclosure was a matter of pride to Richard Carew of Antony, writing his 'Survey' or study of Cornwall late in Elizabeth's reign: Speed had access to Carew's work when writing his remarks to accompany the county map, and thus the accuracy of his remarks is greater than in other areas where he could not draw upon such a fund of local knowledge. Even until fairly recently Cornwall lacked roads, goods being carried by packhorse or transported by ship.

If poor agriculturally, Cornwall was rich in mineral resources. It had deposits of tin, copper and silver, which could be abstracted by diverting the water from nearby streams and washing the ore free from its surrounding matter. Water-power was also used in some of the smelting-houses where the ore was purified and cast into 'fothers' for sale to tin-merchants at the regular sales

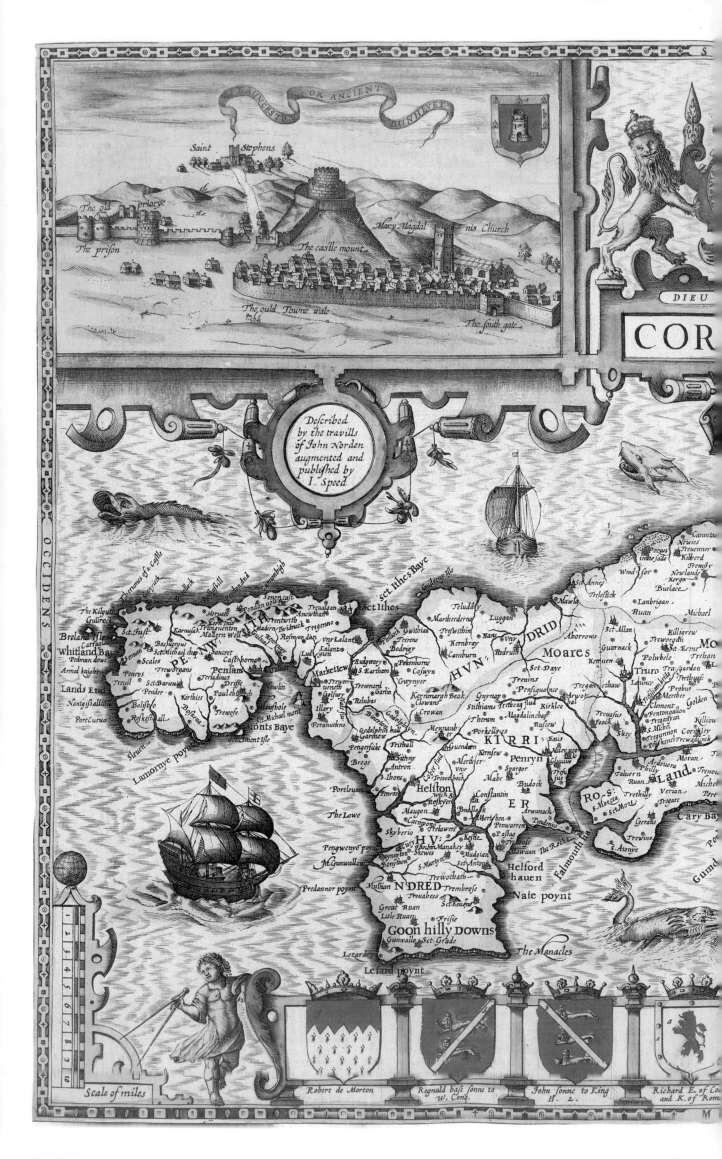

held at the coinage towns of Bodmin, Helston, Liskeard, Lostwithiel and Truro, from where it was taken by sea throughout England, Wales, Ireland and the entire Continent. For administrative reasons, and as a safeguard to the producer as well as to the buyer, the various processes of mining, preparing and selling were regulated by the Stannaries, an association representing the large mine-owners and tin-dealers, with its own warden, court and assemblies. The Stannaries, with their extensive rights and jurisdiction, overlapped with the Duchy of Cornwall, the feudal fiefdom created to provide the heir-apparent with an income of his own, and from which in many respects they were largely indistinguishable: in 1611–12, when Speed published the *Theatre*, the revenues of the duchy were being enjoyed by Prince Henry, and the profits of tin-mining were being used to offset the soaring costs of his household, building works and artistic patronage. During the sixteenth century it had become clear that the surface deposits of tin and other ores were nearing exhaustion, and from the 1540s engineers from Germany were called in to advise on the latest techniques to enable deeper mining. Cornwall was one of the most heavily industrialized counties in Tudor and Stuart England.

Much of the shipping accommodated in Cornish ports came from far afield, some from Spain and Portugal and the Mediterranean, and some from the Baltic. The seas off the peninsula were rich in fish, and pilchards caught by Cornish fishermen were particularly prized. Fleets also came to fish Cornish waters from Brittany, and from the Iberian Peninsula; their intrusion caused a certain amount of resentment in Cornwall, and an excuse for Cornishmen to indulge in piracy against the hated intruders. Cornish seamanship was put to good use in the sporadic wars with Spain and France throughout the sixteenth century, the most celebrated incident in which Cornishmen were involved perhaps being the attack upon the Indies fleet at Flores in the Azores in 1591, when Sir Richard Grenville of Kilkhampton died aboard the *Revenge*. Cornish expertise in mining was put to equally good use by the army. To protect mining and fishing interests, and the vessels tied up in the Fal estuary—sometimes numbering over a hundred ships—Henry VIII had constructed forts at St Mawes and Pendennis and on the Scilly Isles. Unlike other forts along the south coast, these were kept in a reasonable state of repair until the peace with Spain at the accession of James I, though the Spanish had been able to land at Mousehole and to burn Penzance in 1595.

Cornish was still spoken in some parts of the peninsula, but the discontinuance of miracle plays in the language and the introduction of the English liturgy in the 1530s and 1540s had sounded its knell, and the diminishing number of Cornish speakers were by necessity bilingual. The introduction of the Prayer Book sparked off the last major rebellion in the area in 1549, but it was not so much the language of the liturgy as the religious conservatism of the region—situated at some distance from its bishop at Exeter—that accounts for Cornish fervour for Catholicism: under Elizabeth I Cornish Catholics such as the Arundells of Lanherne and their kin were imprisoned for their recusancy.

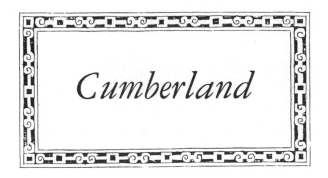

Cumberland

With the Union of the Crowns in 1603, Cumberland with Westmorland lost its historic function of defending England against Scotland as part of the western marches. After the treaty of Edinburgh in 1560, the two countries had co-existed in uneasy peace, but as long as the problem of the English succession on the death of Elizabeth I had remained unresolved, there had been a possibility that Cumberland would have to revert to a more or less permanent war footing. Although the accession of James VI of Scotland ended that possibility, it is doubtful if the inhabitants of the county had realized the long-term significance of the Union for them and their children by the time of the publication of the *Theatre*.

Cumberland's ancient role as a frontier or military zone was reflected in a number of peculiarities which it shared with Westmorland, Northumberland and Durham. On account of its inhabitants' obligation to defend the county against incursions from the Scots whether war had been officially declared or not, men there were permitted to own and to carry firearms and other weapons, a right which farther south was being deliberately eroded or carefully regulated; the county was also exempted from much of the taxation which the rest of the kingdom paid. Recurrent hostilities had meant that local government had not evolved in Cumberland on the same lines as in most of England, and like the other border counties it lacked hundreds, or their equivalents, an omission which Speed duly noted, but it was divided into administrative units called wards, largely for military purposes. For much the same reasons the sheriff was not so important a figure in county management there as elsewhere, playing a subordinate role to the Lord Warden of the Marches, whose authority ran through the entire border area.

There were still men alive in 1612 whose memories stretched back to the last phase of recurrent warfare with the Scots and to the battle of Solway Moss in 1542 when James V of Scotland was killed. Under Henry VIII the fortifications in the northern part of the county had been updated, and the map of Carlisle shows clearly the modernization of its defences in the 1540s with the construction of a citadel and batteries to mount artillery. Even with these improvements the fortifications in Cumberland lacked the sophistication of those in Northumberland, and their neglect during Elizabeth I's reign left them obsolescent and worthless by early seventeenth-century standards. What system of defence there was involved a series of some sixty castles, which

L SEPT. SEVERVS. PIVS AVG. BRIT

THE PICTS WALL

BER LAND

THE PICTS WALL
The ancient and outmost limitts of the
Romane Empire, was first made of Turffs and
Stalks by Hadrian the Emproure. Afterwards by Seve:
rus much strengthned and extended through the Maine euen
from Sea to Sea, a worke soe famous, that the tith Britannicus
was geven a Surename to the Emproure. And lastly in the
declining estate of that Empire. It was built of firme stone 8.
foote brode and twelue foote hygh, beginning in the West at Boul:
nes nere the Baye of Itune, and continewed unto the mouth of
Tyne in the East. Running through vast montanes, for the most
part in a straight lyne ascending and descending over steep,
Craggs and hye hills. conteyning in length nere 100 miles.
The tract whereof in many places yet appeareth, only
dispoyled of his Battlements. In it were built watch
towres, distant 1000 pases rithe from other, wherein
were souldiers kept, for the securing of the con:
fines from the incursions of the
enemy.

VOLANTII VIVAS

The Earles of
CARLILE

| Marcatus E. | Ran. Meschems | Andrew Harkley |

PART

OF

WESTMORLAND

EAST

This Countye being the uttermost Limits
of the Romane Empyre, and a: fenced
with that admirable wall as is aboue
sayd, was continewally frequented with
their Legions and Souldiers, whoe in tyne
of peace, or after victoryes acheiued, buylt,
many monuments and Altars, with in:
scriptions to their Idole Gods, for the
prosperity of their Emperours and them
selues, many of them yet remaynyng in
diuers places there, are to be sene, and
some of them according to their true for:
mes here expressed, as they haue bene,
most carefull and exactly taken by men
of wothy note and credite.

Performed by Iohn Speed, and are to be
sould in Popes-head Alley, by the exchan:
ge by I. Sudbury and Georg. Humble
Cum Privilegio Anno Domini 1610.

Eden flu

CARLILE

Cauda flu

A The Castle
B Caldoe gate
C St Cuthberts
D St Maryes
E The Shambles
F The Mote hall
G Rickard gate
H Highe Streete
I Bother gate
K Almer well lane
L Castle gate strete
M Fishmarket
N Battaull holme
O The Citadell
P Castle orchard

were primarily the homes of local families and the centres of estates and lordships, with military functions coming second. These castles were supplemented by pele-towers, defensible stone structures adjoining houses and farms, and by 'bastles', which were essentially farm-buildings that could be put to defensive use in an emergency. The churches of the region were also capable of being defended to varying degrees, and fairly typical of this precaution was the church at Boltongate, erected in the early sixteenth century and provided with stone-tunnelled vaults clearly with occasional defence in mind. Although many of these buildings were militarily out of date by Speed's time, they continued to have some basic value in maintaining law and order as long as cattle- and sheep-rustling by both English and Scots remained a feature of the region. The illicit trade across the Solway Firth between Cumberland, Dumfriesshire and Wigtownshire was unaffected by the Union and, if anything, smuggling seems to have benefited from it.

Cumberland fell into three distinct zones with uplands in the south, a less bleak and more habitable and self-sufficient central part, and a more desolate area broken with hills in the north adjoining Scotland. Speed commented on the chilliness of the county, the piercing air and the amount of snow that fell there. Agriculture was largely pasture for cattle- and sheep-raising, with some corn production. Although the coastal areas were not renowned for their fishing, mussels 'gaping and sucking the dew' in the estuary of the river Irt produced a type of pearl for which there was a ready demand. More important were the copper mines in the neighbourhood of Keswick, which belonged to the Crown and which had recently been developed by German engineers; and the abundant deposits of lead in the southern upland 'whose plenty maketh it of no great esteem'. The general poverty of the county was reflected in its having only nine market towns, and by the modest income enjoyed by the Bishop of Carlisle. Cumberland was distinctive in that nearly all its buildings, even those of the poor, were built of stone covered with roughcast and with stone roofs.

Like Camden and other antiquarians, Speed was fascinated by Hadrian's Wall, then known as the Picts' Wall, which he carefully delineated on the map, and which he described at some length in a roundel. He also illustrated as adornments to the map four samples of the Roman altars and inscriptions which had come to light through excavation, noting that many more 'as yet lie hid'. His antiquarian interest in Cumberland was not limited to the Romans as his description of Long Meg and Her Daughters, a prehistoric monument near Glastonbury, attests, but its remarkable collection of Anglo-Saxon antiquities such as the Bewcastle Cross, passes without mention. This omission is particularly odd when one remembers the nascent interest in Dark Ages England and the strong sense of nationalism prevalent among his circle of friends and his potential readers.

Derbyshire

With the mountainous grandeur of the Peak, the flatter and less eventful landscape towards Nottinghamshire and the rolling scenery towards Leicestershire, Derbyshire is a county of contrasts. Except for the moorland in the north west of Derbyshire, described graphically by Speed as 'black and mossy ground', the county was heavily wooded and forested with no less than thirty-six parks for the keeping of deer. Hunting was the favourite pastime of local families from the Earls of Shrewsbury downwards, and in 1592 Sir Thomas Cokayne of Ashbourne published 'for the delight of noblemen and gentlemen' his *Short Treatise of Hunting*, a compilation of hints deriving from fifty-two years' experience of pursuing 'the buck in summer and the hare in winter'. Unfortunately, not all the deer were slain as the culmination to a hunt, some being trapped in a temporary arena such as that shown in the town plan of Derby before being killed. In the south and west the land was predominantly arable, and cattle and sheep were pastured throughout the county.

'Besides its woods and cattle, sheep and corn', Derbyshire was a producer of lead mined in the vicinity of Wirksworth, Matlock, Bakewell and Hope. Mining was regulated by custom, individual miners being free to search for lead provided they registered their finds and paid the Lord of the Field a thirteenth of their production. Exploration was certainly encouraged under this system, and large areas of the countryside are littered with pits and spoil heaps showing how the miners followed the veins of lead, sometimes for miles. A by-product of this mining was the production of antimony, which alchemists held 'in great esteem' for their work. Coal and iron were also mined. At Chellaston there were quarries for alabaster (which when first dug is soft and easily cut, but later hardens and is capable of being polished like marble): in the Middle Ages Derbyshire alabaster, carved and painted, was highly prized for objects of devotion throughout England and Europe, but following the ban on the worship of images at the Reformation, its use was restricted to the production of tombs with recumbent figures, and some domestic items. Much of the county's mineral wealth was in the ownership of the Duchy of Lancaster, and many of its inhabitants were in the service or employment of the Duchy, or else its tenants.

The water springs at Buxton had been known since before Roman times for their medicinal properties. 'Great cures by these waters have been done,' Speed

THE ARMES of all those Honorable Famylyes, as have borne the Dignitye and Title of Earles of DARBYE, from the tyme of the Normans Conquest unto this present

William Ferres

Ed. E. of Lācastre

Iohn of Gant D. of L.

Thomas Standley

PART OF CHESHIRE

SHIRE

PART

HIGH PEAK

The Wood head

Dynett

Hollingworth

Mersee flud

Howden howse

New Chapp

Glossop

Woodland

Motteram

Darwen chap

Chalesworth

Edall

Nonstool hill

New flud

Meller cha

Tharsethall

Nether Bouth hill

Aston

Branssord

Merpull chap

Bothumsall

Owlerset

Heathfeld

Hope

Thornell

Hyghlow

Beardhall

Castleton

Burghe

The Castle in Peake

Shatton

Bradwall

Abney

Goyt flud

Yerdesley hall

Elden Hale

The Chamber

Little Hucklow

Folowe

Wyleybrid

Mersh hall

The Chappell in y Firth

Peake forest

Great Hucklow

Tiddeswall

Eham

Shawcrosse

HUND.

Gynlowe

Stony Middle

Tax Hall

Ridge Hall

Whoston

Lytton

Warelow

Rowland

Overton

Wedingwell

Tunsted

Faiers feld

Mylnhowse

Lottgston

Buxton

Kingestarndelle

Wormchill

Wye flu

Newmedow

Warmsawdale

Ashford

Goythowses

Staden

Cowlow

Blakewall

Three Shire stones

Fernhowses

Cowdale

Chelmerton

Taddington

Bakewell

Foxholes

Sheldon

Haddon H

Over Haddo

Dovehad

Therlsbouth

Flaghowses

Monyashe

Lathkell flud

Nollogreu

Staruddle

PART OF

Longnor

Crongston

Myddeton

Nedam Grange

Bradford flud

Gratto

Shene

Pilsbury Grange

Hethcott

Harryngton

Wulscote

Parwidge

Ballid

Eaton

Bradl

Narrodale

Allsop

The Lea

Ausienfeld

Hussingdon Grange

Tissinton

Ilam

Thorpe

Fenny

Maplinton

Blore

Okecover

OF

Calwiche

Ellaston

Suciiton

Narbury

Birchups

park

Rowchester

Rawston

Styd

Cubley

Cambridge

Marston

HUND.

Somershall

Crackmarsh

Less H

Eaton

Sidbury

Uttoxater

Doueridge

Marchinton

STAFFO

SHIR

DARBYE

Darwen flu.

Olde Brooke

A Schale of pases

40 80 120 160 200 240

YORK SHIRE

Sheasfeld
Healey Bridge
Gledles
Beghton
Wales
Harthill
The Shire Okes
Kilmarsh
Norton
Bechif Abbey
Woodhouses
Eckinton
Barlebrugh
Whitwell
Dronfeld
Stubley
Clowne
Belghe
Holbek
Whittenton
Clowncrich Creswell
Hounfeld
Ourifton
Netherho
Woodthorp
Elmeton
Morehouses
Barlow
Shittle
Osfrost
Creswell
SCARSDALE
Dunfton
Brimmin
Inkerfell
Wood
Whalay
Newhold
ton
Woodhowfes
over Langwith
Chester
Topton
Boulfouer cast
Nether Langwith
Brampton
feld
cast
Duck Marton
Scanlyf
Palterton
Holmehall
Furland hall Sutton
Sherbrok
Wadshelfe
Houghton
walton hall
Normanton
Glapwell
Wingerworth
HUND.
Henrli
Harwood Grange
Williamsthorp
Sambye
Huckney
Rewthorp
chap
Pilfley
Hardwick
Woodthorp
Maunsfeld
Elkiston hall
Stretton
Twonsall
Aultem
Hanley
Tibshelfe
Wolley
Hucknall
Darley Hall
Mylnton
Ogston
Morton
Blakewell
Hall
Tanfley
Trenju chap
Higham
South Normanten
Matlok
theddik hall
Brakenfeld
Shirland
Carlingthwat hall
Banteshall
Washington
Alfreton
Wheat Croft
South Winfeld
Pynxon
Crumforth
Wakebridge Hall Winfeld
Swanwick
Somercotes
Selston
Watstanwel
Criche
manner
Wansley
Bridge
Frithley
Prentofet
Codnor cast
Alderwashley
Codnor
Butterley
Middleton
Newlan
Ripley
Laser
Brunfley
Ashley hay
Morley park
Henop
Wirkefworth
Shotley
Crich
Langley
Estwood
Cawley
park
Kidley
Auton
Darwen flud
bey park
Shipley
Cofsall
Irelon
Pofter
Belper
Denbye
Ikeston Erewalke
wood
Kilborn
Langley
Turndiche
Smaley
Hughpark
Hellbrok Horsley
Morperley
Wineley hill
Makerley
Horeston
Halam
Kirk Halam
Trowell
Muggington
cast
Maperley
Mercaston
Dunfeld
Morley
Stanton
Weston underwood
Little Ireton
MORLE
Stanley STON
Brades
Alistre
Dale
ford
Quardon
Bradsall
Chadesdon Hopwell
Stapleford
Koddis
Darleygh
acre
Langley
Ston
Little
Ockbrock
Sand
hall Langley
Chester
Spoundon
Risley
Attenton
Maikworth
Marton
Dalbury Leies
Darwen flud
Allvaston
Longeaton
DETRIE
Darbye
Lytehurch
Braston
Redborne
Great Oure
Little Welne Swaley
Thurnastons
Little Oure
Osmaston
Oslaston
Bowlton
Elueston
Ambaston
Trusley
Normanton
Thurleston
Sutton
Barwardcote
Synfoll
Chelaston
Great Welne
Elwall
Arlaston
OFAP
Barrow
Sharlow
Ashe
PLE
Aston
Howe
Pinderns
Twlyh
Weston
Hihton
Twiford
HUND
Merston
Willinton
Farmarke
Newton
Egginton
Myleton
Melborne cast
Castle Dunnyngton
Titburry
Rowfston
Repton
Melborne
cast
Streton
Newtonfony
Brathye
Ticknall
Wightmere
Wynshill
Bredon on f Hill
ton upon Trent
Harteshorn
Cauke
Stannton
REPPINGTON
Swadlingcote
The
LECESTER
Stanton
Smethik
Great
Draklow
Blaughorby
park
Candwall
Grayfley
Ashbye de la Zouche
Walton
Castle Grayfley
Reaulafton
Lynton
Wilsley
Packington
Catton
Over Seal
HUND.
Coton
Nether Seal
Croxall
Scale Grange
Moscham
Normariton
Dallington
Stretton
SHIRE
Chileote
Applebye
Iodocus Hondius celavit

Part

of

Notting

ham

or

Shire

PART

OF

Anno
DARBIESHIRE
described
1610

The Scale of Miles

Performed by John Speede, and are to be sold in
popes head Alley by Iohn Sudbury and G. Humble

BUXTON

Sainte Annes well

A Cold Spring

commented, 'daily experience' being good for the stomach and for sinews, as well as immersement and bathing in them being 'very pleasant'. The bottom right-hand corner of the county map has an insert showing the main contemporary facilities at Buxton: a square tower of ashlar and many windows situated over nine springs, a smaller structure nearby with a tenth spring, and an eleventh, a cold spring, bubbling not far away. The cults and superstitions which had evolved around the springs during the Middle Ages had shocked the Protestant Reformers under Henry VIII, who had the altars and shrines with their statues and offerings removed, but the celebrity of Buxton survived the Reformation for it to become a spa patronized by the nobility and gentle families for rest and relaxation as well as for medical treatment in the late sixteenth century. Its most famous visitor from that period was Mary Queen of Scots who came to Buxton during her imprisonment at Chatsworth, Hardwick and South Wingfield. The presence in Derbyshire of the Catholic claimant to the throne was a catalyst to the innate Catholicism of the area, and the descendants of Judge Fitzherbert of Norbury, the author of *La Grande Abridgement*, *The Book of Husbandry* and *The Book of Surveying*, were not atypical of the recusant element in Derbyshire: Thomas Fitzherbert (d. 1600) fell victim to that scourge of Catholicism, Richard Topcliffe, and of Thomas's brothers, Nicholas was secretary to Cardinal Allen, Francis a friar, George a Jesuit, and Anthony—according to Topcliffe—'a traitorous felon'.

The most famous resident in Derbyshire until her death in February 1608, shortly before the publication of the *Theatre*, was Bess of Hardwick. The fourth surviving daughter of a lesser country gentleman, she married four times, each husband richer than his predecessor, and she ended her career as Countess of Shrewsbury, scheming for the crown for her own family. Bess's real passion, which the wealth of her successive husbands enabled her to indulge without restraint, was a mania for building, and her houses at Chatsworth, Hardwick and Worksop were among the greatest achievements of the age, only Hardwick New Hall surviving today more or less intact. Her enthusiasm for building was shared by other members of her family who were egged on by her to build as boldly themselves: of these the fairy-tale castle at Bolsover with its rusticated terraces, vaulted chambers, frescoed walls and battlemented turrets, built for her son Charles Cavendish and grandson William by the Smithson family of architects and started about the time of her death, is as justifiably famous as her own creations. The Cavendishes had a secondary passion for horsemanship, which they shared with Prince Henry and others, and at Bolsover they constructed a riding school of their own.

All buildings in the north of Derbyshire were of stone, often with distinctive stone slabs for their roofs (such as are extant today), but in the south only the castles, manor houses, and domiciles of the great were stone-built, the rest being of timber infilled with lath and plaster. Of the castles built by the Duchy of Lancaster and others during the Middle Ages, seven survived in reasonable repair at the time of Speed's survey.

Devonshire

The overwhelming impression of Devonshire is of hills, woods and lush combes, wedged between the waters of the Bristol Channel in the north and the English Channel—or British Sea, as Speed (following contemporary cartographic practice) called it—in the south. From north to south the colour and tones of the landscape vary from grey to red, reflecting the underlying rock, with outcrops of darker-toned granite in Dartmoor. For the most part the soil is agriculturally poor, and in Speed's time difficult to farm, requiring considerable expenditure of labour and money in the application of manure and sea-sand before yielding a meagre crop and small financial returns. Devonian gentle families dependent upon land and farming for their income were noticeably poorer than their peers in other southern counties. The rural depression of the area can be gauged by the survival of the longhouse (a building with accommodation for the farmer at one end and quarters for livestock at the other) well into the seventeenth century, when it had long fallen into disuse elsewhere. Corn was the staple product of the valleys, and sheep and cattle were grazed on the hills. With the introduction of better breeds of sheep with finer fleeces in the late Middle Ages, not only had wool production become more profitable in Devonshire, but the weavers had prospered, producing a fine kersey much in demand, unlike the coarser cloth or straits which until then had been their mainstay. To this business was added in Elizabeth's reign the manufacture of lace (introduced by Flemish émigrés fleeing religious persecution), thus making Devonshire one of the leading textile counties.

There was also mineral wealth. In and around Dartmoor there were veins or lodes of tin, which were mined by means of shafts, or exposed by cutting a trench across likely ground and then diverting a stream into it. Both of these methods marked the landscape, and the damage done by tinners and smelters refining the ore was a cause for growing concern throughout the sixteenth century. As in Cornwall, the production was regulated by the Stannaries, with a Lord Warden whose jurisdiction included the four Devon stannary courts as well as the five Cornish courts. Although the deposits of silver at Bere Altson, Bere Ferrers and Combe Martin had been exhausted by open digging at the end of the Middle Ages, new techniques in extracting the metal had led Adrian Gilbert to reopen the mine at Combe Martin in 1587. The Mines Royal, set up in 1568, had also discovered iron at North Molton and Mollam.

With inadequate roads (and dependence on packhorses for transporting the

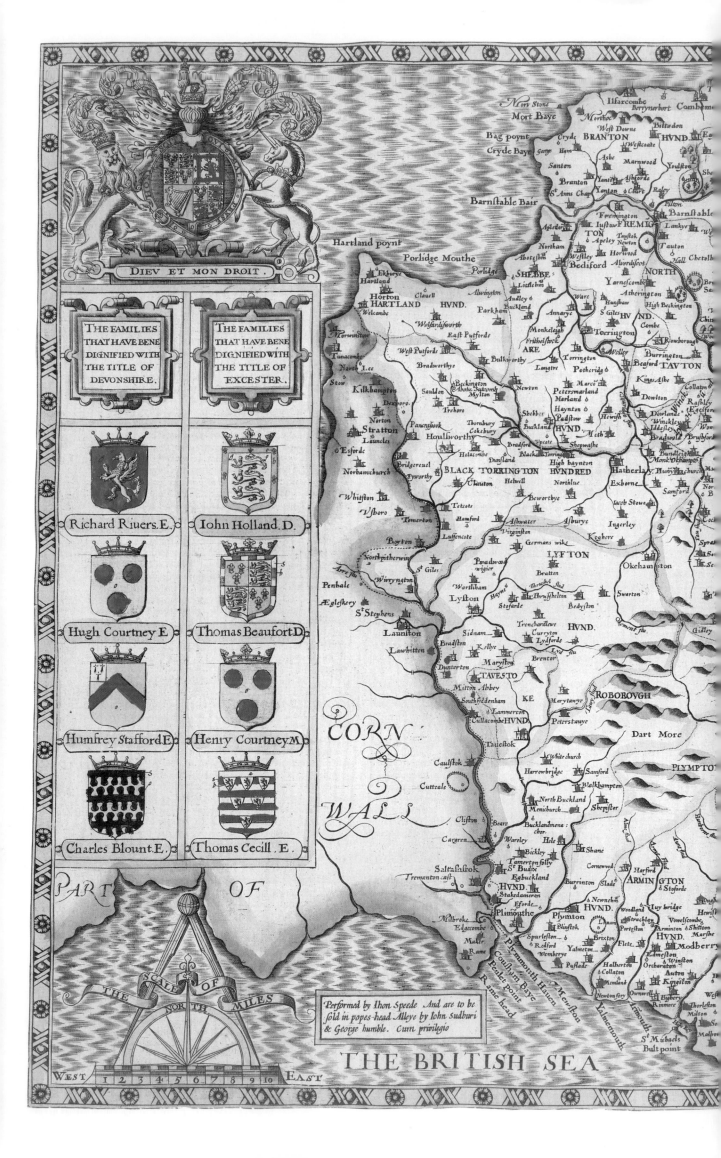

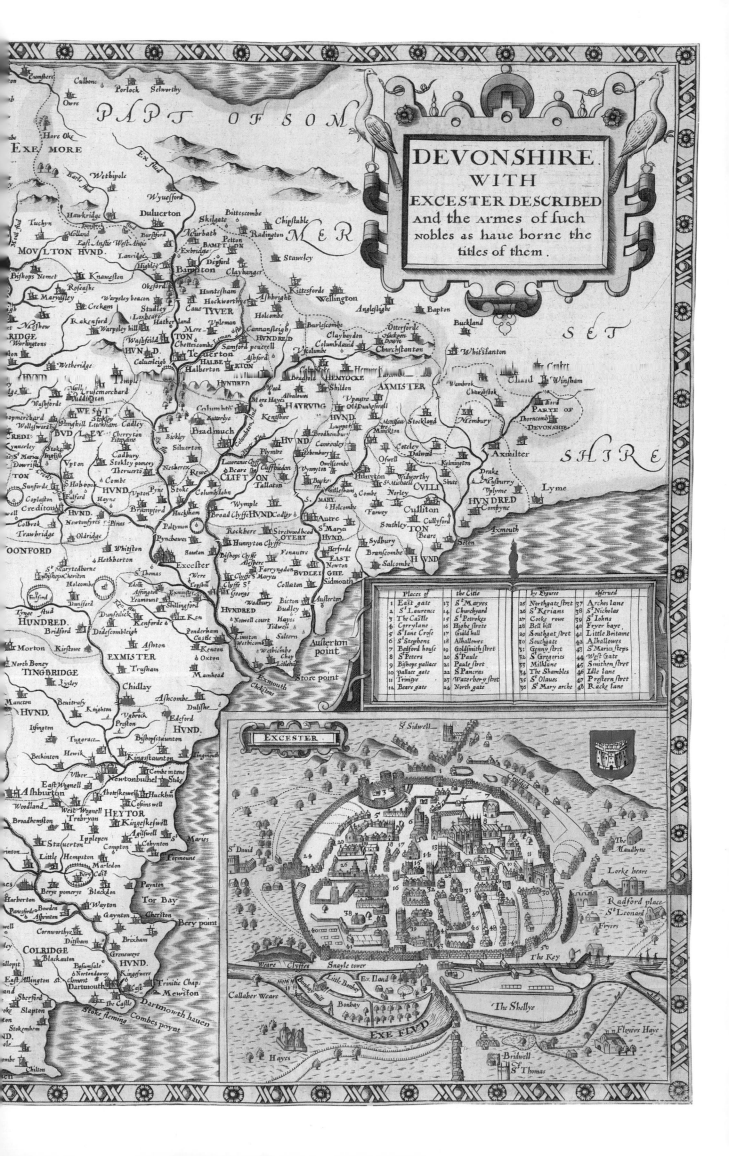

county's textiles and metals along those roads), Devonshire's numerous ports provided a better means of distributing these goods for sale elsewhere. Under the Tudors these ports flourished. The already considerable coastal-trade shipping was further augmented by fishing fleets operating from the same ports and specializing in pilchards from the English Channel and herrings from the Bristol Channel. In times of war this considerable marine expertise was granted licences to privateer or to augment the Navy (as during the Armada crisis of 1588), but however distinguished the role played by seafarers from Devonshire at such times, it was their contribution to mercantile expansion, to voyages of discovery and exploration and to colonial settlement which in the long term was more significant. The slaver and privateer Sir John Hawkins of Plymouth broke into the monopoly of trade enjoyed by Spain and Portugal in North America, ruthlessly using force to obtain his ends, and Sir Francis Drake from Buckland began his celebrated three-and-a-half-year circumnavigation of the globe from Plymouth. In 1583 Humphrey Gilbert, born at Greenaway, founded at Newfoundland the first English colony in North America, and after his death his half-brother Sir Walter Ralegh continued his work of settlement in America and Ireland. Devonians gave their names to places stretching from the Arctic Circle down to Virginia, John Davis of Sandridge naming the Davis Straits after himself.

The city of Exeter, with a population nearing 10,000 in 1600, surpassed any other town in Devonshire in size and prosperity, and with its cathedral and its town houses for local magnates it was in a sense the capital of the entire south-west. Not only was it supreme in the area; Exeter enjoyed a position without parallel elsewhere, free of the urban malaise and recession which inflicted other communities of its size and importance, such as Bristol and Newcastle upon Tyne. It was symptomatic of its well-being and self-confidence that the city commissioned a series of portraits of its own citizens at a time when it was still rare for a merchant to be painted, and inaugurated a programme of public improvements by laying out the Northenhay in 1612, thereby revealing a knowledge of similar works recently completed abroad. As the main city of the area, Exeter had been the natural object for investment by the Cornish and Devonian rebels of 1495 and 1549, and with its neglected and dilapidated walls it had come near to being captured on the latter occasion. At the time of the Reformation the city had been sympathetic towards Catholicism, but under a series of enlightened Bishops both it and the county had been guided into an acceptance of the Elizabethan Church Settlement which was remarkable for its wholeheartedness. This process was doubtless helped by the Protestantism of the Russell family, which had acquired the estates of Tavistock Abbey almost intact in the 1540s, thus becoming one of the leading families in Devonshire.

The map has a serious mistake in its engraving. The area around Mount Edgecombe or West Stonehouse on the Tamar estuary is shown in Cornwall, whereas it was in Devonshire. This is correct in the map for Cornwall.

Dorset

On visiting Dorset, Speed was struck by the quality of the air, which he described as 'good and of an healthful constitution'. He was equally impressed by the fertility of the county. Its northern parts were still heavily wooded and well stocked with deer and game, or else bare hills lush with grass supporting flocks of sheep; the central zone was grassland, where cereals were cultivated and with some meadows; but the coastal area, bleak and windswept, was hardly less productive. Heathlands in the vicinity of Poole and Wareham yielding furze and ling for fuel were economically important to the local community. What Speed overlooked was the string of small ports hugging the coast—Lyme Regis, Bridport, Weymouth and Poole—which figured in the coastal trade plying up and down the Channel and which were centres for fisheries, particularly for mackerel. Bridport also specialized in making rope for the Navy and for more local requirements. The absence of good navigable rivers prevented the ports from acting as outlets for the county's produce, and as a result of this defect the economy of Dorset was orientated northwards, making the road linking Sherborne and Shaftesbury with Salisbury one of the south-west's main highways. There were eighteen market towns, of which Dorchester (the shire town), Wimborne, Sherborne and Shaftesbury were the most important.

Open-field husbandry was widely practised in Dorset: the arable land in a village was divided up into large fields which were subdivided into furlongs, and these furlongs were further divided into strips. The holding or farm of each peasant lay not as a single block of land surrounded by hedges or walls, but in strips scattered throughout the full extent of a village. Whereas the open-field system had to a great extent been replaced in the rest of the country, with attendant agrarian discontent, Dorset had escaped this trouble in retaining the practice. The county was also free of the religious unrest which so marked Devon and Cornwall during the same period.

The Dorset coastline is distinguished by a series of geological curiosities ranging from Chesil Beach and Portland Bill to Lulworth Cove and Kimmeridge Bay. These did not interest Speed, beyond their proper inclusion in his map, and several generations were to pass before map-buyers wanted to know about such phenomena. During the invasion scare of 1539 Lord Russell interested himself briefly in them and in the vulnerability of the county's shore to enemy landings, as a result of which he recommended the construction of artillery

DORCHESTER

The ruins of the guild wals

S. Peters
Trinite
West Strete   Guild Hall
Alhalens church
Fre Schole
A Scale of Pases

PART OF SOM SHYRE

Trent
Oburne
Sherborne
Nether Compton
Over Compton
Evill
Clyston
Glasen Bradford
SHERBOR
Thornford
Lillington
Bearchagard
Yeatminster
HUND
Long
The vaile of whit or Blackemore
Ryme
Lyght
Lewcombe
Melbury osmod
Chetnoll YEAT
MINSTER Heremitage
Melbury bud
TOT
South parret
Halstoke
Part East Chelborduch
West Chelborough of Evershot
Great Mintc
Cheddington
Corscombe
Vlcombe Mortpuers
Batcombe
Samford
Mosterne
REDHOAVE
Bemis
Chantmerls
Frome Quintan
Ex flud
HUN ter
TOLLERFORD
HUN
Vpcer
Forde
BEMIS
Tollardwelme
Rowsham
Wraxhall
South Chalmington
S. Nichos Sidling
Part of Devoshire
Brodewindsor
Bemyster
Iske
Vpsidbing
Thorncombe
Burstoke TER
Mapertin
Kencombe
Catstoke
WHITE CHURCH
Churche stoke
Lewson hill
Paunhin
Chilfrome
Stockland
Pillesdon pen
Abbots Lstoke
Netherbury
HUND
Great Tollard
Little Tollard
HUN
Maiden nowton
Membury
Bettescombe
GODER
Milton
Porestoke
Frome
Hawkchurch
Pillesdon
Great Tollard
Hon.church
Frampton
Daswood
Creklad park
Melplash
Wenford
Crokwey
Lambert castle hill
Marshwood park
Burph
THORN
West Compton
Southover
Muckelford
Bradford
Axmyster of Devon
Marshwoodvale
Whitchurch
Simmesboro
Nethercombe
Longlother
East Compton
Kilmington
Wotten
HUND
Birdport
EGGARDON HUN
Shute
Part
Waldishc HUN
Askerswell
Longhrida
Stepien
Musbury
Charmouth
Stanton Gabriell Chediok
Baunton
Chilcomh
Winterborn
Little Broddi
Shyre
Uplyme
Shipton Vorton
Lytton
Cullyton
UGSKOMB HUND
Lyme
Punkcnall
Swire Beksinton
Portesham
Abotsbury
THE
Roddon
Langton West Chcker
BRI

Osmund E. Dorsed   Ioh. Beauford Mar.   Thomas Grey Mar.   Thomas Sackuil E.

WEST

PART OF WILT:

DORSETSHYRE

With the Shyre-towne Dorchester described, as also the Armes of
such noble families as have bene honored with the Titles there
of since the Normans Conquest to this present Anno 1610.

Pen
Loug lane
Mill
Stoke
Sylton
Gillingham
Wynecaunto
REDLANE
Cuckkington
Bugley
Buckhorne Weston
Kyngton
HUND
Stourewestouer
Stour Estouer
Stoure prouest
The Fyue
Bridges
Fishead
Stoure Stou

Mere
Mere
park
UP WIMBORN
Gillingham
Forest
Motcombe
Ham
Shaftesbury

SHYRE
Tollandrioll
HUND. Can

Craneborn Chace
Sexpenny Hanley
Pantridge
Blagden
park
Damarum
Woodcotes
CRANEBORNE
Farnham
Munkton
Alhalowes Wimborn
Craneborne
Bonridge
Edmondesham
S. Andros Glisset
S. Michaell
Glisset
Bereson
S. Giles Wimborn

Twiford
Compton
Hargraue
Melbury
Ashmere
Stepington
Chettle
Tarranthinton
Longturchell
Morechurch
KNOWLTON HUN
Kenton
Worthe
Horton
Chabury
Wirtwood
Forest
Holte
Mannyngton

NEWTON
Tudboro
Marnhull
HUN
Bedcister
Westorchard
Manston
Estorchard
Flintenell
Sutton
Shrawton
Stoure payne
Pimpern
Launston
Munketon
Rauston
Wichamton
BADBURY
Hotl
Hinton
Martell

Stalbridge
andelpurse
Thornhull
DOWNE
Stirton
Caundell
Lyllynch
HUND
Stoke
Holwell
Pulham
Hasilbere
WHITWAY
Stokewake
Welland
Quarleston
Howton
Cleuston
Stichland
HUND
Carleton
Spesbury
Craford
Barnesley
The Lodge
Shopwick
Winbornmister
Berforde
Corfe
Lake
Canford
Kynston
Percy
Little Cauford
HUNDRED
Preston
Longham
St Leonard
Little Hinton

Duddle
flu
Newton castle
Shillingaukford
Durweston
Belchalwell
Ibberton
Fippennyaukford
Knighton
Brianston
Blandeford
PIMPERNE
Turnwood
Blandeford
Maries
Langton
Caynston
Tarrant

Maypouder
Helton
HUND
Middleton
Binghams
Milborn
Winterborn
Anderston
Tomson
Charbarow
Sturmynster
marshall
Corfe
COGDEANE
Lechiot
Becon
Longflet
Hickford
Parkston
The Mynes
CANFORD LAWNDES
HUND
Poole

Plushe
Horses Melcombe
Cheselborne
Deuelishe
PUDDLETOWN
Piddlchinton
Burston
Milborn
Tolpuddle
Turnars piddle
Beer
BEER HUND.
Muston
Kingston
Morden
Bloxworth
RUSHMORE
Holton
South Lechiot
Hauworthy

Walterstow
Pudlton
Athelhamston
Tinkleton
Aspudle
Hyde
Keysworth
Aren poynt
Brankfey Island
North Hauen poynt
Brankfey cast
South Hauen poynt

Stynford
Bochampton
Woodford
Morton
Straford HUND
Knyghton
Burton
Wareham
Wongret
East-Holme
Stowboro
Aren
St Elyns
slepe
Newton
Owre

Came
Witecombe
Brodmayne
WINFRITH
Woll
Stoke
West-Holme
HASLER HUN
Sherfordbridge
PURBEK

LIFORD
Warmwell
Owre
HUN.
East chaldon
Helwarden
Bindon
Combecaues
West-Holme
THE ISLE OF
The Lodge
Crechharrow
Corfe Cast
Studland Castle or
Hanfast poynte
Studland

Sutton
Osmanton
Pokeswell
Ringston
Mountpoynynas
West Lulworth
East Lulworth
West creech
Pouington
Barnston
Church Knoll
Bradley
ROWBARROW HUND
Hareston
Sandwich Baye
Steple
Kingston
Langton
Sandviche
Preston
Est Lyncha
Egleston
Kimbridge
Worthe
Faucrel poynte
Encombe
Adams chap

Waymouth
legis
TISH
andessoote castle
SEA
Portland Castle
Cheselton
Portland
Iland
Portland church
lauit Cum priuilegio

The Scale of English Miles
1 2 3 4 5 6 7 8 9 10

PART OF HAMSHIRE

EAST

forts and bulwarks along the coast. Although several of these were built by the Crown or, as at Brownsea Island, by private enterprise, none was ever put to the test. The French burnt Lyme Regis in 1525, but the nearest that Dorset came to a major emergency was in August 1588 when the Armada sailed up the Channel, several of its straggling ships being engaged by the English Fleet off Portland.

Dorset had figured unexpectedly in national affairs when in 1506 the Archduke Philip was forced to land at Weymouth during a storm and the gentle families in the locality had to entertain him before he proceeded to a meeting with Henry VII at Windsor.

With its chalk and its limestone, Dorset had better building material readily available than most counties. Smaller buildings for the poor were invariably made of cob, and many of these with their thatched roofs survive until today. Limestone, preferably from Ham in Somerset, was the choice of the well off, who employed it in the construction of a type of country mansion with a mixture of gothic and renaissance detail that is distinctive to the area; the Horseys' house at Clifton Maybank, the Strangeways' at Melbury, the Knoyles' at Sandford Orcas and the Trenchards' at Wolfeton being fine examples of such mansions. As elsewhere, monastic houses were converted into private dwellings at the Reformation, but however successful the work of conversion at Abbotsbury and Milton Abbas, it is the lodges built in the 1590s and early 1600s by successful courtiers and politicians (often outsiders to the county) to established houses or parks, with their esoteric and cabbalistic references and design, that prove more memorable: Sir Walter Ralegh led the way at Sherborne, and he was imitated by Sir Robert Cecil at Cranborne and by Viscount Bindon at Lulworth. Portland stone was already in demand as far afield as Exeter, but despite Inigo Jones's current enthusiasm for it the stone did not become popular nationally until Sir Christopher Wren selected it for the rebuilding of St Paul's Cathedral.

With his interest in early monuments, Speed is known to have visited Maiden Castle where he remarked on the corn growing within the ramparts, but if he saw any of the other remarkable hill forts in Dorset, or features such as the Cerne Giant, he does not single them out for mention. Speed shows the county's boundary with Devon and Somerset before it was rationalized for easier administration by the respective sheriffs and justices of the peace.

Durham

The County Palatine of Durham had been created by the Norman kings to secure the disputed borders with Scotland, and its distinctive liberties and rights, administered by the Bishop of Durham, survived the Union of the Crowns in 1603. As Speed aptly put it: 'Over the county the bishops thereof have had the royalties of princes.' Attempts to bring Durham more into step with the rest of England in the years following the Reformation had been resisted by successive Bishops as diminishing their power, and one of the consequences of this resistance was that alone of the English counties Durham lacked any representation in Parliament.

Aesthetically Speed's map of Durham is one of the most accomplished in the *Theatre*, notable for its clarity and the undoubted primacy of the map over the secondary features—the royal arms, the compass and the depiction and description of the battle of Neville's Cross—which embellish it. The division of the county between upland and lowland is immediately apparent, the city of Durham with its episcopal castle and medieval cathedral at the intersection of the zones. The west of the county was fell and moorland with ancient forest, deer-parks and scattered farmsteads or hamlets. The agriculturally richer Wear valley separated it from the more fertile plateau to the east with its villages. Lush farmland to the south adjoining the Tees, was characterized by townships with open fields. Livestock predominated in uplands, mixed husbandry with crops of wheat and rye in the lowlands.

The county was comparatively well developed industrially. Coal was mined in a line of pits stretching upstream nearly eight miles from Newcastle and Gateshead. Fleets of 'keels' carried coal downstream from the collieries with their riverside 'straithes' or wharves to the quays of Newcastle and Sunderland for distribution by sea throughout England and across the North Sea to the Continent. To meet the ever-increasing demand for coal, improved pumping machinery was being introduced to facilitate the mining of deeper seams, and other pits had been opened along the river Wear. Quarries supplied sandstone for building, and in an area without much woodland stone was used even for the dwellings of the poorest. On the coast salt was produced at South Shields.

Resentment against the new Tudor policy of appointing bishops from among men outside the County Palatine and of giving key positions in local administration to courtiers (rather than to old Durham families such as Neville, Hilton and Lumley)—combined with unease over the long-term consequences of

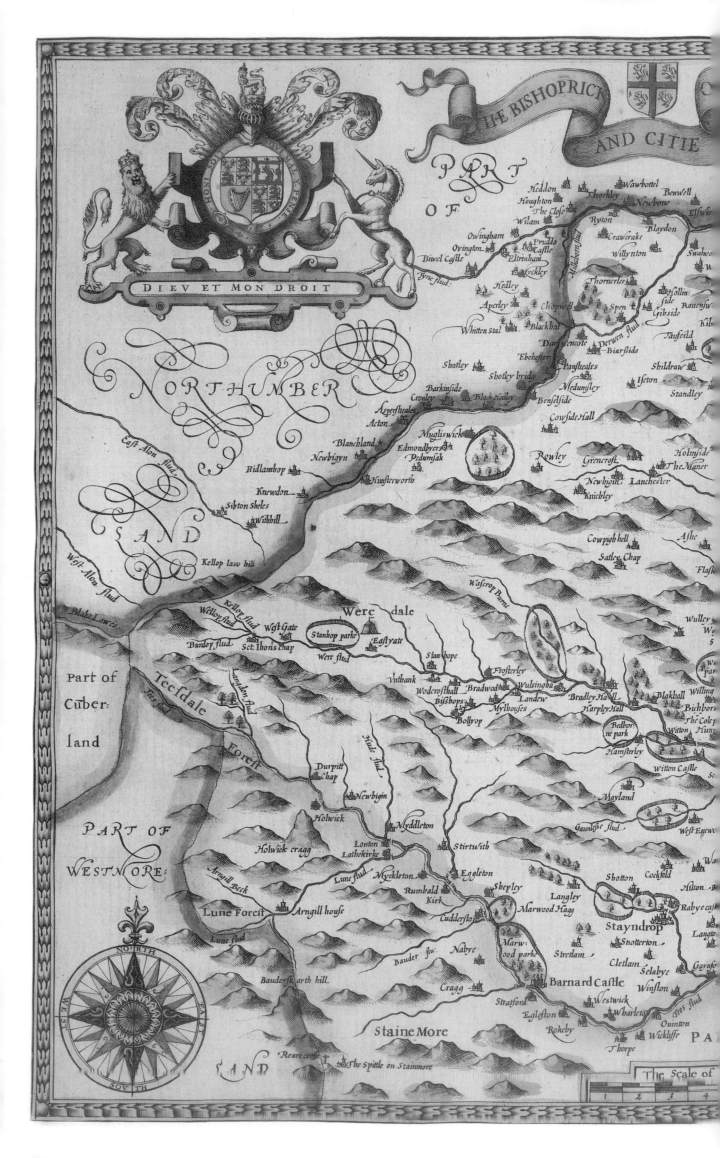

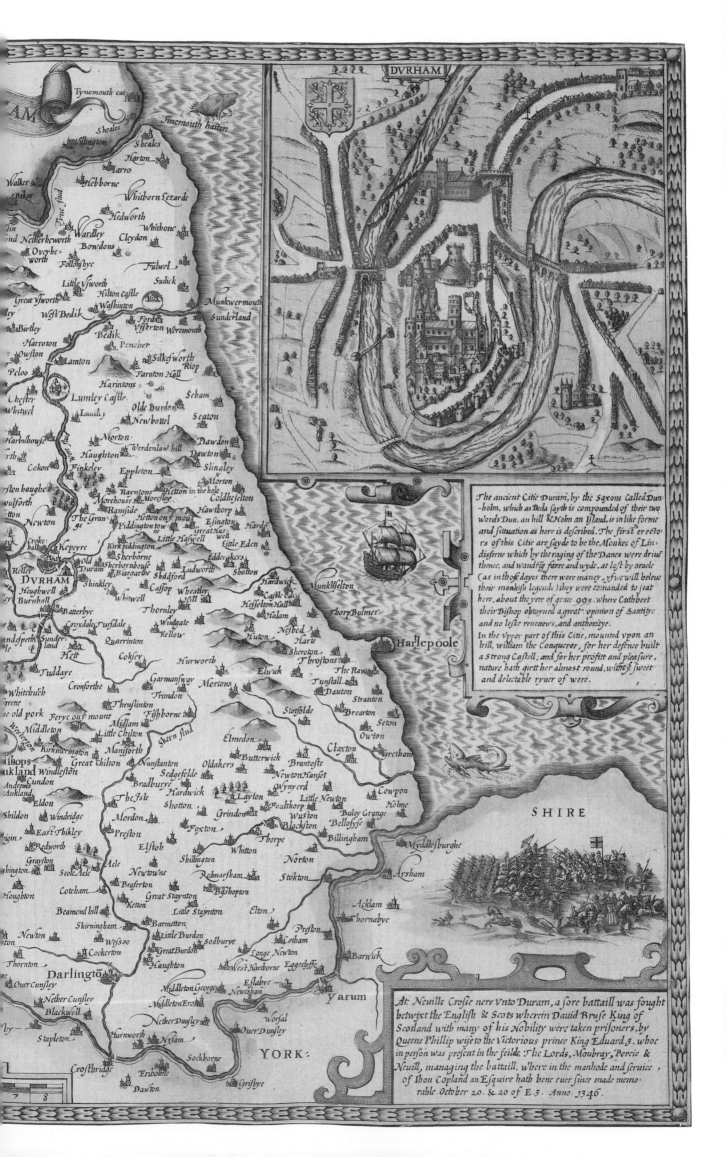

DVRHAM

The ancient Citie Durani, by the Saxons called Dun-holm, which as Beda sayth is compounded of their two words Dun, an hill & Holm an Iland, is in like forme and situation as here is described. The first erectors of this Citie are sayde to be the Monkes of Lin-disferne which by the raging of the Danes were driuē thence, and wandrig farre and wyde, at lest by oracle (as in those dayes there were maney, yf we will beleue their monkish legend) they were comanded to seat here, about the yere of grace 995. where Cuthbert their Bishop obtayned a great opinion of Santitye and no lesse reneuews, and authoritye.
In the vpper part of this Citie, mounted vpon an hill, william the Conquerer, for her defence built a strong Castell; and for her profitt and pleasure, nature hath girtt her almost round, with a sweet and delectable ryuer of were.

At Neuills Crosse nere vnto Duram, a sore battaill was fought betwixt the English & Scots wherein Dauid Bruse King of Scotland with many of his Nobility were taken prisoners, by Queene Phillip wife to the Victorious prince King Eduard 3. whoe in person was present in the feilde. The Lords, Moubray, Percie & Neuill, managing the battaill. Where in the manhode and seruice of Ihon Copland an Esquire hath bene euer since made memorable. October 20. & 20 of E.3. Anno. 1346.

the suppression of the monasteries and with distaste at the growing need to defer to the Crown in the affairs of the County Palatine—led to Durham's open involvement in the Pilgrimage of Grace, many thousands from the area marching behind the banner of St Cuthbert to join the Pilgrim host in Yorkshire during 1536. The Northern Rebellion of 1569 was a later expression of the same pent-up feelings, but it collapsed when its potential leaders submitted to Queen Elizabeth, leaving only the Earls of Northumberland and Westmorland to commit treason by restoring the mass. By making religion their cause the two earls invited the prospect of a religious war in England such as France was then experiencing, and even those with Catholic sympathies realized the folly of such a course of action. The collapse of the Northern Rebellion left the bishop the trusted agent of the Crown in the County Palatine, as he had always been, and ensured the acceptance of the Anglican settlement there.

One of those briefly imprisoned in the Tower for involvement in the 1569 rebellion was the 6th Lord Lumley, a bibliophile, antiquarian, and for fifty years High Steward of the University of Oxford until his death in 1609. Although Lumley lived mainly in Surrey, he remodelled Lumley Castle incorporating self-conscious medieval as well as renaissance features and adorning it with the arms and portraits of his ancestors and 'a marble pillar' of his pedigree and an equestrian statue of his Saxon ancestor Liulph in full armour. In Chester-le-Street church he set up an aisle of mainly spurious funeral effigies commemorating the Lumleys from Liulph to his own father. On his journey southwards in 1603 James I stopped at Lumley Castle, and on being told of the family's antiquity he exclaimed: 'Oh, mon, gang na further: let me digest the knowledge that I have gained, for I did na ken Adam's name was Lumley.' Despite the king's acid remark, Lord Lumley only typified one of the abiding passions of the age, but with his collection of family portraits and his erection of funerary monuments he was something of a pacesetter in what became the two lasting artistic interests of English families from the seventeenth century until the present day.

Essex

Rather like Surrey, Essex was curiously isolated from London. The river Lea with its many courses and its largely undrained wetlands near the river Thames served as a barrier between the capital and Essex, which the series of bridges at Stratford atte Bow and the highway that they served running from London to Colchester did little to diminish. The rise of Harwich as a port with important Continental trade links had led to its recent creation as a parliamentary borough by Queen Elizabeth in 1601, but if anything this had only reinforced the county's isolation, as Harwich dealt in the export of the fine cloth produced in the small towns lining the Colne and Stour valleys in the north of the county, and its ties with London were of secondary interest. Both Colchester and Maldon, situated high up on tidal estuaries, played a more significant role than Harwich in the extensive coastal trade that plied the whole east coast of England and served as outlets for local goods sent to London.

With its heavy clays, inland Essex was still predominantly oak woodland, and its low-lying coastal areas marsh, with a number of islands such as Canvey, Foulness and Mersea cut off from the mainland at high tide. The combination of wood and marsh made communications between neighbouring villages often difficult, and with the exception of the system of roads radiating out from Colchester and dating from the Roman occupation, Essex lacked the thoroughfares so necessary for both trade and agriculture. More than with most shires, the decision not to mark the roads in the *Theatre* was a true reflection of their comparative unimportance in Essex. Barley, wheat and corn were cultivated throughout the county, and in the vicinity of Saffron Walden the crocus used for flavouring food and for dying cloth (and which gave the town its popular name), was grown. More important to the area's well-being were sheep and cattle production, the fleece supplying wool for the weavers in the north of the county, and the milk being turned into a 'great and thick' cheese which was marketed in London and elsewhere. Fowl and fish caught along the coast and oysters produced in the inlets (particularly near Colchester) were sent by boat to feed Londoners.

The extensive woodland and numerous parks and forests well stocked with deer made Essex an attractive area for noble families and successful officials to have residences. Although the de Veres, Earls of Oxford, had long been the leading family in the county and hereditary Lord Chamberlains of England, the 17th Earl (d. 1604) had spent his time largely in court and in pursuit of his

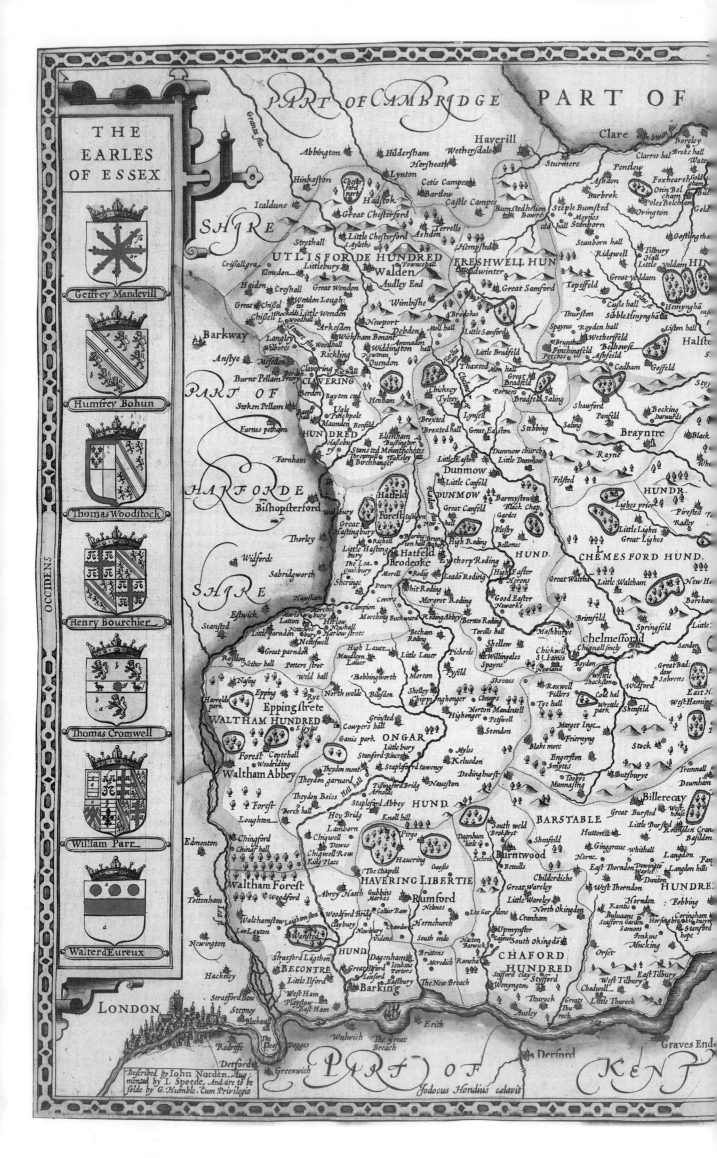

THE
EARLES
OF ESSEX

Geffrey Mandevill

Humfrey Bohun

Thomas Woodstock

Henry Bourchier

Thomas Cromwell

William Parr

Walter d'Eureux

OCCIDENS

PART OF CAMBRIDGE PART OF

SHIRE

PART OF

HARFORDE

SHIRE

UTLISFORDE HUNDRED
Walden
Audley End

FRESHWELL HUN

HIN

HALSTE

HUNDR.

Braintre

DUNMOW

HUND.

CHEMESFORD HUND.

HUNDR.

Chelmesford

ONGAR

BARSTABLE

Billerecay

HUNDRE

WALTHAM HUNDRED

Epping strete

Waltham Abbey

Waltham Forest

HAVERING LIBERTIE
Rumford

CHAFORD
HUNDRED

BECONTRE

Barking

LONDON

Described by Iohn Norden, Aug
mented by I. Speede, And are to be
solde by G. Humble, Cum Privilegio

PART OF KENT

Iodocus Hondius cælavit

ESSEX, devided into Hundreds, with the most antient and fayre Towne COLCHESTER Described and other memorable MONUMENTS observed. Anno 1610.

scholarly, poetic and dramatic interests, thus letting the Earl of Sussex with his house at Boreham and the Earl of Suffolk at Audley End assume a greater role there. Audley End, which was under construction at the time of the publication of the *Theatre* and eventually cost £200,000, was built with the intention of entertaining James I and his court there: when James did see it in 1614 he exclaimed that 'it is too much for a King, but may do for a Lord Treasurer'.

Sadly, little remains of Audley End today to illustrate James's comment, but even now it is immediately noticeable that in a county notoriously lacking stone the house is stone-clad. The natural material and obvious choice for building was timber. Flint had been used in the construction of churches until the advent of brick, which was also used for the houses of the wealthy like Sir Richard Rich at Leez Priory, Sir William Petre at Ingatestone Hall, and Sir Thomas Smith at Hill Hall. As brick did not become generally available for domestic use in Essex until the mid-seventeenth century, timber or wood with a daub infill remained the only option for the majority. After four hundred years the quantity of timber-framed building in Essex remains impressive, particularly the farmhouses with their barns, such as Temple Cressing with its medieval barley and wheat barns.

The Thames estuary and the adjoining coasts of Kent and Essex had figured in the national scheme of defence planned in 1539, and at Tilbury (where there was a ferry across the river) a fort was constructed. In 1588 this fort was strengthened by 290 pioneers in less than three weeks when there was a fear that a Spanish army would be transported from the Netherlands by the Armada, and it was there that Queen Elizabeth so famously rallied her hastily mustered troops before it became known that the Armada had been driven off course by winds in the North Sea. Apart from its proximity with the Netherlands, Essex had been selected for disembarking Spanish troops on account of the known Roman Catholicism of many of its inhabitants, whom it was presumed would support the downfall of Elizabeth and of the Anglican Church. Interestingly, equally strong Protestant groups coexisted, sometimes in adjoining parishes, and Puritans from these communities, disliking the Church of England almost as much as the Roman Catholics did, were among the first settlers to go to North America early in the seventeenth century.

Speed's aerial view of Colchester reveals a town of some prosperity with its castle, churches, dwellings and former religious houses somewhat uncomfortably straddling a circle of walls of Roman origin. Despite his interest in Roman antiquities—and the knowledge of the importance of Camulodunum in Roman Britain—Speed seems not to have been aware of the interest of much that survived there, preferring to depict coins bearing the heads of the Emperor Constantine and his parents Constantius and Helena, all Romans born in Britain, than of the Emperor Claudius who had incorporated Britain in the Roman Empire and who had visited Colchester, on account of Constantine's part in the adoption of Christianity as the official faith of the Roman Empire.

Gloucestershire

Gloucestershire is divided into three distinct zones: from west to east, the Forest of Dean with its red sandstone, the valley of the river Severn with the associated vales of Gloucester and of Berkeley, and the Cotswolds with their limestone. Economically the county was equally distinctive. The Forest of Dean with its abundance of oak, elm and beech was rich in iron-ore deposits near to the surface, and from the Middle Ages it had shared with Sussex the honour of being one of the two main centres for iron production in England. The lower reaches of the Severn valley were good for corn and cattle, and its dairy produce was much in demand; higher up-river near Herefordshire and Worcestershire apple and pear trees were cultivated. On the Cotswolds grazed innumerable flocks of sheep which yielded the most highly prized wool in England. With its fast-flowing streams and river the valley of the Stroud was a centre for weaving, though this industry was established in most towns and villages throughout the county. At the Dissolution of the Monasteries Sir Thomas Bell set up a cloth manufactory in the former Blackfriars in Gloucester. During the Tudor period the older urban areas with their regulations and restrictive practices made several attempts to curtail the expansion of the cloth industry, but to no avail. At the end of the sixteenth century glass production was revived at Woodchester to meet the local demand for the commodity. The period was one of great prosperity as can be seen from the perpendicular churches built at Northleach, Chipping Camden and Fairford by the Forley, Grevel and Tame families respectively, and by the boom in small domestic buildings with their distinctive gabled first-floor windows. Stone from the Cotswolds quarries was in great demand as a building material and as chips for the county's highways. Gloucestershire was also something of a pacesetter in modern horse-breeding, which Sir Nicholas Arnold (d. 1580) of Highnam made very much his own interest, and encouraged his friends to imitate.

Gloucester, with its small industries, its market and its quays, was the commercial outlet for the marcher counties along the banks of the river Severn, which was navigable for light craft almost as far as Shropshire. Silting downstream led merchants to prefer Bristol to Gloucester as a port supplying the Severn basin, but the liability of the highway between Bristol and Gloucester to flood and its general disrepair, combined with the difficulty of transporting goods across the river to Monmouthshire at a crossing lower than Gloucester (the ferry at Aust being unreliable), ensured that Gloucester preserved some

The Armes of ý Cittie   NORTH   GLOCESTER

Walsham   Meyn ham

Were houle

Poole Meade

West Bridge

Oxlease

The Castle Mead

The riuer of   Seuern

Whit friers

Marben pke

The Butts

Gaudy Green

Grounds belonging to the Priory of Lanthony

SOVTH   EAST

A. The College
B. Cathedrall Chu:
C. S. Oswald
D. S. Mary ante po
E. S. Nicholas
F. S. Bartlemew
G. S. Mary grace
H. S. Trinyty
I. S. Albalowes
K. S. Michaell
L. S. Johns
M. S. Aldames
N. S. Mary Christ
O. S. Owens
P. Castle Gate
Q. Black friers gete
R. The Key
S. The Colledge gate
T. K. Edw: gate
V. The Bishoppallas
W. The Deans house
X. The high Cross
Y. South gate
Z. West gate
1. North gate
2. East gate

This Citty is not great but standeth holsomly and sweetly, as it were vpon a hill, the streets descending euery way from the Crose. It is gouerned by a Mayor, two Shirifs, and 12 Aldermen, hauing both sword and Macees borne before them. It is accounted one of the hundreds of the Shire: but indeed it is a County within it selfe of great comaund, hauing 2 other Hundreds adioyned vnto it viz Kings Berton & Dudsto the which conteyning 30 Townes & Hamlets, lying rounde about the Cittye, ý Mayor & Cittizens haue the comand of all ý inhabitants ther dwelling. the liberty therof is called ý Inshire, as more euedently is seē in ý Mapp

Besides the 2 plottes of Glocester and Bristow (which are exactly sett out with euery Church Street Lane and place of note you must note also that the whole Shire is contriued into 53 Hundredes, all which are deuided by certeyn pricks according to auntient custome and Records Now besids ý diuisions aboue specified the Shire is quartered into 4 parts ý which also is explayned & seuerered by a litle round Circle contayning ý number of Hūdreds within euery diuision

Part   of Mō   mouth

After many deadly battells fought betwixt Canut the Dane, and Edmund Ironsyde King of the English Saxons: the last was tried by single Combate betwixt them in the Ile of Alney nere Glocester, wherin they valliantly a while fought, & in ý end accorded to parte ý Kingdō: & they ioyntly gouerned, till treason took away the lyfe of K. Edmund, & left ý Dane sole Monarche.

shire

At Tewkesburye was fought the last battell betwene King Edward 4 and K. Henry 6. wherin prince Edward ý generall was slaine, and Quene Margaret ý maintayner of those quarels taken prisoner. ther died also in ý battayll Tho E. of Deuonshire Iohn Mar: Dorset, ý L. Wenlake, & Edmund D. of Somerset ther taken & beheaded. This was fought 1471.

The Scale of Miles

WEST

PARTE OF   WOR   TER   FORD

PARTE   OF   HERE

Maluern Hills

Vpton

Longden

Twyn

Bushley
Forthamp
Passage

Pendock

Eldersfeld

Chaseley

Turley   TEWK

Losse cour
The Haw passa

Preston
Niarche

Bamsbrugh

Lidbyry

Ledenssu

Dimock

BOTLOW

Kempley

HVN

Oxnoll

Pantley

Vpleadon

Stanton

Hasfeld
Cosse cour
Cossewood

Vpton

Newent

Hartbury

Aston

SHIRE

Gotheridge Ca

Wasford

Maistmore

Ledencot

Ashelewort

Laisinton

Taynton

Tibberton

Radford

Ouer

Huntley

Bulley

The Lea

Longhope

Abenhall

Churcham

Blayson

Minster worth

Wellsbicknot

Whitchur

Dixto

Pant

Jbam

Ruarden

Monmō

PARS

Mansi hope

Dean mag

Dean pua

Flaxey

Westbury

Elnore
Longney

Hardwick
Haresfeld

Mortonwo
Standish

MVNMOVTH

Staunton

Newland

S. BRE

English Bicknor

THE FOREST OF DEAN

Newnhā

WESBVRY

HVN

Aure
Blakney

Frethern
WHISTON
HVN

Frampton

Stonbou

Whitmyster
Estlinton

Pennalt

VELLSH
Churewall

S. Brewells Cast

Lydney

Preston pass

Aylberton

Gatcomb

BLE
DISLOWE

King Stanley
Leonard

Cambridge
Stanley

Cowley
Frocetet

Llandago

Tyntern

HVN

Hewels field

Aulyberton

Alvingtō

Slimbridge

Wansvvell

Nymfeld

Tyntern:
Abb

Brokwer

Wuttaston

Hame

Barkley

BARKLEY

Stinch:
combe

Pentery

Lancante

Whitley Purke

Ny bley
HVN

Durfley

WOTTON HVN

The New worke

Chepstow

Tydenham

Shperdine

Stone

New Parke

Micklewood Chase

Bradley

Wotton Vnderedge

Mathorn

Settes ley pass

Rockhāpton

Favlesfeld

Tort worth

Charfeld

Kingeswood Alderley

Sudhrok

The Treacle

Oldhury

THORNBVRY

Littleton

Thornbury
HVN

Crumball

WILT
PARS

Apscro

Wekewar

GROMBOLDASH

Baa
Horton

Badmant

Sherston rock

Aust

Aust passage
Aylverton

Allaston

Tetheringtō

Rangeworthe

Acton yate

Chesell Pill

HENBVRY
Tuckington
Vicote

Ouleston

Satirige

SVYNSHEAD
& LANGLEY

Chippingsodbury

Old Sodbur

Wapley

Aunsbury

Frampton Cottrel
HVN

Westerley

Codington

Compton
Grenuyld

Ouer

HVN
Winterborne

PVCKLE
HVN

Hinton

Do

HVND:

Stoke gua
Stoke

Teysford

Pucklechurch

Durhā

The River Sabrine

Kinges rode

Porshut Poynt

Laurence
Weston

Charlton
Henbury

CHVRCH
Ahoteston

Durhā lo

Weston
Regis

Fylton
Horfeld

Stoke Loda

Hambrok

Syston

Durbī ma

Crockhampill

Sye

S. Blase Chap

Shirehampton
Ridlam

Mangsfeld

The forest of

Coldaston
lodge

Rownam passage

Clifton

S. Vincents
rock

BARTO
HVN

Kingelwood

Walland

Wyke

Catarn

Sangris

Colg

PARTE OF   SOM Caneshā   Bedminster

BRISTOL

W. Hanham

Bitton

Stoke

MERSET SH

PARTE OF WARWICK SHIRE

PARTE OF OXFORD SHIRE

PARTE OF WILT SHIRE

DIEV ET MON DROIT

The Vale of Evesholme

Coats of arms (right column, with captions):

Rob. Fitz Hamont Erle of Glou.	W. Mandevile Erle of Glocest.	Robert de Millent Erle of GL.
Richard de Clare Er. of glouces.	Raff Monthermer Erl of Glocest.	Hugh Spencer Er. of glocest.
Hugh d'Andley Erle of Glou.	Thom of Woodstock Erle of GL.	Humfry Duke of Glocester
Richard Duke of Glocester		

Richard Duke of Glocester

EAST

Bristol key:

A. Greate St Augustin	G. St Ihons	N. Allhallowes	T. St Thomas
B. Litle St Augustin	H. St Lawrence	O. St Mary port	V. The Temple
C. The Gaunte	I. St Stephens	P. St Peters	W. Ratcliff gate
D. St Michaell	K. St Leonard	Q. St Phillip	X. Temple gate
E. St Iames	L. St Warburgs	R. The Castle	Y. Newgate
F. Froomgate	M. Christ church	S. St Nicholas	

BRISTOW

NORTH

The Armes of ye Citty

Froome fluvius

The Key

Auon flu.

The Marsh

The Bucke

WEST

EAST

Redclif

SOUTH

BRISTOW is one of the greatest and famous Cittes in England, the greatest parte thereof standeth in ye boundes of Glocestershire ye rest in Somersettshire: but the Bristollians will nott be counted in eyther, but wilbe a County or Shire within themselfes It standeth vpon the Riuer of Auon which 4. myles from thenc falleth into Seuern, it hath a fayre bridge of stone with howses on each side like London bridge and almost halfe so long although but 4. Arches In the East end of ye Citty is ye Castle, which they confes to stand in Glocestershire Ther is no dunghill in all ye Cittie nor any sinke that cometh from any house into ye Streets but all is conueyed vnder ground, neyther haue they any Carts, but cary all vpon Sledds theris in ye Citty and Suburbs 20 fayre Churches whereof 18. are parish Churches, It is gouerned by a Mayor Aldermen and Shirifs hauing Sword and wearing Scarlett as they doe in Glocester, London and other Cities vpon great high and feastiuall dayes in ye yeare. A towne of great Marchandise The chiefe kay standeth vpon ye lesser Riuer called Froome which ebbeth & floweth some times 40. foote in height bringing in Shipps of very great burden. The Castle was builded by Robert Consul of Glocester, bastard sonne of Kinge Henry the first.

Anno Domini 1610.

Performed by John Speede And are to be sold in Popes head Alley against the Exchange by John Sudbury and George Humble Cum Privilegio

of its former regional supremacy well into the seventeenth century. The Reformation with the abolition of the local cult of the martyr-king Edward II, assassinated at Berkeley Castle in 1327, ended an important source of money to Gloucester, but the elevation of its former abbey to cathedral in 1549 went some way to compensate for this.

At the southern extremity of the county and on the river Avon, Bristol had a markedly different character from the rest of the county. With a population of about 10,000 in 1600, it was one of the largest towns in England, and as a commercial centre it served both the Severn basin and the Avon hinterland of Somerset and Wiltshire. It was also an international port. The trade with Spain and the Mediterranean had diminished to insignificance under the Tudors, but in its place new links with North America had developed, while the colonization of Ireland under Elizabeth I had revived Bristol's Irish business and its flagging coastal trade with South Wales. Above all, it enjoyed what amounted to a monopoly on the supply of cod. Like Gloucester, Bristol became the seat of a bishopric under Henry VIII, with an anomalous diocese situated largely at some distance in Dorset.

As with all other counties on the Severn, Gloucestershire fell within the administrative orbit of the Council in the Marches of Wales, and at least during the presidency of Princess Mary (later Queen Mary) the council frequently met there, the princess often residing at Thornbury during the 1530s. If Henry VIII was the last monarch to visit Gloucestershire with regularity, it became the home of his sixth and last wife Catherine Parr, who after the king's death lived with her new husband Lord Seymour at Sudeley Castle until her death in 1548: Speed, with his strong royalist sentiment, strangely omitted the fact of Catherine's burial at Sudeley in his commentary on the county. Sudeley Castle, a magnificent building dating from the mid-fifteenth century, which Edward IV had not scrupled to secure for a palace, passed into the possession of the Chandos family which during the 1570s further embellished it. However, the most interesting buildings in the county from the sixteenth century were not the baronial castles of Thornbury and Sudeley, though these were spectacular, but a group of houses associated with men in the service of Henry VIII who ensured that Gloucestershire retained its regional pre-eminence in artistic fashion almost until the compilation of the *Theatre*: at Horton Thomas Knight, who went to Rome in the hope of advancing Henry VIII's divorce, added adornments and a loggia to his house reflecting what he had seen in Italy, and at Iron Acton and Newark Park Sir Nicholas Poyntz, who had his portrait done by Holbein, put up a house and a hunting lodge clearly influenced by current architectural ideas in London and at the court.

At the Union with Wales in 1536, the boundary between Monmouthshire and Gloucestershire was rationalized, but several anomalies remained on the east where the county incorporated outliers from Worcestershire, Wiltshire and Berkshire, while limbs of its own were detached in Worcestershire and Oxfordshire. These administrative oddities are clearly shown on Speed's map.

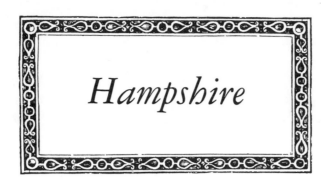

Hampshire

With its chalk uplands, gravels and thin soil Hampshire would seem to have lacked the basic requirements for a prosperous agricultural community, but this was not the case. Much of the county was woodland, particularly the New Forest in the south-west and the area to the north of Portsmouth running eastwards to the border with Sussex and Surrey. However, this extensive woodland with its timber, deer, game and birds was not the chief source of income to the county's proprietors: the soil responded to careful husbandry, yielding an abundance of corn and of grass pasture where cattle grazed; the many rivers were spawning-grounds for freshwater fish, and had long been celebrated for their sport before Izaak Walton sang the praises of the river Itchen, and the ubiquitous sheep provided wool for export and for weaving. Towards the east of the county there were deposits of iron near to the surface of the ground which could easily be extracted; and on the coast were saltpans, which provided an essential commodity for cooking and the preservation of food. As Speed put it, the diversity of these commodities was to 'the county's great benefit and England's great praise'. The wealth that they produced goes a long way in explaining the enormous revenues enjoyed by the bishopric of Winchester during the Middle Ages, so that even after the depletions of the Reformation Winchester remained one of the richest sees in the kingdom.

The material and economic advantages of the county and the disposal of church property at the Reformation made Hampshire an obvious choice for men successful in the service of the Tudors and anxious to consolidate their fortunes and to invest their newly acquired wealth. With the exception of the Countess of Salisbury with a house in Warblington, Hampshire lacked a lay magnate resident in the county at the beginning of the sixteenth century. Two men of local origin, William, Lord Sandys, and William Paulet, Marquess of Winchester, consolidated their family holdings and built homes befitting their new status at Mottisfont, the Vyne, Basing and Netley, but it was the outsider from London who rose to be the King's Secretary and Lord Chancellor, Thomas Wriothesley, Earl of Southampton, who perhaps made the greatest impact when amongst other properties he acquired the estates of Titchfield Abbey virtually in their entirety. Significantly Speed, who did not normally mark houses on his maps, made an exception for Titchfield and its park.

With its commodious houses and many facilities, Hampshire was a favourite county for progresses with Tudor and Stuart kings and queens. It was also the

Winchester

Index of Winchester plan:
1. Hyde Church
2. Hyde Abbey
3. Hyde street
4. Iury stretz
5. Tanners stretz
6. Ruell Chappell
7. Walles strete
8. S. Maryes Abbey
9. S Johns hospitall
10. S Johns stret
11. Tens Lane
12. Water Lane
13. S. Peters church in c.
14. S Peters strete
15. Colbrok strete
16. S. Peter Colbrok
17. S Mary Callender
18. The Gail prisone
19. Staple Garden
20. S. Morts Church
21. S Lawrence
22. S Thomas
23. S Bartholomewes
24. S. Clementes
25. Wolsey House
26. The Colledge
27. Colledge mill
28. Kings Gate
29. South Gate
30. The minster
31. Paradise
32. The Castle

60 120 180 240
PASES

CLITON a Saxon Earle of Winchester

SAER QVINCY Earle of Winchester

HUGH SPENCER Earle of Winchester.

LODOWICK BRUGET Earle of Winchester.

WILLIAM PAULET Marques of Winchester

The warrs betwixe Maud the Empresse (intituled Lady of England unto whom all the Nobility had sworne Aleageance) And King Stephen Earle of Bolloigne her Cosin germane, was prosecuted with such variable fortunes in many conflicts on both partes: that Stephen himselfe was by her taken prisoner and reteyned in Irons with other extremityes used, But successe of warr altering, Maud the Emprese to save her owne life adventured throwe the Host of her enimie, layde in a coffin fayned to be dead, and soe was caryed in a horse-litter from Winchester to Lutegershall Vices, and Gloucester; and thence to Oxford, whence the yere following she escaped as dangerously by deceaving the Scout watch in a deepe snowe. Anno 1141.

PART OF BAK

SE

PART OF EVINGER HUNDRED

PASTRAE HUNDRED

ANDOVER HUNDRED

HORWELL HUNDRED

BUDLESGATE HUDRED

BARTON STACYE HUNDRED

THORNEGATE HUNDRED

SOMBOURNE Hundret

WEST Forrest

WALTHAM HU

Woodhay
Highclere
Ashemansworth
Newton
Earleston
Burghclere
Sidmanton
KIN

Nastwood
Combes
Fakeham
Paston
Woodcote
Lichsfeild

Ninkenholt
Upton
Egbury
Henley
Bindley
Langley
Stoke
St Maryborn
Whitchurch
Frisake
Charlecote

Hetherden
Charlton
Swamplon
Wyke
Husborne
Tyston

Rednan
Aylecha
Chute Forrest
Charlton
Clanfeild
Enchem
ANDO.
Witham
Husborne
Penton
Weyhill
VER HONDR.
Andover
Long parish
Bram
Barton Stacye
Sutton
Wunston
Olds

Truxton
Tidworth
Kimpton
Offield
Coldton
Saughton
WITHOUT HUNDRED
Munkeston
Platford
Abbotsham
Gallare
Whorwell
Chilbolton

Shipton
Anporte

Quarley
Grotley
Clatjord
Dunbury hill
Goodworth Clatford
Kings
Leckford
Crawley
Littleton
Hedborneworth

Uperwallop
Nether Wallop
Longstoke
Stokbridge
Uper Somborne
Somborne
Bearewecke
Pitt

Browghton
Bossington
Little
Kingsomborne
Ashley
Fairelcigh
St. Crosse
Compton

Buckholt Forrest
West Titherley
Mottesfont
Hundret
Hursley

East Titherley
Brooke
Lunford
Maxwell

East Deane
Michelmersh
Otterburne
Crowdhill

Lockerley
Anseild
Badsley
Toothill
Beacon
Bistoke

Timsbury
Stanbridge
Persunt
Rumley
Chilworth
North Stonham

Sherseild
Brodlands
MANSBRIDGE
Durley

Wellow
Morcot
Nursting
Grove place
South Stoham
WALTHAM HU

Setchfeild
Hale
Warke
Paltons
Winston
Redbridge
S. Dionics

Charforde
Whisbury FORDIC
Branxe
NEWFORREST
Linwood
Testwood
Milhrokhill
Sct. Maries

Rockborne
BRIDGE
Fritham
Totton
Itche

Burgate
Fording bridge
Malwood castle
Minsted
Elinge
REDBRIDGE
HUNDRED
Southampton

HUN:
Beckam
DRED
Tach Burye

Migiam
Newe
Lindhurste
Debdon
Hyth

Horbridge
Ibsley
Parke
Hobury
Beaulieu

Mloyles Court
Burley
Brokenhurst
Raydon
Fowley

RINWOOD
Ringwood
Selborne
Beacon
Battramsley
Boldre
Leape
Exbury

Winton
For:
HUN: DRED.

HUNDRED
CHRISTCHURCH
rest
Lymington
Badsley

Longham
HUNDRED
Bisterne
Arnwood

Parlieu
Winton
Avon
Tuddiford
Hurst castle

Preston
Holmhurst cap.
Sopley
Burton
Hurton
Milton
Milford
Hordwell

Isforde
Somerford
Nash

Heath
Christchurch
Black Cliffe

Bascomb copperashouse
PART O

Allam house

WIST SHIRE

Parte of Dorset Shire

T

scene of the meeting of King Henry VIII with the Emperor Charles V in 1525, and of the marriage of Queen Mary with Philip of Spain in 1554, both events taking place at Winchester. If it had not been for its castle, cathedral, episcopal palace and college, Winchester would have been little different from other market towns in Hampshire. Winchester College—founded in 1382 by William of Wykeham to provide a system of tuition with his co-foundation of New College, Oxford, for boys from early adolescence to manhood—had been unprecedented in England and had provided a model for other less lavish foundations: such was the fame of the college that pupils came to it from far outside Hampshire. At the Reformation Winchester College was recognized as an institution of exceptional merit, and like Eton College and the two Universities, it survived the fate that so disrupted the teaching of children in mid-sixteenth-century England.

Throughout the Middle Ages Southampton had been a port second only to London, but with a decline in the export of wool for weaving abroad and the collapse of its trading links with Gascony, Italy and Spain, it had lost its earlier prosperity, and by the 1590s its population had shrunk to some 4,200. Speed's aerial view of the town (an insert in the map of the Isle of Wight) reveals considerable uninhabited areas within its walls, and what housing there was is known to have been in a poor state of repair. The experience of Portsmouth was very different from that of Southampton. Long a base for naval expeditions, Portsmouth under Henry VII became for the first time a dockyard of some complexity and permanence, with docks and shore installations, victualling stores with their breweries and bakeries, and the fortification of the town. Henry VIII further developed his father's idea of a defensible naval base which was later to be so important in Britain's subsequent sea power. With the fleet harboured there the defence of Portsmouth and its approaches became a major preoccupation of the Crown: in the 1520s Portsmouth was provided with one of the earliest artillery defences in the country, and following the invasion scare of 1539 an integrated system of forts was constructed for the protection of the Solent, Southampton Water and the Isle of Wight. This system was repaired and modified throughout the century in accordance with the latest military thinking. With the development of alternative bases in the Thames estuary at Deptford, Woolwich and Chatham, Portsmouth lost its hitherto unchallenged position as the headquarters for the Navy, but even so it remained a town of great importance in the nation's defensive network. That notoriously indolent king, Henry VIII, had taken a keen personal interest in Portsmouth, and it was during one of his visits there in 1545 when the French fleet attacked that the *Mary Rose* capsized and sank. Concern over the marine approaches to Portsmouth and its defence made the Hampshire coast one of the most surveyed stretches of the kingdom, and this accounts for the higher degree of accuracy than usual achieved by Hondius in his delineation of the county's shoreline. The county map also marked the beacons used in emergencies to warn of enemy landings and to galvanize the local musters to repel the invaders.

Isle of Wight

For general purposes of civil administration the Isle of Wight was considered part of Hampshire, from which it was separated only by the waters of the Solent. For purposes of national defence it was the historical linchpin of a system of defence nominally in charge of the governor or captain of the island with headquarters at Carisbrooke Castle and with a jurisdiction extending as far as the Scilly Isles in the west and the Channel Islands in the south. The development of Portsmouth as a naval base by the early Tudor kings and the creation of a complex system of fortifications commanding the marine approaches to Portsmouth, and including the island, diminished the importance of the governorship, but that the appointment remained one of significance to the Crown is clear from its being given by Queen Elizabeth to her kinsman Sir George Carey, later 2nd Lord Hunsdon.

Under Henry VIII the vulnerable northern shore of the island was protected by a series of small artillery forts, blockhouses and bulwarks extending from the Needles Passage to Sandown Bay, the earliest and least successful being Worsley's Tower opposite Hurst Castle on the mainland. At first Carisbrooke Castle did not figure in the new system of fortifications, being left to endure the general neglect which was the fate of ancient castles in the early sixteenth century, but the arrival of Carey in 1583 brought that to an end. Admittedly Carey attended initially to putting his quarters in good repair, but the worsening of international relations with Spain led to the surveying and repair of the castle. After the destruction of the Armada in 1588, the island remained a likely target for a Spanish landing, and this possibility led to the engagement of the Italian engineer Frederico Grenebelli to remodel the castle in accordance with the latest ideas on artillery fortification, the work being completed shortly before the accession of James I and the new King's peace treaty with Spain, so that Grenebelli's work was never put to the test. During the Civil War the castle was considered comfortable and secure enough to house and to hold Charles I and three of his children after their capture by Parliamentary forces.

The island had long since been recognized as a hazard to the shipping entering Southampton and Portsmouth and to the coastal trade that plied along the south coast of England. This was further complicated by the double high tide which is a phenomenon of the Solent and Southampton Water. Much of the island's own southern coastline was made up of sheer chalk cliffs with rocks offshore, and rocks and sandbanks and mudflats made its northern shoreline

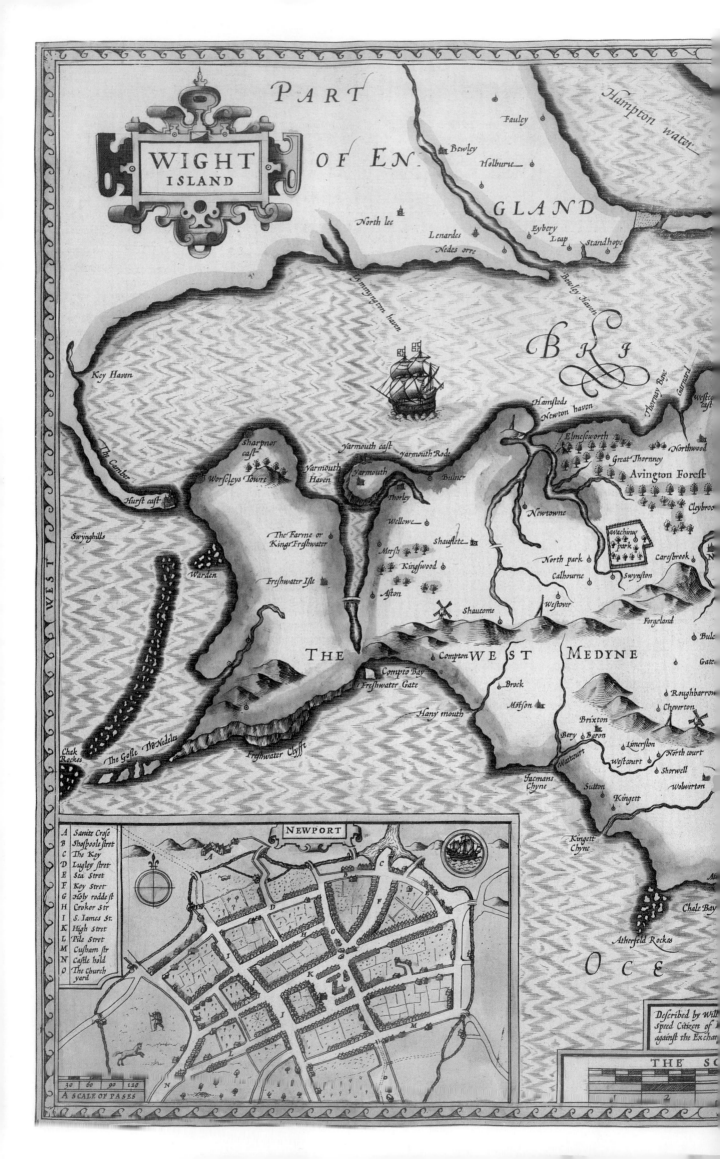

The Isle of Portsmouth   The Isle of Haybuge   The Byll

Latiyston Haven   Chichester Powler

Gosport   South Sea cast   Stoks Baye   Browne Downes   Tychefeld haven

THE   The Horse   ISH

The Brambles   No Mans lande

Medhol   Shofleat   Wootтом haven   Sands heale   Black Rocke

Nettles Hythe   S. Hellens haven   The Myxon

Wootone Park   Fishhouse   Quarr   Pouppoll   Trablesfeld   Ride   Whitfeld   S. Hellen   Hill

Bindsted   Neunam   Smalbrok   Binbridge Isle

EAST   Standen   Comley   Ashe   Nounwell   Brading   East Forland

ME DYNE   Mitton

Keughton   Kerwn   Ageston   Averston   yaverland

Ahorton   Merston   Haslley   Newchurch   Sandome cast   Coulver Clyffes   The White Clyffe

Redway   Pagam   Hall   Langhorn   Fleshland   Slutter

Godshill   Apse   Langford   Shanklin   Shanklin

Bridg court   cliffe   Roxall   Luckome   Bannose

Stynburne   Apton Combe   Weeke   Whitwell   Dane   Done Mosse

Katherm   S. Laurence   park

ugmented and published by Iohn
be solde in Popes head alley
and G. Humbell. Cum Privilegio.

ENGLISHE MILES

5   6   7

SOVTHHAMPTON

A Scale of Pases   20 40 60 80 100

A	Witter Gate	Y	Simnel stret
B	Custom house	X	Biddles Gate
C	Gods house	Z	The Castle
D	Gods house gate	2	Castle lane
E	Gods house grene	3	Castle Gate
F	The Friers	4	Barr Gate
G	The Friers Rum	5	Englist stret
H	S Iohns church	6	East stret
I	Brod Lane	7	Broker lane
K	French strete	8	East Gate
L	West Gate	9	Alhallowes
M	Bull strete	10	Athal without
N	Bull hall	11	Canshut lane
O	West Hall	12	The Butts
P	West Key	13	Beyond y wale
Q	Lords lane	14	Bargrewe
R	Fish market	15	S Mary stret
S	S. Michaels	16	Orchard lane
T	Holy Rode	17	S. Maryes
V	S. Laurence	18	The Chantree
W	New Corner	19	Salt Marshe

20

Will Fitz Osborne L

Rich. River E of Devon

Hen. Beauchamp K of Wight

Rich wooduill E. Riuers

EAST

no less easy to sail. With an eye to navigational needs, Speed and William White, upon whose earlier work Speed drew, marked all these features as well as the main natural and man-made features, such as beacons and windmills, which served as navigational guides. Given this, their omission of the lighthouse at St Catherine's Down, which survives today from the fourteenth century, is somewhat curious. The series of beacons up the island was interlinked with that on the mainland as part of the national warning system.

Despite its fortifications with their soldiery and its marine hazards, the island was not a bleak place to live. As Speed noted, its 'air is commended both for health and delight', and he went on to observe the longevity of the inhabitants, without signs of the decrepitude that marked the elderly elsewhere in Britain. Not only was the island a salubrious place to live, it was a fruitful one too. Within its small compass it had land in the south suitable for growing corn, in the centre for grazing sheep 'whose wool the clothiers esteem the best' after that produced in Leinster and the Cotswolds, and in the north for pasturing cattle. Everywhere there were rabbits, hares, partridges and pheasants. Timber for building and wood for fuel were scarce, however, and had to be brought across the Solent to meet the islanders' needs. As if to compensate for this deficiency the island had a source of good limestone for building at Quarr, and the stone houses of its inhabitants were the cause for comment by visitors. Sea-birds and fish in large numbers completed the basic amenities of the place, providing food for the islanders and for sale throughout Hampshire. In addition to Newport in the shadow of Carisbrooke there were two other market towns, and all in all thirty-six parish churches. The port of Southampton was the natural point of distribution for the produce of the island, and it was perhaps for this reason that Speed included an aerial view of that town together with that of Newport in the two bottom corners of his map of the island.

Herefordshire

As is evident from Speed's map, Herefordshire has a rolling landscape broken by isolated hills, with its western flank rising gently into the foothills of the Welsh mountains, and it is crossed by innumerable brooks, streams and rivers feeding into the main artery of the river Wye. The county is still heavily wooded, disafforestation since the seventeenth century being limited to the former royal forests and deer-parks. Much of the woodland was made up of oak, elm and beech, but some of it was orchard, producing apples and pears. It was also good arable country, specializing in growing wheat, but the rural economy of Herefordshire rested not on its fruits and cereals but on its livestock—the cattle and sheep which grazed its hills. The cattle were bred largely for meat destined for sale in London and the sheep for their fleece woven into fine yarn and cloth, 'Lemster Ore' being among the best quality short-staple wools. With its water-power the county was well supplied with mills for grinding corn and fulling wool, and whereas other regions had disturbances sparked off by enclosures, in Herefordshire similar riots and incidents were often connected with attempts to restrict the number of such mills. In addition to weaving, the many small towns also specialized in the curing and tanning of hides, and those communities were not infrequently split between the opposing interests of the clothiers and the tanners. The comparative wealth of Herefordshire's twenty-eight market towns and their commercial rivalries led to a spate of constructing town-, market- or guild-halls under the Tudors and Stuarts, often spectacular structures which, where they survive, continue to impress today's visitors. In the Middle Ages glass had been produced in the county mainly to supply the windows of its churches but when the industry was re-established in the late sixteenth century, its products were used entirely for domestic purposes.

Until the Edwardian conquest of Wales, Herefordshire had been an area subject to frequent Welsh incursions, and to protect the county as much as to provide a springboard to mount offensives against the intruders, it had been defended by numerous castles, such as Goodrich. In Speed's day twenty-eight of these fortresses with their feudal appendages survived intact and were occupied as homes by their owners. The Welsh had ceased raiding Herefordshire in force, so that these fortifications had now lost much of their original *raison d'être*. But herds of cattle and flocks of sheep were subject to thieving from across the border: the full extent of this thieving (which was by no means

HIRE described
...eford, as also the
...ne intituled with

PART OF WORCESTER SHIRE

PART OF WORCESTER

SHIRE

HEREFORD

A Alhallowe
B St Peters
C St Iohns
D S. Ethelberts minst
E St Nicholas
F Kirryes Hospital
G St Gilles Almeshous
H St Ethelberts Almes
I St Ethelberts Well
K High Causye
L Wyebrigd stret
M Pipewell strete
N King Diche
O Brode strete
P Wroughtall
Q Packers Lane
R Bewall strete
S Gilford stret
T Northgate stret
V Beyond the wall
W Castle strete
X Abbaye lane
Y ...way stret
Z The Castle
3 Bowse lane
4 Wydmarsh strete
5 Towry lane
6 S Thomas stret
7 Olde stret
8 Britons stret
9 Wye Bridge
10

Black Friers

Wydmarsh Gate

Bisters Gate

S. Onyns Gate

William Hospital

S. Onyns

S. Gilles

Bartesham prebend

Eygne Gate

Friers Gate

White Friers

Wye flu.

A SCALE OF PASES
50 100 150 200

EAST

William Fitz Osborn

Robert Bossu E.

Miles Consta of Engl.

Henry Bohun E.

Henry Bullingbrok D.

Stafford

Upon the Virge of this Shire betwixt Ludlow and little Here ford, a great battail was fought by Iasper Earle of Pembrooke and Iames Butler Earle of Ormond and Wiltshire, against Edward Earle of March; In which 3800. men were slaine. The two Earles fled, and Owen Teuther taken and beheaded. This feild was fought upon the daye of the Virgin Maries Purification in Anno 1461. Where in before the battell was strok, appeared visibly in the firmament three Sunnes which after a while ioyned all together and became as before: for which cause (as some have thoight) Edward afterwards gave the Sunne in his full brighenes for his badge and cognizance.

GLOCESTER SHIRE

Whitborne

Kinghtwick

Teme flu.

Suckley

Bysshops Stanford

Cowley

Actonbeacham

Cradley

Byssfrome

Mathern

Easbache

Malvern Hills

Castle frome

Bosbury

Canfrome

Coddinton

Colwall

RADLOWE HUND

Asperton

Munsley

Lidenstu...

Esnor

The worlds end

Pixley chap

Lidbury

Aylton

Bransill cast.

Little Marcley
Marcley hill which re moued in Ano 1575

Dunnynton

Kinnaston chap

Putley chap

Preston

Bransbourgh

GREYTREE

Great Marcley

Dimmok

Salers hope

Yatton

Kempley

PART OF

How Chapple

Upton

Newent

HUNDRED

Brampton

Rudhall

Lynton

Ecklesvall

Ayton

Weston

The Lea

Rosse

Penycard cast

Coughton chap

Hope Manesell

Walford

Part of
Mounmth
...shire

Ewelshe Bicknor

English Bicknor

1 2 3 4 5

restricted to the Welsh) is hard to estimate as the livestock in the foothills of Wales was moved to different pastures according to the season, as was the standard practice in Wales but not in England.

The county's castles were stone structures as were its parish churches and the cathedral at Hereford, but most buildings were timber-framed with distinctive cusped wind-braces, which are stylistically a feature of Herefordshire. The vernacular houses in the countryside are unlike the standard pattern for England, but adhere to a type common throughout Wales—that of the 'unit' house, where domestic accommodation is duplicated in another range either facing the main block across a yard or adjoining it at one corner, but without internal communication between the two blocks. The 'unit' house reflects a family structure slightly different in Herefordshire from the rest of England in that different members or elements of a large or an extended family were given a measure of independence from one another without the sense of kinship being lost.

Like other marcher counties, there were anomalies in the extent of Herefordshire. It had outliers in three adjoining counties and itself incorporated a part of Monmouthshire. Several further oddities had been ironed out at the Union of England with Wales in 1536, but those remaining were largely resolved by Herefordshire falling within the jurisdiction of the Council in the Marches of Wales, which had its headquarters just across the Shropshire border at Ludlow. Many of Herefordshire's gentle families, such as the Crofts, provided generations of officials for the Council in the Marches.

In his commentary on Herefordshire, Speed recorded an incident of great oddity. In February 1571, he alleged, 'Marley Hill ... with a roaring noise removed from the place where it stood, and for three days travelled from her first site to the great amazement and fear of the beholders' but without harm to trees, or animals. This phenomenon, one feels, fascinated him, and unfortunately distracted him in the checking of his proofs: the armorial border decorating the right-hand side of the map contains an unusually high number of errors: the 2nd Earl of Hereford was not Robert Bossu, but Roger de Breteuil, and the Bohun earldom was not inherited by the Stafford family. A viscountcy in favour of the Devereux family, descendants in the female line from the Bohuns, was created in 1550, but Speed was not interested in recording honours lower than earldoms, and moreover the family had later acquired the earldom of Essex. This elevation is passed over on the county map for Essex—presumably on account of the 2nd Earl's rebellion and execution for treason in 1601. The embarrassment caused by the link between Herefordshire and the most recent but unsuccessful *coup d'état* may account for the mythical Stafford creation at the bottom of the column of heraldic arms, and for Speed's decision to include a depiction of the battle of Ludford Bridge (actually fought in Shropshire in 1461) in the Herefordshire map as a deflection from this unfortunate connection.

Hertfordshire

One of the smallest counties in England, Hertfordshire is the watershed for rivers which flow north, west and south, a fact made clear by the map's careful delineation of watercourses rather than our more modern emphasis on roads. Of the county's many rivers by far the most important was the river Lea, which went south via Waltham Abbey to the river Thames. Between 1609 and 1613 Hugh Myddelton canalized the Lea from Great Amwell and directed it along a new cut (aptly called the New River) down to Islington in Middlesex, where it fed a number of conduits supplying London with fresh water.

As in the case of Middlesex, the economy of Hertfordshire was geared to providing the foodstuffs so much in demand in London. Its corn went to make bread for Londoners and its hay fodder for their horses. The county bred cattle in large numbers for sale as beef at Smithfield, and supported a larger number of cattle driven down from the North for fattening up before completing their journey to London. Market gardening figured less than in Middlesex, but the county's watercress beds were already famous, watercress being recognized as an antidote to the scurvy which inflicted so many Londoners. Woods as sources of timber and of fuel and parks for deer and for pleasure completed the amenities which led Speed to say of Hertfordshire that it was 'destitute of nothing that ministreth profit or pleasure of life'.

With roads from London traversing it northwards, Hertfordshire was country much favoured by government officials and administrators, and historically it has always had a disproportionately high number of country houses, both great and small, which were built as bolt-holes from London. Since the climate was 'neither too hot nor too cold and with air temperate, sweet and healthful', Londoners often withdrew there during outbreaks of plague, and Hertford, which was a modest market town with a neglected castle, became the headquarters of the Exchequer at such times. Of the many new arrivals in the sixteenth century the two most important were the Bacon family, which built a house at Gorhambury, and Lord Burghley, who constructed Theobalds. Erected between 1564 and 1585, Theobalds in its size and design not only testified to the meteoric rise of the Cecil family, but was one of the most handsome palaces in an area where there were no royal residences of importance. Like Queen Elizabeth before him, James I was a frequent visitor to Theobalds, and to its many virtues could be added its accessibility to the roads leading to and from his Scottish kingdom: such was its appeal to the King,

E DESCRIBED
, and the moſt an:
le actions as have happened

PART

VEROLANIUM

OF

ESSEX

MIDDLESEX

Place names (selection, as labelled on map):

Little Cheſill · Great Cheſill · Barley · Newſels · Minſtonbury · Abbotſbury · Cokenhatch · I. Claueing · Barkwaye · Gigging · Meeſden · Anſtie · Burnt Pelham · Whit Barnes · Benehce · Stokenpellam · Helſhams hall

EDWINSTRE HUNDR. · Withiall · Dogſhead · Redgwells · Great Hormed · Pelham furnix · Little Hormed · Milfords · Aldboryhall · Quenbery · Grauesend · Aldbery · Patmerhall

king Beachams · Ryſton · ngley · Aſpenden · Buckland · nnus · Buntingford · Westmill · Braghing · Puckeridg · auliric · Standon · Uphall · Hadhamenaſh · Little Hadham · Bishops Stortford · Waymer caſtle · Hockerell · pollrooke · Thorley

Collies end · Berwick · Bartrams · Satridge · Caſtullbery · Great-Hadham · Shingle hall · Tednambury · Sabſworth · Sidehall

High Croſe · Tunwell · Thundridg · BRAGHING HUNDRED · Bleakſway · Peſchery · Geldeſden · New place · Newhall · Wadeſmill · Wildford Mallocks · Hunſton · Eaſwike · Harlow

Rickneſſe · Ware parke · Widboro hill · Engee · Ware · The Beacon · Hily · Amwell · Margett · Stanſted · Little Prenden · Briggens · Stantherk · Great-Prenden

Hart ford · Little Amwell · Holey · Roydon · HARTFORD HUNDRED · Hodſdon · The Ree

Barkhamſted · Reyford · Broxebourne · The Baſe · wood · Naſing · Cheſton Nunery · Punſburne · Newgateſtret · Wormeley · Cheſton park · Cheſton · woode · Woode Grene · Thyebald · Nimhall · Northhaw · Cuhollgacee · Waltham Abbey

Enfeilde Chace · Waltham Croſe · Hadley · Enfeild houſe · Enfeild · East-Bernet · Edmunton · Poteredge

In this Countie at three ſeverall tymes, three mortall and bloody Battells of Englands ciuill diſſentions haue bene fought. The firſt whereof chaunced the 23 of Maye Anno 1455. in the towne of St Albons by Richard Duke of Yorke, with his aſſotiats, the Earls of Warwicke, and Saleſbury, and Lords of faw co̷brigg, and Cobham, againſt King H 6. In whoſe defence Edmund Duke of Somerſet, Henry Earl of Northumberland, and Iohn Lord Clifford with 5000 more loſt thei̷ lives, the king himſelfe was wounded in the neck with an arrowe, the Duke of Buckingham and Lorde Sudley in their faces. Humfrey Earle Stafford in his right hand, and the Earle Dorſet almoſt ſlaine. On the Dukes part only 600. were ſlaine. The king by them was brought to London, and a reconciliation made by their aduancements unto dignityes and Offices.
The ſecound Battell was likwiſe fought in the towne of S. Albons by Queene Margaret, againſt the Duks of Norfolke, and Suſſolke, the Earls of Warwicke, and Arundell, that by force kept with them the king her huſband, with whome by conſtrayt he held, and on their ſyde fought untill the feild was loſt and the Lords fled, when with great ioye he was receiued by his Queene and younge ſone Prince Edward this Battell fell the 17. of February being Shroueſtueſday Anno 1461.
The thrid and laſt battell was fought nere unto the towne of high Barnet upon the 14. of Aprill being Eaſter daye, by the Earles of Warwicke, and Oxford, and Marques Montacule againſt King Ed. 4. whoe led with him king H. 6. his priſoner unto that feild, and obtayned that daye the victorye againſt his enemyes. There were ſlaine in this bloody Battel Richard Nevill the Stout Earle of Warwicke with his brother the Marques and the Earle of Oxford put to flight. & the Duke of Exceſter ſore wounded, and leeſt in the feild for dead. On King Edwards part were ſlaine, the Lords Cromwell, Boucher, and Barnes. And on both parts the number of tenn thouſa̷ men. Anno 1471.

7 · 8 · 9 · 10

that in 1607 Sir Robert Cecil exchanged Theobalds for several properties including Hatfield, where in the next five years he built a new—equally impressive and more modern—house which (unlike Theobalds) survives today. Hatfield had previously been a favourite residence of Queen Elizabeth, who had persuaded her brother Edward VI not to sell it but instead to give it to her: it was at Hatfield that Elizabeth spent much of her semi-captivity during the mid-1550s, and where she received news of her accession to the throne in 1558. In addition to Theobalds, James I owned an extensive but rambling hunting lodge at Royston, which straddles the county boundary with Cambridgeshire. Mary I had shared her sister's enthusiasm for the county, having a house at Hunsdon from which in 1553 she escaped from Queen Jane's supporters in the initial stages of successfully claiming the crown for herself.

The presence of so many administrators in Hertfordshire and the frequent visits of the court may explain the interest shown in learning in the county. There had been a school of some importance attached to St Albans Abbey until the Reformation, but, as with others in the county, this did not survive the Dissolution of the Monasteries. As early as 1541 the town of Berkhamsted had established a new school, with a schoolroom and accommodation for the master and usher, and the excellent example was copied elsewhere in the county so that by 1600 Hertfordshire was in the forefront of English counties in its provision for education, most of it being free to children living in the immediate vicinity of each school.

St Albans excited the curious visitor perhaps more than anywhere else in the county. Its great abbey church rebuilt at the Norman Conquest, had survived the Reformation, although the shrine to St Alban, Britain's first saint, had not. It was not the structure of the church that then attracted notice, but the fact that the dead from two battles (1455 and 1461) fought at St Albans during the Wars of the Roses and—familiar to Speed's contemporaries through Shakespeare's plays—had been buried in the church, and there was in it a font of solid brass looted by Sir Richard Lee at the siege of Leith in 1544. The remains of Verulamium also attracted attention, but the belief subscribed to by Speed that the Roman ruins had been levelled by the abbey on account of thieves and prostitutes consorting there was unfounded, the brick and stone from the ruins actually being used in the construction of the abbey. Barnet, which in 1471 had witnessed an even bloodier battle than the two engagements at St Albans, shared the interest of visitors to Hertfordshire, and all three battles were accordingly marked, illustrated and described on the county map.

Huntingdonshire

With its uplands, vales, woodland, arable, pasture and fen, Huntingdonshire had in 1600 a complexity and diversity of terrain which was disproportionate to its small size. Its prosperity as an agricultural community was mirrored by the existence of six market towns providing points for the sale of local produce and the purchase of goods varying from fresh and dried fish to coal, brought upriver and across marsh by small inland craft. For most people, not resident in the county but familiar with it, Huntingdonshire meant two things, the Great North Road traversing the county from north to south, and the Fens on its eastern flank. Speed's map reflected these two features.

With the exception of the Huntingdonshire stretch of the Great North Road and the major road junction at Chesterton, Speed showed no roads in the *Theatre*. The reason for this notable exception lay in the nature of the provision for the maintenance of roads: the inhabitants of a parish were expected to maintain a road running through the parish. By the standards of the time this system worked reasonably well in remote, rural parishes, far from any busy thoroughfare, but for places on the main highways the burden was intolerable, and the Great North Road was in a constant state of disrepair in Huntingdonshire, Cambridgeshire and Hertfordshire, the problem being worst in Huntingdonshire where the road skirted the edge of the fenland and where the volume and weight of traffic using the road was greater than anywhere other than the immediate approaches to London. The problem of maintenance, and the realization of the uselessness of presenting and indicting parishioners at assizes and quarter sessions for failing to repair the common highway, was to lead those parishes responsible for the Great North Road later in the seventeenth century to promote an innovative solution to the problem whereby road-users paid tolls, the receipts of which were to be used by specially appointed surveyors to maintain and repair the road. After its initial rejection by Parliament, the idea was accepted in 1663, when the first Turnpike Act was passed: the original measure was meant only as a temporary expedient, but its successful application to the Great North Road led to its general adoption throughout Great Britain.

The Fens were largely undrained, and although their abundance of freshwater fish and fowl and their supply of reeds for thatching houses or for covering floors were economically important, these advantages were often outweighed by the dampness and wetness of the area, which slowed down travel other

HUNTINGTON

50   100   150   200
THE SCALE OF PASES

Waldeof, by William Conque-
rour whose sisters dochter by
the mothers syde he had maried,
was created Earle of Huntington, whose elder daughter and
Coheire named Maund, maried
Simon de St Lizio, to whom
she brought the Earldome, &
a sonne that bare his father
name, Maund after death of her
first husband maried David, brother to Maund Queene of England
whose sister was King of Scotland

unto whome she bare Henry, y caryed awaye y honnor of y Earldoe.
fro his halfe & elder brother, But
Prince Henry dying before his father,
by y mutablytye of fortune & favour
of Princes, y Dignitie was agayne restored to y Lizoars, & agaye to y Scotish, as to Malcolne & willm both
Kinges of Scotlad. To David and
Iohn surnamed the Scot, Earle of
Chester, & lastly to Alexander 2.
King also of that nation. After
ward y Earldome was possessed
by these Nobles here under writte.

Waldeof E of Hunting	Simon de St Lizio	Henry Prince of Scotl.
William Clinton E	Guysard Angolesme	Iohn Holland E
Thomas Graye E	William Herbert	George Haslings

WEST

HUN... BOTH S... TOWNE... ELY

PART

NORT

OF

NORT

HAMP

TON

SHIRE

Upton
PETERBOROW
Caster
Durobrius
Water newton
Fleton
Alerton
Chesterto
Overton Waterwill
Bodulph Bridge
Overto Longuill
Farset
Elton
Haddon mill
Yaxley
Elton mill
Haddon
Haddon
Beton
Marborn
Folkesworth
Ogerston
washingle
Calcot
Stilton mill
Stilton Stilton Fen
Denton & Calcot
Oundle
Lutton
Denton
Glatton
Hemington
Conington
Saltrey mill
Saltry Beynes
Saltrey moynes
Saltrey abbey
Luddington
Thorning
NORMAN CROSSE
Great Gidding
Little Gidding Mill
Saltrey Iudeth
Knights mill
Little Gidding
Saltrey Grange
Clapton
Wiruik
Steple Gidding
Copinsford
Salom Wood
Hamerton
Upton
Hamerton mill
Old Weston
Buckworth Grove
Buckworth
Weston Crowe
Weston mill
Leighton mill
Buckworth Becon
Alkmundbury
Molesworth
Brenton
Leighton
Barham
Woolly
Bithorne
Keston
Spaldwick myll
LEIGHTENSTON HUN.
Great Catworthe
Spalwick
Catworthe mill
Stowe
Ellington
Wabridge
L. Catworth
Easton
Sibthorpe
Coynyton
Grasham
Hargrave
Birthime ladg
Calfe wood
Tilbrok
Kimbalton
Priory Stowy
Agden Mill
Over Benz
Swinshead
Peterhill
Newpark
Great Stoughton
Creudgesbery
Melchborne
Little Stoughton
The Mare
Haleweston

PART OF BED:
FORD SHIRE

Eaton
Rekkesde

Performed by Iohn Speed
And are to be sold in Popes:

Berforde

LINCOLNE

TON
ND SHIRE
E ANCIENT
BED.

ELY

A Scale of Pases

50   100   150   200

Mersh

by Bishop Morton   S. Eldernall
Whitlesey   Maden lood

Whitlesey Kings delfe   Wunlington

Ramsey Kings delfe   Dunnyngton

Ramsey mere

Benwik mere   The fyrthe Dike

Botley
Ramsey

PART OF

Ramesey Fenn
Common to many townes   Charters

Bigen   Upwood   Bury   Mepole

HUND.   Upwood mill

Warboys Fen   THE ISLE

Wistow   Rowcy
Warbois woode   Somersham Fen

Reveley   Warbois

Broughton wood   Fenton   Pidley   Somersha parke   OF ELY

Ripton   Ould Hurst   The Chase   Colnt

Saply parke   Wood Hurst   Blantham

Herford   Erith

kley   Witton   Boughton   St Ives   Holiwell

ington   Holywell Fen

Hennyngford   Oise flu.

Godmanchester   Owre   Owre fen

Durosponte   Homnyngsford

Fenny Stanton   Fenny Draton

Beggers Bushe   HUNDRED

Gravely   Hilton

Cunyngton

Papworth Annes

BRIDGE

Papworth Euered

Elsley

ngani   Croxton

SHIRE

Great Gransden   Stow

Litle Gransden

Gamlingay

Text panel

Although this Citie of Ely is not in this Countye of Huntington, but in Cambridge-shire: yet because that place wo'uld not permit, to be see fully explayned. I have thought good here to insert it, as in other Countryes I am forced to the lyke: neither doth it greatly varye from the true place of situation, the Iland it selfe being bounded on the West with the Shire of Huntington.

This Citie is ancient, and hath bene better inhabited and frequented, whose beauty is much increased by the most magnificent minster dedicated to St. Peter the Laterne whereof & the Mount are ever beheld w. admiration and deserveth to be comended with a better stile then in this ould verse made by her monk Quatuor Elia, Lanterna, Capella, Maria,   Atque Molendinu; recno das vinea vinum.

EAST

DIEV ET MON DROIT

HONI SOIT QVI MAL Y PENSE

THE SCALE OF MILES

| 1 | 2 | 3 | 4 | 5 | 6 | 7 | 8 | 9 | 10 |

Jodocus Hondius Cælavit Anno Domini 1610

head alley against the Exchange by George Humbell. cum Privilegio.

than by boat and undermined health. It was with these issues in mind that Speed carefully delineated the extent of the Fens with their mears, islands, rivers and dikes, with the result that the representation of the Fens in the Huntingdonshire map is better than the one for Cambridgeshire: Speed himself was aware of this, and realizing the arbitrariness of county divisions he extended his fenland survey to cover the waterlogged areas as far as the Isle of Ely. This practical approach to map-making explains why Speed included a ground plan of Ely as well as that for the county town of Huntingdon as inserts in his county map of Huntingdonshire: the view of Huntingdon is interesting for its reliance on a survey of 1572 used selectively by Speed to show the town's bowling green and gallows, but omitting the full extent of the housing.

The Dissolution of the Monasteries—bringing with it the suppression of Ramsey Abbey and other religious houses which had done so much to control the Fens—had affected Huntingdonshire more than most counties. The site of the Benedictine nunnery at Hinchingbroke was acquired in 1538 by Richard Williams *alias* Cromwell, the husband of Thomas Cromwell's niece, and he converted the nunnery into a private dwelling of some comfort: Williams's grandson, Oliver Cromwell, was a Puritan lawyer attached to the households of both Anne of Denmark and Prince Henry when the *Theatre* was published, and Oliver's nephew and namesake born at Huntingdon in 1599 was to lead the Parliamentary forces to victory in the Civil War and to become Lord Protector. The Cromwells were fairly recent arrivals in the county: more established were the Wingfields, who had a tradition of service at court and in the county, at home and abroad, in peace and at war. Their principal home, acquired in 1522, was Kimbolton Castle, which once repaired and extended became the final home of Catherine of Aragon, and it was there that early in 1536 Catherine, separated and divorced from Henry VIII, died.

The entry for Huntingdonshire was not of Speed's own composition, and it lacks his literary charm. It was received from 'a right worthy and learned friend' whom he did not name, and whose lacklustre and lengthy essay he presumably feared cutting and thereby offending his friend.

Kent

John Leland's summary of the 'commodities' of Kent in about 1540 as 'fertility . . . rivers, havens with ships . . . royal castles and towns', ending with 'the faith of Christ there first restored', was still accurate when Speed produced the *Theatre* seventy years later. Geologically Kent is made up of clay and sands with outcrops of sandstone and limestone, and of chalk in the North Downs stretching from Surrey to the cliffs of Dover, with an outlier in the Isle of Thanet. Although lacking any mineral deposits save iron in the Weald, where the ore was both mined and smelted, the county was a prosperous one, with much of its ancient woodland still surviving. Then as now fruit trees predominated, and sheep grazed in the orchards. Hops and vegetables were staple crops and cattle vied with sheep for pasturage. The fleeces were cleaned, spun into yarn, and woven into broadcloths which were sold in London or exported to the Continent. Refugees from political and religious persecution abroad had already made Kent their home, and they brought with them new techniques improving cloth production. Fisheries flourished particularly in the Thames estuary near Whitstable, famed for its oysters and mullet that found a ready market in the capital.

An extensive coastline with numerous creeks and havens, together with proximity to France and the Netherlands, gave Kent unrivalled advantages for trade and made it a bastion for defence. This pre-eminence was reflected in the association of the Cinque Ports, made up of Dover, Hythe, Romney and Sandwich in Kent, and of Hastings, Rye and Winchelsea in Sussex, which under a lord warden of royal choosing enjoyed a measure of autonomy from the rest of the region. Dover Castle had long been a linchpin in the defence of the realm, but most other castles in Kent were made redundant when in the 1540s Henry VIII constructed a series of modern artillery forts like Deal and Walmer to protect the anchorage of the Downs which the Navy had recently taken to using. The adoption of other fleet-anchorages along the Thames and the Medway, and the establishment of dockyards at Deptford and Woolwich by Henry VIII, and at Chatham by Elizabeth I, turned Kent into the best defended area in the kingdom throughout the Tudor and early Stuart periods. Not only were the anchorages good for shipping and the rivers still largely navigable, but the deep channels isolated the islands of Grain, Sheppey and Thanet from the rest of the county. Much of the county was still marshland, or wetland, with Romney Marsh in the process of being reclaimed.

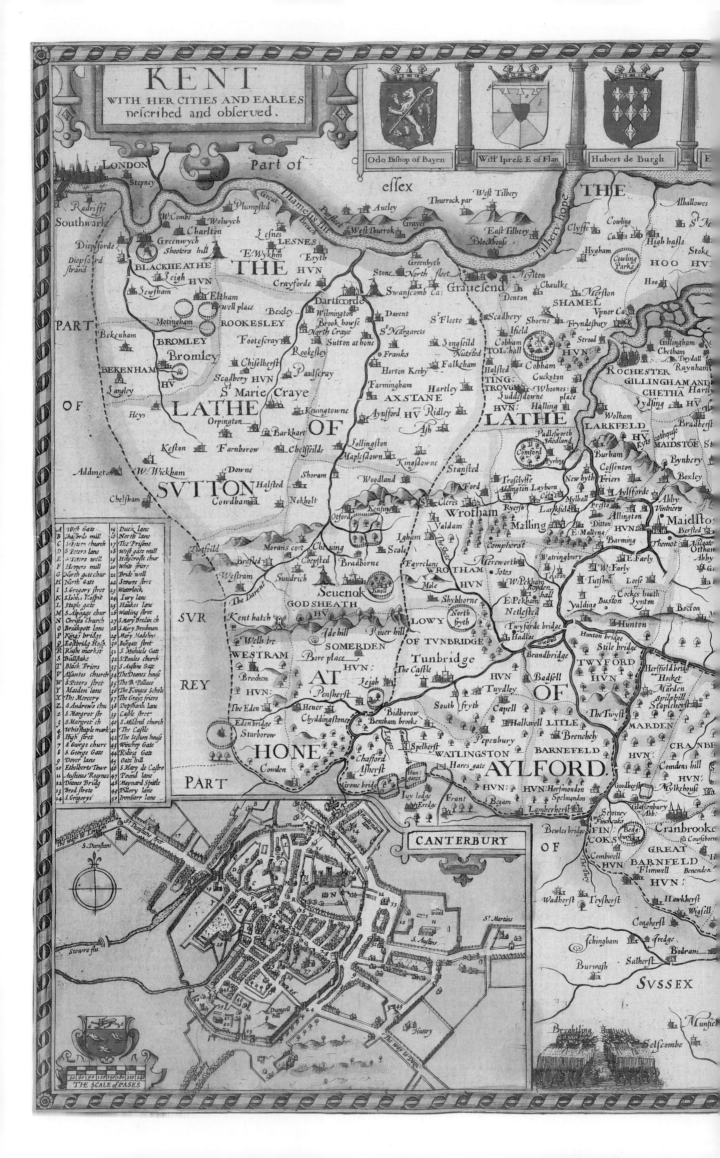

With two major palaces at Eltham and Greenwich and a host of subsidiary ones, Kent was a favourite county for courtiers and government officials to have residences, particularly in the lathes nearest to London. Both natives and new arrivals invested profits from office and land in a sequence of new houses and homes which in its continuity and extent was virtually unparalleled elsewhere: these buildings ranged from clothiers' dwellings through to the Clement and Boleyn domiciles at Ightham and Hever, to the Cheney and Baker mansions of Sheppey and Sissinghurst, and to the Brooke and Dorset piles at Cobham and Knole. These splendid houses were used as homes, partly as retreats, partly as political or social powerhouses, partly as places of entertainment for monarchs on progress or for visitors passing through Kent on their way to London. The receptions accorded to the Emperor Charles V and to Anne of Cleves were exceptional even by sixteenth-century standards, but these were outshone by that given to the Elector Frederick when he arrived to marry the Princess Elizabeth in 1612. However, travel in Kent was by no means easy, and Shooters' Hill on the edge of Blackheath was notorious for highwaymen. The rebellion of 1554 raised by Sir Thomas Wyatt came near to capturing London and to toppling the Marian regime.

Perhaps the first famous native of Kent in the Tudor period had been Sir Philip Sidney—darling of the Elizabethan court, soldier, statesman and poet—born at Penshurst in 1554 and fatally wounded at Zutphen in 1587. Even better known to Speed's contemporaries were the celebrated murders of Thomas Arden in 1551 at Faversham by his adulterous wife and her lover, and of Christopher Marlowe, the dramatist, in 1593 at Deptford during a drunken brawl: Arden's death was immortalized in Holinshed's *Chronicle* which in its turn supplied the plot for the earliest surviving murder play in English, *Arden of Faversham*. Speed did not mention any of these matters, Faversham for him being the burial place of King Stephen: he was, however, steeped in the historical researches of his fellow antiquarian, William Lambarde, whose *Perambulation of Kent* had appeared in 1576.

Speed completed his county map with ground plans of Kent's two cathedral cities, Canterbury and Rochester. Of Canterbury he remarked—as a good Anglican—of Thomas à Becket's tomb 'that for glory, wealth and superstitious worship equalized the pyramids of Egypt, or the oracles of Delphi, yet now with Dagon is fallen before the Ark of God'. He does not seem to have been aware that Sir Thomas More's head was preserved in the Roper chapel at St Dunstan's, Canterbury.

Lancashire

The map for Lancashire has long been greatly admired and esteemed. As with Lincolnshire, Speed and his engraver were faced with a long, fairly narrow county oriented north–south which did not fit the layout of the *Theatre*. As with Lincolnshire, their resolution of the dilemma was to use a much smaller scale than their usual, so that the county seems at a cursory glance to be little larger than Rutland. Despite its small scale, the map is remarkably uncluttered, yet nothing has been sacrificed to the accurate depiction of its coastline, rivers and other physical features, which are rendered clearly. The extensive areas not used for the county map proper were employed for the conventional plan of a town—in this instance Lancaster—heraldic arms, ships and marine monsters. A border, unique to Lancashire, portrayed the kings of the Houses of Lancaster and of York, with the inscription 'Blessed are the peacemakers' over the portraits of Henry VI and of Henry VII, celebrating the pacific nature of the former and the triumph of the latter in bringing the Wars of the Roses to an end.

Since the making of the map, the work of reclaiming the marshlands and mudflats south of Morecambe Bay down along the coast to the Mersey estuary, which before 1600 had not achieved much, has been brought to a successful conclusion, transforming the coastline and its immediate hinterland. In the south of the county the draining of Chat Moss at the conjunction of the rivers Irwell and Glazebrook proved even more problematic and defied technology until the nineteenth century. In Speed's day much of Lancashire was still heavily wooded in Wyre Dale and Bowland in the north and Simonswood in the south, but steady small-scale enclosure and clearing under the Tudors was changing the uplands into a landscape of small hedged or walled enclosures, and of isolated farms. More conservative than most, Lancashire landowners tended their remaining woodlands 'very carefully', and in this they were helped by the deposits of coal in the south and by peat or turves from the moorlands or marshes which provided fuel for warmth and cooking. Farming divided into arable in the lowlands and stockbreeding in the uplands. These were celebrated for cattle of 'large proportion' and 'goodly heads and horns', of which each year 'many thousands' were driven south to London for sale. Fish and fowl were also plentiful, and these were important staples in the local diet of a population largely on the verge of poverty and subject to high mortality through starvation after recurrent poor harvests. In the

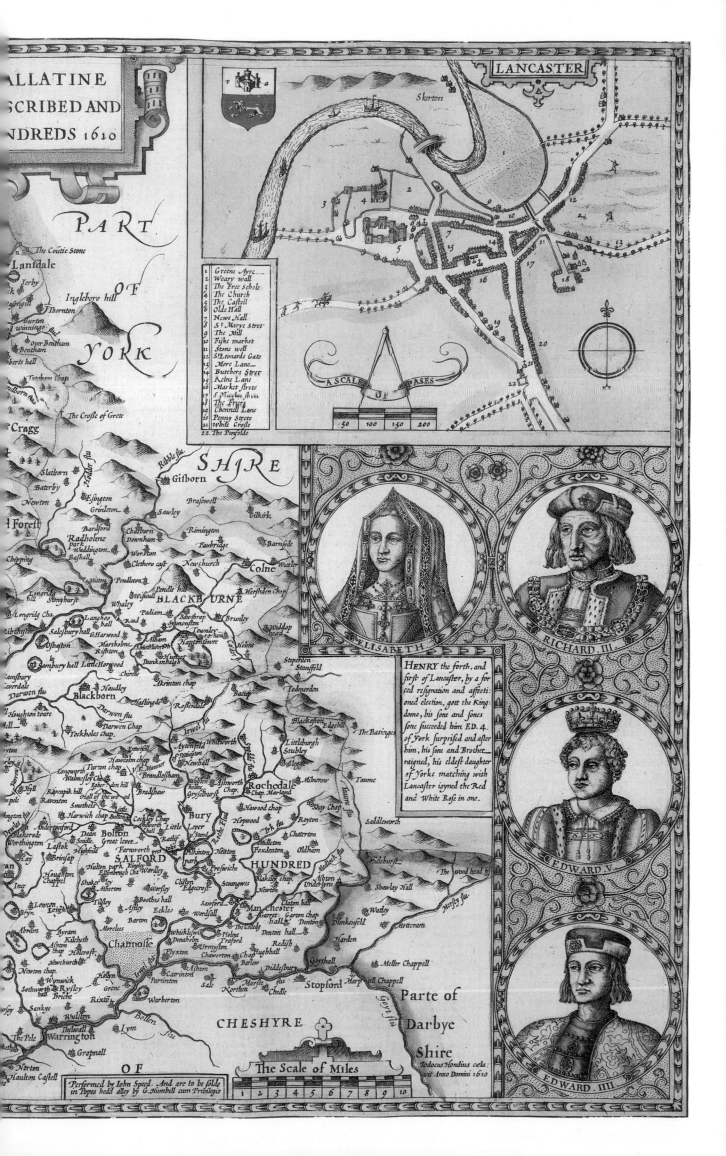

ALLATINE
SCRIBED AND
NDREDS 1610

PART

OF

YORK

LANCASTER

1	Greene Ayre
2	Weary wall
3	The Free Schole
4	The Church
5	The Castell
6	Olde Hall
7	Newe Hall
8	St Marye Stret
9	The Mill
10	Fishe market
11	Stone well
12	St Leonards Gate
13	More Lane
14	Burchers Stret
15	Kelne Lane
16	Market Strete
17	St Marye Stret
18	The Friers
19	Cheninal Lane
20	Penny Strete
21	White Crosse
22	The Pinfolde

Skerton

A SCALE OF PASES

| 50 | 100 | 150 | 200 |

The Coutie Stone

Lansdale

Ingleboro hill

The Crosse of Grete

SHIRE

Gisborn

BLACKEBURNE

Blackborn

SALFORD

Bolton

BURY

ROCHEDALE

HUNDRED

Manchester

CHESHYRE

Parte of
Darbye
Shire

OF

WARRINGTON

HENRY the forth, and
first of Lancaster, by a forced resignation and affecti-
oned election, gott the Kingdome, his sone and sones
sone succeeded him ED. 4.
of Yorke surprised and after
him, his sone and Brother
raigned, his eldest daughter
of Yorke matching with
Lancaster ioyned the Red
and White Rose in one.

ELISABETH

RICHARD. III.

EDWARD. V.

EDWARD. IIII.

The Scale of Miles

| 1 | 2 | 3 | 4 | 5 | 6 | 7 | 8 | 9 | 10 |

Iodocus Hondius cæla:
vit Anno Domini 1610

Performed by John Speed. And are to be solde
in Popes head alley by G. Humbell cum Privilegio

county's many poor families unable to make ends meet solely by agriculture, women and children spun, wove and knitted, Liverpool and Manchester with their neighbourhoods already being established centres for textiles. Lancashire weavers did not specialize solely in woollen cloth production; linen was made from flax grown in the county or else imported from Ireland *via* Liverpool. On the coast some salt was produced by boiling seawater over turves, and near Manchester there was a nascent glass industry.

The relatively high number of market towns—fifteen—did not reflect any prosperity, but simply the need for outlets for each district's produce, however meagre, and in its modesty Lancaster was not atypical of most towns in the county, even though its castle housed the headquarters for the duchy and for the shire. Liverpool, with its Irish trade, was larger, but Manchester, with its clothiers, market and former collegiate church, already surpassed in size and wealth all other places in Lancashire. Most housing in the county was made up of small two- or three-roomed cottages, with a number of large manor houses, for gentle families elaborately timber-framed, or else built of stone. Throughout the sixteenth century these families had continued building houses at Speke and elsewhere in the earlier tradition of Odsall and Rufford, but despite their small incomes and geographical isolation—hemmed in by uplands and inadequate river-crossings and restricted by poor roads—they showed themselves abreast of current fashions in the construction of Hoghton, Stonyhurst and Gawthorpe. Under the Tudors brick had become an increasingly popular material for building where supplies of sandstone or limestone were not readily available. The boom in church building which had resulted in such spectacular perpendicular churches as Sefton and Manchester had spent its force by the Reformation, and no further work was done to its parish churches and many chapels of ease until the Laudian programme for church improvement started after Speed's death. One of the peculiarities of the county was its lack of castles or dwellings fortified by anything more than a wet moat dating from the Middle Ages: this unusual absence perhaps reflected the overall control of the county by the Duchy of Lancaster.

Lancashire had an unenviable reputation for lax morality, with a high rate of concubinage and of illegitimacy, and with loose living practised by all social classes. This reflected an inadequate parochial structure in the county; its twenty-six parishes covered extensive areas and were crippled by clerical non-residence, often aggravated by poor incomes. Lack of religious instruction or supervision combined with the inherent conservatism of the inhabitants and the recusancy of its clergy left it one of the most Catholic counties in the kingdom, except for the area in the south-east where Protestantism and trade seem to have gone hand in hand: 'Hence it is,' wrote Thomas Fuller, 'that many subtle papists and Jesuits have been born and bred in this county which have met their matches, to say no more, in the natives of the county.'

Leicestershire

Unlike the counties adjoining it to the west and north, Leicestershire had few trees and hedgerows, its most heavily wooded areas being the ancient, but much reduced, forests of Charnwood, Dalby and Leicester. It also had few deer-parks, these for the most part being maintained by the owners of nearby country houses for their general recreational use, rather than specifically for hunting. The processes of disafforestation, disparking and enclosure of common land had gone on uninterrupted since the Middle Ages to the benefit of the county's agriculture, which specialized in growing barley and pulses with some acres given to wheat, and in pasturing an 'abundance' of cattle, particularly in the more sparsely populated hills to the north of the river Wreak, and sheep. Such improvements as these processes had brought were, however, counterbalanced by increasing hardships for the smallholders and cottagers who lost their grazing and sowing rights. Leicestershire was thus one of the most disaffected agrarian counties in the Midlands, and disturbances and riots connected with enclosure were common throughout the Tudor and Stuart periods. The fact that Leicestershire was a wool-producing county but not a cloth-weaving one meant that its countryfolk lacked the sort of cottage industry that supplemented the incomes of farming communities elsewhere in England. The rural poverty of the area was reflected by the one-roomed cottages still common for its peasantry and the use of clay mixed with straw and waste for their construction. In the north of the county there were extensive deposits of surface coal, and in the absence of wood or turves, coal was the fuel used for heating and cooking. In the neighbourhood of Belvoir stone heavy with fossils was readily available, and this was very much in demand in Speed's time for decorative purposes.

Of its twelve market towns, the county town of Leicester, with the regional headquarters of the Duchy of Lancaster, was by far the most important. Leicester had long been established as a centre for the leather trade, and the quality of its goods and of the cattle and horses for auction at its sales often attracted purchasers from as far afield as London. However, Leicester's commercial fame was overshadowed in popular imagination by the notoriety of two figures buried there. Of this pair, the more recent was Cardinal Wolsey, who died at Leicester Abbey in 1530 while on his way to London to answer charges of treason and had been buried in St Mary's church. The other was Richard III, who in 1485 had left the town with an army to fight Henry of

PARTE OF DARBYE SHIRE

WEST GOSTCOATE

Swarlston · Trent flud · Hemington · Lockington · Radcliff
Castle Dunington · Kinston
Melborne castle · Isley Walton · Ketworth · Norm.
Wilston
Bredon on the hill · Dyseworth
Stanton Harald · Langley · Hatherne
Tong · Long Whalton · Thorpacre
The great parke · Worthington · Merill Grange · Belton · Dishley Grange · Knightthorpe
Blaugherby · Newbold · Osgathorp · Garenton · Lon
Prestope parke · Collerton · Thrinkston · Shepeshead · Blackbroocke · Burley parke
Ashby de la Zouth · Overton saufy · GraceDieu · Charnwood
Overseale · Alton Grang · Swanington · Bewmanner
Cliston · Packington · Part of Darbyshire · Dunington · Whitwike · Charley · HUNDRED · Quar
Stretton · Raunston · Huglescote · Ulvestroft Abbey · Woodhouse
Part of · Thorpe · Normanton · Snihston · Pikering Grange · Bardon hills · Forest
Comberford · Little Appleby · Appleby · Swebston · Horsepoole Grange
Staf ford · Newton · Snareston · Newton Nethercote · Heather · Stanton Under Bardon · Markfeild · Switw
Tamworth · Seckington · SPARKENHOE · Ilstoke · Bagh worth park · Horshool · Cropstor
Shire · Austre · Hogges Norton · Shaxton · Oddeston · Nelson · Thornton · Newton
Shuttenton · Bramcote · Bilston · Cunston · Baghworth · Whittington Grange · Ansty
Aminton · Orton · Gropestill · Carlton · Barleston · Stanton · Groby
Poole · Polesworth · Morebarne · Twicrosse · Osbalston · Naneby · Newbold verdon · Glenfeil d
Willineote · Grindon · Great Shepey · Tem ple · Coton · Bosworth · Botcheston · Rathy · Kirby
Little Shepey · Whellesborow · Shenton · Gadeby · Desford · Leicester · Abba
Sence flud · Sibsdon · Upton · Kinge Richards · Barn park · Brantingthorp westedits
Ratcliffe Culey · Atterton · RedMore · HUNDRED · Sutton Cheny · Braunston
Witherley · Kingefeild · Teckleton · Forest · Lubsthorpe
Fenny · Draiton · Dadlington · Kirby malory · Stapleton · Thurlaston · Elstor
Lindley · Stoke · Erlshil ton · Norman · Enderby · Huncot
Higham · Barwell · Toly park · Narborow · Whet ston
Cauant · Wikin · Elmsthorpe · Croft · Blaby
Inker flud · Hinckley · Little thorp
Burbach Potters marston · Stonystanton · Cosby
Nun Eaton · Sketchley · Sapcotte · Countisthorp
Aston flavil · Sutton Thorpe · Stour flud
Copston · Wigston little · Broughton Astley · Willughby waterlet
High crosse · Frolesworth · Dunton Basset
Wisitoft · Clabroke · Ulsthorp · Great Ashby · Little
Wethibroke · Little Ashby · Gilmorton · Bra
Newnham · Bitesswell · Kincot
Willey · Lutterworth · Walcot
Chester over · Bensford bridge · Misterton
Harborow · GUTHLAKESTON DRED
Church over · Cotesbach · Nor
Cofford · Newton · Shawel · Swineford · South
Newbold · Brounsover · Catthorp · Stan
Cliston · Lilhorne
Avon flu. · Rugby · Parte o
Bilton · Hilmorton
WARWIKE SH.

Cheife places of y Citie by figurs noted	
1 S. Leonards	18 S Martins street
2 Leicester Abbay	19 Alhallowes
3 Abbay gate	20 High street
4 Sundaye Bridge	21 Huntington place
5 North gate	22 Woole Hall
6 North gate street	23 Graye fryers
7 Sinuis gate	24 Graye fryers gate
8 The Spittle	25 S Nicholas
9 S. Margrets	26 S Nicholas shambbes
10 Churche gate	27 Redd crosse street
11 Belgrave gate	28 S. Maryes
12 Humberston gate	29 The Castell
13 East Gate	30 Castell street
14 Swines market	31 Black Ffyers lane
15 Satterdayes market	32 Ould Hospitall
16 Cankwell Lane	33 The newe warke
17 S Martines	34 The Grange

LEICESTER

The old Stoure · Stoure Fluvius
wensdayes mark · High Crosse Street
Sceyvington house
Horse faire layes
Horse faire lane · Cockpitt
London Way · South Gate · Monte Bradsty

Performed by John Speede, and are
to be sold in popes head Alley by John
Sudbury and George Humble anno 1610

The

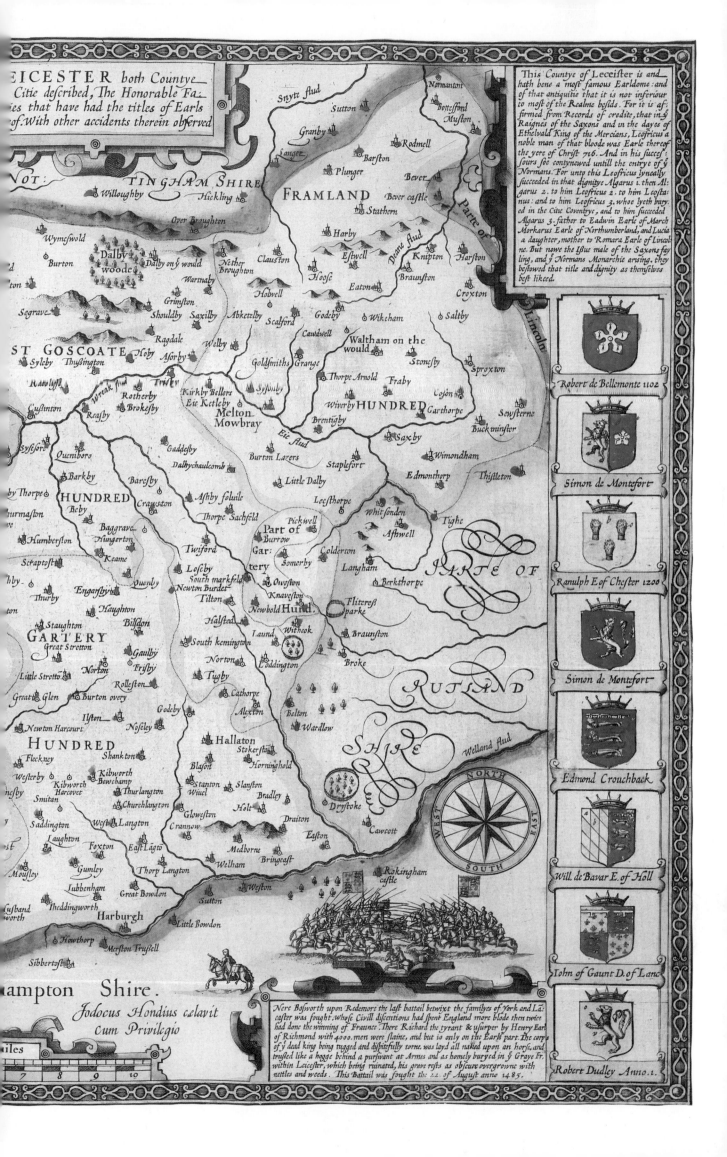

LEICESTER both Countye
and Citie described, The Honorable Fa:
milies that have had the titles of Earls
therof. With other accidents therein observed

NOT:

TINGHAM SHIRE
Willoughby · Hickling
Over Braughton

FRAMLAND

Snyte flud
Sutton
Granby
Langer · Barston
Plunger · Bever
Bever castle
Stathern
Normanton
Bottesford
Muston
Rodnell

Wymeswold
Burton
Dalby woode · Dalby on ý would
Wartnaby
Nether Broughton
Clauston
Hoose
Harby
Estwell
Eaton
Knipton
Braunston
Harston
Croxton
Deane Aud

Segrave
Grimston
Shouldby Saxilby
Ragdale
Abketelby Scalford
Welby
Godeby
Cawdwell
Wikeham
Saltby

ST GOSCOATE Hoby Asorby
Syleby Thussington
Trive
Rotherby
Reasby Brokesby
Kirkby Bellers
Eie Ketleby
Melton Mowbray
Goldsmiths Grange
Waltham on the would
Thorpe Arnold Fraby
Stonesby
Sproxton

Cusinton
Quenboro
Barkby Baresby
Ragdale
Gaddesby
Dalbychaulcomb
Crawston
Ashby foluile
Thorpe Sachfeld
Humberston
Baggrave
Hungerton
Keame
Quenby
Loseby
South markfield
Newton Burdet
Tilton
Knaveston
Newbold
Halsted

HUNDRED
Beby

Crayston
Twiford
Part of Burrow Gar: tery
Pickwell
Somerby
Colderton
Somerby
Langham
Berkthorpe
Whit sonden
Ashwell
Tighe
PARTE OF

Wreak flud
Sysfore
Gaddesby
Eie flud
Burton Lazers
Little Dalby
Leesthorpe
Staplefort
Wimondham
Edmonthorp
Thistleton

Wiverby HUNDRED
Brentigby
Saxby
Garthorpe
Sewsterne
Buck minster

Thurby
Engarsby
Haughton
Staughton
Bisfdon
GARTERY
Great Stretton
Gaulby
Frisby
Norton
Little Stretto
Rolleston
Great Glen
Burton overy
Ilston
Godeby
Newton Harcourt
Nofeley

HUNDRED
Fleckney
Shankton
Westerby
Kibworth Beawchamp
Kibworth Harcover
Smitan
Saddington
Laughton
Foxton
East Lagto
Gumley
Lubbenham
Great Bowdon
Theddingworth
Harburgh
Howthorp
Merston Truffell
Sibbertoft

South kemington
Norton
Tugby
Cathorpe
Alexton
Belton
Wardlow

Hallaton
Stokerston
Blafon
Horninghold
Stanton
Wiuel
Slawston
Bradley
Holt
Gloweston
Crannow
Draiton
Welham
Bringeast
Medborne
Weston
Sutton
Little Bowdon

Laund
Witheok
Flitreß parke
Braunston
Broke

Newbold Hund
Loddington

RUTLAND
SHIRE

Drystoke
Welland Aud

NORTH
WEST · EAST
SOUTH

Rokingham castle
Cawcott
Easton

AMPTON Shire.
Jodocus Hondius cælavit
Cum Privilegio

Miles
7 · 8 · 9 · 10

Parte of Lincoln

Robert de Bellemonte 1102

Simon de Montefort

Ranulph E. of Chester 1200

Simon de Montefort

Edmond Crouchbaek

Will. de Bavar E. of Holl

John of Gaunt D. of Lanc

Robert Dudley Anno. 1.

Nere Bofworth upon Redemore the laft battail betwixt the familyes of York and Lā:
cafter was fought. whofe Civill diffentions had fpent England more blode then twice
had done the winning of Fraunce. There Richard the tyrant & ufurper by Henry Earl
of Richmond with 4000. men were flaine, and but fo only on the Earls part. The corps
of ý dead king being tugged and difpitefully torne. was layd all naked upon an horfe, and
truffed like a hogge behind a purfivant at Armes and as homely buryed in ý Graye Fr.
within Leicester, which being ruinated, his grave refts as obfcure overgrowne with
nettles and weeds. This Battail was fought the 22. of Auguft anno 1485.

Richmond's expeditionary force at Bosworth (marked King Richard's field on the county map), and whose body 'naked and torn' had been brought back to the town 'and with contempt without tears obscurely buried' in the Greyfriars. At the Reformation the site of Richard III's grave had been lost, but Cardinal Wolsey's continued to be pointed out to interested travellers.

Leicestershire was remarkable for its being controlled politically and socially more or less by two leading families at any given time during the century preceding the issue of the *Theatre*: the Hastings Earls of Huntingdon from Ashby de la Zouche were powerful throughout; but after 1554 the Greys Marquesses of Dorset and Earls of Suffolk from Groby and Bradgate were replaced by the Manners Earls of Rutland from Belvoir. As each generation of this trio of families distinguished itself at court, in government and in war, Leicestershire and Leicestershiremen were often in the thick of—or at least witness to—the great national events of the period. At no point were they perhaps nearer than in 1553 when Lady Jane Grey (who had been reared at Bradgate and educated by Roger Ascham) was willed the crown by her kinsman Edward VI and was Queen for ten days before losing it through an uprising in favour of Princess Mary. Whether Jane Grey was the paragon of learning described by Ascham is a moot point, but there can be no doubt she shared the Protestantism of her family and died on the block in 1554 professing it. The religious persuasion of the three families, and in particular the puritanism of the 3rd Earl of Huntingdon, with what amounted to a monopoly on the presentation to ecclesiastical livings in the county, meant that by 1600 Leicestershire was almost Anglican to a man, in marked contrast with the curve of northwestward counties from Warwickshire to Nottinghamshire abutting on it.

As with so many counties, the administrative reforms of the sixteenth century had not ended pockets of jurisdiction outside the control of Leicestershire's sheriff, and at Ravenstone there was a detached limb of Derbyshire.

Lincolnshire

Geographically Lincolnshire was divided into six zones when described by Speed—a western lowland stretching south from the Isle of Axholme along the river Trent to the Vale of Belvoir; the narrow upland of Lincoln Cliff carrying Ermine Street; the valley of the river Ancholme; the wider uplands of the Lincolnshire Wolds; the fenlands in the south (since drained); and the coastal strip of the Lincoln Marsh running from the Humber to the Wash. These zones did not coincide with the county's three ridings (Holland in the south, and Kesteven and Lindsey in the north), or with the wapentakes (rather than hundreds) into which the ridings were subdivided. The county's economy was largely dependent on the breeding and rearing of livestock—cattle, sheep and horses being grazed throughout all three ridings, with rabbits in the uplands—with some corn-production. Little cloth was woven in Lincolnshire, the short and fine fleeces produced there being sold almost immediately on shearing to clothiers outside the county.

The extensive fen and marsh produced reeds which were used for thatching and covering floors and flax for making linen, and supported freshwater fish as well as a large bird population, mallard being particularly prized for eating and geese for their feathers. Whereas the inhabitants of the marshland tended to be prosperous yeomen and husbandmen, and relatively few, those of the fenland were smallholders or landless cottagers, and numerous. These latter occupied one-roomed cottages built of mud, and their existence was threatened by the schemes being advanced in the late sixteenth century to drain the fen. As can be seen from the map, the Lincolnshire coast with its many inlets, sandbanks and mudflats was a hazardous stretch of water to coastal shipping, and both the county's littoral trade and its fisheries were losing in competition with Yorkshire ports to the north and Norfolk ones to the south. The extent of the wetlands along the North Sea and inland made Lincolnshire highly susceptible to mists and fogs, but having commented on these disagreeable aspects of its weather, Speed went on to say that its climate was 'therewithal very moderate and pleasing'.

An overall economic depression was shared alike by town and country. The last great programme of church-building in the perpendicular style came to an end in the marshland of the county's north-east with the Reformation, but the grandeur of the recently completed churches at Addlethorpe, Burgh-le-Marsh, Croft, Ingoldmells, North and South Somercote, Theddlethorpe All

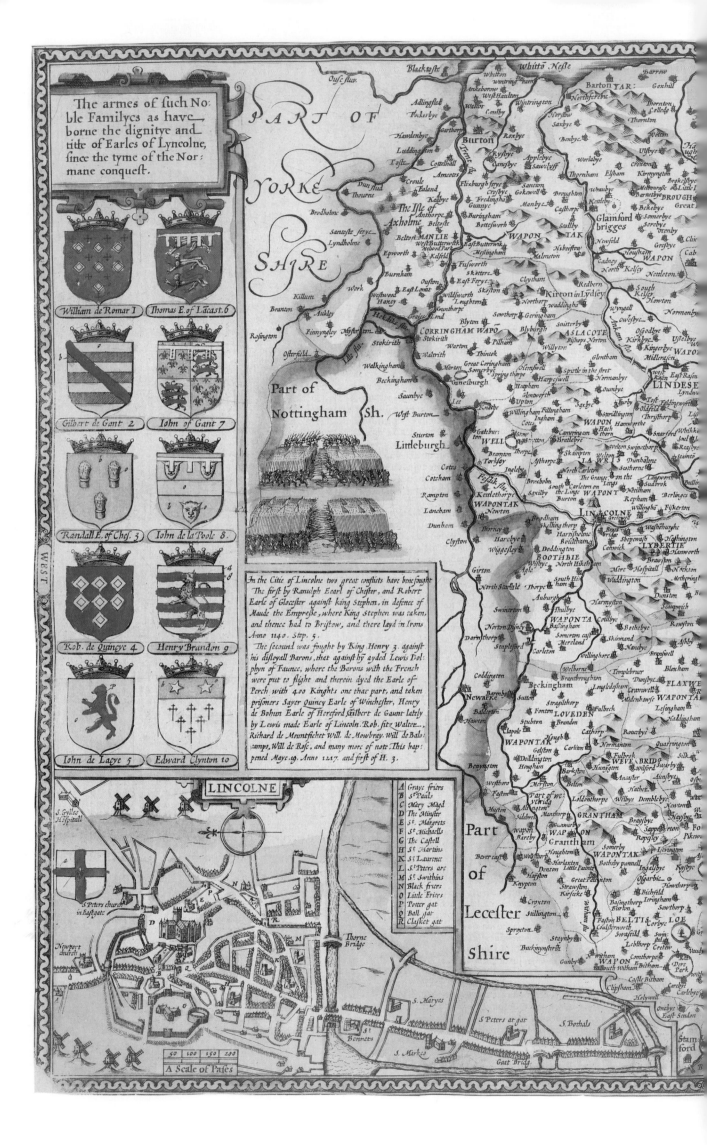

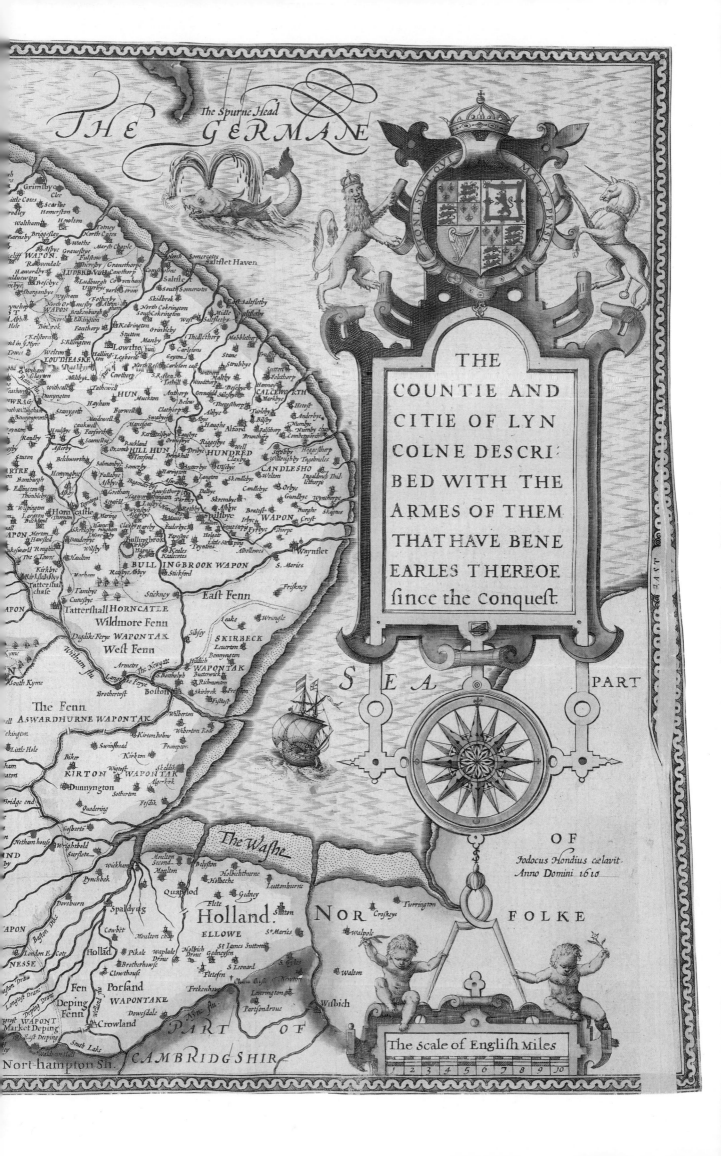

Saints and Wainfleet St Mary served as reminders of not-too-distant prosperity. More significant than the impact made by these churches and by the derelict religious houses, more than the visible decay and recession of the thirty-one modest towns, and more than the problems arising from erosion or silting to its ports, was the psychological impact made on the visitor to Lincoln, which with its cathedral, castle, houses and industries had in Speed's words been 'more magnificent as her overturned ruins doth appear'. The shrunken extent of Lincoln is apparent from the plan of it in the left-hand corner of the county map. During the sixteenth century Lincoln had lost to Nottingham its former pre-eminence in the North Midlands, and its decline had not been reversed when its enormous and wealthy medieval diocese reaching south to the river Thames had been reduced at the Reformation. More than in most regions the Dissolution of the Monasteries had dislocated the local economy and further accelerated decline. Enclosure also exacerbated the inherent and apparently insoluble problems of the area, and twice (in 1536 and 1546) there had been uprisings sparked off by these persistent tensions, the Lincolnshire rebellion of 1536 even briefly threatening the security of Henry VIII as king.

Notwithstanding the many problems besetting the county, Lincolnshire did not miss out in the house-building boom which was such a feature of sixteenth-century England. In this Lord Hussey, who was executed for failing to suppress the rebellion of 1536, had led the way at Sleaford, where he built a house of timber and stone, thereby reviving a tradition of spectacular building not witnessed in Lincolnshire since Lord Cromwell had completed Tattershall Castle in the previous century. Hussey's example was followed by others, particularly by families with court connections, and by Henry VIII's brother-in-law, the Duke of Suffolk, whom the King had encouraged to settle in the county. Brandon's Grimsthorpe was followed by the Earl of Lincoln's Sempringham, and by a series of houses at Glentworth, South Kelsey, Snarford, Sudbrooke and Torksey. Most of these houses were of brick, after limestone and sandstone the material increasingly favoured for building in a county notable for its lack of woodlands, trees being marked only in the Isle of Axholme on the county map.

The convention of orientating a map north-south and the restrictions caused by the size of the paper used in producing the *Theatre* posed a number of problems in presenting Lincolnshire, which were settled by adopting a much smaller scale than that generally employed throughout the atlas. The success of this solution, which was also adopted for Lancashire, can be gauged from the outcome, where neither accuracy was forgone nor details skimped, as scrutiny of the coastline and inclusion of inland ferries with their names reveal.

Middlesex

By far the richest shire, Middlesex shared with Gloucestershire the unusual distinction of not being a predominantly farming county, with its inhabitants dependent wholly or largely upon agriculture for their living. This is not to say that farming was unimportant; the townships and villages encircling the capital and the seat of government at Westminster were geared to producing foodstuffs for sale in London or to fattening up the cattle, sheep, pigs, chickens, ducks and geese raised elsewhere but intended for marketing there. Wheat and hay were the main products, the best wheat being grown at Heston whence—according to John Norden—Queen Elizabeth had 'the most part of her provision'. Where the ground was poorer and more gravelly, market gardeners concentrated on growing parsnips, carrots, cabbages, turnips, peas, beans and 'all kinds of salad herbs'. This intensive cultivation meant that Middlesex was one of the least wooded counties, although some areas of extensive woodland remained, mainly at its edges, largely for pasturing livestock or for deer. Of the county's ten surviving deer-parks, the greater number belonged to the Crown—which, with its enthusiasm for hunting as a pastime, guaranteed their survival against encroachments for more land for food production.

The overwhelmingly rural atmosphere of Middlesex was not disturbed by its popularity among courtiers and government officials for country residences, except along the north bank of the Thames where easy access to water transport had resulted in an almost uninterrupted series of such residences and palaces from above Hampton Court downstream to London. The city of London had long since overspilled the walls dating from Roman times, and at the accession of James I housing stretched westwards along the Strand to Westminster, northwards to Clerkenwell and eastwards to Bethnal Green. After Henry VIII's decision to give up Bridewell as a royal palace, no succeeding monarch was to live in the city again, and this fact—along with general overcrowding—led peers, courtiers and officials to seek more salubrious accommodation outside London's wall, leaving the medieval city to its merchants, craftsmen and artisans with their warehouses and industrial premises. Not only was London the most heavily industrialized town in England, with products ranging from pottery through leather and cloth goods to guns and body armour, but it was also a port of national and international consequence 'whose traffic for merchandizing is like that of Tyre', with good communications by road or water anywhere in the kingdom, and with London Bridge, a stone bridge of

WESTMINSTER

MI...
do...
WITH T...
C...
LONDON

St. PETERS

THE Churche of WEST
MINSTER was antiently the
Temple of Apollo as sayth
Sulcardus, which by an earth
quake in ye raigne of Anto
ninus Pius was overthrowe
Of whose ruines Sebert K of
ye East Angles built another to
S. Peter: and ye beyng destroyed
by the Danes, Edward Con
feſſor raised againe to greate
beautye wch was lastly takedow
by K.H.3 & new built W.50.w
res labor as nowe it standeth.

SAINT PAULES

THE Churche of St PAULS
is thought to have bene some
tymes ye Temple of DIANA, wch
oppinion is strengthned by
an incredible number of oxes
heads digged up there in the
raigne of K.E.1. their bodyes
supposed to have bene ſacri
ficed unto her. This Churche
Ethelbert K of Kent newe
built and converted to Chri
ſtianite; And after him Mau
rice Biſ. of Londō raiſed it to thi
greatnes, whoſe ſteple was 114
foote hye & hath bene twiſe
coſumed by fiere frō Heave. And

SAINT PETERS

PART OF HAR...

Bedmondt
Shenley
Langley Abbey
Kings Langley
Aldnham
Brokeley
SHIRE
Bushye Heath · Watford
Bushye
Highw
Little
Cannons
Gret Stanner
Pynner
Woodhall
GOARE HUN
Kenton
Chalfedt
Ryslipe
Ascot
Breakſpears
Harrow, on
the hill
Part of
Harſeyld
Ickenham
Swakleys
Wembly Hill
Morehall
ELTHORNE HUND
West
Denham
Brokenborowes
Little Hellingdon
Northhall Lodge
Grat
Hellingdon
Greneforde
Northolt
Periwale
Uxbridge
Cowley
Hayes
Nercote
Dormans Well
Sautholde
Hanwe
BUCKINGHAM
Wewrſley
Colham
Nortwoode
Drayton
Hamworth
Synſon
Cranford
bridg
Osterley
Parke
ISTLEWO
HUN
Colnebrok
Harlington
Hiſton
Hurſlow
Worton
SHIRE
Stanwell
Cranford
Eaton
Eueney forme
West Bedfont
Babe
Bridg Whitton
Datchet
East Bedfont
Aſhford
Feltham
Wraſbury
Stanſchurch
STANES
Feltham hill
Aſtleham
Hanworth
Twi
Littleton
Windſore
SPELT
HORNE HUNDRE
Newhouſe
PART OF
Lalam
Charlts
Kenton
Sunbury
BERKSHIRE
Egham
Windelore
Cherſey
Hanforde
Thames flu
Walton
West Mo
Parke
Thorpe
Shepperton
Otlandes
Cum Privi

Jodocus Hondius cælavit

SEX
d
FAMOUS
MINSTER

LONDON

The large circuite, w
multitude of streets be:
sydes the beautifull &
stately buildings in this
sayre, and most famous
Citie LONDON: can no
wise be demonstrated
in soe little compasse,
as here I am inforced
to shewe. But as Her:
cules his bodye might
he measured by his
foote, and the univer:
sall Globe drawe in a

smale circle: Soe in this
rather conceit the mag:
nificens thereof in myde,
then curiousely seeke
satisfaction by the sight,
whose pleasant situa:
tion, beautye, and rich
blessings both for soyll
and sea equals (ys not
exceeds) any Citie un:
der Heaven. The
trew plott whereof
I purposely reserve to
a further leasure & larger
Scale.   And.

Fol.   142

SAINT PAULS

Theoball
Waltham Abbey
Whitwch   Waltham Crosse
WalthamForest
Potters Bare
Southmyns   Morehatch
Durhams   EDMONTON HUDR.
Ancerfhill   Enfeild Chace
Riekefend   Enfeildt
The Folde   Ponders End
Grenestret   Durance
                              Chigwell
High Barnet   Chingford
        East Berner   Winchmorhill
                 Buryftret
        Whetstone   Edmondstret   PART OF
Tatteridg   Edmonton   ESSEX
        Fryarn Barnet   Wyer hill   Pymes
North End   Fryarn manner   Woodford
East End   Cony Hatch   Tottenhamstret
Brownswell   Hollick   Tottenham Ducoats   Muckings
Finchley   Muswell hill   Dorfty Sars
FYNESBURY   Harnesey   Tottenham highe   Walthamstow
n house   Lodge   hill   Cruch Ende   Wansted
        Chittes hill   Highgate   Layton
Daleson hill   Hamsted   Halways   Newington
d Kylborne   Belssse   Newington Grene
ysedon   Chalcot   Kentishtown   Shackerwell
arleston Grene   Canbury   Clapton
AND   Pancras   Kinsland   Hackney
Paddington   Iftington   Hockesdon
Westborne   Marybone   Totten Court   Shordich   Mercstret   Oldeford
LAXBARNE   St Gylles   Clerkenwell   Byshops hall   Stratford
East Acton   Hyde Park   WESTMINSTER   LONDON   Stepney   OSULSTON
                              Bednall   Blackwall
Padingwike   Kensington   StIames   Lymehouse
RTIES   Brompton   Lambeth mersh   The Isle
the Hospitall   Hamersmith   Lambeth   Southwork   of Dogges
ard   Chelsey   Parsons Grene   HUNDRED
l   Chefwike   Charleton
        Fulham   Batterfey   Newington   Grenewich
Morshlake   Barnes   Clapham   Detford
        Bartelms   Wansworth
                Putney
PART OF SUR   REY   PART OF KENT

Thamis flu.

Described by Iohn Norden, Augmēted by I. Speed
Solde in Popes head alley against the Exchange by
George Humble.

nineteen arches crossing the Thames, 'for length, breadth, beauty and building, the like again not found in the world'. However, it was not its population of 200,000 (some ten times larger than the next nearest city, Norwich), its dirt, its atmospheric haze or its scavenging kites that visitors best remembered, but its absence of up-to-date artillery fortifications. This lack marked it out from any city of equal importance or size on the Continent. Fighting in the city during Wyatt's rebellion in 1554, and more recently the 2nd Earl of Essex's desperate attempt in 1601 to raise London and to seize Queen Elizabeth, had resulted in measures for reviewing the militia, but not in plans for modern defences.

From Henry VIII's reign the principal royal palace in Middlesex was that at Whitehall, a hotchpotch of buildings in the traditional English style and lacking the architectural symmetry favoured abroad, but conveniently near the more ancient, medieval palace of Westminster, which by 1600 had been taken over almost exclusively for administrative and judicial purposes by the government offices and courts housed there. The accession of James I, with a household modelled on principles different from those guiding his Tudor predecessors, with an influx of courtiers and administration from another kingdom and the need to accommodate them suitably, and with the new fad for masques (starting with Ben Jonson's *Masque of Blackness* in 1605), called for a radical rebuilding; however, this with its long-term aesthetic implications had not received serious consideration before the publication of the *Theatre*. Hampton Court, the other palace equally favoured by Tudors and Stuarts alike, was also originally constructed by Cardinal Wolsey, but in the meantime it had undergone repeated transformations and further elaboration. It was there that James I summoned a conference in the hope of reconciling the different elements within the Church of England, and where the idea of producing a good modern translation of the Bible in English took seed, eventually emerging as the Authorized Version, published about the same time as the *Theatre*. Henry VIII's other favourite palace, St James's, had become in 1604 the home of the heir-apparent Prince Henry, and a library to house Lord Lumley's books and a riding school, representing two aspects of the prince's many interests, were built there before the prince's untimely death in 1612.

Speed embellished the Middlesex map with plans of the cities of Westminster and London and with depictions of Westminster Abbey and St Paul's Cathedral, with a set of brief notes on each. The details are not entirely reliable, but the picture of St Paul's shows the cathedral with the hastily repaired lantern after the loss of its spire in 1561 and before restoration by Inigo Jones in the 1630s.

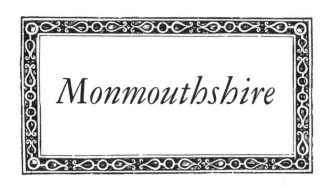

Monmouthshire

The county of Monmouth was the last of the English shires to be created, being formed in 1536 by joining Gwent with the district of Gwynllwg beyond the river Usk. Notwithstanding its recent creation, Monmouthshire had an outlier wedged between Herefordshire and Gloucestershire, while Herefordshire had another wedged between Monmouthshire and Breconshire. Although Gwent and Gwynllwg were largely Welsh-speaking above the coastal plains, Monmouthshire was in essence orientated on the Severn estuary, and thus its outside links economically, socially, culturally and politically were undoubtedly English. This curious situation had been recognized as far back as the reign of Edward I, when the area had been placed within the English assize system, and it had been further confirmed at the Union with Wales, when the new county was placed within the jurisdiction of the court of Chancery and its sheriff made directly accountable to the Exchequer, unlike the new counties made in Wales at the same time. As with all the counties off the Severn basin (and all the Welsh counties during the Tudor and early Stuart period), the administration of Monmouthshire was supervised by the Council in the Marches of Wales, from its headquarters at Ludlow in Shropshire.

Divided between the mountains in the north, the uplands of the central district and the low-lying coastal plains, Monmouthshire was a predominantly farming county. Cattle and sheep grazed its hills and pasture, and wheat, barley, oats and rye were cultivated in its valleys and plains. There was much dairy farming and flannel production, while several towns had flourishing tanneries. Its extensive woodlands supplemented the charcoal needed in the ironworks in the Forest of Dean just over the county's eastern border in Gloucestershire, as well as in some iron and brass production in Monmouthshire, but the quality of the oak there led to its being reserved for use in the royal dockyards in Hampshire and Kent, the port of Chepstow serving as an outlet for Monmouthshire wood. The juxtaposition of supplies of water-power and wood for charcoal had also resulted in the Company of Mines Royal selecting a site near Tintern on the river Wye for a factory for wire; although relying on German craftsmen to start with, this factory prospered. By 1600 it had some 120 staff and was producing wire that could be used to make a range of items from pins and needles to teeth for combs used to prepare wool for spinning or to card cloth.

Monmouthshire's six market towns had grown up around marcher castles,

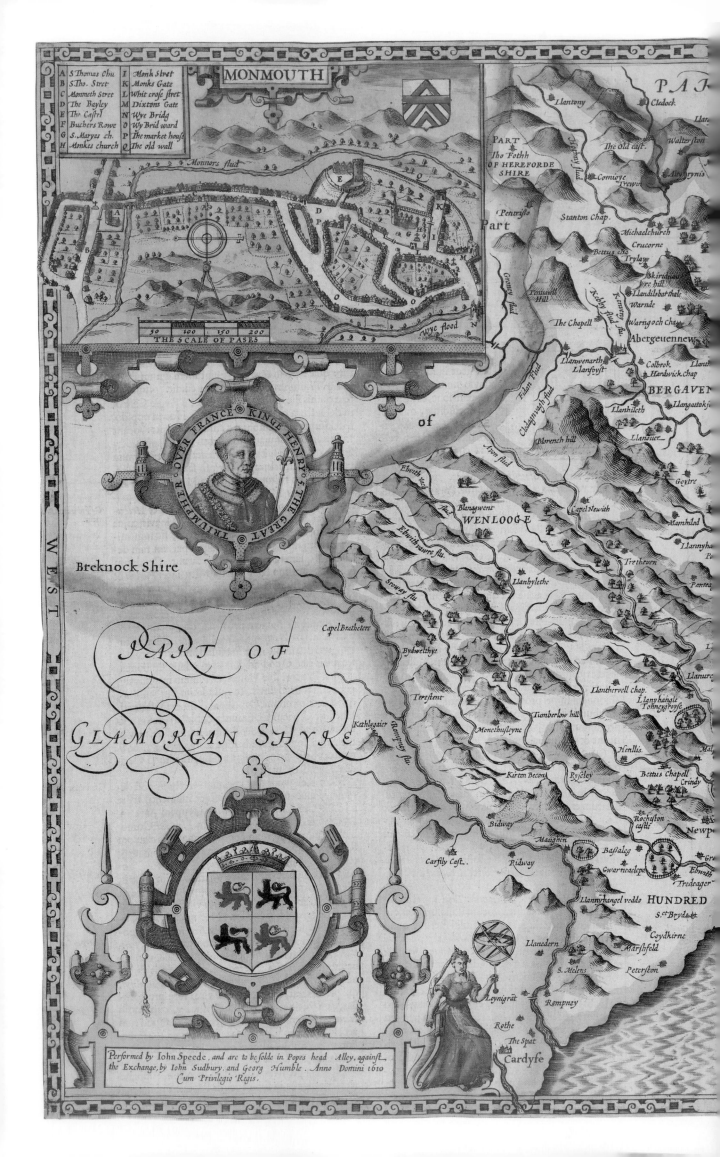

MONMOUTH

Monnors flud.

THE SCALE OF PASES
50   100   150   200

TRIUMPHER OVER FRANCE KINGE HENRY ⁵ THE GREAT

Breknock Shire

WEST

of

PART OF HEREFORDE SHIRE

Iho Fothh

Part

PART

Llantony
Cledock
The old cast.
Walterston
Comioye
Trewin
Alterynis
Pentriso
Stanton Chap.
Michaelchurch
Crucorne
Bettus cha
Trylay
Pentuall Hill
skirtidu wre hill.
Llandilobat thale
Warnde
The Chapell
Waringoch cha
Abergeuennew
Llanwenarth
Llansoyst
Colbrok
Hardwick Chap.
Llanth
BERGAVEN
Llanhileth
Llangattoksi
Llanouer
Blorench hill
Goytre
Avon flud
Ebwith flud
Blanagwent flud
Capel Newith
Mamhlod
WENLOOGE
Llannyha
Po
Ebwith vawre flu.
Llanhylethe
Tretheven
Srowey flu.
Pantea
Capel Brathetere
Bydwelthye
Llanthervell chap.
Llanyhangle Tohnegroyse
Terestent
Tamberlow hill
Kethlygaier
Rompney flu.
Monethusloyne
Henllis
Llanure
Mal

PART OF GLAMORGAN SHYRE

Karten Becon
Ryseley
Bettus Chapel
Crindy
Rocheston castli
Newp
Bidway
Maughen
Carsily Cast.
Ridway
Bassaleg
Gwarneaelepa
Ebwth
Tredeager
Gr
Llannyhangel veddo HUNDRED
S. ct Bryda
Coydkirne
Llanedern
Marshfeld
S. Melens
Peterston
Rompney
Loynigrat
Rothe
The Spat
Cardyse

Performed by Iohn Speede, and are to be solde in Popes head Alley, against the Exchange, by Iohn Sudbury, and Georg Humble. Anno Domini 1610 Cum Privilegio Regis.

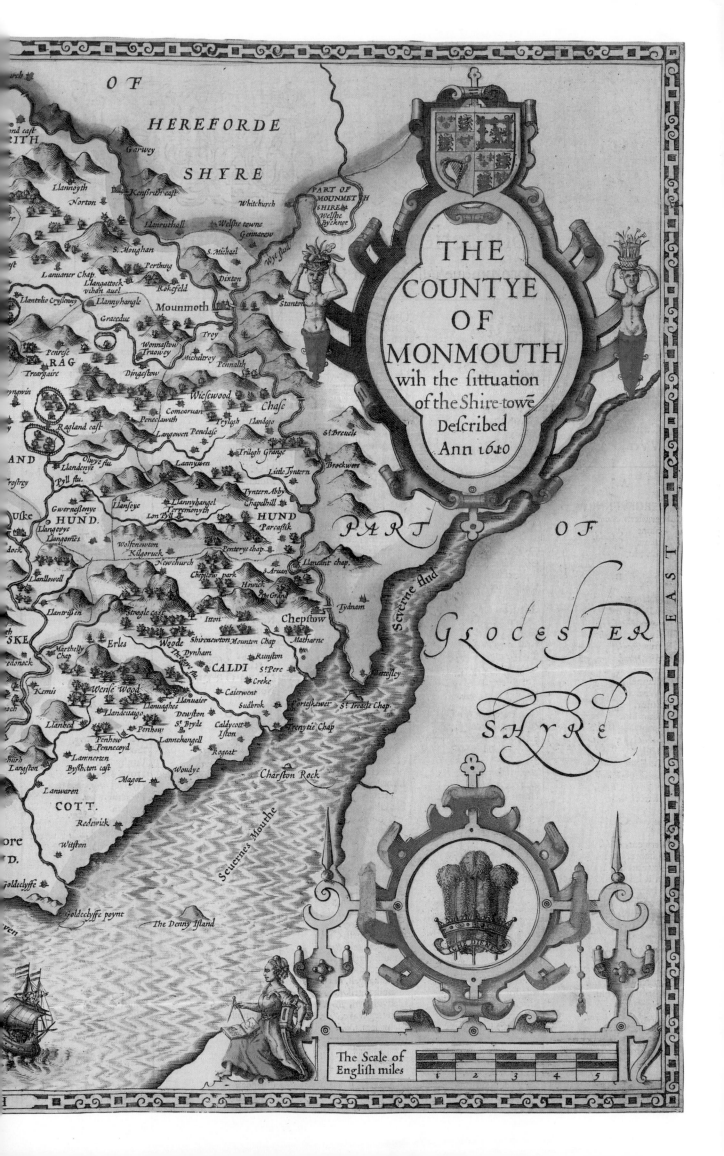

but by Speed's time the castles were in a ruinous condition, Monmouth castle being described as 'no better than a regardless cottage'. The exception to this statement was Raglan Castle, which had been recently and lavishly modernized by the Somerset Earls of Worcester. The 4th Earl, although an openly professing Roman Catholic, had been a favourite with Queen Elizabeth, who said of him that 'he reconciled what she believed impossible, a stiff papist to a good subject'. Regarded as the best horseman of his time, he was Master of the Horse successively to Elizabeth and to James I, and he also held many offices of state. A man of letters, he was patron of two of the outstanding figures in Elizabethan literature and music, the poet Edmund Spenser and the composer William Byrd. He was also a keen gardener, the gardens at Raglan being designed with gazebos and 'pleasant walks', the one surrounding the castle moat being 'of the Roman Emperors in arches of divers varieties of shell-works'. The Catholicism of Monmouthshire's leading resident peer meant that his fellow believers in the county did not share the persecution suffered by others elsewhere for their recusancy in the years following the papal excommunication of Queen Elizabeth in 1570 and the arrival of seminary priests five years later. However, the Catholicism of the Earls of Worcester did not prevent them from acquiring monastic property at the Dissolution, notably Tintern Abbey, and retaining it.

Probably what interested Speed most was that the Duchy of Lancaster castle at Monmouth had been the birthplace of King Henry V, and to balance the Prince of Wales' feathers in the county map he had included a portrait of that king. The Monmouthshire map is completed by a ground plan of the county town and the arms of the Earls of Worcester.

Norfolk

Speed's map and description of Norfolk are unusual in his acknowledgement of indebtedness to others, the map to the cartographer Christopher Saxton but 'augmented' by Speed, and the description to the antiquarian Sir Henry Spelman, who lived at Congham in the county until moving to London in 1612. The result of this combination of talents is that the county map, although not among the most aesthetically pleasing in the *Theatre*, is singularly accomplished in its delineation of the coastline, the course of rivers and the boundaries of the hundreds, as well as in its positioning of towns and villages.

As with the rest of East Anglia, Norfolk is sometimes best remembered for its winds, or—as Spelman put it—'the air is sharp and piercing' especially in the marshland to the south of the Wash and along the coast. Windmills were so profuse, and so important in the local economy in the grinding of grain, that they were taken for granted and did not figure in the map. The terrain was diverse, the underlying soil being clay or chalk and often well watered. While the marshland was devoted largely to pasture and rearing cattle and sheep, the area running north from Thetford on the border with Suffolk to the cluster of villages called the Burnhams was a mixture of first-rate arable land, woodland and heath, while the eastern seaboard area was a region set aside for corn production. The upland area west of Thetford, known as the Breckland, was natural heathland and contrasted with the rest of the county, being 'naked, dry and barren', but even so it was hardly less profitable to its landowners since it was suitable for warrens where rabbits, a major source for meat and for cheap fur, were bred and kept. The low-lying areas to the east of Norwich had been a source of supply of turves and peat for fuel for London until coal from Durham and Northumberland had ousted them, but still continued to furnish the hearths and ovens of East Anglia. Careless maintenance of dikes and a succession of freak high tides in the late fifteenth century had resulted in the flooding of the exhausted peat-cuttings and the creation of the Broads.

The river Yare was navigable to shipping beyond Norwich, which had wharves for the loading and unloading of merchandise, and many other towns in Norfolk were similarly served by the other rivers there. Not only was there extensive inland waterway traffic, but the lengthy coastline had a series of suitable and safe havens and mooring places for sea-going vessels. Of the numerous small ports and fishing towns along the coast, the two most important

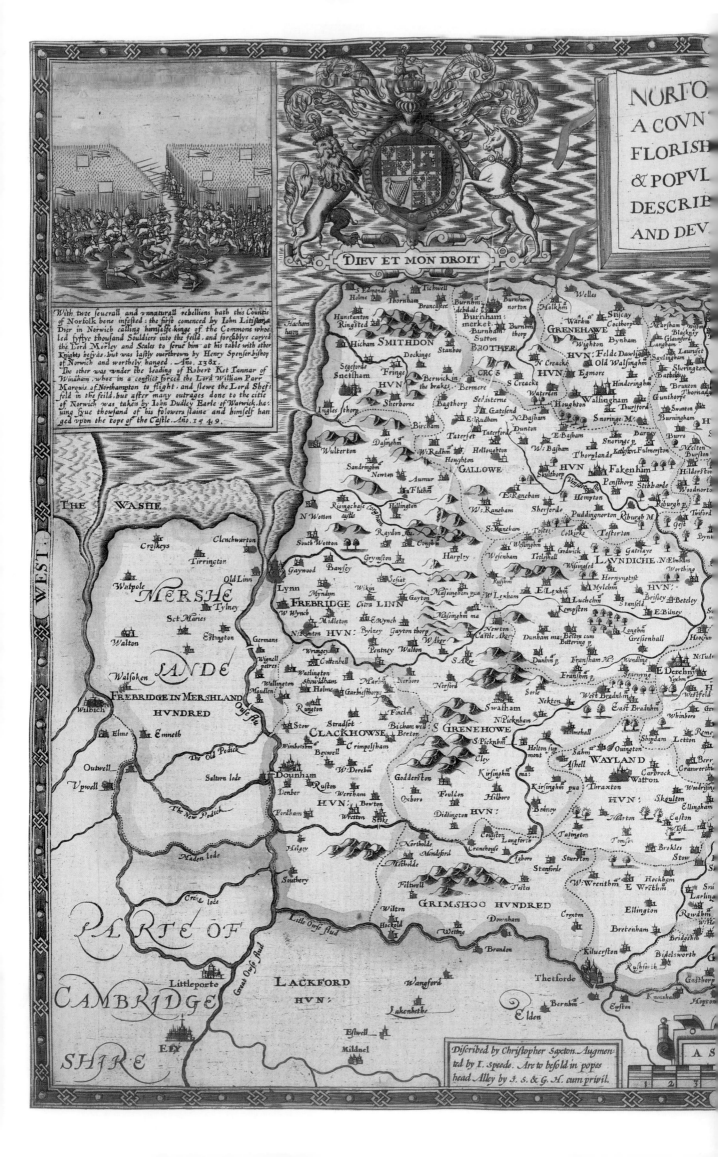

TH THE
ES OF SVCH
E FAMILES
AVE BORNE
E TITLES
THEROF.

The Armes of Norwiche

NORWICHE

Verus flu

PLACES within the Cittie obſerued by Letters.

A.	S. Leonards	N.	S. Michaels.
B.	Biſhops gate	O.	S. Iohns at the gate.
C.	The Cathedrull Churche	P.	S. Stephens.
D.	S. Martins at ſ Pallis gate	Q.	The Market place.
E.	S. Botholds	R.	S. Gyles gate.
F.	S. Clements	S.	Hell gate.
G.	S. Auguſtins	T.	S. Benets gates.
H.	S. Martins at the Oke	V.	S. Stephens gates.
I.	The Caſtle	W.	Pockethorpe gate.
K.	S. Peters Permanitgate	X.	The New Milles.
L.	S. Martins on the hill	Y.	Chappell in the feilde.
M.	S. Iohns on the hill	Z.	S. Martins gate.

Ri: Guet Earle of Norf:

W. of Boleign E. of Nor:

Hu: Bigod E. of Norfolk

Th: Brotherton E. of N:

Th: Moubray D. of N:

Ri: of Shrowesbury D of N

Lo. Howard D. of Norfolke

EAST.

Hope
Runton Cromere
Elmerton Oxtrand Syftrand Trimmingham
N. ORPINGHAM S. Reppes Gimmingham
Gresham Roxton N. Reppes
Melton Mounſley Paſton
HVN Thorpe Knapton Backton Walcote
Hanworthe Braſeld Edingthorpe
Antingham Swafeld Didlington Witton Hapſburg Eckles
Hempſted
Prumſted Pauling
N. Wallhm Croſtwick Ruſton Stalham Ingham Leſingham Waxham
TVNSTED Honyng Horſey
Wurſted Sutton Hickling Hayhm
Skeyton Weſtwick Dilam Smalbore Vrſted HAPPINGE HVN Somerton Winterton nelse
Somerton Martham Himmesby
Releſbye WEST FLEGG Scrutbye
Burtas HVN Ormeſbye Sct Michaell
Reppes Ormeſbye
Filbye Mandbye
EAST FLEGG
TAVERHAM Waxham Thiergohye Runham
Crostwick bridge Woodaſtwick Chſſhye Stokeſbye Caſtor
Hellesden Sprotto Heliington St Walſhm Vpton HVN
Fiſbley Hauergate Yermouth
Wilton Blofeld HVN Wickhmton
BLOFELD HVN
Lingwood Sowthwood Tunſtall Gorleſton
Strumſfall Lympenhowe Moulton Belton Burgh Caſtle
Redehm Fritton
Hierus Freithorp Sct Olaues Hopton
Lownde
Hardley LOVINGLAND Corton
Langley Aſhye Thurlton Leſtoffe
Chedgraue Hadſco Oldton
CLAVERINGE & LODDON
HVN Windell
Beckles Pakesfeld
Keſland
DEPWADE HVN
Mutford
Henſted
ERISHAM HVN
Bungay Benacre
Harleſton Coue hithe
S. Coue
DIS Saterley
Sowowld
HVN
DIS Haleſworth Bliboro Walderſwick
Hoxon Wenhaſton Dunwiche
Horhm Heueningham Sibton

PARTE OF SVFFOLKE

7 8 9 10

were King's Lynn and Great Yarmouth. In such a prosperous region it was not surprising that parish churches proliferated (660 according to Speed) and that the many small towns producing cloth and the thirty market towns were 'common well built and populous', Norwich, Lynn and Yarmouth 'being of that worth and quality, as no shire of England hath the like'. At the time of the compilation of the *Theatre*, Norwich was the second largest city in England, with a population approaching 20,000. With its thriving cloth trade and numerous industries, Norwich was one of the few urban centres which could not be said to be in decline at the time: evidence of its civic vitality can be seen in the imaginative arrangements for the poor and elderly made in the city in the 1550s and subsequently modified through experience, which were scrutinized and accepted as the model for the Poor Law system for the whole kingdom by Parliament in 1571.

Although Speed mentioned the two great uprisings in Norfolk in the early modern period—the Peasants' Revolt of 1381 and Ket's Rebellion of 1547, both of which revealed the uneven distribution of wealth between families of noble or gentle birth and the peasantry, and imbalances between town and country—he said nothing of Norfolk's crucial part in the succession crisis of 1553, when Princess Mary withdrew into the shire to Kenninghall. There, with the support of the Howard family, their dependants and other Catholic sympathizers, she rallied a force before starting an eventually triumphant march south to Framlingham and then on to London. Kenninghall figured in a national crisis again in 1571, when the Duke of Norfolk was arrested for conspiring with Mary Queen of Scots against Queen Elizabeth I.

James I became instantly enamoured of the county on his first visit to it in 1604, and it was said that he was 'so far in love with the pleasures' of Thetford that he meant to have a house there. Three years later the King ordered that all the game within a twelve-mile radius of Thetford should be preserved for his personal use, but another two years elapsed before he actually bought a house there. The frequency of James' visits to Norfolk encouraged Lord Chief Justice Hobart to rebuild his house at Blickling between 1616 and 1627 as a suitable place to receive the King, and to employ as architect and designers much of the team which had previously worked at Hatfield House.

As in Suffolk, the absence of a good indigenous stone meant that most building was timber-framed, only the more costly being in knapped flint with stone dressing. What stone there was came from across the Fens, from Barnack, Clipsham and Ancaster—ample evidence of the good internal waterway links that existed well into the seventeenth century. Brick was also a much favoured material; Sir John Fastolf's castle at Caister, built in the 1430s with his profits from the Hundred Years War and later dishonestly acquired by the Pastons, had been erected in brick, as was Sir Henry Fermor's remarkable house with its elaborate mouldings at East Barsham in the 1520s.

Northamptonshire

With its limestone uplands Northamptonshire was one of the few areas in England with limited access to navigable rivers. Thus largely denied direct lines of communication with the coast and the sea, it was geographically more isolated than many other counties. This sense of isolation was further enforced by the lack of a major highway serving the heart of the county, such important roads as there were being situated along its peripheries.

Apart from the quarrying and preparing of its high-grade stone, which was in demand as a building material not only locally but in most of its adjoining counties, Northamptonshire was a predominantly agricultural area. According to Speed the 'soil was champion, rich and fruitful' but in actuality it was not well suited to ploughing and grain production. What it proved ideal for was the breeding and rearing of cattle and particularly of flocks of sheep 'loaden with their fleeces of wool'. Of the sheep Speed laconically commented: 'notwithstanding the simple and gentle sheep, of all creatures the most harmless, are now become so ravenous, that they begin to devour men, waste fields, and depopulate houses, if not whole townships, as one merrily hath written'. While it is true that Sir Thomas More never meant his rhetorical aside to be taken seriously, many genuinely feared that the increase in size of flocks and the acceleration of the process of enclosing common land benefited only the sheepowners, not the community at large, and riots against such enclosures in Northamptonshire and elsewhere in the Midlands had led to the Crown's instituting commissions of enquiry into enclosure in 1517, 1545, 1566 and 1607. Although the enquiries did reveal ample evidence of fraud and coercion, it was clear to the commissioners that the land involved was often poor, difficult to farm and sparsely populated, and no effective action was taken to stop further enclosure or to restore enclosed land to its previous use. The wealth deriving from the rationalization of land-holding and from ownership of cattle and sheep is to be seen in the size and quality of the county's numerous medieval parish churches with their distinctive towers and spires, and in the general availability of finely prepared stone for building and of stone slabs for roofs even among the dwellings of the relatively poor inhabitants of the county, William Camden noting how Northamptonshire was 'passing well furnished with noblemen's and gentlemen's houses'. Perhaps the most spectacular fortune made from grazing in the county was that of the Spencers who had bought Althorp by 1508, and had intermarried with the peerage by the end of the sixteenth century.

A St Andrews mill
B S. Andrews Abbey
C North Gate
D St Sepulchres
E sheepe market
F S. Edmonds end
G Marhold
H Graye Friers
I The Drapery
K S Kathrens
L The Checker
M The Castell
N The Hermitage
O S. Iames end
P Bridge stret
Q St Iohns
R Alhallowes
S St Peters
T The Towre
V Darngate
W St Thomas well
X St Gylles
Y Free Schole
Z The Mill

40 80 120 160 200 040
Scale of Pases

This towne of Northampton
hath thrice felt the ruins of civill diſſentions. The 1. was by R.
Wil. And Henry brethren and
ſones to the conqueror, who
ſpoyled it, and the Courtye ad-
ioyning Anno 1106. The 2. was
by king H. 3. whoe ſurpriſed it
againſt his rebellious Barons
and brake downe the walles
thereof. Anno 1263.

And laſtly therin was taken
King H. 6. by the Earls of
Warwick and March ſuppor-
ters of yᵉ title of Yorke where
were ſlayne Humfrey Stafford
D. of Buckingham. Iohn Talbot
Earle of Shrowesbury and Lᵗ.
Beamount, and Egremount,
with mamore. The King was
by Lords conueyed to Lõdõ
Anno 1459.

WEST

PART OF WARWICKSHIRE

Performed by Iohn Speed and
are to by ſold by George Humbell in
yᵉ Popes head alley. Cum Privilegio.

1 2 3 4 5 6 7 8 9 10

Parte of Oxford

PAR

OF SECESTER

NO S

Medborn
Wellan
Ashley
Weston
Sto
HigherBowto
Sutton
Brampton
Lubbenham
Herboro
Dingly
Pipwell
Fedingworth
Merson, Truſſell
Howthorp
East Farndon
Little Bowton
Brabrok Caſt
Rushto
Bosworth
ROTHE Oxendon WELL
Daiesboro
Rothw
North Kilworth
Sibbertost Ardingworth
Harinton
Clypston HUND.
Kelmersh
Loddingto
South Kilworth
Sulbye
Maidwell
Swineforde
Wilford
Naſlybye
Haſlbich
Draughton
Cransl
Faxton
Cathorpe
Stanford
Clayatton
Cold Aſhbye
Thurnbye
Hanging
Houghton
HU
Lylborn
West Haddon
Raunsthorp
Codesbrok
Creton
Newton
Yeluertost
Winwick
Teton
Scaldwell
Brixworth
Clyſton
Hilmorton
Kilsoye
Guleſburgh
WE
Stratton
SPEL
HOE
PART FAUSLEY
Watford
HUN
Holdenbye Braÿton
Iſford
Berbye
Aſhbye Legers
East Haddon
Althorpe
Buckton
Dunchurch
Wetton
Loſing Buckbye
Wilton
Church
Brynton
Harleston
Kingsthorp
Willye
Braundſton
Duſton
Abbington
Wes
Granboro Widsfneore
Flexnoo
Ovencote
Norton
NEWBOTLE
Leme flud
Staverton
Dodford
Newbottle
Brokhole
S. Iames
Upton
OF WAR
Daventre
Hartple
GROVE HUND.
Northam
Shughoro
Badbye
Newnham
Euerton
Wedon
Flowre
Killingbury
Hardington
Wotto
Napton
Caiſbye
Nyne
Forthinston
Hosfordes
Thorpe
Milton
WICK
Hellindon
Stowe
Gayton
Collingtrough
Blisworth
Merston
Faluſley
CESTER
Rode
Corter
Hardwick
Cherwelton
HUND
Lichbord
Coldhigham
HUND
Wormeleighton
Byfeld
Preſton Capes
Madford
Stoke Bruant
Aſhton
Boddingtonn
Woodford
Adſon
NOR.
Grene norton
Easton
CLELEY
Graſto
Cleydon
Aſton
Aſhbye
Blakesfel
TON
Towceſt
Farmeboro
WARDEN
Eydon
Morton pynckney
HUND
Aldrington
Chipping warden
HUND
Slapton
Athrop
Whittle
Wardenton
Edgecot
Culworth
Wedon
Silverton
wood Forest
HUND
yardly
Choperedye
Soulgrave
Wapnicham
Whittlebury
Pett
Lillington Louell
Danes more
Thorp manduill
Aſhwell
Syſam
Paſſenham
Chalcombe
Middleton Cheyney
Helmedon
SUTTON HUND
Werkworth
Duſſeld
Lillingtõ Dorrell
wkins
Werkworth
Merston
Radſton
Bidleſdon
Whitfelde
Lekhamſted
Fernyho
Banbury
Stone
Turweſton
Bodycot
Hinton
Brackley
Westbury
Buckingam
Kings ſutto
Charlton
Fulwell
Adderbury
Newbottle
Finmere
Imley
Ayno
Mixbury
Ouſe flu:
Croughton
Jodocus Hondi
Clyſton
Souldern
Beddington

WILD FOREST

Part of

PART OF — LINCOLNE — SHIRE
Crowland

Rut
land WILLI

Stanford
Tinwell
Burghley
Baddingto
Beruak
Easton
Collyweston
Duddington
Wyttering Wyttering Heth
Thornhow
Suly Lodge Walmsford
Tickover
Wakerley
Kinges
Finftead
Haringworth
Loxton
Bulwick
Rokingam
Denethorp
Glapthort
Denifeld
Weldon
Lyfden
Stanyon
Brustok
Wadenhoo
Oldwinkles
Sudboro
Luffwick
Slipton
Islip
Draton
Twiwell
Thrapfton
Woodford
Cranford
Great Adding
Burton
Little Addington
Artleboro
Thyndon
HUND
HIGHAM
Rushden
Newton
Higham park
FEYRES
Archefter
Wolafton
Winnyngton
Poddington
Souldrop
Strixton
Bofiat
Woodhill
Hanrold
Chellington
Launden
Bradfeld
Oulney park
Oulney
Ouse flu:
PART OF BED
FORD
CKING SHIRE

West Deping Tallington
Uffington
Maxey caft
Etton
Burghley
Glynton
NASABURGH HUND.
Ufford
Woodcroft
Marham
Pafton
PETERBURG
Mylton
Upton
Sutton
Cafton
Verwell
Stibbington Water Newton
Allerton
Chery orton
Yaley
Haddon
Marhon
Tanfour
Lutton
POLBROOK
Oundle
Pokbrok
Bernwells
Hemnyngton
Glatton
Great Gedding
Liddington
Thurnyng
Winwick
HUND
FORD
Clapton
Bythorn
Kofton

Market Deping
Waldram hall
E. Deping
Nerboro Prakirk
Singlefale
Thorney mill
Eye

PART
OF HUN
TINGDON

At Edgcot in this county upon Danes more
a bloody battell was fought, by the Lords of
the north, their Captaynes being Sir Iohn Co:
mers, and Robbin of Ridfdale, againft King E.
4. William Harbert Earle of Pembrok there
his Generall, Whoe together with his brother
Richard and Richard Wooduill Lord Riuers
brother to the Queene, with his fonne were
there taken and all foure beheaded and 5000.
of their men flayne the greateft part where
of were Welchmen. This Battall was fought
Iulij 26. Anno 1469.

The armes of all those honorable Fa milies that have bene created Earles of Northapto, since y Normans conqueft.

Siward E. — Simon Sentlis E.
William Bohun E. — Humfrey Bohun E.
Thomas Wooftok — Humfrey Stafford
William parr M — Henry Haward E.

EAST

PETERBOROW

A Borrow Bery
B Weft gates ftret
C Swane Poole
D Bungate
E Bungate hoole
F Saxon Barne
G St Iohns
H The Market
I The Prison
K St Peters minft
L Prefgat Laine
M High ftrete

A Scale of pafes
50 100 150 200

1610.

When Speed visited Northamptonshire he was impressed by the number of churches and windmills to be counted from any vantage point there. Scrutiny of the map reveals how extensively it was still wooded, and its many parks and forests. Three of the forests—Rockingham, Salcey and Whittlewood— were still in royal ownership from the Middle Ages, and Henry VIII's predilection for the hunt led him to buy Grafton in 1526, even though he had inherited a splendid house at Fotheringhay from his Yorkist forebears. Grafton was memorable for being the last meeting place of the King with Cardinal Wolsey before the minister's downfall. Over a period of thirty years starting in the 1550s Sir William Cecil transformed his grandfather's modest house at Burghley into one of the largest and grandest in England, with the avowed purpose of entertaining Queen Elizabeth there on her progresses through the kingdom. Kirby Hall was begun in 1570 for Sir Humphrey Stafford for the same reason, but passed quickly into the ownership of another of the Queen's favourites, Sir Christopher Hatton, who built a further 'prodigy' in its vicinity at Holdenby: finished in 1583, Holdenby was bought by James I from the Hattons in 1608 for his own use with a remainder to his second son, Charles, Duke of York. Castle Ashby was similarly rebuilt from the 1570s, and Lord Compton entertained James I there on three occasions before becoming Earl of Northampton in 1618. Despite the fame and the grandeur of these buildings, the best known buildings from the sixteenth century in Northamptonshire are the series of curious structures erected by Sir Thomas Tresham, a convert from the Church of England to Roman Catholicism who was obsessed with theology, architecture and allegorical conceits, and whose buildings illustrate his fanaticism: these at Lyveden and Rushton survive today.

The royal castle at Fotheringhay was the final prison of Mary Queen of Scots, and it was there that on 8 February 1587, after nineteen years' imprisonment, she was executed, dying 'for the honour of [God]'s name and of his Church, Catholic, Apostolic and Roman'. As the collegiate church there with its royal mausoleum had already been largely demolished, Mary was buried at Peterborough, where Catherine of Aragon had been interred in 1536, and which had been raised to cathedral status in 1541. When Speed went to Peterborough while preparing his commentary, he saw the tombs of both Queens draped in black, but by the time that the *Theatre* was published, James I had had his mother's body removed to Westminster Abbey.

Northumberland

'The air', wrote Speed, is 'subtle and piercing', Northumberland being 'exposed to extremity of weathers, as great winds, hard frosts, and long lying of snows', only ameliorated by its proximity to the North Sea and by its seams of coal mined and burnt for heat. The collieries mainly situated near Newcastle or along the coast supplied fuel not only for local consumption but also for the rest of England, particularly for London, being transported in 'cats', deep barges with a narrow stern and projecting quarters, along the north-east coast to their destination, or else across the North Sea to the Netherlands and Scandinavia. The prosperity of Newcastle, which was the subject of the town plan in the top right-hand corner of the county map, rested upon this trade and upon supplying the troops often present to keep the borderlands with Scotland quiet and in order until the Union of the Crowns.

The Northumbrian landscape varies from the moorland of the Pennines in the west and of the Cheviots in the north through rough country cut with rivers to the coastal plain. Its agriculture reflected the landscape. The bleak uplands supported flocks of sheep and herds of cattle, which were moved to different pastures according to the seasons. Some areas still had their medieval forests and woodlands, which were as important for their horse population as for their deer, the horses being used to mount lighthorsemen to fight the Scots and to pursue rustlers. Most of the soil was poor, needing much manuring, and only in the Tyne valley and along the coast did it repay the hard labour of farming with crops of cereals and other foodstuffs. The coastal plain was an area of open-field husbandry, each township having three open fields of its own which remained unenclosed well into the seventeenth century.

Like the other border counties Northumberland fell under the jurisdiction of the Lord Warden of the Marches, and in recognition of their military obligations, its inhabitants were exempted from the regulations for carrying arms and from taxes which applied to the rest of the kingdom. With its long frontier against Scotland the county was well supplied with castles kept in reasonable state of repair, and with pele towers and bastles, and at Berwick-upon-Tweed (recovered from Scotland only as late as 1482) there was a fortress, repeatedly redesigned in the light of current military knowledge from the 1530s but in need of updating in the 1590s. It had a permanent garrison until the accession of James VI of Scotland to the English throne in 1603, when the fortress lost its *raison d'être*: the defences dating from 1569 can clearly be seen

A.SCALE.OF.PASES.
40 80 120 160

The Armes of such honorable Families, as have borne the Dignity, and Title of Earles, and Dukes of Northumberland, since the Normans' Conquest.

A	Castle	I	Middle mount	S	Copens Tower
B	Whyt wall	K	Search house mount	T	Shore-gate
C	S. Marie gate	L	Cow gate	V	Maison deeu
D	Bell Tower	M	Mill mount	W	Bridge gate
E	Lordes mount	N	z. Store houses	X	Kinges Stables
F	The Grenes	O	Hunsdons new moūt	Y	Tolbooth and state house
G	West mount	P	Hunsdons mount	Z	Parado
H	New Marie gate	R	Pallace Tower	1	Pallace

WEST

Waldeof Earl. Northum.

Robert Mowbrey E.

Henry sonne to David K. of Scot.

Hugh pudsey Bishop of Durham

John Nevill E. of Northum.

Henry Percy Earl. of Northum.

John Dudley Duke of Northum.

Thomas Percy Earl. of Northum.

A.SCALE.OF.MILES.
1 2 3 4 5 6 7 8 9 10

SCOTLAND

PART OF

Hume cast.

The whele kirk

Packirhaugh

Kirsop Fell

Flights chap

Whithaugh Towre

Mangerton

Kirsop flu.

Kirsop foote

Lamford

Cristinbury Crag

The gele Crag

The Horse head

Bew Cast

PART OF CUM:

THE PICTES WALL

Lenercost

Naworth cast

CARLISLE   Irthing fl.

Overdenton

Thirlwall

Blenkensop cast

BER:

SAND

Tweede flu.

Cupup

Edgerton

Aumond hill

The Carter

Robbes crosse

The Whele Fell   Chetlop Burne

Tyne head
Belkirk   Redes   Dale

Butterhaugh

Flights Fell

Shele flu.

Leaplish

Emothaugh

Shilborn   Yarro
haugh smalburn

Tyndale

Grenesed

Dala cast

Chirden

Whitchester   Brearidg

Shitlinton   Bellerley

Workesborn   Water yate

Roseborn

Spi Crag

Middleborn

River hall   Wall Town

The Fo:rest of Lowes

Sewensheld

Bradley hall

Stone   Chesterwood

Widon   Mel   Eriche

Unthank   Whily   Snotewsill

Bellister   Allons   Groue

Cast   Penpughe

Hartley flu

Sibbenes   Fethersto
haugh   Conewood
chap

Lamley

Knaresdale

Thornhope

Gilderdale

Whitlaton

Eldes

Williamston

Kirkhaugh   Alneburne

Hawcople   Mowat

Whitlaton

Auschmūore

Whitfeld

Whitfeld Hall

Toddewood

Munk

Permandley

oūston

West Alnẃ

Spartewell

Newshile
Whinnelrau

Allenton

Harsney flu.
Strauert peale

Nobok

Hexham

Grindrigg

Doteland
Hamburnhall

Esheoles

Stelhall flu.

Douols flu.

Sindrop

Sibton Sheles   Knewdon

Ridlamhope

Whetley Sheles

Kelloplaw

PART

Long Bridgham   Caldstreame
Rydam   Spylawe
Carram
Pryssan
Hawdon   Windram
Holefelde   Padston
Timpetlaw   Graydon   Kila

Nattons   Hethpole

Whit squir: hill

Maiden Crosse
Blak Brea

Coket flu

Kemblepeth hill
The red squire   Ridley flu.

Lynbridg
Hoclugh

Wullaw

Rochester   Durt:
Steubes   chorn
Greene chester

Rattenraw   Otter:
Smal burne   burne

Theeam Snepe   Overa

Hollin head   Troughwhen
Grenehaugh old Towne

Tarset   Charleton   Corsenside

Blakelaw   Leame
Kinsingh

Nuke
Birkes   Bellin
gham

Dunterley   Reasid

Lee Hall

Carohouse
Burtley

Hathcinton   Wark

Gunnerton

Ruthester

Barraford

Marele Pawle   Black   Chipechase
Nether morley   Haughton

Simon burne cast
Carrow tower

Walwick
The Syde   Newburghe

Haydon   Wharby
pynters   Wardel
Black Hall   Woodhall
Beltingham   Castley
Hadon Bridg   Longhope
Less   Langley east

Dukepill
Plankford
Penpughe

Caddon   Oldrown

Kmeleysid

Knewdon

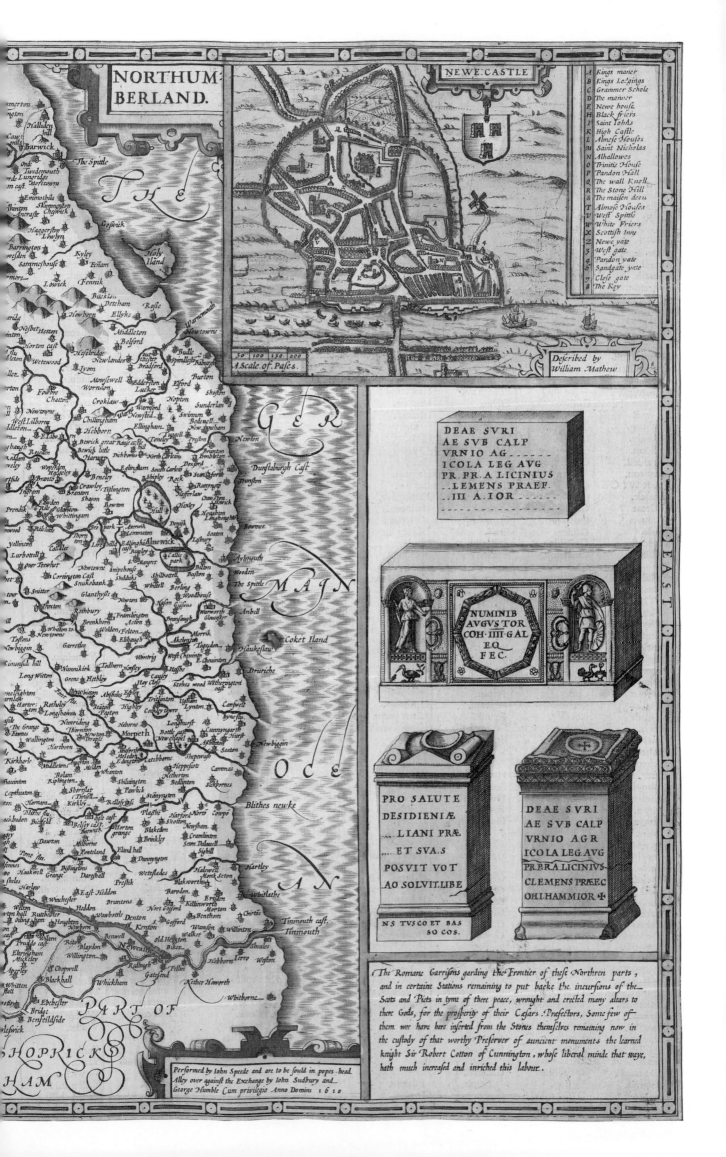

NORTHUMBERLAND.

NEWE CASTLE

A Scale of Pases. 50 100 150 200

Described by William Mathew

A Kings maner
B Kings Lodgings
C Grammer Schole
D The maner
E Newe house
F Black friers
G Saint Iohns
H High Castle
I Almese Houses
K Saint Nicholas
L Alhallowes
M Trinitie House
N Pandon Hall
O The wall Knoll
P The Stone Hill
Q The maison deeu
R Almose Houses
S West Spittle
T White Friers
V Scottish Inne
W Newe yate
X West gate
Y Pandon yate
Z Sandgate yate
1 Close gate
2 The Key

DEAE SVRI
AE SVB CALP
VRNIO AG......
ICOLA LEG AVG
PR. PR. A LICINIVS
...LEMENS PRAEF.
...III A. IOR.......

NVMINIB
AVGVSTOR
COH · IIII · GAL
EQ.
FEC.

PRO SALVTE
DESIDIENIÆ
... LIANI PRÆ
.... ET SVA. S
POSVIT VOT
AO SOLVIT.LIBE
NS TVSCO ET BAS
SO COS.

DEAE SVRI
AE SVB CALP
VRNIO AGR
ICOLA LEG AVG
PR.PR.A LICINIVS
CLEMENS PRÆC
OHI.HAMMIOR

The Romane Garrisons garding the Frontier of these Northren parts, and in certaine Stations remaining to put backe the incursions of the Scots and Picts in tym of there peace, wrought and erected many altars to there Gods, for the prosperity of their Cesars Prefectors, Some few of them we have here inserted from the Stones themselves remaining now in the custody of that worthy Preserver of auncient monuments the learned knight Sir Robert Cotton of Cunnington, whose liberal minde that waye, hath much increased and inriched this labour.

Performed by Iohn Speede and are to be sould in popes head Alley over against the Exchange by Iohn Sudbury and George Humble Cum privilegio Anno Domini 1610

in the town plan in the top left-hand corner of the county map. The vulnerability of Northumberland to incursions from the Scots (the last major invasion being that of 1513, halted at Flodden Field through the prompt action of Catherine of Aragon), and the prevailing violence of the area, meant that not unsurprisingly wholly domestic habitations were few, and that the house-building boom common to most counties in England during Elizabeth's reign passed Northumberland largely untouched. In several of the wilder parts of the county, notably North Tynedale and Redesdale, men grouped themselves as late as the 1580s into a 'clan' or surname system for their own mutual protection, and to threaten their neighbours. Thieving, particularly of livestock, was so extensive as to amount to a way of life, and 'as a cautionary note for such as have cause to travel that way' Speed recorded that 'Busygap is a place infamous' for hold-ups and robbery. As to the intense conservatism and Catholicism of the region, he made no remark.

Contrary to his normal practice Speed marked all the Northumbrian castles with their names on the county map. He also marked the course of Hadrian's Wall, which (like William Camden) he called the Picts' Wall. The armorial border has the arms of successive holders of the earldom and dukedom of Northumberland, ending with those of the duke who had been unable to prevent the accession of Princess Mary to the throne in 1553 and of the earl who had led the Northern Rising in 1569 with the Earl of Westmorland: both these men were beheaded for treason, but their crimes were things of the past compared with the ignominy of the imprisonment in the Tower of the current holder of the earldom, Henry Percy, about the time of the issue of the *Theatre*, on suspicion of complicity in the Gunpowder Plot of 1605, in which his kinsman Sir Thomas Percy had a chief part. Speed completed the county map with the town plans and illustrations of four Roman inscriptions in the possession of his friend, Sir Robert Cotton of Connington in Huntingdonshire 'whose liberal mind that way hath much increased and enriched this labour'.

Nottinghamshire

From the tenth century Nottinghamshire had been known as 'the shire with the wood', and since Sherwood accounted for over a quarter of its area seven hundred years later, the description was apt. As can be seen from the county map the woodland extended northwards from Sherwood right up through the county to its border with Yorkshire and Lincolnshire. Being sand or clay, the soil was poor (rather than 'rich', as described by Speed) and since it was able to sustain little ploughing, was largely given over to deer and rabbits, hunting being the chief pastime of the area. To obtain crops of cereals and grasses, patches of heathland had often to be broken up and cultivated for periods up to five or six years, after which they were allowed to revert to pasture by cattle, raised for their hides rather than their beef or milk. One commodity for which there was a culinary and medical demand grew well in Nottinghamshire, and this was liquorice, cultivated in the neighbourhood of Worksop. However, inadequate supplies of food grown locally meant that Nottinghamshire was more vulnerable than most English counties to famine, and an inadequate diet even in times of relative plenty presumably accounted for the high mortality rate during epidemics and the shortness of its inhabitants' lives. The economy of the county depended principally on coal and iron mining, but also on a variety of smaller industries such as leather curing and tanning, the making of hose (done throughout the county), and the carving of alabaster (in the town of Nottingham.)

The timber felled in Nottinghamshire woodlands was neither much good nor plentiful, and for a predominantly forested county, Nottinghamshire is odd for its lack of a rich tradition in vernacular timber-framed building. Much of the building done for peasants and tenant farmers was made up of slight timber frames embedded deeply in a mixture of wet mud and straw, which was then allowed to dry and was afterwards whitewashed to protect the mud-and-stud. In the absence of good timber, brick and tiles had been adopted for building houses by the early sixteenth century, long before they became common elsewhere, a good example of this being Sir William Pierrepont's house at Holme Pierrepont, built in the 1510s. It was perhaps in response to local difficulties that houses with small entrance lobbies giving on to a central chimney stack which heated two rooms by having two back-to-back fireplaces, and with a staircase beyond the chimney giving access to the upper floor, evolved earlier in Nottinghamshire than in the rest of England, where they had become

PART OF YORK

NOTTINGHAM

A SCALE OF PASES
40 80 120 160

I	Bearward Lane	T	Midle pauement	7	worser Lane
K	S Iames Lane	V	Highe pauement	8	Newark Lane
L	Whitfriers Lane	W	Pepper strete	9	Barker lane
M	Hen Gate	X	Bridlesmith	10	S. Marie Gat
N	wheelwright Lan	Y	Woller Lane	11	Pilcher gate
O	Castle Lane	Z	Flesher Gate	12	Hallifax Lane
P	Broad marsh	1	Lynby Lane	13	Stony Stret
Q	Narrow marsh	2	Chalers Lane	14	Bellar gate
R	Vaule Lane	3	Swine Grene	15	Fisher Gate
S	Lowe paument	4	Gosse Gate	16	Malin Hill

A	S. Maryes chur.	D	Carter Gate
B	S. Peters church	E	Cowe Lane
C	S. Nicholas	F	Griddlesmith
		G	Corne market
		H	Timber Hill

SHIRE

BASSETLAWE

WEAPONT.

PART OF

At Stoke in this County, nere unto Newark, was
fought a great Battell, against King H. 7. by the
Erectors of Lambert: a conterfet Warwick. where
Iohn Dela Pole Earle of Lincoln, Francis Lord
Louell, Tho. Garadyne. Chaunceller of Ireland,
Martyn Swart, and Sir Tho. Broughton, with
4000. of their naked Irish lost their lyues. Lambert was there taken, and made a turne spitt in
the Kings kitchyn, and lastly one of his ffalconers
This conflict was fought the 16. of Iune Anno
1487. and in the third yeare of H. 7.

Iodocus Hondius cælavit
Anno Domini 1610

BROXTOWE WEAPONTAK

Forest of

She

DARBY

NORTH
EAST
SOUTH
WEST

The Scale of English miles

1 2 3 4 5 6 7 8 9 10

SHIRE

RUSHCLIFF WEAPONT

Part

THE COUNTIE OF NOTTINGHAM described THE SHIRE TOWNES SITUATION AND THE EARLS THERE OF observed

THE Armes of such Honorable Familyes as have borne the titles of Earles of Nottingham

Robert Ferrers — Iohn Mowbray

Rich. D. of Yorke — Will. Barkley

Henry Fitz Roy — Charles Howard

Performed by Iohn Speede and are to be sold in Popes head Alley by Iohn Sudbury and Georg. Humble Cum Privilegio 1610

common by the seventeenth century. Stone imported from Ancaster in Lincolnshire was the material favoured by the Holles, Cavendish, Talbot and Willoughby families in the spectacular series of Elizabethan prodigy houses erected by them at Haughton, Worksop, Welbeck and Wollaton. Of these only Wollaton (costing £8,000 and paid for out of the profits of coal-mining) survives, with its all-round symmetry and raised central hall with turreted prospect room above, but the impact made by Worksop can be gauged from extant prints of it and the fact that on the map it is marked and described as The Manor, a distinction accorded to few other country houses in the *Theatre*.

After journeying through a landscape of small villages, travellers arriving at Nottingham were impressed by the size of the town. Speed saw 'a town seated most pleasant and delicate upon a high hill, for buildings stately and number of fair streets surpassing and surmounting many other cities': he was impressed with its 'spacious and most fair market place' and recalled 'the many strange vaults hewed out of the rocks', particularly one with carvings allegedly done by King David II of Scotland while held captive there. The castle had been a favourite residence of Edward IV, and under the early Tudor kings it had continued to be the main royal fortress in the north Midlands, in 1536 serving as a base for the suppression of the Lincolnshire and Yorkshire rebellions, but later it was allowed to decay. Notwithstanding the neglect of the castle during the late sixteenth century, Nottingham with its industries and crafts flourished, and replaced Lincoln, which was in decline, as provincial capital of the region. Between Nottingham and Gainsborough the river Trent was navigable by flat-bottomed ketches drawing no more than three feet of water yet capable of transporting fifty-ton cargoes. However, records from the period show that local highways were in sound repair and more goods were carried by road than by water. Some damage to roads caused by moving goods too heavy for them led to a remarkable innovation, the full potential of which was not to be realized for another two centuries, when a railway for wagons bearing coal was constructed in Nottinghamshire in 1598.

Nottinghamshire played a significant part in national history when in 1487 the supporters of Lambert Simnel were defeated at Stoke Field, an event duly marked and commented upon by Speed. It played no part of equal importance until in 1642 Charles I raised his standard at Nottingham Castle at the opening of the Civil War.

Oxfordshire

Until the early nineteenth century, Oxfordshire was one of the most heavily wooded counties in England. The royal forest of Wychwood—or Shotover as it was sometimes called—which had been created by the Norman kings, survived almost intact at the accession of James I and covered almost two-thirds of Oxfordshire. The forest, with its many deer and the promise of good hunting, had ensured the county's favour with medieval kings, who had made the manor at Woodstock one of the most desirable residences in their possession. Both Edward IV and Henry VII had lavished considerable sums in modernizing and improving the house and its grounds, but their successors did not share their enthusiasm for Woodstock. For Elizabeth I this is readily understandable: while still a princess she had been detained there during 1554–5 as a prisoner on her sister Queen Mary's command. In spite of her unhappy memories of the place, Elizabeth I was an occasional visitor to Woodstock, and was entertained there by Sir Henry Lee in 1575. At her reception at Ditchley, Lee's own house, in 1592, the Queen had symbolically made her way through an enchanted wood and released Lee from a punishment for failing to protect 'enchanted pictures', which perhaps included the portrait of Elizabeth I standing on a map of England with Ditchley at her feet.

Oxfordshire not only had hills 'beset with woods' and provision for 'all kind of game for hound and hawk', but was well watered with streams and rivers, and its valleys and level ground were good for grain-growing and fruit-farming. However, its enormous prosperity depended upon its pasturage of cattle and sheep, particularly in the Cotswolds adjoining Gloucestershire, where some of the highest-quality wool in the country was produced. The wealth obtained from grazing sheep can be gauged today from the number of fine large churches in the county at places such as Burford, Chipping Camden, Chipping Norton and Witney, and by the quantity of surviving houses from the fifteenth and sixteenth centuries—some quite modest—often with ground floors built of stone and upper parts timber-framed. Because of the extensive forest, good arable land not limited in its potential use by forest law was at a premium, and attempts to enclose such land in order to increase sheep production and profit margins were bitterly resented by yeoman farmers in the county, with the result that Oxfordshire shared the agrarian discontent so common in the Midlands. Disputes and rioting over enclosure were endemic there, yet Speed's encomium, 'both heaven and earth accorded to make the

inhabitants healthful and happy' affords no hint at a problem that formed the subject of repeated commissions of enquiry in his lifetime. Stone quarried at Burford and Twyford was in demand throughout the county and beyond its boundaries, and several quarries provided stone slating for roofs long before modern roof tiling became readily available.

Of its ten market towns, the shire town of Oxford with its stone bridge crossing the Thames was the most important. From the early twelfth century this thriving commercial centre, with plenty of accommodation available and with protection from a castle and fortified walls, had attracted scholars for occasional courses of lectures, and within the following hundred years the University had developed from these small beginnings. Hostels for students were established first, and later colleges for teachers, the earliest probably being Merton, although Speed favoured the tradition that gave the honour to Balliol College. In his nationalist fervour Speed believed the University of Oxford to be older than it was, having 'long been the glorious seat of the Muses', the British Athens, and 'learning's wellspring' with a patron in King Alfred, but in this he was mistaken. William of Wykeham's foundation at New College in 1379 was innovative in providing accommodation for teachers and students, and the string of colleges established in the sixteenth century followed this model, the most famous being Cardinal Wolsey's foundation of Christ Church in 1525. As a University Oxford had shown an early fascination for Protestantism which had alarmed the authorities in Church and State and led to a series of visitations meant to suppress the heresy, the last of these being under the Catholic Queen Mary. The establishment of Jesus College in 1571 did not succeed in reversing the long-term consequences of the Marian visitation, and it was Sir Thomas Bodley's hope that the library that he set up in 1602 would prove a Protestant lighthouse in a world still tainted by Catholic ignorance and waywardness.

Speed's map is dated 1605, and thus the arms decorating its borders do not include those of Wadham College, which was in the process of construction by the time that the *Theatre* was issued. As with the map for Cambridgeshire, Speed adorned the map for Oxfordshire with figures in academic dress and holding dividers indicating the scale.

On account of its easy accessibility from London, Oxford had been chosen repeatedly in the sixteenth century as a place for trying and burning heretics, whether Catholic or Protestant, the most famous being the so-called Oxford Martyrs of Queen Mary's reign. Following the condemnation of Ridley, Latimer and Hooper in 1554, Archbishop Cranmer's courage failed him and he recanted, but on going to the stake he repudiated his recantation and put his guilty right hand into the fire withdrawing it only briefly to wipe his face. Despite the impact that this deed had upon those witnessing it and upon the country as a whole, a number of families in Oxfordshire, such as the Stonors, remained true to Catholicism, and for hiding priests and participating in the mass they were imprisoned or executed during Queen Elizabeth's reign.

Rutland

The map for Rutland differs in a number of respects from the other maps for English counties in Speed's *Theatre*. Not only is the scale larger than any other place save for Holy Island off the Northumbrian coast, but the map is not dependent on the work of a professional surveyor such as Christopher Saxton or John Norden, but on that of the gifted amateur John Harington, who lived at Exton in Rutland and who was created 1st Lord Harington of Exton by James I in 1603. Harington, who lived to see the publication of the *Theatre* shortly before his own death in 1613, had drawn his own map 'in his younger years'. For this reason not only are all the hills with their distinctive outlines carefully delineated, but the scatter of trees within the county's many parks together with the coppices and launds or open spaces are equally carefully shown: the hunting lodges in Leefield Forest are all marked and named, as are the watermills throughout the county; and the church at Tixover is depicted standing within an embanked enclosure or park. Harington also helped Speed with information for the county commentary.

The agriculture of Rutland was divided into arable and pasture in the lowlands and valleys 'besprinkled with many sweet springs', and into grazing on the hills for herds of cattle and flocks of sheep. The fertility of the county had long been famous, and the revenues obtainable from its corn, its livestock and its woodland explain why Edward the Confessor had settled Rutland on his second wife with a reversion to Westminster Abbey, and equally why William the Conqueror broke the settlement. Notwithstanding the Conqueror's high-handed action Rutland continued to have a reeve or sheriff of its own, and thus it survived as England's smallest shire. Rutland had two market towns, one of which was its shire town with a castle housing the assizes and a gaol at Oakham.

Early in the Middle Ages the Ferrers family, which later became so powerful in the north Midlands, had had their seat in Rutland. The badge of the Ferrers was a horseshoe, but whether horseshoes were adopted by them because they were domiciled in Rutland or the horseshoe became the symbol of the county on account of its Ferrers lords has never been satisfactorily resolved. Even today the great hall of Oakham castle is adorned with horseshoes, some of monstrous size but none exceeding the one five and a half feet high, which stood behind the presiding justice's seat in Speed's time. Many of these horseshoes were the product of an ancient custom enforced by the Haringtons,

OUKHAM

A	Norgate
B	Finkle ſtret
C	Deans Lane
D	Tythe Barne
E	Bargate
F	Free Schole
G	Shire Hall
H	The Caſtell
I	The Market
K	Malt mill ſtret
L	Gilber Gate

A Scale of Paſes
50   100   150

RUTL
OUKHAM a
bordering N.

PART OF

DIEV ET MON DROIT

WEST

Edw. ſone to Ed La | Edw. ſone of Ric D. y | Thomas Mannours

ECES

Thiſtelton

amundthorp

Markel Ouerto

Tyghe

Barowe

Wenton

Wiſſenden

Aſhwell

Loudall

Cotſmöre

Weſtlar

Auſthory

Rankeſborowe hill

Auſthory
Groue

Burley
wood

Multey hill

The vale

Langham

Burley

Ruſhep
wood

Coldouertoñ

Barhythorp

Catmouſe
mill

Oukham

Barinſdal

Coldouertoñ
parke

Knoſton

Edgeton

OUKHAMSOOK
HUNDRED

Knoſton
Brande

The wiſhe
Leefeilde

Braunſton
Brooke

Gunthorp

Wadeland ſhi:

Withcöck

Martinſthorp

Manton

MARTINSLEY H

Launde

The kings
lodge

Lee lodge

Chater flu

Wi

Bittewell

Riddlington

Preſton

Coldeleyes

Ridlington
park

Stirwood

Lamley lodg

Aiſton

Gla

Forest

Vppinhā
park

The

Belton

The Hermitage

Depe
dale

Vppinghā

Biſbrook

Wardley

Beau
mount

Redgate

WR

Stokerſto

Brdegatt

Seyto

Liddington
parke

road

Kings

Leſhare

Priſley hill

Stike

Liddingtoñ

The

Little Ey flu

Bee hill

Weland

Snewton

SHYRE

Caldecote

FER

HIRE

RD her
ly described.

Part of Lin‡

STANFORD

A Scale of Pases
50   100   150   200

Q   The Nunery
R   Water Gate
S   S. Georges Church
T   S. Michaells
V   S. Johns Church
W   Whitmoat mar
X   S. Peters hill
Y   Peters ſtret
1   Peters Gate
2   Auſtyne friers
3   Nunnery
4   Kings mill
5   Th. Caſtle
6   Caſtell ſtret
7   Mawerly lane
8   S. Maryes well
9   S. Peters well
10 Buggell lane
11 S. Maryes church
12 Chani lan
13 Tenter Mdw
14 L.Burleys Almes
15 S. Martins

A   Clemens gat
B   Alhalows
C   Beaſts market
D   Bruins Almeſ
E   Clement Stret
F   Silver lane
G   Nowgate
H   Stabe lane
I   Free Schole
K   Braſenoſe coll
L   Poſts Gate
M   Gray friers
N   St Georgs gate
O   Black friers

Lytrall wood · Clipſham
·stretton
Oſburneall wood
Fauldal wood
Newall wood
e mille croſſe
Croſe mill · Pickeworth
Wolfsky wood
Hardwick
Turnecouſe wood
Ezenden
Brokenell wood coln
Woethead wood
Frith wood
· Horne
Eſt wood
Ryall · Belmsthorp
Boyal wood
Thokthorp
Rullors Stone
· Little Caſterton
Empingam wood
· St Botulphe
Tikencote
neill Caſterton Bridge
pingham Ingthorp
Shire
ell

EAST HUNDRED
Wicheley Heath
Stanford
Weland flu
Normanton
Tymwell · Burghley
· Edyweſton
· Eaſton
Newbotle
Ketton
Chater flu: Geeſton
Kelthorpe
Tofters Bridge
Coliweſton
North Luffenham
South Luffenham
Didington
ton
Tyxover
Moorecote
Barongdon hey
Baroughdon · Waggerley
HUNDRED

PART OF NORTHAMP‡

groorth ‡ON SHYRE

E·AST

SEMPER EADEM

1   2   3   4   5   6
THE   SCHALE   OF   MILES

Performed by Iohan Speede, Solde by M.
John Sudbury and George Humbell, in Popes head
alley againſt the Exchange. Cum Privilegio.

whereby any nobleman entering Rutland had to forfeit a shoe from the horse that he was riding as a homage to the holder of the lordship, unless he preferred to pay a monetary fine instead: most of these real horseshoes were affixed to the door of the great hall. From his nephew and namesake's *Nugae Antiquae* or recollections, it is evident that Harington had a sense of fun which others did not always readily appreciate: one instance involved Henry Clinton, Earl of Lincoln, who starchily 'refused to forfeit the penalty or to pay the fine' and for his unsporting and ignoble conduct was threatened by Harington with a lawsuit which was still pending at the *Theatre*'s publication, and which only lapsed with Harington's death.

As an adherent of Protestantism and an enemy of Catholicism, the 1st Lord Harington was a firm believer in the virtues of learning, and the education of James I's daughter Elizabeth was placed in his charge. Harington's own daughter was Lucy, Countess of Bedford, the constant companion of Queen Anne of Denmark from her arrival south in 1603, and a discerning patron of poets and painters, and his son John 'the most complete young gentleman of his age this kingdom could afford for religion, learning, and courteous behaviour' and the friend of Prince Henry, with whom he shared many common interests, particularly in 'the study of histories, the art of war, mathematics and navigation, wherein he attained to a great measure of perfection'. The 2nd Lord Harington's premature death at the age of twenty-two in 1614, only two years after Prince Henry's, caused an outbreak of grief second only to the mourning at 'the untimely death of that Prince of Wales, the flower of his house, the glory of his country and the admiration of all strangers', and which is best conjured up today by John Donne's *Obsequies to the Lord Harington*. With their interests in education and in promoting the reformed faith, the Haringtons co-operated with the Cecil family over the provision of sound schooling in Rutland and over the presentation to its fourteen parishes, so ensuring a higher degree of literacy and numeracy among its inhabitants and a moderate puritan ministry among its clergy.

The county map is one of the *Theatre*'s more pleasing achievements, with its clarity and its balancing border-designs headed respectively with town maps of Oakham and Stamford. Although Stamford is in Lincolnshire, Speed presumably justified its depiction with Rutland on account of its being barely over the county border, and of the residence there on its outskirts of the Cecils at Burghley.

Shropshire

In his commentary on Shropshire Speed remarked, 'Wholesome is the air, delectable and good, yielding the spring and the autumn seed-time and harvest in a temperate condition, and affordeth health to the inhabitants in all seasons of the year'. In his anxiety to mention only advantages, he did not refer to the bitter cold of Salopian winters, although while praising Cheshire's more even climate he took for granted Shropshire's unenviable reputation for being the coldest area in the kingdom.

The county consists of upland, with isolated hills of considerable grandeur such as the Wrekin, and the Sliperstones. Shropshire is crossed by the Severn, into which run numerous tributaries. Not only was there bream of great size in Combermere, but according to John Leland Shropshire's rivers and streams were full of pike, tench, perch and brace, and there was some trout. The countryside remained heavily wooded and attempts to disafforest it failed to get approval until long after the publication of the *Theatre*. The celebrated marcher wool from Shropshire sheep produced high-grade cloth, and milk from its cows was made into butter and cheese. Where the land had been cleared there were ploughlands with wheat and barley growing abundantly. Shropshire also had extensive deposits of coal and iron, and some lead, all near the surface and easily extracted in open-cast mines, and the Wrekin had veins of copper.

The river Severn was navigable downstream from Shrewsbury to the port of Bristol where its estuary joined the Bristol Channel, although it was narrow and had rapids, shoals and banks of mud and sand. Its reaches were plied by barges called 'trows' peculiar to the river; they were fitted with square-rigged sails, but in the absence of wind were hauled upstream by men and rowed downstream. Its position on the Severn and its ease of access across the border to Wales made Shrewsbury, with a population over 4,000, not only the shire town for Shropshire, but in a sense the capital of Wales. Shrewsbury was not only commercially well suited to this task, with its many small industries and crafts, but also culturally since it had a school founded (or more correctly refounded) by Edward VI in 1552 serving both the town and, indeed, the whole of Wales. Shrewsbury also had bookshops which as yet were uncommon in most towns; the school's own collection of books was housed in a purpose-built library erected in the 1590s. 'Inferior to few of our cities: her buildings fair, her streets many and large, citizens rich', the prosperity of Shrewsbury can be gauged from the aerial view of it included by Speed in the

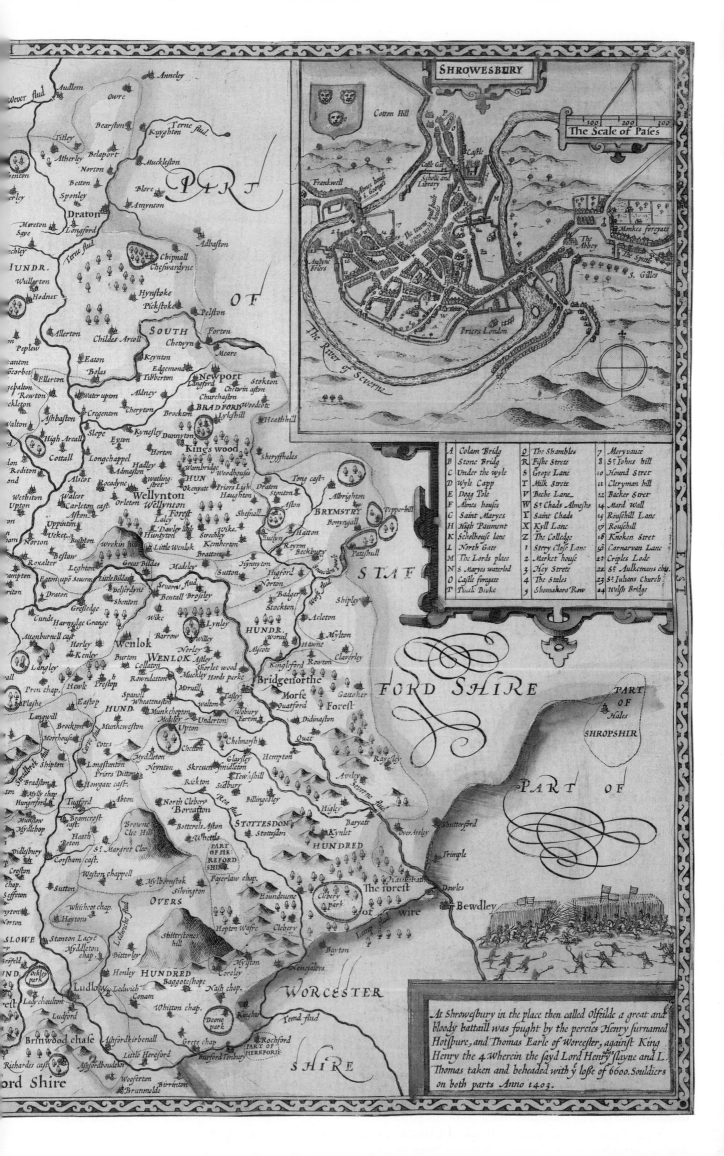

SHROWESBURY

The Scale of Paces

A	Colam Bridg	Q	The Shambles	7 Meryvauce
B	Stone Bridg	R	Fishe Strete	8 St Iohns hill
C	Under the wyle	S	Grope Lane	10 Hound Stret
D	Wyle Capp	T	Milk Strete	11 Cleryman hill
E	Dogg Pole	V	Beche Lane	12 Backer Stret
F	Almes houses	W	St Chads Almesho	14 Mard Wall
G	Saint Maryes	X	Saint Chads	15 Rouschill Lane
H	High Paument	Y	Kyll Lane	17 Rouschill
K	Scholhouse lane	Z	The Colledge	18 Knoken Stret
L	North Gate	1	Story Close Lane	19 Carnarvan Lane
M	The Lords place	2	Market house	20 Criples Lode
N	S. Maryes waterlod	3	Hey Strete	22 St Aulkemans chu
O	Castle foregate	4	The Stales	23 St Iulians Church
T	Puch Bloke	5	Shomakers Row	24 Welsh Bridge

At Shrowesbury in the place then called Olfeilde a great and bloody battaill was fought by the perceies Henry surnamed Hotspure, and Thomas Earle of Worcester, against King Henry the 4. Wherein the sayd Lord Henry was slayne and L. Thomas taken and beheaded with y loße of 6600. Souldiers on both parts Anno 1403.

top right-hand corner of the county map, and from the surviving timber-framed houses built by its residents, particularly clothiers, in the sixteenth century. Because of its social, political and trading importance, Shrewsbury was considered for the seat of a bishopric at the Reformation, but the idea came to nothing. Moreover, in spite of the town's advantages, the Council in the Marches of Wales preferred a headquarters in the south of the county at Ludlow, more central for its administrative purposes, making only occasional visits to the town. During the sixteenth century the Council's presidents had included Prince Arthur, Henry VIII's older brother, who died at Ludlow in 1502; Princess Mary during the 1520s, and Sir Henry Sidney (the father of that Elizabethan paragon of virtue, Sir Philip) from 1559 to 1586. In addition to Shrewsbury and Ludlow there were twelve other market towns.

The pacification of Wales by Edward I had brought a degree of law and order previously unknown, but it had not led to the neglect of the medieval castles which lined the county's borders with Wales. Although there had been no major incursions by the Welsh since 1403, when Owen Glendower had been defeated at the battle of Shrewsbury, some Welsh passed through the county with Henry of Richmond's expeditionary force when on its way to Bosworth in 1485, and cattle rustling by the Welsh remained a serious problem. With extensive properties there belonging to the Duchy of York, Shropshire had figured prominently in the Wars of the Roses, a fact familiar to Speed's contemporaries with their thirst for chronicles telling the tales of the wars, and from William Shakespeare's popular history plays catering for the same taste. After some doubt as to whether peace would last, Salopians began in the mid-sixteenth century to build themselves country houses similar to those found in the rest of England. Two of these—the Corbet family house at Moreton Corbet of the 1570s, and Justice Owen's Condover Hall of twenty years later—were as elegant and sophisticated as anything elsewhere. Like the castles from the Middle Ages, but unlike most domestic buildings in the county, these new country houses were built of stone rather than timber, which was the standard material locally for building. If Salopians proved themselves not to be backwoodsmen with these new houses, their waywardness and conservatism in religion was such that Bishop Aylmer wished puritans to be banished there to wear out their zeal on the papists.

The county map reveals that Shropshire was not exempt from the administrative anomalies of the marches, having a detached outlier of its own wedged between the borders of Staffordshire and Worcestershire, and itself incorporating a detached limb of Herefordshire. On its northern edges it had the separated part of Flintshire which Speed had drawn with the same attention to detail as Shropshire, even though the Flintshire limb received proper attention in its due place. Speed completed the Shropshire map with a monumental compass supporting the arms of the Earls of Shrewsbury, a cartouche, and the royal arms—all done in the latest fashion; a highly detailed plan of Shrewsbury and a humdrum battle scene showing the 1403 engagement outside the town.

Somerset

Somerset is a county of considerable physical diversity. Its terrain rises towards a sequence of watersheds, which separate it from the adjoining counties of Devon, Dorset, Wiltshire and Gloucestershire, yet the heart of the county—Sedgemoor and the Somerset Levels, in the neighbourhood of Glastonbury—is low-lying, and sometimes below sea level. At the Dissolution of the Monasteries the work of draining the central marshland remained unfinished, as the reader can see from the size of the mear on the map near Glastonbury. These wetlands provided pasture for livestock, birds and fish, and reeds for thatch and matting; thus the attempt to resume drainage in 1618 met with such fierce opposition from the commoners, who felt their livelihood to be threatened by the project, that nothing was accomplished for another century. Cattle and sheep were reared throughout Somerset, and its dairy produce was shipped up and down the Bristol Channel or sent inland to neighbouring counties. Cereal production was also important. In the north of the county there were valuable mineral deposits in the Mendips: of these the most important was lead, for which Somerset was the chief source with Derbyshire, the lead additionally valuable by containing occasional veins of silver and semi-precious stones called St Vincent's Rocks (which could substitute for diamonds in jewellery). Coal was also to be found near the surface, and about the time of Leland's visit in the 1540s, iron had also been discovered. Using the local supply of coal, both the iron and the lead mined there were smelted on the spot before being sold and transported away. At Ham and elsewhere good building stone was quarried. There was also some weaving, but the attempt to improve the quality of production by settling Flemish weavers in the conventual buildings of Glastonbury Abbey at its suppression had come to nothing. The wetness of Somerset made the maintenance of bridges and highways particularly important, but the resources available for their upkeep were inadequate, so that complaints about their disrepair were frequent. More than in most counties the rivers in Somerset were vital for travel and transporting goods, and perhaps for this reason they were all somewhat unusually named on the county map.

To Speed's contemporaries Somerset did not mean a supplier of foodstuffs and raw materials for the region and the nation, but Bath with its thermal springs. In the early 1540s, John Leland had commented: 'The colour of the water of the bains is as it were a deep blue seawater, and reeketh like a seething

BATHE

The forme of the Kings Bathe

The forme of the New Bath

AVON FLV.

Ham Gate

The horse Bathe

Southgate Strete

Southgate

Gascoms Towere

West Gate

The forme of the Crosse Bathe

The forme of the Hotte Bathe

Lazours Bathe

S Michaels

Broad street

Northe Gate

The Armes of Bathe

The Boate stall

Bathwick Mill

East Gate

Monkes Mill

DIEV

Flatholmes Island

Shepholme Island

Stert

PORLOCK BAY

Botestall poynt

PAR.

Oure
Porlock
Culhone
Almesworthy
Mynhead
Watchet
Kulue
Lystoke
Kilton
Stokland
Otterhampton
CAN
Stokland
Luckum
Wotton Courtnay
Timbercomb
Dunster
St Decombs
East Quantokehead
Strenxton
Stokland
Stokgussey
Ex more
Stoke pero
Carhampton
Old Cleue
Williton
Donyford
West Quantokhead
Alfoxton
Houlford
Nether
Eiddington
Stowley
TON
CARHAMPTON
Cutcombe
Luxborough
Wethicomb
Nettlecombe
Quantoke hills
Doddington
Cannington
Exford
Leighland
Samford
Combe
Bicknaler
Ouer Stowley
Coripole
HVNDRED
Ex flu
Trebora
Monksiluer
Stoke Gomer
Crokam
Ashholt HVNDRED
Spaxton
Ch
Winesford
Exton
Wethihill
WYLLITON &
Elworthye
Enmore
Barle flud
Wethpole
Brupton regis
FREEMANNOR
Vpton
Lawrenchiddear
Bagboro
Brumfeld
North Peth
Haukridge
Dunsbrook flud
Haddon beacon
HVNDRED
Hewishe
Clatworthy
Tolland
Combeflorye
Cotheleston
ANDRESFEH
Kingston
Thurloxte
Hastercomb
Iuchen
Molland
W. Ansty
E. Ansty
Duluerton
Bittescomb
Chipstable
Campston
WthELLCOMB
PART OF NORTH
Bishops
Fieshead
Haulse
Lediard
TAVNTON
Monkton
Cheddon
Creche
DEVON:
Combe
Bushford
Langridge
Skilgat
Murbathe
Exbridge
CVRRY
MILVERTON
Miluerton HVNDRED
Hethfeld
Oker
obridge
Staple
grove
Hilbushop
Wilton
TAVNTON
SHI.
Highley
Dipford
Petton
clayhanger
Baunton
Stauleygh
Langford
Badleton
Mynhead
Bradford
Trull
Mary Stok
Orchard
Thurlebare
CVRRY HVND
Bickn
Readdington
Hull farrence
Poundsford
RE.
Ashbrittell
Margretsthurne
Kittesford
Runton
West Buckland
PART OF NORTH
CVRRY
Wellington
Angellsley
Pitmyster
Corse
Sta
Barton
HVNDRED
Burland
Holcombe
Samford
Black Down hylls
Burlescomb
Otterford
Yarcombe
Stokland
Whit
Long

Renold de Mohun Lord of Dunster. & E. of Somerset.

Iohn Beauford Duke of Somerset.

Henry fitz Roy Duke of Somerset.

Edward Semer Duke of Somerset.

Phillip Chandew

Iohn Bouchier Lord fitz

Henri Dauhney

pot continually, having a somewhat sulphurous odour and a somewhat unpleasant savour.' Whatever their drawbacks, the therapeutic value of the springs had long been recognized, and alone of the spas in England Bath had been largely unaffected by the Reformation since the religious cults there were secondary to the more important medical and social facilities. Speed's splendid ground plan of Bath shows the city virtually confined within its medieval walls with its several parish churches and the abbey church (co-seat of a bishop with the cathedral at Wells) unfinished at the time of the abbey's suppression. Four of the city's five open-air baths with their springs and alcoves for the bather to sit immersed to the neck in the warm waters are depicted in larger separate inserts in the bottom corners of the view of Bath. Outside the walls was a horse bath, where horses and other animals received attention: this is shown with a horse in it on the map. In addition to its two hospitals for patients requiring longer treatment than most visitors, there were gardens to stroll in and tennis courts for play. Bath catered for the many needs of those who went there for a cure and relaxation. 'A place of continual resort for persons of all degrees and almost of all disease.' Its waters were supposed to be particularly good in helping barren women to conceive, and on that pretext Bath was patronized by two queens in the sixteenth and seventeenth centuries—by Catherine of Aragon in the 1520s and Mary of Modena in the 1680s.

Like many modern tourists Speed was fascinated by the tales of King Arthur which had long been a staple of English literature, and by the associations of Arthur with Somerset. Not only did he mention Glastonbury Abbey as being the burial place of Arthur and his wife Guinevere, but he went on to identify the impressive hill-fort at South Cadbury—'a very steep place to be ascended'—with Camelot, a plausible identification corroborated by more recent scholarship. Speed drew upon the antiquarian researches of the Lyte family for his commentary on Somerset, particularly the work of Henry Lyte (d. 1607) whose contemporary fame rested more upon his *New Herbal* of 1578 and the extensive gardens created by him at Lytes Cary rather than his historical and archaeological speculations: Thomas Lyte shared his father's passion for genealogy, and for tracing the descent of James I from the Trojan Brutus, that king rewarded Thomas with the Lyte Jewel, a miniature of himself by Nicholas Hilliard set in gold and diamonds, which is now in the British Museum. More important than the Lyte family house was the palatial structure built with the profits of the law at Montacute by Sir Edward Phelips during the 1590s. Even then Montacute was quite exceptional in a county more noted for its many small manor-houses and stone dwellings and its earlier perpendicular churches than for large country houses.

Staffordshire

Staffordshire is the source of the Trent and many of its tributaries, and the shape of the county is defined by them before the Trent descends eastwards through Derbyshire to feed eventually into the North Sea. This network of waterways can be clearly seen in Speed's map, and it is perhaps in Staffordshire that the *Theatre*'s emphasis on rivers as the life blood of an area in supplying fish and fowl for food, reeds for thatching, and means for communication and transport as well as boundaries for manors, parishes and counties is more justified than almost anywhere in England. Once off three main highways from London to Carlisle, Chester and Shrewsbury, the traveller faced roads poorly maintained, often liable to flooding and with inadequate river crossings, the bridges notorious for impeding the movement of traffic.

The north of the county adjoining Cheshire and Derbyshire was largely moorland, and the remainder was more level. Much of Staffordshire was heavily wooded, and in addition to the ancient forests of Brewood, Cannock, Kinver and Needwood, there were chases and parks for the preservation of deer. Grasses and cereals were grown in the central zone, pasture with some corn-production predominating in the south. With its numerous waterways, meadow was particularly important in Staffordshire, and during the sixteenth century new techniques were devised to flood them with such success that their grasses remained green even in the depth of winter. Cattle and horses were bred throughout the county. More important than agriculture in this thinly populated and poor county were mineral deposits. Much of the coal and iron was at or near the surface and could be obtained from open pits, or by digging into the hillside. Such mining was wasteful and haphazard, and the digging of a succession of shallow pits in close proximity to one another had succeeded in turning the south of the county into a desert of water-filled pits and smouldering waste heaps even by the early seventeenth century. With both coal and charcoal readily available, the iron mined was smelted near by, and cast or hammered into bars or rods suitable for transport or into nails or chains for sale and distribution. There was also some glass production. But the speciality for which the county was famous was the carving of alabaster at Burton-upon-Trent: until the Reformation the Burton carvers had produced religious statues and panels for use in churches and chapels, and when such items were condemned as idolatrous they specialized in funerary monuments and more domestic fittings, such as chimneypieces and sculpted friezes. One

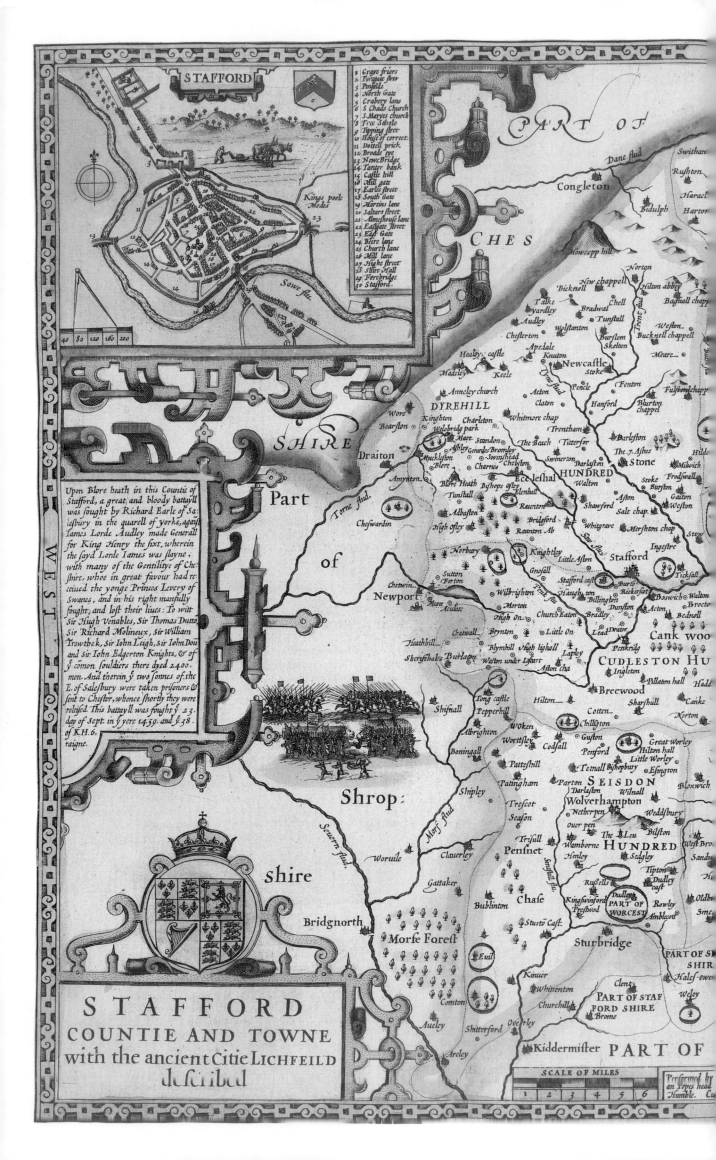

STAFFORD

1 Grave friers
2 Torgate ftrw
3 Penfolde
4 North Gate
5 Crabery lane
6 S Chads Church
7 S Maryes church
8 Fre Schole
9 Tipping ftreet
10 House of correct.
11 Doifell prick.
12 Broade eye
13 Newe Bridge
14 Tanter bank
15 Castle hill
16 Mill gate
17 Earls ftrett
18 South Gate
19 Martins lane
20 Saltars ftreet
21 Almeshouse lane
22 Eaftgate ftreet
23 East Gate
24 Beire lane
25 Church lane
26 Mill lane
27 Highe ftreet
28 Shire Hall
29 Forebridge
30 Stafford

Kings poole Medes

Sowe flu.

40 80 120 160 200

PART OF

Dane flud

Congleton

CHES

Mowcopp hill

Congleton

Swithan
Rushton
Harael
Hartor

Bidulph

Norton

Bicknoll
Talke yardley
Audley
Chesterton
Healiey castle
Madeley
Keele

New chappell
Bradwal Chell
Wolftanton
Burflem
Skelton
Apedale
Knuton
Pencle
Acton
Claton

Hilton abbey
Baghall chapp
Weston
Bucknell chappell
Newcastle stoke
Meare
Fenton
Hanford
Blurton chappel
Fulfoonchappy

Anneley church
Wore
Bearfton
Kinghton
Charleton
Welobridge park
Maer
Ashley Standon
Muckleton Blore
Amynton
Blore Heath
Tunftall
Adbafton

DYREHILL
Whitmore chap
Trentham
The Beach Titterfor
Swinerton

The .7. Ashes
Barlefton
Stone
Stoke Frodfwall
Milwich

SHIRE
Draiton

Genardes Bromley
Swinfhead
Chartes
Bifhops ofley
Elenhull
Rawiton
Bridgford
Rantron Ab
Whitgrave
Merfhton chap
Darlafton
Walton
Shawford
Salt chap.
Afton Weston
Gaiton
Burfton

HUNDRED
Ingeftre
Stafford
Tickfall

Part
of
Shrop
shire

Torne flud

Chefwardin

High ofley

Norbury

Sutton Forton

Knightley Little Afton
Gnofall
Stafford caft
Wilbrighton
Morton
Itigh On
Church Eaton
Bradley

Stafford
Burfti
Rickerfort
Haughton
Billington
Dunfton
Drayton
Lead

Boswich Walton
Brocto
Acton
Bednoll

Cank woo
CUDLESTON HU

Chettwin
Newport
Meane
Aculate

Heathhill
Sherifehales Burlagn
Chaiwall
Blymhill Ifigh lighall
Weston under Lifeart
Afton cha
Lapley

Ingleton

Penkrid

Pillaton hall
Hadd
Canke
Norton

Breewood

Shifnall

Tong caftle
Pepperhill
Albrighton
Boningall

Hilton

Cotten
Chillgton

Sharfhull

Woken
Worttfley
Codfall
Pattefhill
Patingham
Shipley
Shrop:
Trefcot Seafon
Trifull
Clauerley
Gattaker
Woruile

Gufton
Penford
Tetnall
Parton
Darlafton
Wilnall
Wolverhampton
Netherpen
ouer pen
Wamborne
Henley
Penfnet

Great Worley
Hilton hall
Little Worley
Bifhopbury Efington

SEISDON

The Leu
Bilfton
HUNDRED
Sedgley
Tipton
Dudley caft
Ruffells
Kingfwinford
Prefwod

Weddsbury
West Bro
Sandu
Oldbu
Sme

PART OF WORCEST

Bridgnorth

shire

Severn flud

Morf flud

Morfe Forest

Euil

Kinuer

Bublinton

Chafe
Sturto Caft

Rowley
Ainblecot

Sturbridge
PART OF S
SHIR
Halefowen
Wefley

Clent
PART OF STAF
FORD SHIRE
Brome

Churchill
Comton
Whitterton
Shitterford
Auckley
Arcley
Oberley

Kiddermifter PART OF

STAFFORD
COUNTIE AND TOWNE
with the ancient Citie LICHFEILD
defcribed

SCALE OF MILES
1 2 3 4 5 6

Performed by
an Iopes head
Humble. Cu

LICHFIELD

Places in the Citie Lichfield by figures obserued.

1	Stowe Church	18	Wade street
2	Stowe Mill	19	Towne Hall
3	Stowe Strret	20	Frogge lane
4	Ioyles lane	21	St. Ihons street
5	St. Michaels chur.	22	St Iohns Hospitall
6	Roüen Rowe	23	The Friery
7	Tamworth stret	24	The Conduit
8	The Chappell	25	The Freeschole
9	The Conduit	26	Grey Marger lane
10	Dams street	27	Greenhill street
11	St. Chads minst.	28	Bakers lane
12	Iayes lane	29	Fruers lane
13	Bacon stret.	30	High Crosse
14	The Almeshouse	31	Stowe Crosse
15	Samford stret	32	Damm Mill
16	Sadlers street	33	Stowe Mere
17	Bore street	34	Damm Mere

This Baronye of Stafford is very anciēt and hath bene an Earldom, the Nobles whereof hath borne the title of Dukes of Buckingham.

further industry had been established during the Tudor period in the north of Staffordshire in the vicinity of Burslem, but at the time of the publication of the *Theatre* the pottery made there was indifferent and only for local use.

None of the county's thirteen market towns was prosperous, and Lichfield with its cathedral had been particularly hurt by the loss of income from the pilgrims who until the Reformation had gone there to pray at the shrine of St Chad. As can be seen from the aerial views of Lichfield and Stafford in the corners of the county map neither place was large. However, the poverty of Staffordshire under the Tudors and Stuarts is best indicated by the smallness of its medieval churches and the poor quality of its black and white timber-framed building when compared with the specimens in Shropshire or Cheshire. The building work done by the Dudleys and the Pagets at Dudley and Beaudesert was exceptional and was funded by twin means, the exploitation of mineral resources and access to money outside the county. Much of the construction in the reign of Elizabeth was work either on small but impressive hunting lodges (such as that at Wootton), or else cosmetic improvements to old properties (such as the gatehouse at Tixall), which survive now when the rest has long disappeared. It is symptomatic of the modesty of their incomes that the gentle families of Staffordshire continued to occupy their ancestral sandstone castles—never fortresses of much consequence—without significant improvements or modifications, long after others elsewhere had been deserted or converted to wholly domestic use. Perhaps the most important castle was the Duchy of Lancaster's at Tutbury, where Mary Queen of Scots was held several times during her nineteen-year-long captivity.

Bishop Aylmer rated Staffordshire barbarous in its Catholicism, and under the protection of Thomas Lord Paget, until the discovery of the Throckmorton Plot in 1583, there was little that successive diligent Bishops of Coventry and Lichfield or the Earls of Shrewsbury could do about such families as Draycott, Erdeswick, Fowler and Gifford, who were penalized for their recusancy by imprisonment or fines. Searches for seminary priests were initiated by the Privy Council at regular intervals, and one of those captured was executed at Stafford in 1588, but this did not stop Edmund Campion, John Gerard, Jasper Heywood and William Holt making visits. One of the most obstinate recusants was Sampson Erdeswick, punished for not attending his parish church at Sandon after Queen Elizabeth's progress through the county in 1575. Excluded from local affairs, he was able to indulge his passion for local history and wrote his *Survey*, the first Staffordshire county history, before his death in 1603. Through William Camden, Speed may have had access to the manuscript which remained unpublished until 1717.

Speed correctly noted the detached part of Staffordshire in the north of Worcestershire, and a number of other points of interest such as the spot where the river Manifold goes underground near Ilam, and the three shire stones marking the conjunction of Staffordshire with Cheshire and Derbyshire.

Suffolk

A county 'most plenteous and pleasant for habitation', Suffolk is separated from its adjoining counties by a series of rivers: from Norfolk by the Waveney and Little Ouse, from Cambridgeshire by the Great Ouse, and from Essex by the Stour. Rivers with sources in its hinterland flow down to the North Sea, and their tidal estuaries provided a series of havens for fishing boats, ships plying up and down the coast and larger vessels crossing to the Netherlands and the Baltic transporting the fine cloths and cheese produced in the county for sale elsewhere. The extent and prosperity of this commerce was reflected in the size and number of the county's ports—particularly Ipswich, 'blessed with commerce and buildings, she might worthily have borne the title of a city' and with a population of about 5,000—and in the splendid run of recently completed perpendicular churches which punctuates the coastline from Lowestoft down to Aldeburgh. The only place not to benefit from the general prosperity was Dunwich, a town and port in irreversible decline as the result of erosion by the sea. Similarly the inland areas wanted nothing 'for pleasure and profit', and the soil was equally good for the cultivation of cereals, for the pasturage of sheep and cattle, and for the management of woodland. Weaving provided some employment in most villages, but in some places (such as Lavenham, Long Melford and Mildenhall) it was the backbone of the local economy, with dynasties of clothier-families such as Spring, Clopton and Branch dominating the towns' business. Magnificent medieval churches are a feature throughout the county.

Despite its many natural endowments, Suffolk is notable for its lack of a good building stone. Until the seventeenth century the bulk of its building was timber-framed and plastered, finished (as today) with colour-washes and with thatched roofs. Parish churches and other prestigious buildings were built from flint, knapped and often set in patterns with the more expensive stone transported from a distance. The shortage of good building stone meant that the county was one of the first where brick became a common material for houses, but up to 1600 brick was restricted in its use to the homes of certain wealthy families such as the Cordells at Long Melford and the Kytsons at Hengrave.

More than many counties, Suffolk had been dominated by a single monastic house until the Reformation—the great Benedictine abbey at Bury St Edmunds. Such had been the ill-will generated by the abbey that its buildings

PART

PET: CEREALIS

A Christs church
B S. Georgs chap.
C S. Margarets
D S. Mathews
E S. Mary Tower
   S. Mary Elms
G. S. Laurence
H S. Stephens
I S. Helens
K S. Clements
L S. Nicolas
M S. Peters.
N S. Mary Key
O Stoke church
P Stoke Bridge
Q Stoke mill
R The Key
S
T Graye Friers

The DVKES, and EARLES of CLARE. created since the Normans conquest.

Gilbert de Clare Earle of Clare

Lionell sonn to KE 3 Duke of Clarence

Thomas Lancaster Duke of Clarence

George Brother to KE 4. Duke of Clarence

NORFOLKE

Downham

Wilton

Hockhold
Wetinge

Litle Ouse Flu.
Wangforde   Downham
Brandon   Thetforde   Rushforth   Ridlesworth
Lakenheathe   Elden   Ouse flu   Gast
LACKFORD HVN   Bernham   Euston   Knatteshall   Hopton
Conyweston   Weston
Esewell   Fakenham pua   BLACK   BORN
Mildnall   Wordwell   Fakenham mag   Hynnyton   Beringham
Icklingham   Leuermere pua   Troston   Sapston   Hepworth   Stanton
Iselham   W. Stow   Leuermere mag   Culsforth   Ixworthe   Berdwell   Langham
Fordham   Worlington   Berton   Hengraue   Ingham   thorpe   Ikesworthe   Hunston
Frecknham   Tuddenham   Lackforde   Fernham   Ampton   Pakenham   Stowlangtoft   Badw
Badlingham   Heringeswell   Flempton   Fernhm omnium   Tymworth   THEDWARDSTRE   Norton
Kennet   Caneham   Sanctorum   Fernham   HVN   Ashfulde
Exninge   THINGOW HVN   mertin Berton   Thurston   Elmeswell
Kenforde   Gaiesley   Saxham magna   Westley   Rougham   Tostok
Westley   Saxhm pua   Rushbrok   Beighton   Wulpet
Newmarket   Ashley   Monlton   Bareowe   Heringherthe   Bure   Drenkeston   Shellane
Cheueley   Denham   Cheuington   Ikesworth   Nowton   Whelthm   Hesset   Ratlesden   Onch
Cutidge   Dalham   Ouesden   Hargraue   Hausted   pua   Mukebradsfeld   Finb
Lidgate   Whepsted   Waltham   S. Cleres   Gedding   mag
Carleton   Cowildge   Rede   magna   bradsfeld
Wyckham brooke   Chedber   Burnebradsfeld   Felsham   Buxhall
Bradley   Debden   Cock   feld   Bretenham   Fin
pua   Brokley   Thorpe   Watteshm   COS   FORD
Weston   Thirlow pua   Bradley   Denston   Lawshull   Kettlebaston   Hitcham
Stradishill   Haukden   HV   Bilson   Bilston
Bernardston   Stansfelde   Somerton   Preston
SHIRE   Wickham   Tallow   Hartyste   Shimplinge   Alpheton   Bumteylie   Munke
wratting   Bernardston   Boxted   Laneham   silue   Chelfie
Horsheath   Witherssfeld   Honedon   RISBRYGE   Stansfed   BABER   Mildinge   Lynsey
Haucrill   Kediton   Poslingforde   Glemysforde   Acton   HVN   Waldingfeilde pua   Co
Shedi campes   Castle campes   Sturmere   HVN   Clare   Melforde   Waldingsfild mag   Edwardston
Wicksoo   Stoke   Bulton   HVN   Assington   Boxford
Burbrok   Ashdon   Sture flu.   Candishe   Chilton   Newton   Stoke
Ouington   Pentlowe   Fixherbe   Lyston   Sudburye   Ney
Poules beltham   Boreley   Bullington   Cornerd   Smalebridge   Stoke
Brundon   Midleton   pua   Henny   Cornerd   Horsley
Lammersh   Buers   mag
Buers hamlet   Warningford   Horsley

PART OF

PART OF   CAM   BRIDGE

1 2 3 4 5 6 7 8 9 10
THE SCALE OF ENGLISH MILES

Cum Privilegi

SUFFOLKE described
and divided into HUNDREDS, The situa:
tion of the fayre towne IPSWICH shewed,
with the ARMES of the most noble fami:
lies that have bene either Dukes, or Earles
both of that Countie as also of Clare

BOADICIA

OF

THE DUKES and EARLES of SUFFOLK Created since the Normãs conquest.

Robert Vfford, Erle of Suffolk

William de la poole Duke of Suffolk

Charles brandon duke of Suffolk.

Henry Gray duke of Suffolk.

Thomas Howard Earle of Suffolke

A SCALE OF PASES

V	Black Friers	4	Barre Gate
W	Chrift Hofpital	5	Old Bar gate
X	Gramer Schole	6	Fifhe market
Y	Poores houfes	7	Kings ftret
Z	Hauford mill	8	Corne hill
3	Bull Gate	9	Broke ftret

Yermouth
Vermouthaue

LOW ING
LANDE HVN.

MVTFORD HV

WANGFORD HV̄

HOXON HV

BLITHING HV̄

Dunwiche

Milmere hauen

ESMERE HV̄

LOES HV̄

TREDLINGE HVN.

PLOMES GATE HV̄

Aldebrough

Orforde

Orford hauen

MERE

CLEYDON HVN.

CARLEFORD HV

IPSWICHE

WILFORDE HV

COLNES HV

SAMFORDE HVN.

Bawdfey hauen

Harwiche

ESSEX

Performed by Iohn Speede and are to be folde in
Popes-head alley againft the Exchang by George Humble

were put to immediate use at the Dissolution as a source for building materials, and of its vast complex little survived when Speed visited Bury. Normally when mentioning monasteries, Speed commented on their wrongdoings, but viewing Bury he was moved differently: 'Whose ruins lie in the dust, lamenting their fall, moving the beholders to pity their case.' That Henry VIII's sister, Mary, Queen of France, later Duchess of Suffolk, and a resident in the county, had been buried in the abbey had not been considered a sufficiently good reason for the preservation of the abbatial church. Many of the leading families had strong Catholic sympathies, but the county was more remarkable for its overall Protestantism, which flourished wherever weaving was important.

Suffolk had played a crucial role in the succession crisis of 1553. After mustering her forces at Kenninghall in Nòrfolk, Princess Mary had marched to the Howard family castle at Framlingham, and it was there that she received the submission of the Privy Council and of leading national figures before travelling in triumph to London. Seeing Framlingham Castle today, its shortcomings as a sixteenth-century fortress had it been invested and besieged by the Duke of Northumberland are manifest, and serve to emphasize the uncertainty of the outcome of Mary's daring bid for the throne. After the Dissolution the Howards made Framlingham parish church their mausoleum, and their funerary monuments in the church rank with some of the finest renaissance products in England.

During one of his progresses in 1605 James I had been much impressed by Suffolk and by the facilities for horse-racing at Newmarket. A year later he bought a small house at Newmarket, which was expanded to meet the needs of his immediate entourage, and which in 1613 suddenly subsided—almost killing the King. The inadequacy of the accommodation at Newmarket for anyone outside the immediate entourage made the town's attraction even greater for a monarch seeking privacy and pleasure, and led to his frequent visits there being dreaded by ministers, courtiers and government officials.

Surrey

Surrey was something of a paradox. It was close to both the capital and the court, yet unlike Kent and Middlesex it was decidedly remote from London. This phenomenon is partly to be explained by the physical barrier of the river Thames, bridged only at Kingston, Chertsey, Staines and Southwark, and by the marshiness of the land south of the Thames in the neighbourhood of London which until the nineteenth century prevented much development beyond Southwark, and which made Southwark something of an exception in Surrey. Situated at the southern end of London Bridge, Southwark was essentially a suburb of London, with its inns and taverns, its palaces and prisons, its leather trade and other crafts, its brothels and its theatres in the 'ancient Roman manner' and 'so designed that the audience could get a good view of any action within them', where so many of the plays of Kyd, Marlowe and Shakespeare had their first performance: the interdependence of Southwark upon London had been recognized as far back as 1327, when its administration had been given to the City of London, but as the borough remained technically within the county of Surrey it was a haven for all sorts of undesirables as well as political and religious refugees. However, it was not the seaminess of the place that visitors remembered, or its theatres, but the approach to London Bridge with its gruesome array of human heads, including in 1612 Queen Elizabeth's former favourite the Earl of Essex, executed for treason a decade before.

The contrast of the air in Surrey, 'most sweet and delectable', with that in London already notorious for its fetidity, access by barges rowed up the Thames, and the plentifulness of game, especially deer, made the county one much favoured for residence by successive monarchs and by courtiers. Henry VII had built a late gothic fantasy at Richmond which became Elizabeth I's favourite residence and where that 'rarest of her sex, the Mirror of Princes' died in 1603, and Henry VIII had created the mannerist confection of Nonsuch. During Elizabeth's reign Nonsuch was occupied by her kinsman, the antiquarian Lord Lumley, who housed his famous collection of books and paintings there, and indulged his passion for gardening. Nonsuch and Lumley's library passed to Prince Henry, who further improved the gardens before his own premature death in 1612: neither the palace nor its gardens survive at Nonsuch, but Lumley's library became the nucleus of the British Library. The fashion for buildings, parks and gardens set by the great and the rich was copied, and

RICHMONT

WILLIAM WARREN Created Earle of SVRREY by wil. RVFVS

WILLIAM Earle of EAGLE sone to King STEPHEN Earle of surry

HAMLIN, BASE SONE to GEFFREY PLANTA-GENET Earle of Surrey

THOMAS MOWBRAY Earle of Surrey i'right of his wyffe Ano 1347

PART OF BUCKINGHAM SHIRE

PART OF BARKE

S DESCRIP INT

PARTE

Heston
West Bedfont
Cranford
Hunslo
East Bedfont
Ashford
Stanes
Ashleham
Littleton
Thames flud
Washbury
Egham
CHER-TSEY
Carleton
Lalam
Shepperton
Buckham Lane
Thorpe
strond
St Annhill
Chertsey
Absoun Walton
Trotworth
Potnol
Adleston
Wesh Esher
Oatlands
Newlodge
Hamhaug
Waybridg St Geory Hill
parke
Winsham
Valley woode
Wodham
Woodhā lane
Esher EMLI
Cobha
Co
Bagshot
Horsyl
Wisley
Bysleet
Basingstone
Cobham
Byfley
Frimley
Purford
HVNDRED
Working
Newark
Ockam
Brookwood
Ripleyss
Sly
Caue
WO
KING
Bradley
Sende
HVN-DRED
Great Prsk
PARTE OF
Purbright
Mayfort
Effingham
Henley park
Sutton
East Horsley
Robarns
Weshwoode
Worplesdon
Stowghton
Burphans
West Horsley
East Clandon
Ashe
Ushot
Amershot
Wanboro
Gulford manor
Stoke
West Cladon
Crundall
Wyke
Katerm hill
Meroc
Guildford
BLACKHEAT
Badshot
Littleton
Tilting
Shere
Tangham
Poyle
Puttnham
Ithesley
Shalford
St Martins Chilworth
Gunl
Ramfold
Shooland
Polsled
Ferncombe
Tangly
Weston
Albury
Sele
Morehouse
Compton
Shackleford
Tangly
Holmbu
Fernha
Compton
gstrd
Peperharo
Godalming
Catteshill
Vsted
Bramley
BLACKHEA
Waurley
Esing
Milford
Mounsted
OR WOTTO
Weeklesham
Tylforde
Oxen-forde
Whelershrete
Burgate
Hascomb
Scotland
Ewhu
Cranler
Fresnham
GODALMI: Enton
Hameldon
Knole
HVN
Thursley
NG
Witley
Farncombe
Nore
Vac
Whitley park
HVNDRED
Loxley
Hyde head
Haslmer
Embhams
Dunsfold
Glashouse
Pytfall
Pophole
Shotouer mill
Chidingfold
Awfold
HAMSHIRE
Warningfold
Sydny
Foxwood
Blacke Downe
Shillingleig park
North chappell
NORTH

Described by the travills of Iohn Norden Augmēted and performed by Iohn Speede

Iodocus Hondius caelavit. Anno 1610. SOVTH

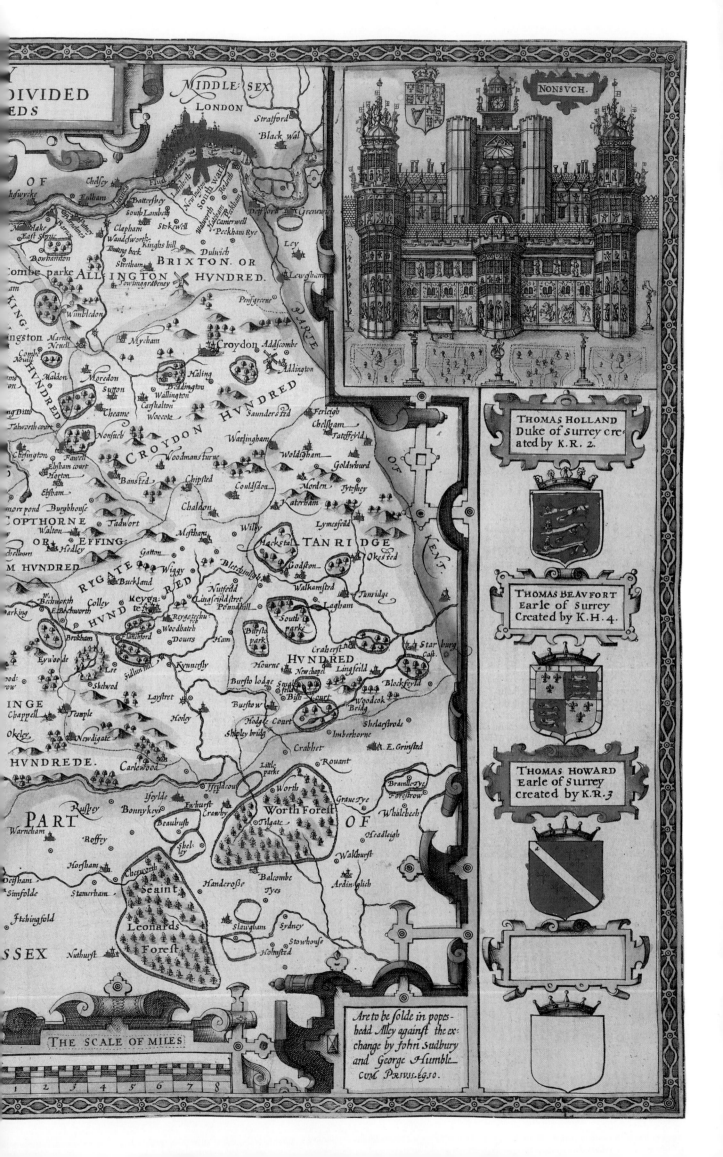

DIVIDED
DS

MIDDLE-SEX
LONDON

NONSVCH.

OF

Chelsey

Stratford
Black wal

Fulham

hswycke

Battersbey
South Lambeth

Combe parke ALLINGTON

Clapham
Wandsworth
Tooting beck
Streatham

South warke
Newington
Waworth Walham
Peckham
Camerwell
Peckham Rye

Deptford
Grenewi

Barnes
Putney

Mortelake
East Shyte

Kings hill

Dulwich

Ley

Bowharron

Lewsham

BRIXTON. OR

HVNDRED.

Wimbledon
Mycham
Martin
Neuell
Combe
Neuell

Penygreene

Croydon Addscombe
Addington

Moredon
Sutton
Cheame

Haling
Bradington
Wallington
Carshalton
Woocote

CROYDON HVNDRED

Saunders fed
Ferleigh
Chelsham
Tatsffeild

Nonsuch
Fawell
Chesington
Elsham court
Horton
Ebham
Banstead
Woodmansturne
Chipsted
Chaldon
Warlingham
Couldsdon
Morden
Katerham
Tytshey
Woldigham
Goldhburd

THOMAS HOLLAND
Duke of Surrey created by K. R. 2.

COPTHORNE
OR EFFING
HVNDRED.

Tadwort
Mestham
Willy
Lymesfeld

Hackstall TANRIDGE
Godston
Walkamsted
Tanridge
Okested
Starbury Caft.

RYGATE
HVNDRED

Wiggy
Buckland
Keygate
Nutfeld
Linascield ftret
Ponhhill
South parke
Lagham

THOMAS BEAVFORT
Earle of Surrey Created by K. H. 4.

W. Bechworth
E. Bechworth
Colley
Reygate church
Woodhatch
Doners
Ham
Brokham
Tanchford
Bursta
park
Craherst ho.
HVNDRED
Hourne
Newchapel
Lingfeild
Woodcok

Eywoode
Lee
Sidlin hill
Kynnersly
Bursto lodge
Smal feild
Bish court
Blockfeyld

Shelwod
Laystret
Burstow
Woodcok Bridg
Shelaystrode

THOMAS HOWARD
Earle of Surrey created by K. R. 3.

Tesaple
Chappell
Okeley
Newdigate
Horley
Hodge Court
Shipley bridg
Crabbet
Imberhorne
A. E. Grinsted

HVNDREDE.
Carlewood

Little
parke
Rouant

OF

INGE

Russhey
Ifeylde
Bonnykeys
Beaubush
Worth
Worth Forest
Tilgate
Graue Tye
Foreshrow
Whalebech

PART
Warncham
Roffry
Shelley
Headleigh

Horsham
Simfolde
Stamerham
Chetworth
Seaint
Handerose
Balcombe
Tyes
Wakhurst
Ardin-glich

Itchingfeld
Leonards
Forest
Slawgham
Sydney
Stowhouse

SSEX
Nuthurst
Holmsted

Are to be folde in popes-hedd Alley against the ex-change by John Sudbury and George Humble CVM PRIVILEGIO.

PART OF KENT.

THE SCALE OF MILES
1 2 3 4 5 6 7 8

less grand houses such as those belonging to the Weston family at Sutton Place and the Carews at Beddington were rightly celebrated for their renaissance terracottas and for their groves of orange trees. Surrey was remarkable for the extent and diversity of its gardens, which by 1600 were attracting a steady flow of visitors from home and abroad. Even George Abbot, Archbishop of Canterbury, a Guildford boy made good—a patron of Speed's perhaps better known for his part in preparing the Authorized Version of the Bible—employed the Tradescants at Lambeth Palace.

Despite the impression of wealth created by the letters and journals of visitors there, Surrey was not a prosperous county, as the absence in 1600 of any town larger than a couple of thousand inhabitants and the small size of its churches indicate. The alluvial soil of the Thames valley was good for corn production and for pasturage. A great deal of the land further south was wooded, much of it maintained for deer and hunting. The stone in the neighbourhood of Reigate was in demand for mill- and paving-stones. The iron deposits in the Weald were exploited, as they were in Sussex and in Kent, and the water of the Thames and other rivers was used to power mills for grinding corn or rolling copper and brass. The ready availability of wood and the corresponding lack of a building stone better than chalk or flint meant that most buildings in the county were timber-framed until long after brick made from the local clays started to become available in the fifteenth century, even Nonsuch Palace being largely a timber building.

The earldom of Surrey created by William Rufus had been held by a notable series of men, and Speed was hard put to select the most distinguished holders for inclusion in the armorial borders to the county map. Even so, he left one shield blank. The reason for this was almost certainly because he had wished to include the much revered poet, Henry Howard, Earl of Surrey in the set, but he had been executed for treason in 1547, and the already notorious conduct of his descendant, Frances Howard, Countess of Essex, at the court of James I made any reference to the poet, even in 1612, seem a lapse in taste.

Sussex

The absence of good roads going northwards into Surrey or Kent meant that despite its geographical closeness to London Sussex was a curiously isolated and somewhat introverted county in the early seventeenth century. The English Channel was still an excellent fishing ground, but the nature of the Sussex coast with few harbours or anchorages prevented the full exploitation of this asset, and what was caught was intended for local consumption only. What harbours existed were uncertain and difficult in their approaches; and the mudflats of Selsey Bill, rocks near Bognor, sandbanks off Pevensey, together with the changes caused by erosion or by silting in the entrances to Winchelsea and Rye, kept the coastal trade which flourished elsewhere to a minimum in Sussex. The scarcity of anchorages was a serious problem even to larger ships (which, unlike small boats, did not hug the coastline), and it was for this reason that the shelter afforded near Pevensey in the lee of Beachy Head was singled out for mention by Speed. The marshes around Pevensey, Bexhill and Hastings were criss-crossed with dikes and drainage ditches: similar reclamation work near Rye had not been so successful. However, the frequency of mudflats and marshland was conducive to birdlife, and Speed noted the enormous number of birds there. He also remarked on the sea-mists, but made no mention of the winds, although these explain the number of windmills depicted on the map.

The difficulties posed by the nature of the coast were not a safeguard against invasion by the French and other enemies. The Normans had started the last successful invasion of England at Hastings in 1066, and with each war between France and England from then onwards, Sussex had been threatened with raids and landings, Brighton being badly burnt in 1543. The threat to the safety of the county and the kingdom caused by such incidents accounts for the division of Sussex into six more or less equally sized 'rapes', each rape with its stretch of coastline, a castle for its administrative and defensive centre, a forest and a river, and each rape being subdivided into hundreds. In addition to these castles the principal houses near the coast were fortified as a general precaution, and the towns of Lewes, Rye, Winchelsea, Hastings and Chichester had walls for their protection. A series of beacons near the coast and up and through each rape were properly kept as warning signals against landings, and these are marked on the map.

The Downs, a narrow but impressive ridge of chalk (and in the sixteenth century largely bare of human habitation and mostly given over to sheep),

173

armes of such
oles as have
e dignified
h the title of
es since the
quest and other
idents therein
erved.

ented by Iohn
d Alley against
able Cum privilegio

DIEV ET MON DROIT

SOIT QVI MAL Y PENSE IOHN

Ashurst Grombridg
Water
Bolbrok Wythyam Eridge Farut Lambhurst
arfeild Stone Hamfild Scrotney
Buck land brid Wadehurst
hurst parc
Whitsden downe Flymwell
ombed Sockney hill Forest Tifhurst Rufhley
Rotherfeild Borsill Eridge
wn Forest Bruckmate Harmar Sendhurst Newnden OXNEY Island Fayrefeild
Duddel Newnd Mayfeild Franchis Itchingham Wigsill Brockland
well park Burwash Salehurst Bodgham Nordien Old Rim
Nutley Crowboro hill Hawk wood Bugsill Fawhurst Tufton Idm Beckley ney
shall PEVENSEY RAPE Hardley Beacon Sockneys Rotherbridg Stapley Beacon Beaturf Plsden Kent Dych
Marsfeild Buckshol Burwash Beacon Abby HASTINGS Gatt Rye Gulford
hing Hemfted Pownsley Dallington Brigling Munsfeild RAPE Ulymere Mershe
Ludsham Frumfeild Cairstreet forest Dallington Selscombe Breede Camberhat Camber Salles
Harlinges Heathfeild Seawood Westfeild Winchelsey Camber cast Camber Salles
Crockfted Blackhouse Warbleton Penhurst Battle Perly Bromeham Maxfeild Pett Bromehill Church decayed
Litle Horsfed Wylie Walderne Crawle Darum Netherfeild wood Baltefting Beacon Pannelbridge Stonelinch Old Winchelsey Drownd
Flisher E. Hoadly Chit man wood Ashburnham Geiling
Parke Haukland Buckstepe Morehale Netfeild Crawhurst Brayrleigh
The Broyle Ringmere Chitingle Hellingle Caitesfeild Ouro
stoneham Vertwood Boreham Chapl Buckhole Hollington Pepplesham
awling Byke Hurstmonscux Hoo Sidly Worsham Hastings
Loughton place Mychelham Bevill Hastings haven
Chiffe Glyne Claverham PEVENSEY MERSHE Warring The Pell intended
Sowcram Mayes Ludley Nordy Cowling
Bedingham Ludley Erlington Chap The Sclece
erring Furle Selmefton Berwyke Wotton Grenely Westham
Alston Middleton Willington Presthaus Peisey Bubserhyth
Hayton Wynton Aldfrifton Feynton Cronble pond Languey
ohouc Denton Froghurle Willington
Ryching Bletchington West Deane Ratten Ebourn
Bushoptstonbh Seaforde Sutton Friston South The beach
Excete East Deane

Chekmere haven

Penfey Haven

BRITISH   SEA

WILLIAM the Bastard, Duke of
Normandy, making his Clayme to the Cro:
wne of England, by affinitie, adoption and
promise, Aeiued at a port in Sussex called
Pensey with 896 shipps furnished for warr
the 28 of September, y yere of Chrifts in:
carnation 1066. And the 14 of October fol
lowing beyng Satterdaye, nere Hastings in y
same Countie ioyned battayll with Harold
King of England, whoe in y feilde valliant:
ly fighting was there slaine by the shott of
an arrow into his braynes: and with him
dyed Gerth and Leofwine his brethren, and
67974 men besydes. The place where they
fought, ever since doth in memory thereof
beare the name of Battayll, where the Hep:
tarchie of the Saxens was Brought to y last
period. Having all their lawes altered, their
Nobles displaced, and all men disherited: all
seased into the Normands hande, whoe made
him selfe Lorde of all, and on y daye of Chr.
his natiuitye in y same yere was crowned at
Westminster King of Englande, which he
gouerned the space of 20 yeres, 8 moun:
thes, and 16. dayes.

Domini 1610.

PHILLIP
Howard Earle
of Arundell.

ROBERT
Radcliffe Ear
le of Sussex

EAST

stretch from the plain west of Shoreham to Beachy Head. A strip of level ground with fertile soil—then, as now, heavily cultivated with meadow, pasture for cattle and with cornfields—runs along the north side of the Downs before the ground starts to rise towards the Weald, where poorer soil and underlying sandstone allowed forests and woodland to survive more or less intact. Deposits of iron ore and other minerals, together with availability of wood and charcoal for fuel and of running water, made the Weald the chief centre for iron production in the period and an important area for the manufacture of glass. Both these industries had expanded considerably during the Tudor period, and the Wealden ironworks enjoyed what was in effect a monopoly over the production of armaments. Few people did not benefit from the ironbacks for fireplaces and the mass-produced glass for windows, which ceased to be luxury items as a casual glance at houses in Sussex dating from 1600 reveals. However, it was not the material advantages that these industries brought, but the disadvantages that travellers commented on, Speed remarking on the devastation of the woodlands. Despite his modern-sounding concern, Speed as a town-dweller had no knowledge of how woodland should be managed—and managed profitably without harm—and the Wealden woods survived without real depredation until the eighteenth century. Although none of the important ironworks or glassworks is mentioned, several of the water-mills connected with industry are marked on the map.

Speed commented on the inadequacy of Sussex roads, simply saying that they were 'ill in winter'. Problems stemming from poor roads and involving administration, defence and trade resulted in the county's somewhat unusually having two shire towns—Chichester in the west and Lewes in the east. The relative wealth of Sussex was reflected in its eighteen market towns, but none of these was populous, as examination of the ground plan of Chichester shows, with the north-western section of the city virtually uninhabited.

An enlightened episcopate early in the Tudor period, followed by the failure of Bishop Curteys and his successors to enforce the Anglican Settlement, meant that the extremes of Roman Catholicism and of Puritanism were both repre-sented in the county. The geographical isolation of Sussex combined with the religious sympathies of its resident nobility and gentle families ensured the survival of Catholicism. Philip, Earl of Arundel, held a prisoner in the Tower for years until his death in 1595 and already noted for his saintliness, was one of the local worthies singled out for inclusion in the border of the map, but the 'Wizard' Earl of Northumberland, who until his arrest for complicity in the Gunpowder Plot had lived at Petworth, was not similarly honoured.

Warwickshire

The division of Warwickshire into two parts by the river Avon was noted by many visitors, including John Leland and William Camden. To the south of the Avon lay the Feldon, to the north the Forest of Arden. The Feldon was champion country with arable, pasture and meadow 'with their green mantles so embroidered with flowers . . . we may behold another Eden', while the Forest of Arden (where Celia and Rosalind took refuge in William Shakespeare's *As You Like It*) was woodland with extensive common rights enjoyed by a large population of smallholders and landless cottagers. Repeated and sustained efforts by improving landlords to enclose this woodland during the Tudor period were bitterly resented by their tenants, and as a result the Forest of Arden was one of the most disaffected agrarian regions in the Midlands, intermittent commissions of enquiry ordered by the Crown providing neither solution nor more than temporary alleviation. The very north of the county, which was 'churlish to yield to the plough', had deposits of coal and iron ore. Quarries throughout Warwickshire yielded good sandstone for building, and at Lower and Upper Shuckburgh astroit, a stone flecked with fossils and prized at the time for incorporation in monuments.

Speed noted eighteen market towns. The chief of these was Coventry with a population of about 6,000 and with many small industries and crafts, varying from textiles and leather manufacture to ironwork. As an expression of civic pride Coventry had constructed defensive walls as late as the fourteenth century, but with the loss of its cathedral and the ending of its cycle of mystery plays at the Reformation it had entered into a period of stagnation and decline in common with other Warwickshire towns, with the single exception of Birmingham. When visited by Leland, Birmingham was no more than a single street about a quarter of a mile long lined with the forges of blacksmiths, cutlers, lorimers, spurriers and nailers 'so that a great part of the town is maintained by smiths'. At Leamington and Kings Newnham there were spas, which provided rest and relaxation as well as therapeutic treatment, and whose contemporary fame was surpassed only by Bath in Somerset and Buxton in Derbyshire.

Apart from its churches and castles built from stone, building in Warwickshire tended to be either black-and-white timber-framing or cob, and as a result its towns were subject to periodic destruction by fire, Stratford-upon-Avon being severely damaged twice in the 1590s, again in 1614, and once

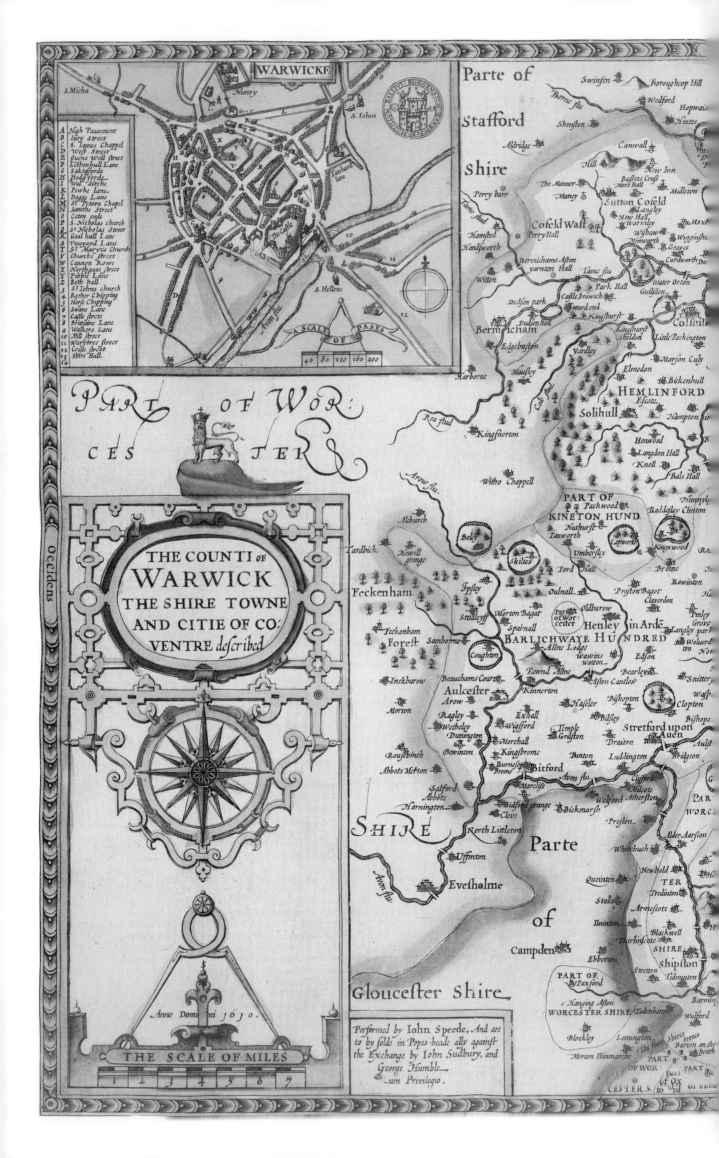

more in 1641. These disasters encouraged the early use of brick in the county, the picturesque and asymmetrical house built at Compton Wynyates by Sir William Compton, Henry VIII's groom of the stool, being something of a trendsetter in the 1520s. More conservatively the Throckmortons, who stuck more firmly to Catholicism than most, rebuilt their house at Coughton about the same time using the more traditional materials of timber and stone. But when Sir Thomas Lucy, who had been tutored by the martyrologist John Foxe and who became a convinced puritan, started to rebuild Charlecote in 1558 he chose brick: Lucy died in 1600 after many years' service on the local bench upholding the peace and Anglicanism, but he is probably best remembered for the incident—of doubtful authority—when William Shakespeare as a youth was allegedly caught poaching his deer.

Until the reign of Edward VI, Kenilworth and Warwick had been two of the principal royal castles in the Midlands: Kenilworth with its superb buildings, its fine apartments and lodgings, its well laid-out gardens, its sequence of lakes and its extensive park had been a by-word for luxury since its ownership by John of Gaunt. After the downfall of the Duke of Northumberland, the two castles reverted briefly to the Crown only to be given by Queen Elizabeth in 1562 and 1563 to two of Northumberland's sons, the Earls of Leicester and of Warwick, who entertained the Queen repeatedly on her progresses through the kingdom—the reception at Kenilworth in 1575 being of the most sumptuous and elaborate of its kind ever mounted in its spectacle and range of entertainments. After Leicester's death in 1588, Kenilworth passed eventually into the possession of his illegitimate son, who in 1611 concluded its sale for £14,600 to Prince Henry, but less than a quarter of this had been paid by the time of the Prince's own death. Seven years earlier the Treasurer of the Navy, Sir Fulke Greville, 'in whose person shineth all true virtue and high nobility', had acquired Warwick and put it in order: Greville had obtained for Speed the post in the Customs which had relieved him from pursuing his trade as a tailor for a livelihood, and thus freeing him for his historical and cartographic interests, and in his commentary on Warwickshire Speed fulsomely acknowledged his debt 'to the procurer of my present estate'. Speed often drew on the work of his antiquarian contemporaries, but whether he did so while drafting his Warwickshire commentary in the case of the recusant Henry Ferrers (d. 1633) of Baddesley Clinton is not known.

Warwickshire incorporated two detached limbs of Worcestershire and one of Gloucestershire's.

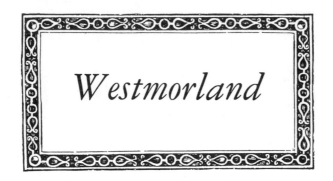

Westmorland

With its bleak hills, moorland and lakes Westmorland was one of the poorest and most thinly populated counties in England. When Speed visited Westmorland there were remnants of the ancient woodland formerly covering the North, at Mallerstang and Whinfell, where survived forests protecting deer. In addition to the woodland there were eighteen deer-parks. Although heather and ling were in plentiful supply, and useful as fuel for warmth and cooking, trees were sparse, and nearly the whole county was wasteland which could 'hardly be brought to any fruitfulness by the industry and painful labour of the husbandman'. In the south, the narrow area between the river Lune and Windermere was not so sterile, and some corn grew there, but not of any quality. Pasture for the grazing of sheep and cattle in the county was at its best indifferent. Lacking even reasonably adequate sources of food, the smallholders of Westmorland were particularly prone to famine and starvation, and a series of bad harvests in the late 1590s took a heavy toll from among them.

As Speed observed, 'The principal profit that the people of the province raise unto themselves is by clothing', which was made in Kendal and every township or village there. In recognition of Westmorland's dependence on one industry and of the quality of the manufactured product, this cloth was exempted from the regulations that governed cloth production elsewhere. Cloth from the area was transported by packhorse throughout England, Wales and Scotland, and at Milnthorp on the Lune estuary it was shipped aboard the small vessels that plied the west coast and crossed the Irish Sea to the Isle of Man and to Ireland. Through Milnthorp came much of the unprepared wool from Wales and Ireland that the clothiers needed for their craft, and also the foodstuffs and other items necessary to life in Westmorland. Of the four market towns, Kendal was the most prosperous, but a glance at the town plan reveals little more than a ribbon development along the confluence of three roads on the opposite side of the river Kent from its medieval castle; Appleby, which had the honour of being the shire town, was no more than 'a poor village, having a ruinous castle wherein the prisoners be kept'.

As part of the northern marches, the inhabitants of Westmorland had been expected to serve in the local musters in the event of an armed incursion by the Scots, and in return for this service regulations governing the carrying of arms in England and Wales did not apply to them. Many of the houses were defensible, often being pele-towers of stone with adjoining farmsteads, and for

KENDALE

A Dockrey Hall
B Crosse Bancke
C Wildmans Gate
D Strickland Gate
E Stramans Gate
F Stramans Bridge
G Brandthwart Lane
H Watt Lane
I The Market
K Leaden Hall
L Finkle Strete
M New Biggen
N Kent Lane
O Wilsons Lanes
P Alhallowes Lane
Q Alhallowes Chapp.
R The Fell syde
S The Mount
T The Battail place
V Rotten Rowe
W The Castle
X The Mill
Y Millers Close
3 Highe gate
4 Abbotts Hall
5 The free Schole
6 Capper Lane
7 Churche Lane
8 The Church
9 Neither Bridge
10 Hersons Lane
12 The Ankeriche

Malcolne Kinge of Scots upon displeasure against ye English entred Cumberland with sword and destruction, forraginge Tesidale, Holdernesse, Weremouth, and Durham, sending from these parts great bootyes into his owne kingdome: in this expedition Edgar Etheling with his sisters Margaret and Chrystian mett Malcolme by whome they were worthyly received, and Margaret the only heire of the Saxons monarchy, afterward married to ye same Malcolme fro whom in lineall right our high & mightie Prince king Iames suceeding, doth in his royall pson unite ye Saxos, Normas, Engl. Scot. Imperiall titles in one.

RAPHE NEVILL

Iohn D. of Bedford   Iohn D. of Somerset   Iohn de Foix

WEST

LAND

BER

CUM

Penreth

Ednell
Langa
Hornby
Carelton
Ninechurches
Wina
Brougham ca.
Whinfeld Forest
Naneworth
Stokbridge
Clifton
Lowther
Milk
Dalemane
Daker cast
Barton
Askhem
Thurnbye
Pole Wethermla
Helton
Crostermond
Heltondale
Rasgill
Shapp
Markendale Chappell
Banton
W
Thornthwate
Wastall head
Burbek flud
Glenkowen flud
Paterdale
Glenkrode flud
Depedale
Hartshope hall
Brederdale
Barrow
Wiborne
Helvillon Hill
Dunbalrase Stones
Gresmere
Langrig
Great Langdale
Claperyate
Little Langdale
Brathy
Ambleside
Kentmere
Sleddale
Fa
Spur flud
Troutbek
Selsted H.
Armeside
Haukesyde
Claffe
Wynandermere
Cowgarth
Chapollon The Inges
Stanlay Colmhead park
Sleel
Barnside
Four nes Fells
Fells
Croke
Kendall park
Lamfwik
Helstonlasthe
Sowthwate
Wynster Chappel
Underbarrow
S. Katherns
Wynster flud
Crosthwate
Siserghe
Newe Bridge
Brigster park
Carp man fell
Witherslak
Leuens Brig
Mylnth
Methap
Be
E
Arneside Toure
Ken Sandes
Wa
S

Kene flu.
Wigh to Lonsda.
Blinde Beck

LAN   CAS
P.

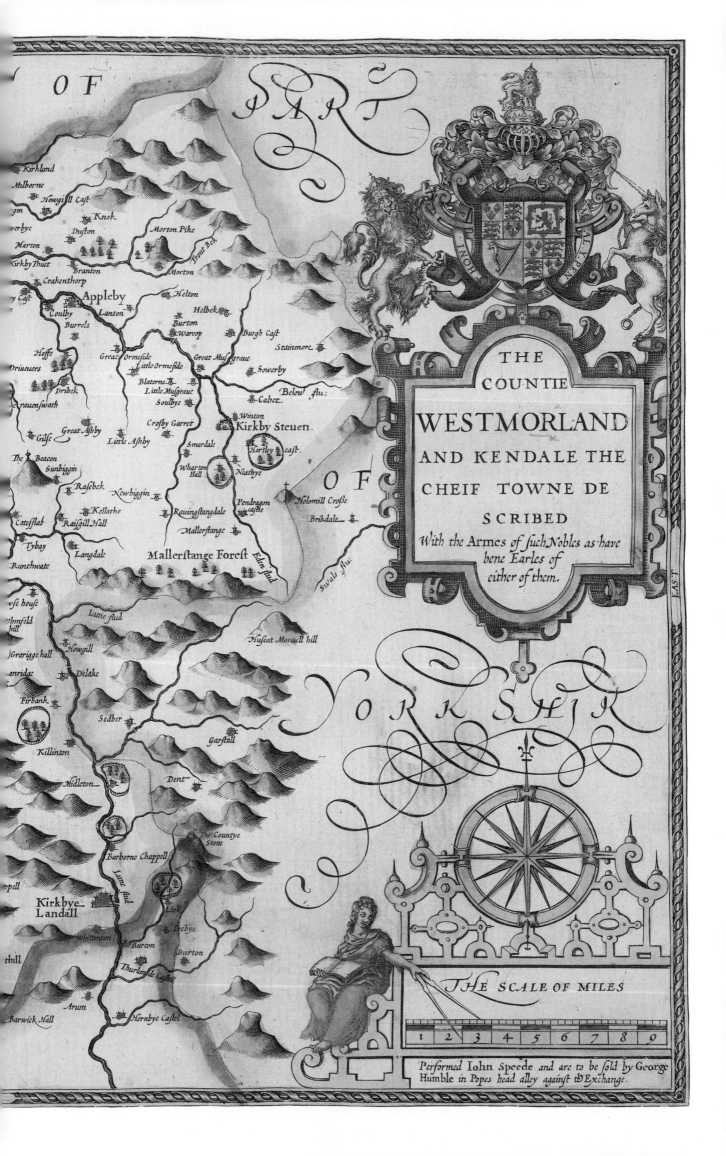

such a modest-sized county there was the surprisingly large number of seven castles, albeit in poor repair when the *Theatre* was published. By 1612 the full impact of the Union of the Crowns upon the economy and life of Westmorland had not been appreciated, and the benefits of the cessation of border hostilities had yet to accrue. The long period of peace between England and Scotland starting early in Elizabeth's reign had enabled the Stricklands to rebuild their ancestral home at Sizergh more comfortably with gorgeous chimneypieces, superlative panelling and patterned plaster ceilings, and James Bellingham rebuilt Levens Hall similarly after his acquisition of the house in 1578: but that these two houses were exceptional was recognized both by residents and outsiders.

Remembering the Roman remains in Cumberland and Northumberland, Speed was disappointed by their paucity in Westmorland. He noted the excavation of some coins and inscriptions at Appleby and surmised a Roman origin for Ambleside from remains discovered there. He seems to have been more taken by the waterfalls near Kendal, where accurate 'prognostications' in foretelling the weather could be made. Cartographic accuracy seems to have lapsed somewhat in the making of the county map: the courses of the rivers are properly shown, but not so the shores of Ullswater and Windermere, which have changed imperceptibly in the last three hundred years, the delineation of the two lakes perhaps being meant to convey something of their grandeur.

Wiltshire

Wiltshire is the watershed for three sets of rivers that run respectively west into the Bristol Channel, east into the North Sea, and south into the English Channel. This watershed is made up of two plains, one being in the north of the county and the other more central with Salisbury at its southern edge, and of downs intersected by deep-running river valleys. Until the programme of disafforestation begun in the 1630s the county was heavily wooded, with an almost uninterrupted belt of forests and woodland stretching across the county from Selwood in the south-west to Braydon in the north-east, and with more woodland on the boundaries with Hampshire and Dorset: today only Savernake survives intact. In the valleys and in the south of the county cereal production predominated, corn and grasses growing abundantly. The great wealth of Wiltshire rested not in its carefully maintained woods and its ploughlands, but in the desolate and windswept plains and downs, devoid of trees, thin of soil and scarce of habitation, yet capable of sustaining 'an infinite number of sheep, whose fleeces and flesh bring in an yearly revenue to their owners'. The wool produced by the graziers was turned into cloth by weavers living in numerous small towns situated by the fast-flowing rivers, whose water-power was put to such good use in preparing the wool and in its weaving, making Wiltshire one of the most heavily industrialized counties in early-seventeenth-century England. The wealth brought to the county through sheep-grazing and cloth-production can be seen in the size and lavishness of its parish churches and in the number of stone-built houses in the towns and villages surviving from the period. The demand for industrial premises for weaving was so great that at the Dissolution the clothier William Stumpe acquired part of the site of Malmesbury Abbey as a cloth manufactory, presenting the townsmen with the nave of the abbey for their parish church, and building a residence in the remainder for himself. With his humble origins, his business drive and flair, and his commercial and social success Stumpe typifies many other similar tales of good fortune deriving from the backs of sheep, not only in Wiltshire but throughout England.

Until the Reformation Wiltshire had been dominated by a set of three great monastic houses at Wilton and Amesbury in the south and at Malmesbury in the north, and by the Bishop of Salisbury, rather than by individual families, although there is no denying the authority of certain families such as Baynton, Darrell, Hungerford and Seymour in local affairs. With the break with Rome

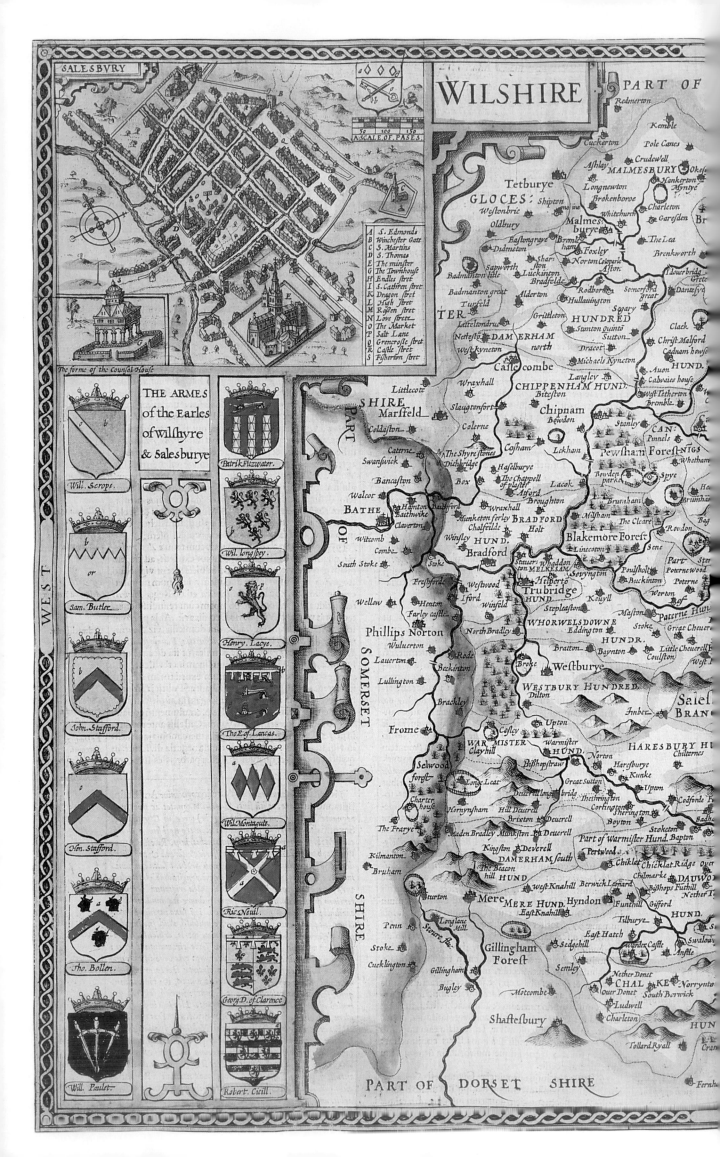

this ecclesiastical dominion ended. William Herbert, Earl of Pembroke, acquired Wilton; Sir John Thynne, Longleat; and Sir William Sharington, Lacock. These men emulated the Seymours, who—after the marriage of Jane Seymour with Henry VIII—began to rebuild their ancestral home at Wolf Hall, near Bedwyn, as part of a spectacular programme of building works. The conversion of Lacock Abbey (funded with money fraudulently taken from the mint at Bristol) into an up-to-date renaissance house with fittings reflecting the latest Continental fashion was nearing completion when Sharington's wrongdoings came to light. Sir John Thynne's redevelopment of Longleat lasted over thirty years, and the eventual design by Robert Smythson was a triumphant prodigy house meant both to accommodate Queen Elizabeth I on her progresses and to impress upon the locality the ascendancy of the Thynnes. Although the new house at Wilton lacked the impact of either Lacock or Longleat, under the 2nd Earl and his brilliant wife Mary Sidney, 'the greatest patroness of wit and learning of any lady in her time', it became a 'college' or haven for poets, playwrights and authors such as Edmund Spenser, John Donne and Ben Jonson. The countess's own interests extended to philosophy and alchemy, and she 'spent yearly a great deal in that study'. Although Sir John Harington said that the countess's own poetry would 'outlast Wilton's walls', John Aubrey less kindly suggested that her interest in horse-breeding—among the earliest recorded—stimulated her in adultery with her followers and other admirers, including even the hunchbacked Robert Cecil, Earl of Salisbury.

The map of Wiltshire omits several outliers in neighbouring Gloucestershire and Berkshire, which are, however, marked appropriately in the respective maps for those two counties. If the Wiltshire map is thus strictly speaking deficient, it still ranks among the *Theatre*'s greatest achievements with its armorial border, its cartouche and its two perspective views of Salisbury and Stonehenge. The view of Salisbury is remarkable for its accuracy and clarity, showing the new town laid out by the bishops in the thirteenth century, its grid of streets and houses (the streams directed through each street to remove unwanted effluent and rubbish), its cathedral and parish churches, market, council house and other civic amenities, which included a gallows and stocks. But it is the depiction of Stonehenge for which the map is more likely to be remembered. Speed shared the fascination of his contemporaries William Camden and Inigo Jones for this prehistoric monument, which he wrongly believed to have been erected by Aurelius Ambrosius, the leader of the British resistance to the Anglo-Saxons, and to be Ambrosius's burial place of 506, and the widespread sales and repeated editions of the *Theatre* go a long way to explain the position which Stonehenge has held in popular imagination since the seventeenth century. The equally magnificent prehistoric complex of Avebury is not mentioned, but the antiquarian John Aubrey was to excavate both sites some thirty years after Speed's death in an attempt to elucidate the historical and archaeological problems they posed.

Worcestershire

Worcestershire consists of a shallow basin cut through by the river Severn and its main tributaries, the Teme, the Stour, and the Warwickshire Avon, and edged by the hills of three uplands, the Malvern Hills, the Clent and Lickey Hills, and the Cotswolds. Its soil was fertile, supporting ploughlands sown with corn, pasture feeding cattle, and extensive woodland. Although sheep were grazed there, the size and number of their flocks were significantly smaller than in adjoining counties, and consequently weaving played an insignificant part in its economy, cloth-production being almost entirely made up of broadcloths manufactured in the city of Worcester, which doggedly prevented the extension of the craft beyond its walls. Much of the woodland was still forest for the maintenance of deer, which were further protected in the numerous small parks and chases throughout the county, but in Pershore with its vale and hundred as elsewhere orchards with crops of apples and pears were common. Pear-trees also grew in the fields and hedgerows and along the roads, and Speed noted that 'with their juice' the inhabitants made 'a bastard kind of wine, called perry, which is both pleasant and good in taste'. Despite the favourable reception given to perry by visitors to the county, Worcestershire was known above all things for its salt-production at Droitwich. It should be remembered that salt was an essential preservative before the discovery of better and more modern ways of keeping food, and an important element in diet, so Droitwich was a centre not simply of local importance, but of national significance, with a system of roads radiating out from it to almost every corner of England and Wales. Beside the river Salwarpe at Droitwich there were three brine springs and nearly four hundred furnaces to dry the salt. Although rated the finest salt, the pollution caused by its production was a source for adverse comment, and John Leland noted that Droitwich was a 'foul' place. The county also had deposits of coal easily mined from the surface, and during the reign of Elizabeth its almost moribund glass industry had been successfully revived. Despite the industrial waste already being dumped in its rivers, these remained well stocked with fish.

The river Severn was an important artery connecting Shropshire and the Welsh hinterland with the Bristol Channel and the port of Bristol, barges being able to navigate the river as far as Shrewsbury. Such was its value as a waterway that the Severn was kept clear of the mills and weirs that congested so many rivers, and from 1532 legislation had exempted the traffic using it from tolls.

WORCESTER

The Scale of Paces
50 100 150 200

A St. Maries minst.
B St. Michaels Church
C St. Clements Church
D St. Nicholas Church
E St. Sythorns Church
F St. Martines Church
G Alhallowes Church
H St. Andrews Church
I St. Albans Church
K St. Helens Church
L St. Peters Church
M St. Iones Church
N Foregate
O Water Gate
P Martines Gate
Q Friers Gate
R Sudbury Gate
S Frogge Gate
T Foregate Stret
V Angell Lane
W Gayle Lane
X Trinitic Lane
Y Doldey Lane
Z Newport Stret
1 Broode Stret
2 Poytes Lane
3 Goſſe Lane
4 Oytmeall market
5 Corne market
6 Bakers Stret
7 Glouers Stret
8 S. Maries Stret
9 Cor Stret
10 Fiſhe Stret
11 Cucking Stret
12 The Key
13 Caſtell Hill
14 The Priſon
15 Frogge mill
16 Sudbury
17 Sudbury Stret

Described by Christopher Saxton, Augmentꝰ
and publiſhed by Iohn Speede citizē
of London, & are there to be ſolde
in Popes-heade Alley againſt the Ex:
change by Iohn Sudbury and George
Humble
CVM PRIVILEGIO

ANNO DOMINI
1610
Iodocus Hondius
cælavit

At Eveſham a ſore battail was
fought, betwixt King Henry 3 &
his Barons, throwe whoſe diſſentions moſt of them were ſlayne as
Simon Mountfort Earl of Leceſter
and 17 Lordes and Knights beſids
Humfrey Bohun E. of Hereford was
there take priſoner A. 1265. Auguſt 5.

OF WARWICK:

SHIRE

Part of Oxford Shire

ORIENS

The whole length of the river, not just the Worcestershire stretches, came under the rule of the Council in the Marches of Wales (with headquarters just across the county border, at Ludlow in Shropshire). During the presidency of Prince Arthur, Henry VIII's elder brother who died in 1502, and later that of Princess Mary during the 1520s, the Council often held meetings in Worcestershire, particularly at Tickenhill on the outskirts of Bewdley. Princess Mary endeared herself to the area which in the succession crisis of 1553 made clear its preference for her as the next ruler. Although Worcestershire showed itself sympathetic towards Mary then, the episcopates of a series of vigorous Bishops at Worcester following Hugh Latimer, who largely supported the Anglican Settlement, ensured the future of Protestantism there.

As in Herefordshire and Shropshire, the favourite material for building in Worcestershire until the seventeenth century was timber, and a wealth of houses and barns, timber-framed with crucks or posts and trusses and painted black and white, survive from Speed's time. Only the parish churches, the cathedral at Worcester, the castles and manor houses were built of stone—usually the local red sandstone, which lends its colour to whole stretches of the county. Unlike the castles of Herefordshire, those in Worcestershire had been neglected since the Middle Ages and by 1600 they were in poor repair. The cathedral of Worcester had largely been rebuilt following the burial of King John there in 1216, and until the Reformation it had been a centre of pilgrimage with its shrine to St Wulfstan, an Anglo-Saxon bishop revered by Anglo-Saxons and Normans alike. Following his death at Ludlow, Prince Arthur was buried there and a chantry was erected to his memory in 1504. As can be seen from the aerial view of Worcester, the cathedral physically dominated the city, which, although it had overspilled its walls, was still a place of many gardens and open spaces, and with its common fields intact: Hondius depicted a ploughman at work with two horses in one of the city's fields, boats with masts on the river, and cranes with pulleys and tackle on the city's quayside to load and unload the passing water freight.

Worcestershire was unusual in its number of administrative areas detached from the main body of the county, with four in Gloucestershire, two in Warwickshire, and one each in Herefordshire and Staffordshire. It also included outliers from Herefordshire, Shropshire and Staffordshire within its own limits.

Yorkshire

One of the criticisms levelled against the work of the cartographer Christopher Saxton had been that in his *Atlas* of 1579 he had often combined adjoining counties, and the maps covering regions rather than counties were difficult to study. John Norden met this reasonable observation by starting to represent each county as a separate cartographic unit in his unfinished project *Speculum Britanniae*, published in the 1590s, and Speed adopted Norden's solution. Unfortunately this gave what might be thought undue prominence to English counties like Rutland and Westmorland or to the Welsh shires as against Yorkshire, which required the smallest of scales used in the *Theatre* in order to fit in with the general approach. To overcome this problem Speed issued two supplementary maps in larger scales, of the West Riding and of the North and East Ridings, but Speed discovered this solution to be not entirely satisfactory when he tried fitting his commentary to the three different maps for Yorkshire.

Yorkshire: North and East Ridings

The North Riding extended from the moors and dales of adjoining Westmorland and County Durham across the Vale of York to the North Yorkshire moors edging the North Sea, while in the East Riding the vale was abutted on its eastern flank by the Wolds, with the plain and wetlands of Holderness and the Humber estuary to the south. The agriculture of the two Ridings was as varied as their geography, the less bleak fells and moorland supporting sheep and cattle, and the lowlands pasture and arable, the East Riding being one of the most prosperous agrarian communities in England. Much of the North Riding was still heavily wooded, with numerous deer-parks, and with careful management, their owners derived greater financial returns from the forests and parks than from their farms and flocks. The veins of iron and coal to be found throughout the uplands were mined, as were deposits of alum and copperas, which were mordants used for stabilizing colours in dyeing. Jet from Whitby continued to be popular for jewellery, and the recent discovery of marcasites near Huntcliffe, also usable in brooches and clasps, had ensured supplies of a semi-precious commodity much in demand throughout England. More important to the regional economy was the knitting of stockings, done around Richmond 'wherewith even the decrepit and children get their living'. Coastal ports from Middlesbrough at the mouth of the Tees to Hull on the Humber estuary were havens of call for the shipping that sailed the east coast of England, and fisheries of some note: with the exception of Hull, whose trade depended more upon catches from off Iceland and the curing of Icelandic cod for general distribution, the Yorkshire ports had been badly hit by the improved techniques of the Dutch in netting herrings from the North Sea and in preserving these for sale, Speed observing 'the Hollanders and Zeelanders do raise unto themselves great profit upon this coast'.

The river Ouse was navigable as far as York, but to ensure its continued use by shipping, York merchants had to prevent the construction of weirs and fishgarths in the river and on the water of Humber, and to regulate tolls imposed at Hull. Not only was the city the county town of Yorkshire, the seat of an archbishopric, and the headquarters of the Council in the North, it was—with its good communications by river and road—the regional and commercial capital of the North. Scrutiny of the ground plan of York in the top right-hand corner of the map for the West Riding reveals the extent of the city, which had a population of about 8,000: the map of the other two Ridings

197

has insets with views of Hull and of Richmond. Besides Hull, Richmond was a modest market town standing in the shadow of its medieval castle. Hull, by contrast, had been a new town founded by Edward I which had prospered. Given its position, Hull was a key-point in maintaining law and order in the East Riding, a fact emphasized by the equivocal part it played in the Pilgrimage of Grace in 1537, and in supplying troops, munitions and victuals for the defence of the northern marches and for the invasion of Scotland. Alone of the ports on the east coast, its defences were adapted for artillery by Henry VIII and a royal residence was built there, these features clearly being seen in the ground plan. At the Dissolution the Crown acquired the former Benedictine abbey of St Mary at York, and converted it into a house for the use of the Council in the North, and for the use of the king during royal progresses, Henry VIII staying there in 1541.

Henry VIII's illegitimate son, Henry Fitzroy, Duke of Richmond, had lived at Sheriff Hutton until his death in 1536, but it was the area's link with Richard III while still Duke of Gloucester that was better known to Speed and his contemporaries, particularly at Middleham. The two Ridings were both peppered with castles and manor houses capable of being defended in an emergency, and many of their 459 parish churches could serve as refuges also. No Scottish incursions taking place in the Tudor period, Yorkshiremen started to build houses more suited to comfort, but with the exception of Gilling, Newburgh, Burton Agnes and Burton Constable, the craze for elaborate prodigy houses under Queen Elizabeth passed them by. The preferred building material was sandstone and, where this was not available, brick and tile; Hull was remarkable for being constructed almost in its entirety from brick. An attempt to develop Ormesby with its medicinal springs as a spa along the lines of Bath or Buxton came to nothing, partly because the Council in the North viewed meetings there as cloaking political or religious malcontent, and partly because local families were less accustomed to such pastimes and dissipations than their southern counterparts. Both smallholders and families supported the Pilgrimage of Grace, and later, in 1596, openly sympathized with the northern rebels.

Since Speed's time the drainage of the marshland of Holderness and of the Humber has been successfully completed, but erosion by the sea also means that the North Sea coastline of Holderness has been significantly altered.

Yorkshire: West Riding

Speed's map of the West Riding is one of the least successful in the *Theatre*. To get the large area covered by the Riding with its 104 parishes into the format adopted for the *Theatre*, Speed used a scale far smaller than his usual standard, and the result is a lack of clarity. This failure is particularly noticeable if one contrasts the map for the Riding with that for Lancashire, where similar problems of production were faced, but more successfully resolved.

The landscape of the West Riding had considerable variety, ranging from the fells and moors of the Pennines adjoining Westmorland, Lancashire and Derbyshire through the dales and deep-cut valleys to more gentle hills, to the central Yorkshire plain of the Ouse valley, to the undrained marshlands near the Humber estuary. Its farming and the economy varied likewise. Although the primeval forest of the Pennines had long since been cleared, forest survived in Bowland, and much of the Riding remained heavily wooded from Knaresborough to Hatfield Chase, even though such woodland was being steadily reduced by the twin processes of disafforestation and enclosure. 'The ragged rocks and swelling mountains' were wastelands, but their slopes were good grasslands for 'great flocks of sheep' and herds of cattle, and 'the bottoms and valleys are not altogether infertile', producing cereals and other foodstuffs. The hills 'barren and bare of corn and cattle' had quarries for limestone, mines for copper, iron and lead, and pits for coal, 'with which they are abundantly furnished'. In the area around Halifax textile production was already established, weaving and knitting supplementing the meagre livelihood to be got from farming, and sixteenth-century efforts to restrict the industry to towns exempted the Halifax district on those grounds. At Sheffield the ironworks were celebrated for cutlery.

Stone was the natural choice for building, but with reeds easily obtainable from the marshlands of the Ouse, Trent and Humber, stone slabs for roofing were common only in the uplands. Yorkshire's proximity to the Scottish marches was reflected in the number of battlefields and of castles and fortified manor houses dating from the Middle Ages to be found in the West Riding. Although none of these buildings was neglected, the improvements made at Skipton Castle in Craven by successive earls of Cumberland during the Tudor period typified a trend throughout the sixteenth century towards greater personal comfort and luxury. The royal castle at Pontefract ranked as the Crown's principal fortress in the North, with its regional headquarters for the

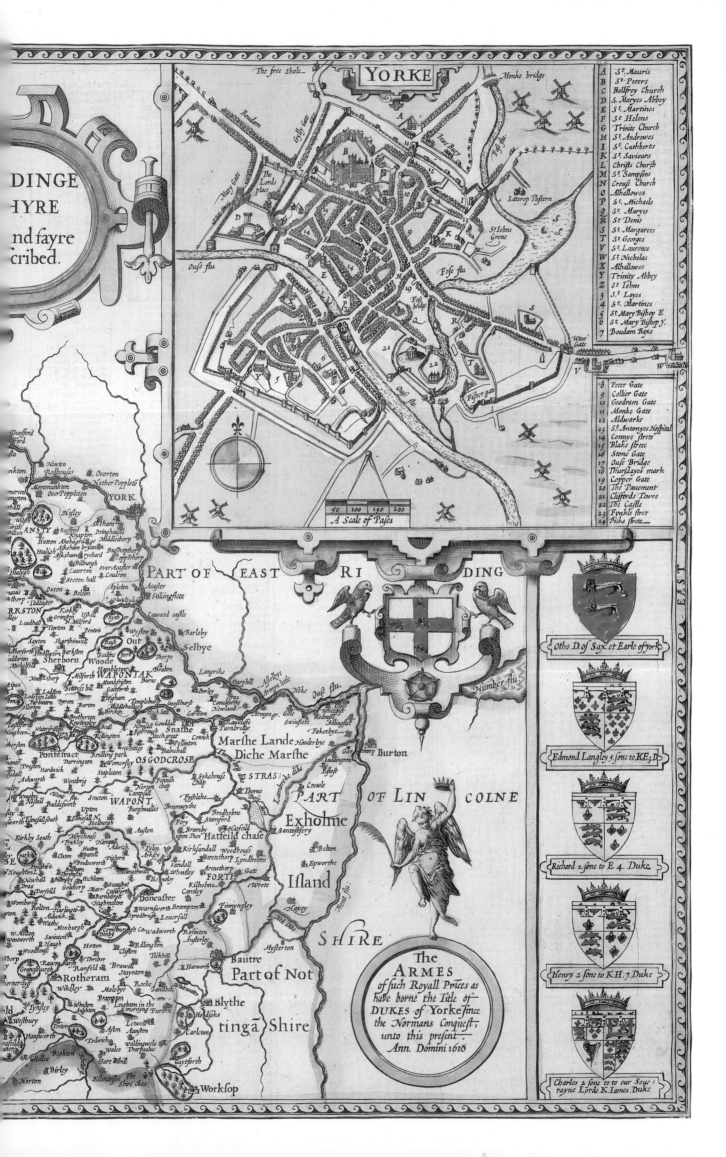

Duchy of Lancaster and royal lodgings. After Henry VIII's visit in 1541 no monarch went to Pontefract on a royal progress until 1603, when James I passed through on his way south to London. Although nothing came of Queen Elizabeth's plan to visit the Riding in 1574, Mary Queen of Scots was an occasional visitor to Sheffield Manor, which belonged to her reluctant host and captor the Earl of Shrewsbury. Sheffield, Thorpe Salvin and New Hall near Pontefract were splendid examples of the new Elizabethan architecture, but more important is the large number of moderate-sized houses (such as Arthington) being constructed at the same time, which reflects the growing prosperity of the region and its increasing stability as a result of the work of the Council in the North with its headquarters in York.

The West Riding was seriously affected by the suppression of the religious houses which had done so much to develop and exploit its economy, and concern at their dissolution combined with the inherent conservatism of the area and its distrust of recent political changes at court and in government under Henry VIII led to its insurrection in 1536: the area did not rally similarly to the support of the northern earls in 1569. Many of its leading families remained lukewarm towards the Elizabethan Church Settlement, despite the example of the Earls of Shrewsbury and of Huntingdon, but the weavers and other small craftsmen, like their fellow practitioners elsewhere, espoused Protestantism, and helped to make West Riding unreceptive to the work of seminary priests and other papists.

Lacking as it did a major township of its own, Speed included in his map of the West Riding the city of York situated just across the river Ouse, and with its castle, minster and walls the regional capital. The set of arms in the heraldic border is more interesting than most armorial borders in the *Theatre*, since from the reign of Edward IV the dukedom of York was reserved for the second son of the reigning monarch, and the arms depicted include those of the young prince murdered in the Tower, of Prince Henry (later King Henry VIII), and of the current holder when the *Theatre* was issued, Prince Charles (later King Charles I).

The Islands

Holy Island

Situated off the north-east coast of Northumberland, Holy Island, or Lindisfarne as it is sometimes called, is linked to the mainland by a causeway at low tide. Bleak and cold and subject to dense sea-mists, it lacked soil sufficiently fertile for cultivation or for pasture, but it did have a supply of fresh springwater which had allowed a Benedictine priory—wrongly called an abbey by Speed—to survive there until its suppression in 1537. Fish and birds abounded. Although the surrounding sea was hazardous with its submerged shelves and outcrops of rock, Holy Island had 'a commodious haven' approachable through a safe channel. This facility with the island's key position against Scotland and in protecting the shipping that plied the Northumbrian coast had meant the island had long been important in the defence of England. The priory had been fortified, and during the Anglo–Scottish hostilities lasting over twenty years from the 1540s a blockhouse and an artillery fort were constructed, the priory with its conventual buildings being modified for the use of the garrison, its stores and munitions: these fortifications were in bad repair at the accession of James I in 1603. For his Holy Island map Speed drew on the work of the little-known surveyor, James Burrell.

The Farne Islands

Some five miles south-east of Holy Island and separated from Bamburgh on the Northumbrian mainland by a sound two miles wide, Farne Island (with nearby Staple Island, Brownsman, North and South Wamses, and their rocky outliers) was a barren place incapable of sustaining life beyond the many birds that colonized it. In this it had not altered significantly since St Cuthbert chose it as his place of retreat in the seventh century. Farne had been fortified and garrisoned by Henry VIII at the same time as Holy Island, but despite regular maintenance these buildings were in poor condition in 1603, only the fish house marked on the map and used by local fishermen being in good repair.

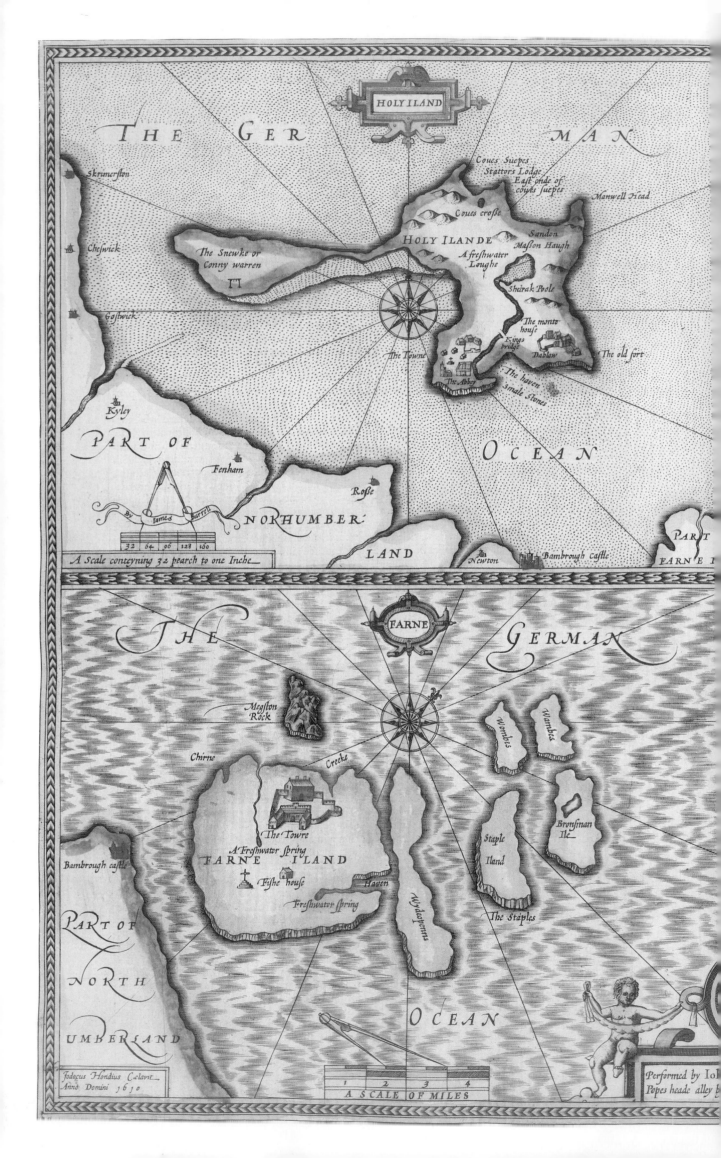

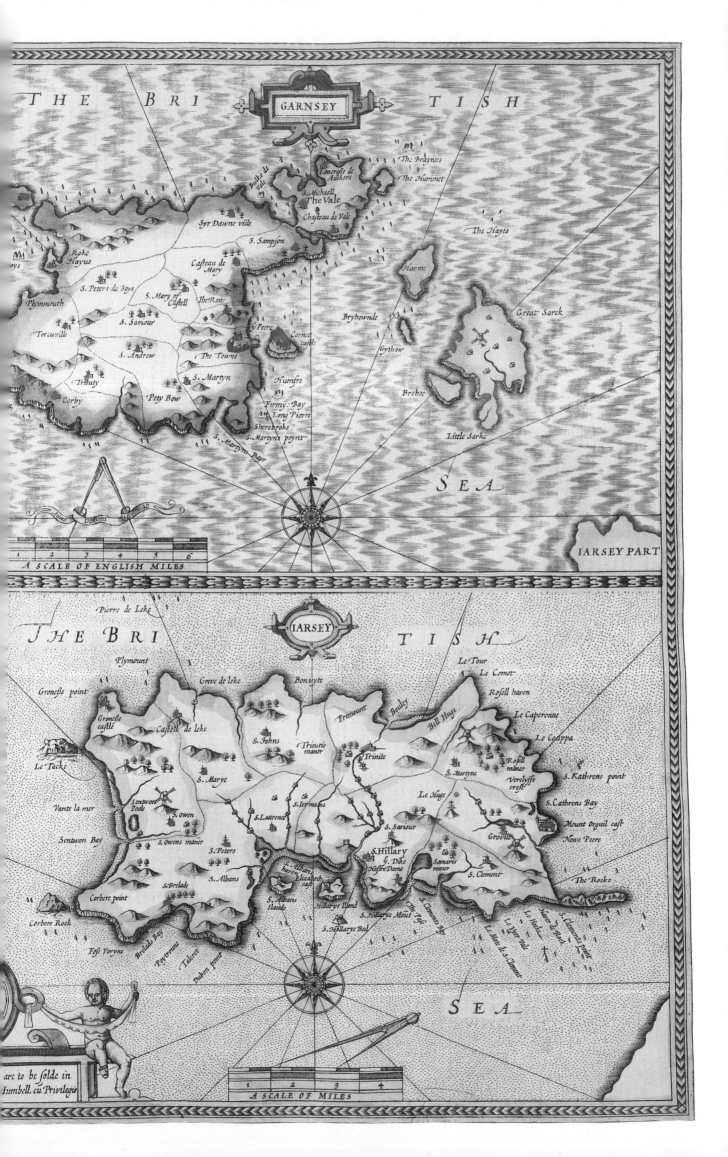

The Channel Islands

Formerly part of the Duchy of Normandy, these islands situated some fifteen miles off the Cotentin peninsula were administered by the Tudor and Stuart monarchs as a miniature dominion of the Crown, with a governor of their own responsible for their safe-keeping and good management. Although coming within the Hampshire legal circuit and nominally subject to the governor of the Isle of Wight, the islands were never incorporated into the system of English local government, and they had kept their own *patois*, described by Speed as 'French though after a corrupt manner' and their own system of law based on the customary laws of Normandy 'without any, or little intermixture, these many hundred years'. Although of limited strategic value, the Channel Islands were useful observation points in time of hostilities, and as outposts of the English Crown in the wars with France and Spain throughout the sixteenth century they often figured in plans for national defence; they were fortified and repeatedly surveyed.

Of the Channel Islands, Speed concentrated on the larger two, Guernsey and Jersey, with Sark, Herm and Iethou being included in the Guernsey map, but with Alderney and nearby Burhou overlooked save for a passing reference in the Guernsey commentary. Speed considered the whole group of islands 'delightsome and healthful'. Agriculturally they were fertile, the fields yielding cereals and grasses in such abundance and so bedecked with flowers in summer time that 'a man being there might conceit himself to be in a[n] Eden': the flocks of cattle and sheep grazed the pasture, the islanders specializing in the manufacture of stockings and other knitwear for sale in England. In Guernsey there was less tillage than in Jersey, but apples grew in orchards and cider was made. In the absence of woodland timber was an expensive commodity in building, but stone was readily available. For heating and cooking the islanders relied on burning turves, furze or fern, and some coal imported at great cost. Fishing was a staple of the islands' economy, their catches of conger eel and lobster being 'the greatest and fattest upon the coast of England'. Also, Guernsey was a source of emeralds, sold not for use as gems but for cutting other precious stones and glass.

In addition to marking the islands' many cliffs, and their interrelated navigational hazards, 'much feared by mariners', this pair of maps showed the windmills, and on Jersey the parishes with their parish churches.

Isle of Man

The Isle of Man had come under effective English rule only following the English victory over the Scots at Neville's Cross in 1346 early in the reign of Edward III. In 1405 Henry IV granted the lordship of Man to Sir John Stanley in return for his doing homage and giving two falcons at the coronation of each king of England. The lordship remained in the hands of Sir John's descendants until the death of the 5th Earl of Derby in 1544. While the dispute as to who should be the new lord of Man was proceeding, Queen Elizabeth took control of the island, and she and her successor James I appointed a series of governors until in 1612 the 6th Earl got the lordship.

Although under English control, Man had remained largely independent. Not only did the Manx speak a language that was not English and dress distinctively, but they retained their ancient customs in law, government and defence: justice was administered by law-men called 'deemsters' who had the laws committed to their memories or their 'breasts'; new legislation was passed by twelve of the 'worthiest men' known as 'keys', and military service provided by a militia system of 'ward and watch' incumbent on all adult males. Man also had a bishopric of its own, which was under the control of the arch-bishopric of York. Speed praised the piety of the inhabitants, but this observation reveals his ignorance about the slow advancement of the Manx Reformation, which was probably due as much to the strong Roman Catholic sympathies of the earls of Derby as to the isolation of the island and the lack of a prayer book in the vernacular.

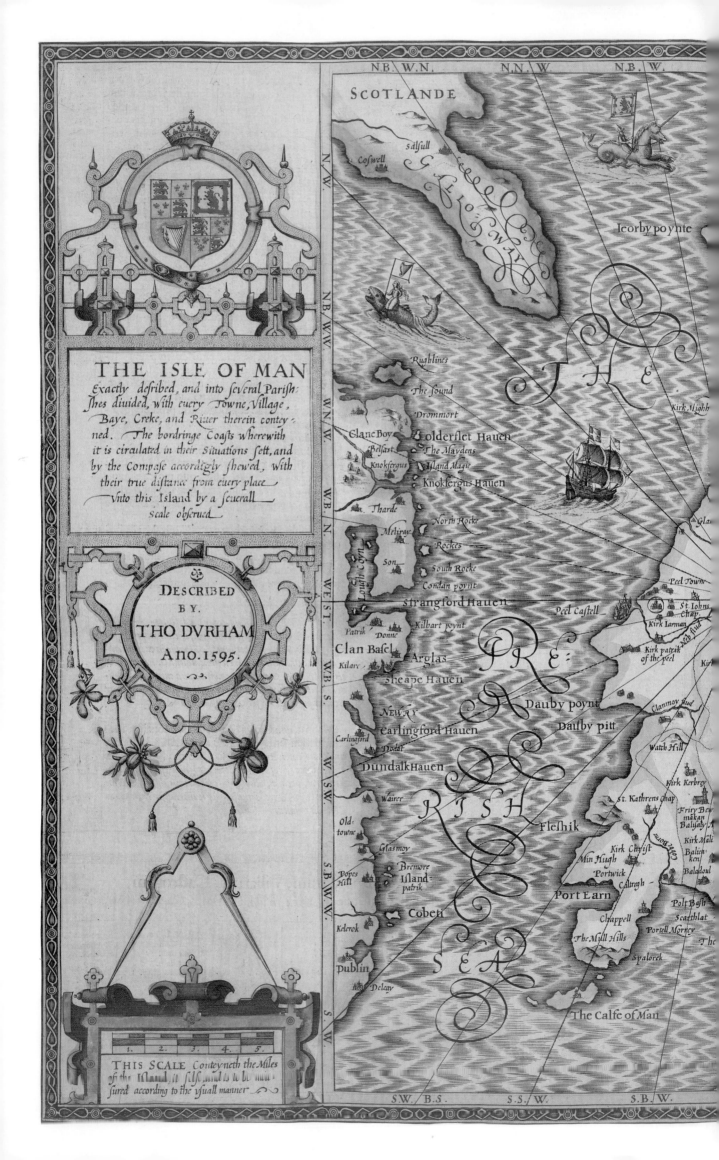

THE ISLE OF MAN

Exactly described, and into several Parish:
shes divided, with every Towne, Village,
Baye, Creke, and River therein contey:
ned. The bordringe Coasts wherewith
it is circulated in their situations sett, and
by the Compase accordingly shewed, with
their true distance from every place
unto this Island by a severall
scale observed

DESCRIBED
BY.
THO DVRHAM
Ano. 1595.

THIS SCALE Conteyneth the Miles
of the Island it self, and is to be mea
sured according to the usuall manner

SCOTLANDE

GALLOWAY

Coswell
salsull

Icorby poynte

THE

Kirk Miahh

Rughlines
The sound
Drommort
Clane Boy
Belfast
Knokfergus
olderflet Hauen
The Maydens
Island Magie
Knokfergus Hauen

Tharde

North Rocke
Melirav
Son
Rockes
South Rocke
Condan poynt
strangford Hauen
Lough Coyn
Peel Castell
Peel Towne
St. Iohns
chap
Kirk Iarman

Kilbart poynt
Patrik
Donne
Clan Basel
Kilare
Arglas
Sheape Hauen
Kirk patrik
of the peel
Glan
Kirk

PRE:

Dauby poynt
Dauby pitt

NEWRY
Carlingford Hauen
Carlingsford
Dodar
Dundalk Hauen
Watch Hill

Kirk Kerbrey

Wairer
st. Kathrens chap
Fleshik
RISH

Friry Bew
makan Balisaly
Kirk Mali
Balichn
ken
Baladoul

Old
towne
Glasmoy
Min Hugh
Portwick
Kirk Chrijt
Calragh

Popes
Hill
Bremore
Island
patrik
Port Earn
Polt Bajh
Scarthlat
Portell Morney

Cobeh
Chappell
The Myll Hills
Syalorek

Kelerok

Publin
Delay
The Calfe of Man
The

SEA

N.B.E.   N.N.E.   N.B.E.N.

poynt of Ayre

Cran:
ston

Kirk Bridge

k Andron

Vark

Shellack poynt

Malar:
lough

Solbe mouth

Ramsy Towne

Ramsy Hauen

Kirk Maghhaules
Heade

Kirk Maghhaul

Workinton

Silsfeld

Egnes

Laxi Baye
Laxi poynt

Miltum cast:

Laxi Towne

irk lennon

Kirk onkon

Egremonde

De pole of
Foodray

Foulay

Douglas Towne
Dowglas hauen

Dowglas poynt

Nunry

Ramsway

St. Mighils
Island

The poynt
Lange nouse

Lerpoole water

Hillbre
Island

DEE FLUD

Prestholme Island

Part of
Flint
shire

PART
OF DENBI:
GHSHIRE

PART
OF
CAERN
ARVANSHIR

SEY

Bewmaris

S.B.E.   S.S.E.   S.E. B.S.

PART OF CUMBERLAND

N.B.E.

N.E.

E.N.E.

E.B.N.

EAST.

E.B.S.

E.S.E.

S.B.E.

S.E.

Part of Lancashire

Part of Chesshire

MAN by Cæsar called Mona, by plini
Monabia, by ptol. Monoeda, and by Gildas
Evbonia, is an Island seated in the Ocean be:
twixt the kingdomes of England, Scotland
and Ireland, it formerly bare the name of a
kingdome, and hathbene populous and well
inhabited very plentyfull of Cattell, Foule and
Fyshe, it is nowe deuided into seauentiene
parishes, many Villages, and de:
fended by twoe Castells.

PERFORMED
BY.
IOHN SPEED
Anno. 1610

5   10   15   20

THIS SCALE is to be measurd from the
Compasse in the midst of the Island vnto
the bordring Coasts of England, Scot:
land, Ireland, and Wales.

With its central spine of uplands rising to over 2,000 feet at Scarfell and broken only by a vale running from Douglas to Peel, the Isle of Man had little good arable land. Farmers depended more on pasturing cattle and sheep than growing oats (used in making an oaten bread which was the staple of the islanders' diet), barley and some wheat: Speed remarked that the cattle were 'smaller in body than we have in England and are much like to the cattle in Ireland'. Hemp and flax were produced in the island largely for export to Lancashire for weaving. In the absence of much woodland or coal deposits the islanders used a 'clammy type of turf' for fuel. Fish and sea-birds abounded, and catching and curing them were long-established businesses. Speed noted the general dependence of the Isle of Man upon Lancashire: the wealthier islanders 'and such as hold the fairest possessions, do imitate the people of Lancashire, both in their honest carriage and good housekeeping: howbeit, the common sort of people both in their language and manners came nighest unto the Irish, although they somewhat relish and favour the qualities of the Norwegians'.

Speed's map of the Isle of Man does not conform with general principles usually followed in the *Theatre*. The explanation for this is presumably the map's dependence on a survey made in 1595 by Thomas Durham, a surveyor about whom little has so far come to light, but who included such items as parishes with their churches and boundaries and the monastic ruins at Bernaken, Douglas and Rushen in addition to such standard features as towns, villages and castles. To Durham must also be ascribed the decision to show on the appropriate edges parts of the coastlines of England, Wales, Ireland and Scotland in complete disregard of their actual distance from the island on the grounds of the map's practical use to navigators in the Irish Sea. The map is embellished with ships in full sail and sea monsters, and completed with the royal arms and the device of the three legs of Man.

Wales

When Christopher Saxton published his *Atlas* in 1579 he had included maps for Wales, but where it suited him Saxton had covered regions, not counties, and he had used a scale which had varied considerably from map to map. Both practices had been adversely criticized. George Owen of Henllys remarked that the combination of Breconshire, Cardiganshire, Carmarthenshire and Radnorshire 'forced ... them so near together – thrusting one town upon another', and the muster commissioners complained about the disproportionate size of the areas assigned to them on account of the failure to take differences of scale into account. In the *Theatre* Speed met these objections: he not only had a separate map for each county, but was more consistent in scale. Moreover, he had the sense to realize that his solutions to critics' objections to Saxton's set themselves called for a regional map to show the

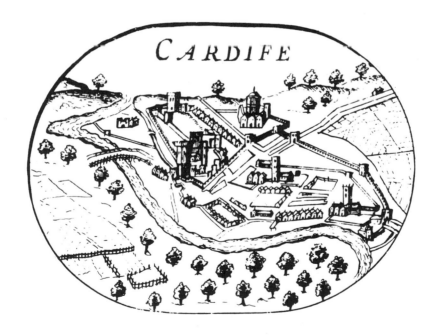

relationship of each Welsh county to the others. The Welsh map does just this as well as showing the main physical features, bridges and settlements. Speed prevaricated over including Monmouthshire in Wales (it was administratively English, although Welsh-speaking), and arrived at a compromise whereby he

included Monmouthshire in the regional map, but excluded the town of Monmouth from his depiction of Welsh shire towns in the borders.

The Welsh map is embellished with the arms of the four diocesans with vignettes of their cathedral cities in its corners and with two vertical bands of six cartouches with vignettes of the twelve shire towns. In his commentary Speed drew attention to the fact that counties in Wales were subdivided into cantrefs and commotes, and not hundreds as in England.

Anglesey

Situated off the north-west extremity of Wales and separated from the mainland by the Menai Strait, the Island of Anglesey is washed by the Irish Sea. Speed thought its air 'reasonable, grateful and healthful, and not generally subject to diseases excepting certain agues at some times, which are occasioned by the fogs and misty exhalations, which arise from the sea'. With no land as high as 1,000 feet, and the greater part less than 400 feet, with extensive marshland but little woodland, Anglesey was dependent upon grazing cattle and sheep, with some cultivation of wheat, oats and barley. There was also some horse-breeding, but suppliers for the army in Ireland dismissed Anglesey horses as nags, so poor as to be worthless. The islanders supplemented their income by weaving, using yarn mostly imported from South Wales. More important economically than cloth production were deposits of stones suitable for milling and grinding, of alum and copperas (used as mordants in dyeing), and of copper and coal. However, there was no denying the poverty of the island: there were only two markets, poorly maintained roads and tracks, and a single bridge giving access to Holyhead. For communications and transport Anglesey relied heavily on the coastal shipping that sailed eastwards to Lancashire and southwards to Pembrokeshire, and on the more substantial vessels crossing over to Ireland.

Its position was strategically vulnerable, and until the Union of the Crowns Anglesey was as much a prey to Scottish raiders as many parts of Ireland. Partly to reduce this threat and partly to pacify the island, Edward I had built his last major fortress at Beaumaris following the shiring of Anglesey and its incorporation into the Principality of North Wales. Although the castle at Beaumaris was never finished, the King's intentions had been largely realized, and there existed at Beaumaris a more prosperous and flourishing borough than many to be found in much of Wales, with among other things a school and a windmill of its own. It was a measure of the general success of the English Crown's policies towards Ireland and Scotland under the Tudor monarchs that the leading gentle families in Anglesey, largely freed from the recurrent military drain on their expenses, were able to join in the house-building boom common throughout most of the kingdom, and put up modest (but not inelegant or old-fashioned) buildings such as those at Plas Coch in Llanedwen, Llangwyfan Isaf in Llangwyfan and Tal-y-Llyn in Llanbeulan. Most of the island's houses were less grand than these gentlemen's residences (as were its

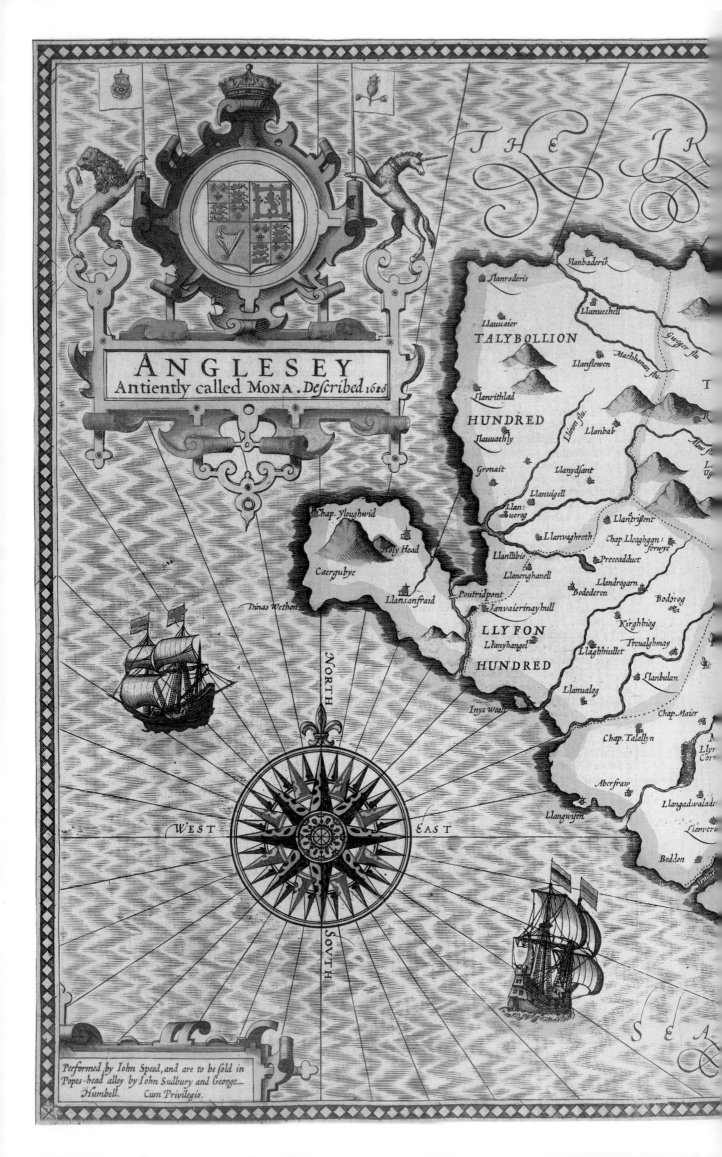

ANGLESEY
Antiently called MONA. Described 1626

THE IR...SEA...

TALYBOLLION

HUNDRED

LLYFON

HUNDRED

Slanbaderik
Slanroderis
Llanuechell
Llauuaier
Gwyger flu.
Llanflewen
Mathhanan flu.
Slanrithlad
Llinon flu.
Llanbab
Nauuathly
Llanydfant
Gronait
Llantuigell
Llan: Suorog
Llantrifent
Llanvaghreth
Chap. Lleaghgan: ferwye
Llanllibis
Preceadduet
Llanenghanell
Llandrogarn
Poutridpont
Bodederen
Bodsrog
Lanvaierinayhull
Kirghhiog
Llanyhangel
Treualghmay
Llaghhiullet
Slanbulan
Llantualog
Inys Weah
Chap. Maier
Chap. Talallyn
Aberfraw
Llangwisten
Llangadwalade
Lianver
Boddon

Chap. yloughwid
Holy Head
Caerguhye
Llansanfraid
Dinas Wethon

NORTH

WEST — EAST

SOUTH

SEA

Performed by Iohn Speed, and are to be fold in Popes-head alley by Iohn Sudbury and George Humbell. Cum Privilegio.

churches), but notwithstanding this Speed was evidently impressed by there being 333 'villages', by which he meant scattered farmsteads as well as the more important settlements marked and named on the map, and seventy-four churches serving the religious needs of the island.

By the accession of James I, Anglesey was more or less dominated by a single family, the Bulkeleys, who had originated in Lancashire. Their emergence as politically and socially the most important family on the island brought to an end the rivalries and feuds which had beset it in the late Middle Ages, and under their aegis Anglesey benefited substantially from the Union with England in 1536 and from the Union of the Crowns in 1603.

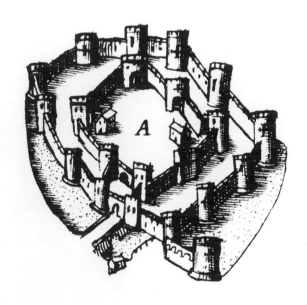

Breconshire

As the county map well conveys, the landscape of Breconshire is dramatic. Speed noted that 'the county is full of hills and uneven for travel', with 'many fruitful springs'. It is the watershed from which the river Usk and many of the tributaries of the Wye flow eastward, and other lesser rivers and streams flow south or west. Between Brecon and Crickhowell the Usk passes through a valley impressive in its grandeur: the Brecon Beacons on its south side rise to almost 3,000 feet; Mynydd Eppynt to the north is smooth, barren and remote; and the Black Mountains to the east divide the county from Herefordshire. Little of this bleak upland was suitable to human habitation; most was left to flocks of cattle and sheep, with herdsmen who moved the animals in rotation to different seasonal pastures. In contrast the valleys, the shores of Llangorse Lake, and the gap where the county's few roads met near Talgarth were all good farming land with settlements and common fields producing 'in plenty both corn and grass'. The Great Forest of Brecon had survived almost intact from primeval times, but much of it was no more than heath or scrubland, its more heavily wooded stretches being clearly marked on the map. Along the Wye there were orchards mainly producing cider apples.

Despite its poor roads Breconshire had three market towns. The chief of these was the town of Brecon, with its castle and college, which had until 1521 been the administrative centre for one of the last great medieval lordships to have survived in Wales, and even after the Union had continued to function as a centre for local management in the marcher counties. Unlike Builth and Hay, Brecon was relatively prosperous, with more inhabitants than most Welsh towns, and from 1541 a school of its own; it was, however, notorious for its lack of accommodation for travellers. Although situated in a county abounding with stone, Brecon is still notable for its quantity of timber-framed building, and this pattern was found throughout the county until the introduction of brick in the seventeenth century. The local stone split easily, thus the stone used for its castles and some of its churches had to be carefully selected or else brought from a distance. As in most Welsh counties, towns in Breconshire rarely dated earlier than the thirteenth century in origin and with the exception of Brecon none of these had prospered. Breconshire was a county of small scattered farmsteads and villages served by a network of fifty-one parishes. The Games, Herbert and Vaughan houses at Aberbran Fawr, Porthmawr and Porthaml were notable exceptions to this general pattern: all these manor

Part of · Cardigan ·

Shire

BREKNOKE
BOTH SHYRE AND TOWNE
described
Ann. Domini 1610

WEST

OF

Part of Cardigan Shire

PART OF

Rayder Gowy

Clarwen flud
Clarwen flud
Clarthy flud

Llanuthel

BEALT HUNDRED

Lleshinan
Kethtalgarth
Capel Llan
prinþabor

Delas flud
Weuery flud

Llanyhangle
Abergweßen

Yrvon flud
Comarch flud

Llanauon
Vawre

Llanthewye
Abergwesten

Llanavan
Vachan

Traufnant flud

Llanurtyd

Llanllowenuel

Po

Llangamarch

Dyhas flud
Yrvon flu

PART

Towye flud

MERTHYE HUNDRED

Flandiloruayne

Llanyhangle
nantbranc

Brane flud

Llywell
Tre Castle

Henud
park

Trallon
Ab

Gwetherik flud

Cappell Ridbruc

Vske flud
Cray flud

Deuinok

Carnlas flud

Slanyhangle

Muthuey flud

Cepel Senny

OF

DYVYNNOCK HUND.

The Black Montayne

Capel Callwe
Neath flud

Traufnach flud
Melas flud

Heyfey flud

Turch flud
Tavy flud

Capel Coyelbryn

Istradwelthye

Neath Vachan flud

ICH · DIEN

CAERMARDEN

Istradqutles

Aberpirgum

Peneder

SHYRE

PART OF GLAMO

Performed by Iohn Speede. And are to be solde
in Popes head alley against the Exchange by
I. Sudbury and George Humbell Cum Privilegio.

RADNOR SHIRE

BREKNOKE

A. Castell lane.
B. Old port inferior.
C. Old port superior.
D. Canterceley ward.
E. Shepe Stret.
F. High Stret superior.
G. High Stret inferior.
H. Lone y posty.
I. Morgannok ward.
K. S. Marys ward.
L. Llanuase ward.
M. The Priorye.
N. S. Iohn Euangelist.
O. St Maryes Chapel.
P. West Gate.
Q. Water Gate.
R. North Gate.
S. East Gate.
T. Watton Ward.
V. Rewredd Ward.

THE SCALE OF PASES
50   100   150   200

The College

Uske flud
Hondey flud

...in this Shire, Leolin (the ... that bare rule over the ...) comminge from Snodowne ... ine by Roger Stranghow, ... head, crowned with iuy, ... on the Tower of London ... yeare of grace 1282, and ... of Ed. I.

Slanelway
Llauarel
Edney flud
SHIRE
Llanthewyecomb
Altemawre
Cunok
Gwendor
Creaderne
Caste Payne
Machaway flud
Llandilo
Lanstephan
Hay
Dulas flud
Llanygon
Glasesbury
Chap. Brengoran
Llangoyd
Wye flud
Aberlleuenye
Elyswen
Pipton
Piateroh Hill
Llandeuathley
Port hamble
Broynclys east
Chap a Fyne
Talgarth
Llanuyllo
TALGARTH HUN.
Cast Dynas
Garthbrengye
Talachdye
Lleveny flud
Llangors
Llanthew Castle
Llangouilog
Kethesden
PART OF HERE FORD The Fothok SHIRE
Breknoke
Llanihanglo
Llanyhangell Cumdy
Comyoye
Talling
Llanwarne
Llyn Sauathan
Langustye
Pentryso
Llanhamlogh
Skethrog
CRICKHOEL HUND.
Blayullynuye cast
Llansanfrayd
Aberkinuelik
Cantreffe
Llaunranach
Uske flud
Llanuygan
Gilston
Tretowre
Gromey flu.
Peterchurch
Creowell
Landdettye
Llangenye
Llangonider
Uske flu.
Llangattok
Llangrones
Slanelye
muchdenny Hill
Capel Tavrechan
PENKELLI HUND.
Tav Vachan flud
Capel Nantyr
Vaynor
Blanagwent
Morlashe Castle
Mounmeth Shire
SHYRE
Runney flud

The Scale of Miles
1 2 3 4 5 6 7 8 9 10

EAST
part of

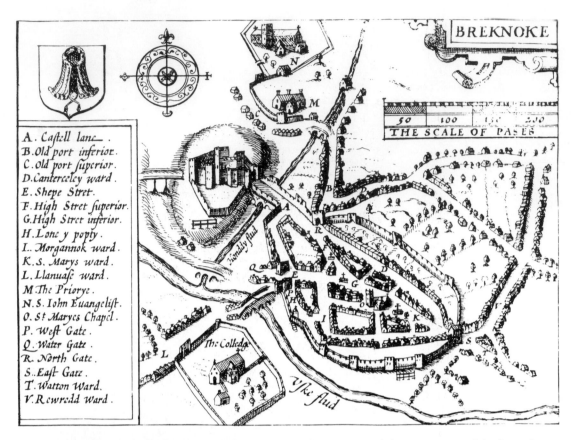

A. *Castell lane*.
B. *Old port inferior*.
C. *Old port superior*.
D. *Cantereeley ward*.
E. *Shepe Street*.
F. *High Stret superior*.
G. *High Stret inferior*.
H. *Lone y popty*.
I. *Morgannok ward*.
K. *S. Marys ward*.
L. *Llanuase ward*.
M *The Priorye*.
N. *S. Iohn Euangelist*.
O. *St Maryes Chapel*.
P. *West Gate*.
Q. *Water Gate*.
R. *North Gate*.
S. *East Gate*.
T. *Watton Ward*.
V. *Rewredd Ward*.

houses had currently fashionable great gatehouses and forecourts added to them in the early sixteenth century, but only that of the county's first sheriff, Sir William Vaughan, now survives in Porthaml.

Breconshire was created at the Union by incorporating the ancient tribal kingdom of Brycheiniog with the cantref of Builth. Speed showed no interest in the county's early history beyond a description of the battle of Builth in 1282, where Llewelyn, the last Welsh prince, had been defeated. He did not note the part that Rhys ap Thomas had played in raising the area in support of Henry of Richmond in 1485, nor that it had been the birthplace of William Aubrey, one of the leading civil lawyers and ecclesiastical administrators of the Elizabethan age, who was buried in Old St Paul's.

Caernarfonshire

'The heart of this shire', wrote Speed, 'is altogether mountainous, as if Nature had a purpose here, by rearing up these craggy hills so thick together, strongly to compact the joints of this our island, and to frame the inland part thereof for a fit place of refuge to the Britons against adversity... These mountains may not unfitly be termed the British Alps, as being the most vast in Britain, and for their steepness and cragginess not unlike to those of Italy, all of them towering into the air, and round encompassing one far higher than all the rest . . . called Snowdon.' Except for the coastal areas in the west of the county, towards Ireland, there was not much arable land, and with little woodland outside the Conwy valley and Pwllheli peninsula, Caernarfonshire was dependent largely on the livestock grazing its uplands. The cloth woven in its scattered villages and homesteads came not from the fleeces of the sheep bred in the county (which were reared for their carcases), but from wool imported from other parts of Wales. There was some fishing, and Speed mentions a 'certain shellfish' producing pearls 'in ancient times more reckoned of than they are now'. In spite of its lack of agricultural produce, Caernarfonshire had five market towns, which relied for their existence mainly on merchants selling wool for spinning and weaving and subsequently buying back the cloth. For outside communication Caernarfonshire relied heavily upon coastal shipping, its roads being poor, often blocked by snow in winter, and lacking bridges except at the county boundaries.

In 1284 Caernarfonshire had witnessed at Nefyn the celebrations to mark the successful subjugation of Wales by Edward I, and not long afterwards the shire was created as part of the new system of government in the region. Together with Merioneth and the Isle of Anglesey, it formed the Principality of North Wales, which was administered from the town of Caernarfon on the shores of the Menai Strait. Both Caernarfon and Conwy, with their castles, walled defences and grid system of streets, had been new towns established at the Edwardian conquest, but unlike so many other towns founded in Wales at the same time they had never stagnated or declined: the plan of Caernarfon reveals a prosperous town spilling out of its walls, and Speed was so impressed with Conwy that he thought it better deserved 'the name of a city than a town'. But this prosperity was not shared to the same degree by other towns: Nefyn was 'a small market town', Bangor the seat of a bishopric with modest-sized houses lining the approach roads to the cathedral, and Deganwy

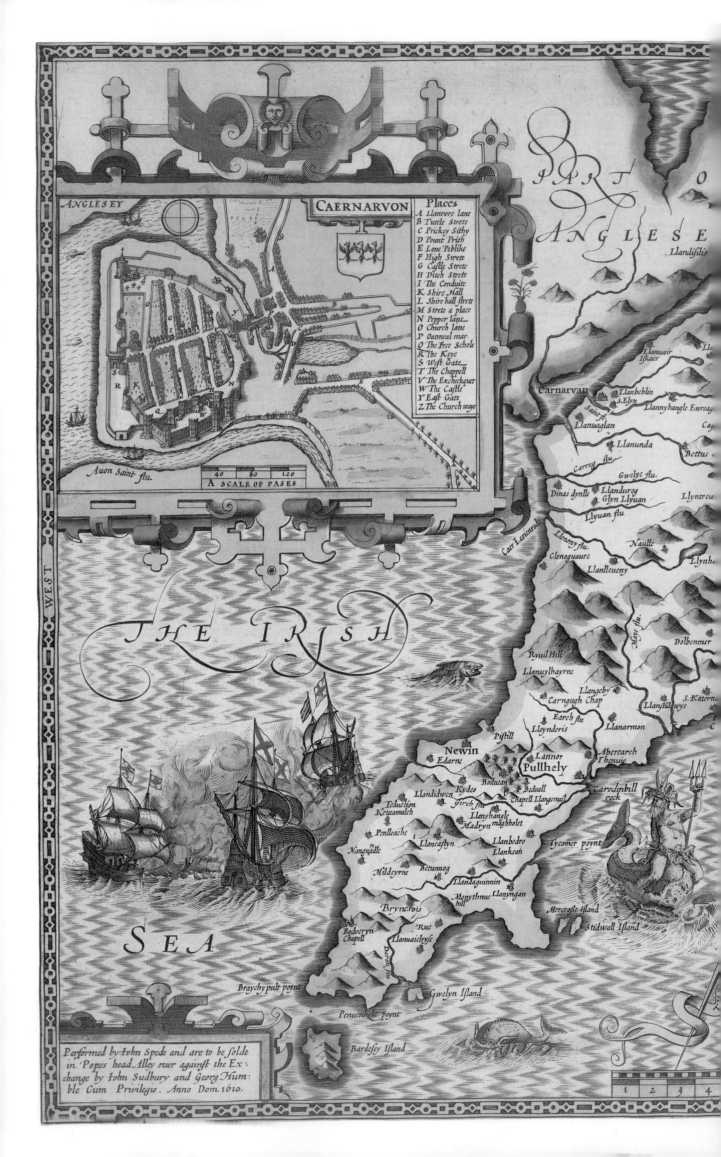

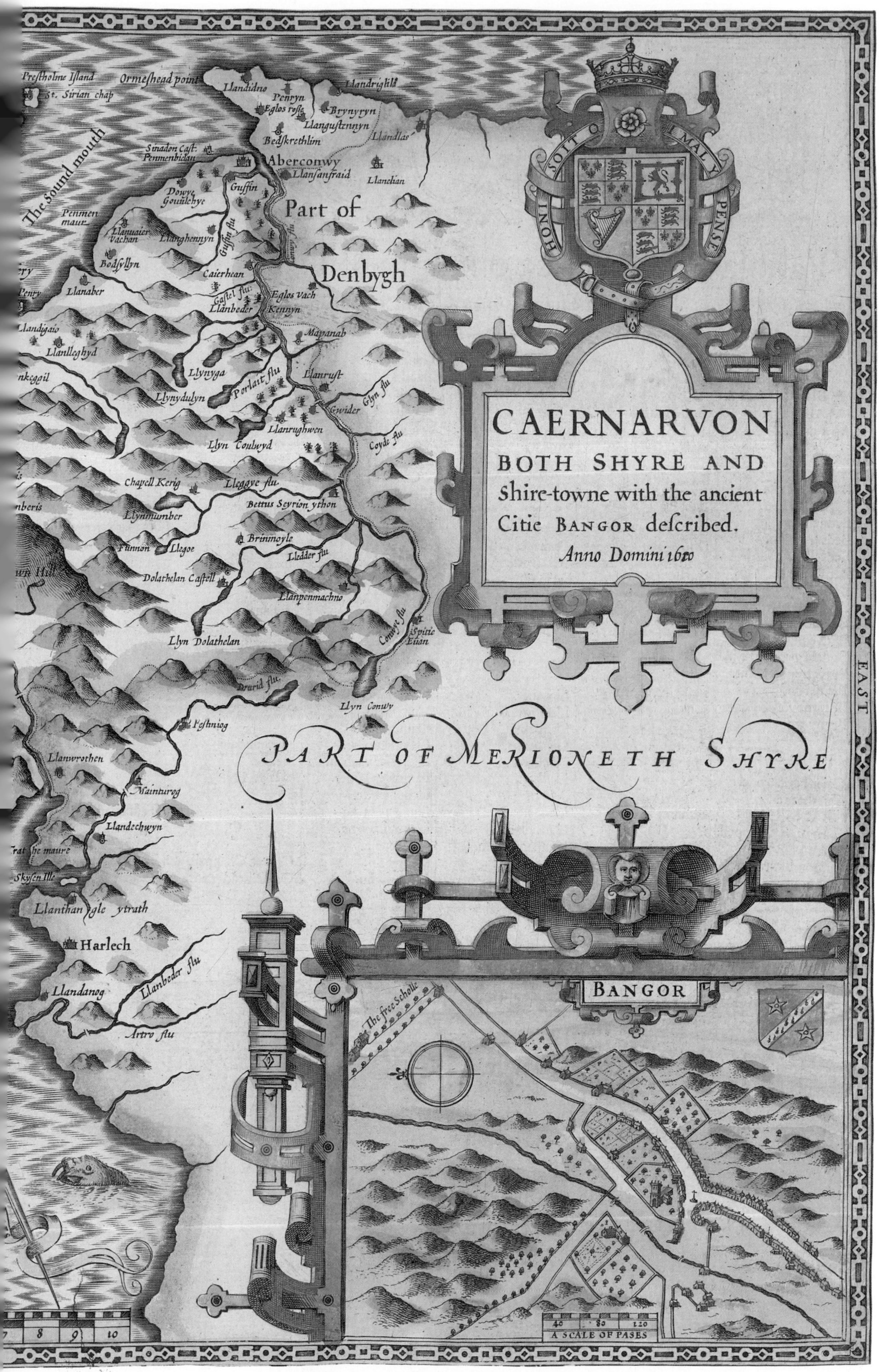
CAERNARVON
BOTH SHYRE AND
Shire-towne with the ancient
Citie BANGOR described.
Anno Domini 1610
HONI SOIT Q MAL Y PENSE
PART OF MERIONETH SHYRE
Part of
Denbygh
BANGOR
The free Scholl
A SCALE OF PASES
40 80 120
7 8 9 10
EAST
The Sound mouth
Prestholme Island
St. Sirian chap
Ormeshead point
Llandidno
Penryn
Eglos rosse
Brynyryn
Llandriglis
Llangustennyn
Llandlas
Bedskrethlim
Aberconwy
Llansanfraid
Llanelian
Sinadon Cast.
Penmenbidau
Guffin
Dowye Gouolchye
Penmen maur
Llanuaier Vachan
Llanghennyn
Guffin flu
Bodsyllyn
Caierhean
Llanaber
Gastel flu:
Llanbeder
Eglos Vach
Kennyn
Llandigaio
Llanlleghyd
Mapanab
Llynyga
Porlait flu
Llynydulyn
Elanrust
Gwider
Glyn flu
Llanrughwen
Llyn Coulwyd
Coyde flu
Chapell Kerig
Lleggye flu
Bettus Seyrion ython
Llynmumber
Brinnoyle
Funnon
Llegoe
Lledder flu
Dolathelan Castell
Llanpenmachno
Llyn Dolathelan
Conwye flu
Spitie Euan
Druid flu
Llyn Conwy
Festiniog
Llanwrothen
Mainturog
Llandechwyn
Trat the maure
Skysen Ille
Llanthanygle ytrath
Harlech
Llanbeder flu
Llandanog
Artro flu

'an ancient city ... many years ago . . . consumed by lightning and made so utterly desolate'. The county was still very much physically dominated by its four main castles, at Caernarfon, Conwy, Criccieth and Dolbadarn, and by its fifty-eight stone-built parish churches. In the more important towns there were timber-framed houses, but much of the population lived in small single-room cabins which were made from clay and turf and thatched with rushes, and which had neither windows nor chimneys.

With his antiquarian interests Speed noted in his commentary the remains of the Roman town of Segontium not far from Caernarfon, and the excavations conducted there by Edward I which had resulted in the discovery of the body of Constantius, the father of Constantine, which the King had transferred to Caernarfon. And remembering his contemporaries' near-obsession with royalty, he drew their attention to the birthplace of Edward II in the Eagle Tower at Caernarfon Castle. One item that he did not mention was whether he met at Clennau Sir William Maurice, who (following the Union of the Crowns in 1603) argued so forcefully for a truly united kingdom of Great Britain. Bishop William Morgan (d.1604), the translator of the Bible and the Psalms into Welsh, had been born at Penmachno.

The county map correctly shows Llandudno together with St Orme's Head to be part of Caernarfonshire, but through a mistake on the part of the watercolourist on the Denbighshire map, this area was erroneously given to Denbighshire. The map is completed with several delightful illustrations—a naval engagement between three vessels, Neptune, and various sea monsters.

Cardiganshire

Thomas Phaer, the crown solicitor to the Council in the Marches of Wales, who lived at Cilgerran just over the river Teifi from Carmarthenshire, described the county simply as very bare and mountainous. Its extensive wastes were grazed by cattle, and some sheep, and what little arable land could be cultivated was limited to the coastal river valleys and to common fields. Rocks and hazardous currents meant that (save for at Aberystwyth in the north and Cardigan in the south) the county had little benefit from the merchantmen sailing the Irish Sea or from fisheries. However, its many springs, streams and rivers abounded with freshwater fish, which (with duck and other sea-birds) augmented an otherwise poor diet for the country's meagre population.

The weaving of a coarse cloth known as 'cotton' supplemented the small incomes to be gained from farming. More important were veins of lead and copper in the uplands adjoining Montgomeryshire, Radnorshire and Breconshire, but lack of supplies of wood, charcoal or coal restricted what refinement of the ore could be done on the spot, and in the absence of good roads the full potential of this mineral wealth remained unrealized. The modesty of the churches and housing extant today from the Tudor and early Stuart periods further attests to Cardiganshire's overall poverty. The county's four market towns served only their localities.

As a county Cardiganshire had been created in response to the Statute of Rhuddlan of 1284, and together with Carmarthenshire it formed part of the Principality of South Wales, which was administered from Carmarthen. The Devereux family, both through its posts in the principality and its estates in the county, remained unrivalled in its political and social domination throughout the century preceding the publication of the *Theatre*, even in the aftermath of the 2nd Earl of Essex's rebellion of 1601. Given their importance in the English conquest of the region, the two royal castles at Aberystwyth and Cardigan, with their feudal honours and planted towns, should have played an important part in county life, but this was not the case. The town plan of Cardigan, based on a survey made by Speed himself, reveals a settlement with single-storey houses lining streets overshadowed by the castle and parish church; of Aberystwyth Speed made no mention in his commentary, even though it shared with Cardigan the distinction of being a venue for the county court, the assizes and the great sessions.

After the turmoils of the Middle Ages Cardiganshire had played a significant

CARDIGAN

Part of Merior

Part of Penbroke Shyre

SEA

PART OF THE IRISH

TREDROIR

HUNDRED

MOYTHEN

HUND

Jodocus Hondius Caelavit

The Scale of English miles

Aberdowye · Dovie flud

Llangüuelyn

Llanyhangle caftle qualter
S. Capel Kilvellen
Gogirthan
Umnu
Aberyfthwyth
Llanbadarnuau

Llannarhairn

LL

Llantyl

Llanthynol
Llarufted
Iftrad

Llanfanfrayde
Blaynpen

Llanbadern · Arthe flud
Aberarthe · Labaddarn · Llangy
Heuenyu
Kilkennyn
Capel Chryt · Llanachayryn · Nantgunlle
Llanynay · Killyaron · Treuilan · Cape Ll
Llanllohayrne · Llanarche · Iftrad · Talaferne · Llanlleir
Llantifilio · Debewid · Bettus Bletherus
MOYTHEN · Sylyan

Pennobadelth point · Llanrannok

Penbryn · Capel Kenon · Llanunnen · The Forest

Mounte · Aberporthe · Capel Llanfra · Capel Llantifilued · Llanwenok
Verwick · Blaynport · Kery flud · Llanumbethex
Cardigan Ifland · Tremayne · Bettus Euan · Tredraier · HUNDRED · Elanlloynye
Penkemmas poynt · Broyngwin · Llanuaier Treligon · Llangynllo · Tyvye flud
Cardigan · Kilgwyn · Llandyffil · Llanuaieralloyne
Llangoidmore · Peneralt · Llandeureog · Hedllandynye Banger
Ofcoidmortimer · Llandogway · Newea.memlyn
St. Dagnels · Capel Llang brid · Kennarth · Llangeler · Penbayre
Kilgarren · Manerdyue · Keuch flud

The Scale of Pafes
40   80   020   060

Tyuy flood

Mylle Brooke · High Street · South Street · Church Street · S. Mary · The Colledg

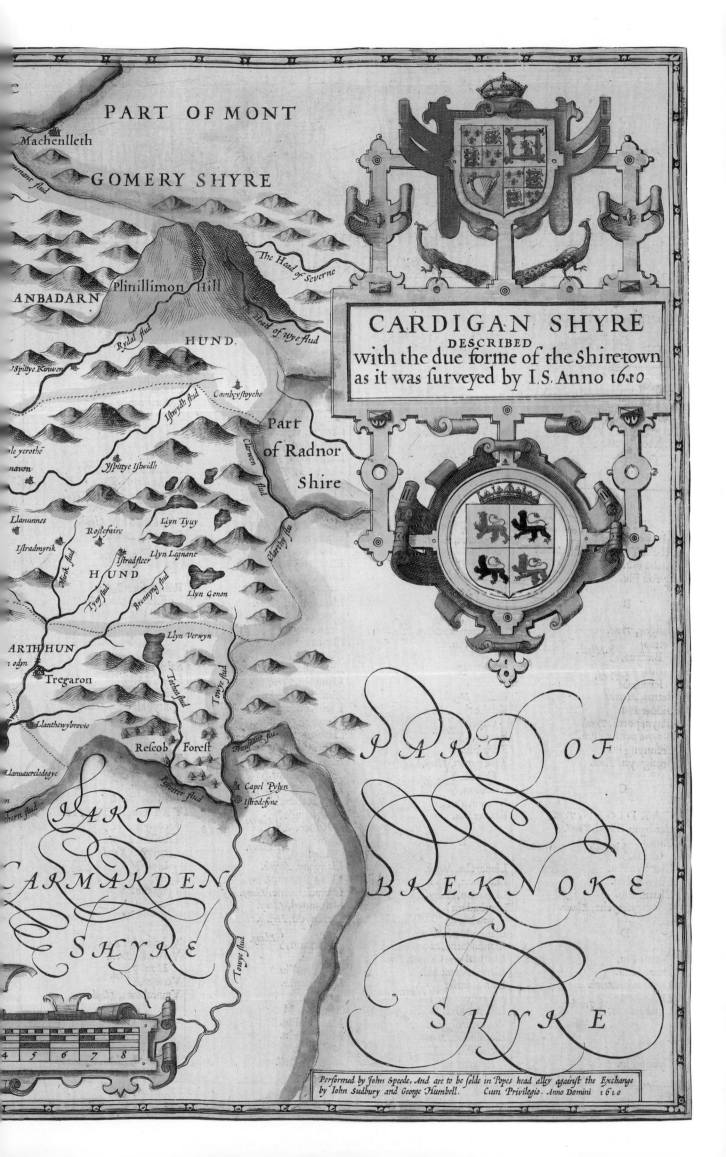

PART OF MONT

Machenlleth

GOMERY SHYRE

ANBADARN

Plinillimon Hill

The Head of Severne

Rydal flud

HUND.

Head of wye flud

Ispiltye Kinwen

Ifbwydh flud

Combeystoyche

Part

of Radnor

Shire

le yerothe

navon

Yspittye Ishwidh

Clarwen flud

Llyn Tyuy

Clartby fiu

Llanunnes

Roffefaire

Istradmyrik

Ifradfleer

Llyn Legnant

Mirik flud

Tyey flud

Brenueyng flud

Llyn Gonon

HUND

Llyn Verwyn

ARTH HUN

n odyn

Tregaron

Torhed flud

Towye flud

Llanthewybrevie

Refcob   Forest

Transfant fiu.

Llanwaereledogye

Egotter flud

Capel Pylyn

hern flud

Istrodefyne

CARDIGAN SHYRE
DESCRIBED
with the due forme of the Shiretown
as it was furveyed by I.S. Anno 1610

PART   OF

PART

CARMARDEN

SHYRE

Towy fiu

BREKNOKE

SHYRE

4   5   6   7   8

Performed by John Speede, And are to be folde in Popes head alley againft the Exchange by Iohn Sudbury and George Humbell.   Cum Privilegio. Anno Domini 1610

part in national affairs only in August 1485, when Henry of Richmond's expedition marched northwards through the county on its way to fight Richard III, but the support that the Lancastrian force got from Cardiganshire was so slight that it cannot have influenced the course of the victory gained at Bosworth.

The Cardiganshire map is one of Hondius's more pleasing achievements in that he resisted the temptation to add to the interest of the area by excessive embellishment (such as he went in for with Lancashire). In its chaste and controlled draughtsmanship and details, the map is as telling about Cardiganshire as is Speed in his equally spare commentary.

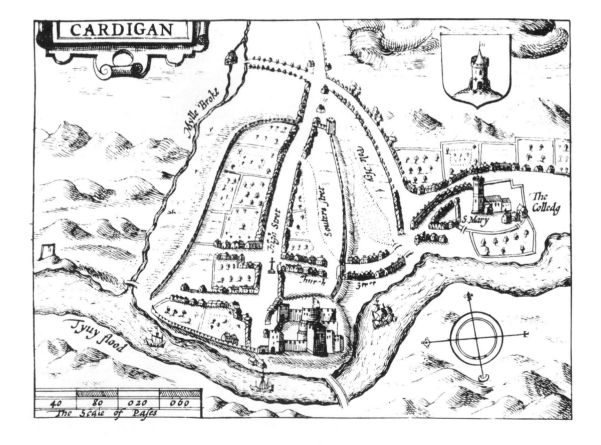

Carmarthenshire

'This shire', observed Speed, 'is not altogether so pestered with hills as her bordering neighbours are, and those that she hath [are] neither so high nor so thick, and therefore is better for corn and pasturage, yea, and in woods also, so that for victuals this county is very well stored.' The common fields of the Middle Ages had survived almost intact, and the process of enclosure which had transformed farming elsewhere in England and Wales had barely been started in Carmarthenshire by 1600. Livestock were bred for their carcases, hides and fleeces rather than for dairy produce, unlike those in Glamorganshire and Monmouthshire higher up the Bristol Channel; its market towns and lesser townships were centres for tanneries and related leathercrafts. The coarse cloth known as 'cotton' was made both in the urban areas and in the isolated farmhouses, and John Leland was impressed by the number of tucking mills for the final dressing of the cloth. Fish, both fresh- and salt-water, provided employment and supplemented diet, the salmon being 'of such greatness and plenty as no place is better furnished'; and duck and other sea-birds were also caught. There were also seams of coal at Llanelli and inland which, when mined and burnt, produced less acrid smoke and dirt than Northumbrian or Durham coal; however, the cost of transporting it to London prevented it from replacing English coal as the main supply for the capital. Silting along the coast was more problematic and economically harmful to Carmarthen and neighbouring ports than to their Glamorgan counterparts, and Carmarthenshire took little part in the extensive trade along the Welsh coast.

Carmarthenshire had been one of the original Welsh counties set up in 1284 and, together with Cardiganshire to its north-west, it formed the Principality of South Wales, Carmarthen being not only the county town for Carmarthenshire but also the administrative centre for the principality, with a chancery and treasury of its own. As can be seen from the aerial view, the modest-sized town of Carmarthen was dominated by a castle guarding the stone bridge across the river Towy and its quays with their shipping: the importance of the town to the region can be gauged from the existence there of a school, which after being maintained during the Reformation by the public-spirited precentor of St David's, lapsed before being re-established in 1576 as the Queen Elizabeth Grammar School. Although Speed found Carmarthen 'pleasantly situated', like many readers of the *Theatre* he was more interested in its being the reputed birthplace of Merlin, and thus associated indirectly with King Arthur, the

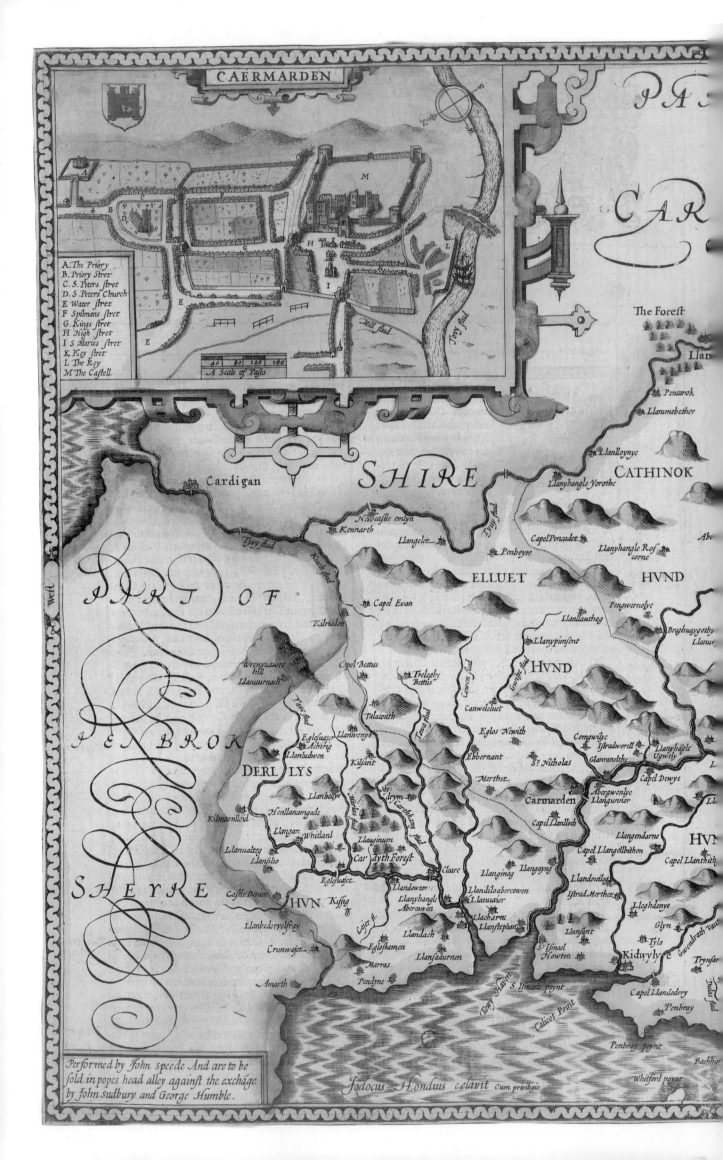

CAERMARDEN

A. The Priory
B. Priory stret
C. S. Peters stret
D. S. Peters Church
E. Water stret
F. Spilmans stret
G. Kings stret
H. High stret
I S Maries stret
K. Key stret
L The Key
M The Castell

A Scale of Pases
40   80   120   160

PA

CAR

The Forest

Llan

Pencarok

Llanumthether

Llanlloynye

Cardigan

SHIRE

CATHINOK

Llanyhangle Yorothe

Newcastle emlyn

Kennarth

Tywy flud

Capel Pencader

Llangeler

Llanyhangle Ros corne

Abe

Penheyns

ELLUET

HVND

Tywy flud

Keach flud

Pengwernolye

Capel Evan

Llanllauthog

Broghuaygothy

Kilriaden

Llanypunsont

Llanur

PART OF

HVND

Wrenyuawer hill
Llanuurnach

Capel Bettus

Trelegby Bettus

Cowyn flud

Canweleuet

Talacouth

Eglos Newith

Comgwilye

Istradworell

Llanyhagle Ugwely

Taw flud

Eglesuaier Achirig

Llanwenys

Llanludwen

Kilsant

Ebbernant

St. Nicholas

Glanranelthe

Capel Dewye

PENBROK

DERLLYS

My drym

Merther

Carmarden

Abergwenlye
Llangunnor

Llanheare

Marlas flud

Carthkay flud

Capel Llanlloch

Henllanamgade

Llangan

Whitlanl

Llauginum

Llangendarne

HVN

Kilmaenlloid

Car dyth Forest

Cloare

Capel Llangellbrithon

Capel Llanthith

Llanualtg

Llansilio

Eglesuaier

Llandewror

Llaniwaier

Llanginog

Llangayng

Llandoutlog

Istrad Merther

SHEYRE

Castle Deran

HVN Kissg

Cajer fl.

Llanyhangle
Abrcowen

Llandilo abercowen
Llanuaier

Llacharne
Llanstephan

Lleghdenye

Glyn

Llanbederyelfray

Llandach

Llansant

Tylo

Crunwajer

Egloskemen

Llansadurnen

St Ismael
Hawton

Kidwyly

Trynsa

Marras

Amarth

Pendyne

Calicot Point

Capel Llandedry

S. Ismaels poynt

Tywy Haven

Penbray

Penbray poynt

Bachhar

Performed by John speede And are to be
sold in popes head alley against the exchäge
by John sudbury and George Humble.

Jodocus Hondius cælavit   Cum privilegio

Whitford povnt

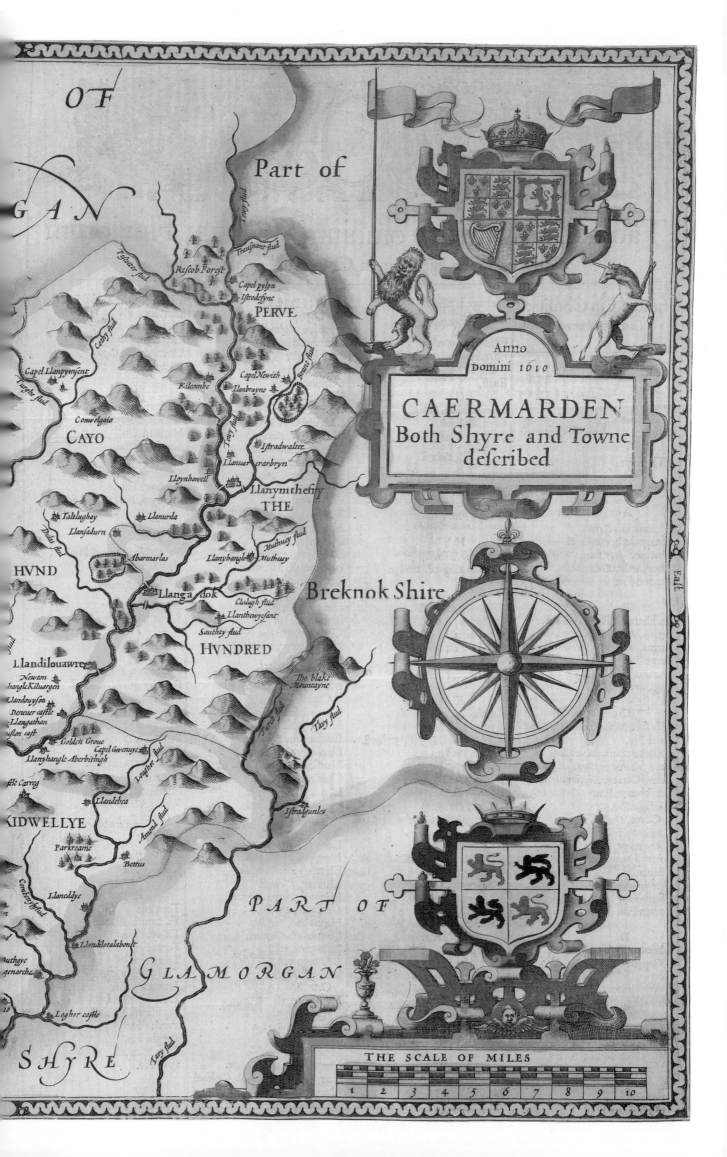

OF

GAN

Part of

Part of

Anno
Domini 1610

CAERMARDEN
Both Shyre and Towne
described

Eaft

Tyway flud
Traufnant flud
Refcob Forest
Capel pylyn
Iftradefyne
PERVE
Tyweter flud
Corby flud
Brance flud
Capel Llanpymfent
Tugghe flud
Kilcombe
Capel Newith
Llanbrayne
Conwelgaio
CAYO
Iftradwalter
Tywy flud
Llanuar erarbryn
Lloynhowell
Llanymthefry
Llanurda
THE
Taltlughay
Muthuey flud
Llanfadurn
Dulas flud
Abarmarlas
Llanyhangle
Muthuey
Breknok Shire
HVND
Llang a dok
Cleluyh flud
Llanthewyefant
Sauthey flud
HVNDRED
Llandilouawrey
Newton
hangle Kiluargen
The blake
Mountayne
Llandouyfon
Deneuer castle
Jarth flud
Tavy flud
Llangathan
uflon cast
Goldch Groue
Capel Gwenuyes
Loughor flud
Llanyhangle Aberbrithigh
fle Carreg
Llandebea
Amand flud
KIDWELLYE
Iftradgunles
Parkreame
Bettus
PART OF
Llaneddyc
Combenyfyflud
genarche
Llandilotalabonft
GLAMORGAN
uthgye
Loghor castle
Tavy flud

SHYRE

THE SCALE OF MILES

| 1 | 2 | 3 | 4 | 5 | 6 | 7 | 8 | 9 | 10 |

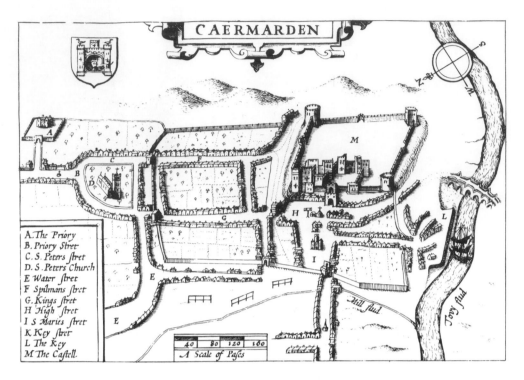

legendary forebear of the Tudor dynasty. The other towns in the county were smaller than Carmarthen, and depended for their existence largely upon the Duchy of Lancaster. Apart from the castle at Carmarthen, the county's ten castles were in poor condition when surveyed for James I.

Although stone was the material most favoured for castles, parish churches and manor houses, timber was more commonly used in Carmarthenshire than in most of Wales. Interestingly, the houses built from timber up to the seventeenth century were rarely timber-framed, but more conservatively made of crucks, where whole trees were propped together in pairs and the intervening space infilled with timber and wattle and daub. If Carmarthenshire lacks the splendid domestic dwellings of the Glamorganshire gentle families, and was notorious at the time for brawling and disorder, two of its residents in the sixteenth century deserve to be remembered. Gruffydd Done was Carmarthenshire born and bred, whereas Thomas Phaer was a Norfolk man who became crown solicitor to the Council in the Marches of Wales. Done was a friend of the antiquary John Leland, and of the translator of the New Testament into Welsh, William Salesbury, both of whom visited him at Merthyr Ystrad near Kidwelli: not only was he a friend of scholars, he was a patron of bards, and of more importance for history at the Dissolution of the Monasteries he assembled a collection of books, mainly in Welsh, which eventually became the nucleus of the National Library of Wales. Phaer's impact was more immediate, as he began the first translation into English of the *Aeneid*, completing the first five books by his death in 1560: Phaer's translation finished by William Wightsman was the one familiar to all English readers until replaced in popularity long after the publication of the *Theatre*.

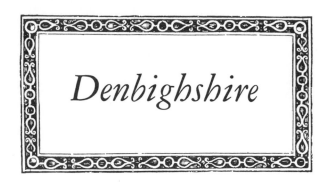

Denbighshire

Denbighshire was the most northerly of the five new Welsh counties created in 1536, being formed by a fusion of the medieval lordships of Denbigh and Ruthin in Gwynedd and those of Bromfield-and-Yale and Chirk in Powys. This fusion was reflected administratively in that the county court had two venues, Denbigh 'the head and shire town' in the west, and Wrexham in the east; geographically, rivers in Gwynedd flowed directly into the Irish Sea while those in Powys fed eastwards into either the Dee or the Severn.

Its valleys, particularly the broad and long Vale of Clwyd, were luscious farmland, William Camden rhapsodizing on the vale's 'green meadows, yellow cornfields and fair houses, standing thick, and many beautiful churches', giving 'wonderful great contentment to such as behold from above'. Speed more prosaically called the vale 'beautiful and pleasant' and gave its dimensions as seventeen miles long by five broad. On either side of the vale there were uplands where Nature was 'very sparing niggard of her favours' but where rye could be grown 'in such plenty as is hardly to be believed', provided the fields had the ashes from burnt turves well ploughed in. The higher hills were bare of trees and shrubs but supported herds of cattle, sheep and goats. And the area around Wrexham was already popularly known as the 'Mines' on account of its many collieries.

Although Denbighshire was thinly populated in the west with only isolated farmhouses, it was one of the more populous and prosperous counties in Wales, its trio of market towns—Denbigh, Ruthin and Wrexham—contrasting with the generality of mean and poor townships elsewhere. At Denbigh the medieval town with its castle and walled fortifications on a hillside had long been deserted in favour of a more comfortable settlement in the valley beneath the hill, where a community of clothiers flourished. The process of building lavish perpendicular parish churches—such as can be seen at Gresford and Llanfarchel—had continued well into the sixteenth century, long after it had been given up in England. Queen Elizabeth's favourite, the Earl of Leicester, while Lord of Denbigh, started to build a monumental church at Denbigh. This church was the first to be built on a new site since the Reformation and reflected current Protestant needs. It is thought to have been meant for a cathedral on the removal of the bishopric from the less convenient St Asaph in Flintshire. Local resentment against Leicester brought the work to a standstill before his death in 1588, and the incomplete shell of

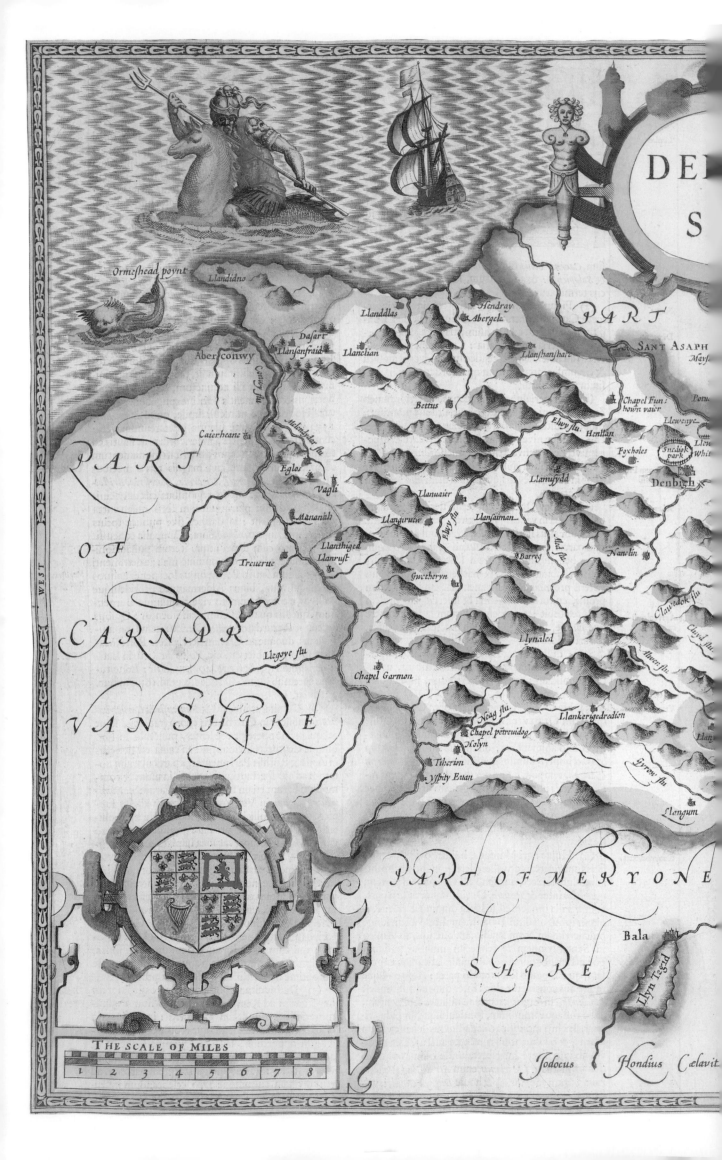

Ormeshead poynt
Llandidno

DE
S

PART

SANT ASAPH
Mayf

Llanddlas
Hendray
Abergele

Dasart
Llansanfraid
Llanclian
Llanshansha?e

Aber conwy
Conwy flu

Chapel Fun:
hown vaier
Potu

Bettus

Elwy flu. Henllan
Llewenye

Caierheane
Foxholes
Sncidiok
park
Llew
Whit

Melenbhar flu
Llanuydd
Eglos
Denbigh
Vagli

Llanuaier

PART
Llangiruew
Elwy flu
Llansaiman

Mananih
Mad flu
Nanolin

OF
Llanthiged
Llanruft
Barreg

Treuerue
Gwetheryn

Clawedok flu
Clwyd flu

CARNAR
Llynaled
Riuer flu

Llegoye flu
Chapel Garmon

VANSHIRE
Noag flu.
Llankerigedrodion

Chapel petreuidog
Holyn
Gyrow flu
Llan

Tiherion
Yspity Euan
Llangum

PART OF MERYONE

Bala
SHIRE
Llyn Tegid

WEST

THE SCALE OF MILES
| 1 | 2 | 3 | 4 | 5 | 6 | 7 | 8 |

DENBIGH

A. Henllan stret
B. Chappell Lane
C. Sandy Lane
D. High Stret
E. Lower Stret
F. Loue Lane
G. Parke Lane
H. Sowter Lane
I. The Chappell
K. The Abbey
L. The new church
M. Lenton Poole
N. The Castle
P. The way to y Church

40   80   120   160
A Scale of pases

OF

Wheler flu
Llangwiuen
Llanganhaual
nu nnis Llanhichian
hinbiu   Llanuerres
ward   Llanbi
der   Moyluiuule hill
thin   Bathauern
arog   Llaruth Llanarmon
Veneghtid   Llauaier   Lleweny flu
canok   Heghyn flu
n flu   Llanelidan   Men Bachan flu
en

FLYNT

Alen flu.

SHIRE

Tagidog flu
Almere
Gresford   Holt park   Holt cast
Common Wood
Abenbury
Wrexham   Iscoid chapel
Gwenurow flu
Bers   Chap. Moynglathe   Hauotwern
Clacuedok flu   Markwiell
Place Cadogan

PART OF CHESHIRE

Worthenbury

PART OF

Bodederis
Llandegley
Egluyseg
Breynegloys
Castell Denas brayn   Ru abon
Llanegwast Abbey   Bystok
Gowyeddeluerne

SHROP   SHIRE

Llandisllio in Dulouree   Llangolleh
Pergwerne
Newhall   Chirk
Chirk Castle

Langer

Llanfanfraid in Glyn

Kenlet flu
Selattyn

Llanarmon Defrune Keriog
Keriog flu   Llansyllyn
Llanarmon   Llancadwalatir
Ryader flu   Place ycha
Llanyader Amoughnant   Llangedwin
Fauat flu

Part of Montgomery Shire

Performed by Iohn Speede and are to be solde in Popes head
Alley against the exchange by Iohn Sudbury and George Hum:
ble. Cum Priuilegio.   Anno Domini 1610

EAST

the church can be seen in Speed's town plan of Denbigh more or less as it survives today. For the town-dwellers and smallholders there was fine timber-framed building in the east, and good-quality stone-building throughout the county.

Although Welsh society was no less male-dominated than English society, Denbighshire had in it a counterpart to Bess of Hardwick in Derbyshire in the person of Catherine of Berain. A cousin and ward of Queen Elizabeth, a substantial heiress, and a forceful personality, she had a matrimonial career paralleling Bess of Hardwick's, marrying in succession John Salusbury of Lleweni, Sir Richard Clough, Maurice Wynn of Gwydir, and Edward Thelwall. Of her four husbands only Clough was wealthier than she, having been a factor to Sir Thomas Gresham at Antwerp, and together they embarked on a spate of house-construction, at Berain and Plas Clough on the outskirts of Denbigh, the latter a remarkable house reflecting Clough's time abroad in the Netherlands and for Wales innovatory for its renaissance symmetry and its use of brick. When Catherine died in 1591 and was buried near Berain at Llanefydd, she was mourned officially as a patroness of the arts by local bards, but by her long-suffering family and neighbours, her death was greeted with unfeigned relief. At Plas Teg, near Hope, Sir John Trevor, Surveyor to the Navy, was building an equally distinctive lodge house in the most up-to-date Jacobean style about the time of the publication of the *Theatre*.

The antiquary Humphrey Lhuyd (d.1568) had been introduced to the Antwerp publisher Abraham Ortelius through Sir Richard Clough, his neighbour at Denbigh, and had sent Ortelius a map of Wales which was later incorporated in the 1573 edition of the *Theatrum Orbis Terrarum*. Speed's own work for the region, however, did not rest on Lhuyd's mapping, but on the slightly later surveying of Christopher Saxton.

Flintshire

Unlike the adjoining Welsh county of Denbighshire, Flintshire owed its origin to an order of Edward I's made while he was staying at Rhuddlan in 1284. Flintshire was made up of two contrasting parts, the larger being the length of the Clwyd hills bounded by the coastal plain of the Dee estuary, and the smaller detached enclave of Maelor Saesneg, or English Maelor, with its gentle farming landscape, separated from the main part by a tongue of Denbighshire known as Maelor Gymraeg, or Welsh Maelor. The areas adjoining Cheshire and Shropshire were intensively cultivated, but with its poor soil and sparse woodland the county was largely given over to dairy farming, milk, butter and cheese being produced in plenty. A speciality of the area was honey, from which 'a pleasant wine in colour like (in taste not much unlike) unto muscandine' was made and called 'matheglin'. Fishing was a major occupation in the towns along the Dee, but silting in the estuary and the lack of good harbours on the north coast overlooking the Irish Sea meant that the county had little benefit from the North Welsh coastal trade or from shipping going to Ireland. Reclamation of marshland and mudbanks in the Dee was well under way, and since Speed's day this stretch of coast has been altered more significantly than any other of equal length in Wales. Some silver had formerly been mined near Holywell, but this deposit had never been of as much value to local landowners (such as the Mostyns, Stanleys, Masseys, Pulestons and Hanmers) as the seams of coal and lead. Even these did not yield much income until the invention of new techniques in mining and smelting during the course of the seventeenth century.

Although thinly populated, Flintshire was a relatively prosperous county, and up to the Reformation its inhabitants invested their wealth in a spate of parish-church building only exceeded by the larger and more magnificent series in Denbighshire. However, the churches built at Holt and Mold stand comparison with their Denbighshire counterparts. The mania for prodigious houses that affected the kingdom during Elizabeth's reign left Flintshire untouched, but for one exception, now largely demolished, at Bach-y-graig near Tremeirchon, where Sir Richard Clough and his wife Catherine of Berain built a brick house round three sides of a court reflecting the mannerist taste of Antwerp where Clough had made his fortune. But, for most visitors Flintshire was a series of isolated houses and of medieval castles in disrepair.

Speed and his contemporaries knew Flintshire for two places, both with

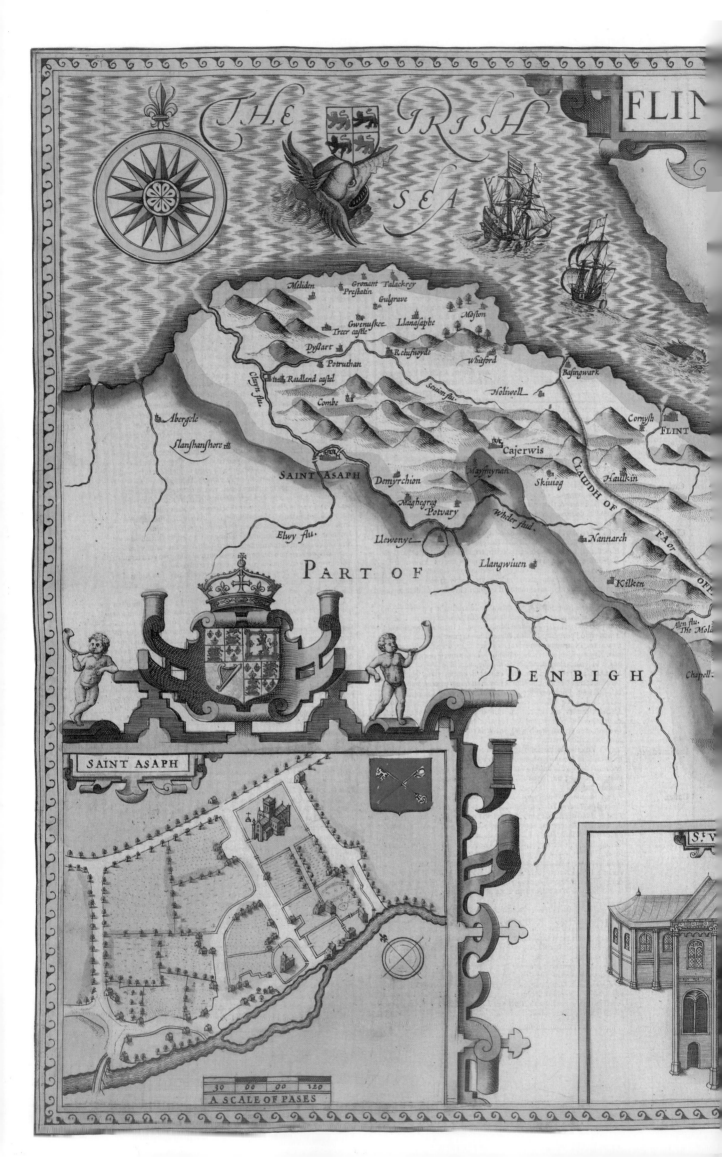

THE IRISH SEA

FLINT

Meliden
Gronant Talackrey
Preſtatin
Gulgrave
Gwenuſker Llanaſaphe
Moſton
Treer caſtle
Dyſſart
Rehuſioyde
Whitford
Cleyn flu.
Rudland caſtel
Seriton flu.
Basingwark
Combe
Holiwell
Cornyſh
Abergele
FLINT
Slanſhanſhore
Cajerwis
Haulkin
SAINT ASAPH
Demyrchion
Mayſmynan
Skiuiog
CLAUDH OF
Maghegreg
Potvary
Wheler flud.
FAOR
Elwy flu.
Nannarch
OF
Llewenye
PART OF
Llangwiuen
Kilken
Alen flu.
The Mola

DENBIGH
Chapell.

SAINT ASAPH

S: V

30   00   00   120
A SCALE OF PASES

HIRE

PART OF CHES

or Dee flu

W CHESTER

Harden Caſt.
Yowley Hall
Bruerton
Old parke
Broughton
Dodleſton
Kinnerton
Horsheath
Tulfonl
Burton
Darland &rene
Alen
Treucalen
Merford
Gresford
Toglog flu
Holt Caſt
Farndon

SHIRE

FLINT

A SCALE OF PASES
30   60   90   120

At Flint Caſtle king R. 2 was ſurpriſed by the falſhode of L. Henry Percye Earle
of Northumberland, and betrayed into the handes of Henry Bullingbrook Duke of Lan:
caſter, whence he was conveyed as priſoner to London: comitted to the Tower: depoſed,
and thence ſent to Leedes Caſtle in Kent, laſtly to Pomſord and there murdered.
Anno 1400. Febr. 13

Shoklidge

SHIRI

Wrexham

Worthenbury
Old Caſt.
Willyngton
Nether
Droitwiche
Bangor
Emher
Hall
Over Droitwiche
Eſcoyde Hall
Whitwell Chap
Whitchurche
Fens Hall

VELL

PART OF FLINT-SHIRE

PART OF

Orton Madok
Penley Chap
Hanmere

Chap aidleſton
Haulton
Bottesley

SHROP
Welſhe Hamton
Elſmere
SHIRE

THE SCALE OF MILES
1   2   3   4   5   6   7   8

Performed by Iohn Speede, are to be
ſold in Popes-head alley againſt the Exchãge
by John Sudbury and George Humbell
Iodocus Hondius Cælavit Cum Privilegio. 1610

royal connections. The castle and town of Flint on the Dee estuary, and the subject of the ground plan in the top right-hand corner of the county map, had been the scene of the deposition of Richard II after his return from Ireland in 1399: this episode had been related at length in chronicles from Froissart onwards, but interest in it had been revived with the recent performances of William Shakespeare's play *Richard II*, in which the inner bailey of the castle is described by the King as the 'base court, where kings grow base'. During the Earl of Essex's revolt in 1601, Queen Elizabeth had specifically banned the play as a possible incentive to rebels. A favourite of the Queen's until 1601, Essex had journeyed through the county at the start of his ill-fated appointment in Ireland, and his charismatic personality had left an impression locally not forgotten by the time of the publication of the *Theatre*.

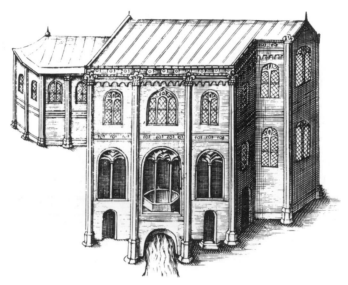

At Holywell, the spring at St Winefride's Well marked the site of the reputed martyrdom of St Winefride 'for resisting the advances of a local prince' and her miraculous restoration to life. The well had been restored and rebuilt by Margaret Beaufort, Countess of Richmond and mother of Henry VII, who was a paragon of piety and learning, and it consisted of a well-chamber with a chapel above, both built in the perpendicular style. When Speed visited the well, the building had not been desecrated, although some of the worst excesses of pre-Tridentine Catholicism had been removed. Speed went on: 'To this fountain pilgrims are accustomed to repair in their zealous, but blind devotion; and divers others resort to bathe in, holding firmly that the water is of much virtue.' Not surprisingly, Flintshire was one of the areas most responsive to the sending of seminary priests, and against such Roman Catholic enthusiasm the bishop of St Asaph, with an inadequate income and without the backing of local families, had little hope of securing the county for Protestantism. Thus, Speed's choice of ground plans of Flint and St Asaph and of a depiction of St Winefride's Well as embellishments for the county map were not only apt, they were more telling than most of his choices elsewhere.

Glamorganshire

Glamorganshire was one of the wealthiest and most populous areas in Wales. Although its uplands, and the poor soil in the Vale of Glamorgan and the Gower Peninsula, were not well suited to farming, the introduction of liming during the Tudor period had improved local grain production, and increased agricultural profits from wheat, oats, barley and rye had led to a belated start in enclosing the common fields of the villages along the Bristol Channel coast. The hills and woodlands of Glamorganshire were well suited to deer which roamed freely, and to herds of cattle, sheep and goats which were tended, and the celebrated dairy produce from these herds was shipped from ports such as Oxwich, Swansea and Porteynon across the Channel to Devonshire and Cornwall, along the Welsh coast as far as Anglesey, or over St George's Channel to Ireland. Both Leland and Speed remarked on the number of streams, brooks and rivers, 'most clear springing waters through the valleys trickling', the quantity of fish in them (notably the salmon to be caught in the river Tawe), and the impossibility of crossing them downstream if there were no bridges or ferries available. Glamorgan was well endowed with seams of coal and iron, which had long been mined, and at Aberdulais there were veins of copper exploited by the Mines Royal since the reign of Elizabeth and smelted in the furnaces and forges of Neath. Unfortunately, this general prosperity and its continuance were threatened by the seemingly irreversible silting of the marine approaches to the Glamorganshire ports, and by the lack of good roads as an alternative means of transport.

With its extensive coastline and many harbours, Glamorganshire was a paradise for smugglers. It was also prone to raids from Welsh and Irish pirates. Thus, unlike other coastal areas where medieval castles had fallen into disrepair through lack of use, Glamorganshire's littoral castles remained occupied and continued to serve their original function as bases to protect their localities: inland the tale was somewhat different, Speed observing of the castles there that 'times and storms have devoured the most'. During the mid-sixteenth century Oxwich Castle was modified and extended by Sir Rhys Mansell and his son, who also converted Margam Abbey into a private house. The comfort and affluence of Oxwich and Margam were not unique to the Mansells, the Bassetts remodelling Beaupre, the Herberts Llanmihangel Place and Neath Abbey, and the Matthews St Fagans equally ambitiously, and in a similar style, mixing late gothic increasingly with early classical architecture. The culmination

CARDYFE.

A. Smithes stret
B. Shomakers stret
C. West Stret
D. Back stret
E. Hummanbye stret
F. St Iohns stret
G. High stret
H. North stret
K. Working stret
L. Porrag stret
M. Frogg Lane
N. St Iohns Church
O. Castell Lane
P. Towne howse
Q. Duke Stret
R. The pootes Releife.

Shire hall

Castell

Black fryers

West Gate

The Key

East Gate   Cokkerton stret

The Spitle

THE SCALE OF PASES
40   80   120   160   200   240

S. Maryes

PART   OF   CARMAR DENSHEYRE

WEST

Bettus

LLAN

Ystradguin.

Capel Kr
NE

Llaneddye   GEVELACH

Llangnis   Kelibebilth

Tawye fud

Dulghe fud

Chelaugh fud

Cadoxtown

Llandilo
Talabont

Llangenarth

Llansamled   Neath Abbay   Llany

Neath
HUN.

Thhle fud

Llatygoyuelach
HUND

Coidfrank
Forest

Briton Ferye
Michael

Bagland

Llanelthye

Noghor Castle

S. Iohns

Swansey

Bachhannis Iflad
Burra flu

SWANZEY HUND

Llannyenwere

Whitford poynt

Ab

S. Kenetts Chap.

Wchley

Pengwern

Llammadok
Cheriton

Llanridien

Ilston

Pennarth

Bishopston

Oystermouth cast.

Mumbles poynt

The Holme

Llangenyth

Park Brewis

Penmayne

Penrife

Nicholas
towne

Pennarth
Cast

Iackinston

Roffilye

WEST GOWRE

Rinolston

Knolston

Llanddewye
cast

Oxwiche

Pennarth point

Wormeshead poyt

Porthynon

Oxwich poynt

Ioudocus Hondius Cælauit

of this spate of building, which was not restricted to the more prosperous gentle families, was perhaps the Jacobean lodge-house or castle started at Rhiwperra by Sir Thomas Morgan not long after the publication of the *Theatre*: at Rhiwperra serious defence no longer counted, all elements of castellation being contrived for effect and decidedly romantic. Hand in hand with this building went the enlargement of deer-parks, both for leisure and as symbols of status and wealth, or even their creation at Beaupre, Nash, Radyr and Y Fan, at a time when many English examples were being disparked. One unfortunate consequence of the leading families' prosperity was a tendency to carry their rivalries to extremes, and to quarrel, their feuds sometimes lasting over several generations and erupting into occasional shows of brutality and force and into litigation. The most notorious incident of this sort occurred at Oxwich in 1557 when the Mansells contested Sir George Herbert's right to the cargo from a wreck, though it is unlikely that the blood-letting, rape and murder so graphically described by the plaintiffs and defendants in the ensuing lawsuit actually took place, these being largely fictions to advance the cause of either side in the legal proceedings. There was undoubtedly ill-feeling and trouble, but allegations as to their full extent should no more be trusted for Glamorgan than for the rest of Wales in the Tudor and early Stuart periods.

Speed, who was not normally interested in monuments dating from the Dark Ages, was impressed by the early Christian memorial stones and crosses in the neighbourhood of Margam, and recorded the local superstition that anyone who could read and understand the inscriptions written in Ogham should shortly afterwards die. He embellished the county map with ground plans of the shire town of Cardiff and of the cathedral city of Llandaff, the two plans bearing out his comments on Cardiff as 'the fairest town of all south Wales' with a castle in good repair, town walls and a quay, and on Llandaff 'wherein is a castle and a cathedral church dedicated to St Talean, bishop of the same, without any other memorable matter worthy the speaking of'.

Merionethshire

Merionethshire was undeniably the poorest and most desolate county in England and Wales. And Speed, who invariably found some feature to commend in each county, was hard put to do so in this case. He found it a 'rough' place, and with few metalled roads and fewer bridges 'unpleasant to see'. He continued: 'The air for great pleasure, nor the soil for great profit, I cannot greatly recommend, unless it be for the many and mighty great winds, that for the most part therein do rage.' With farmland in the valleys barely yielding enough to subsist on, and with woodland sparse and restricted to the neighbourhoods of Llanegryn, Dolgellau and Machynlleth, what little wealth there was derived from the 'fruitful flocks of sheep, besides neat [oxen] and other cattle' that grazed the country's rugged uplands and mountains in abundance. As with other poor areas in Wales freshwater fish played a vital part in diet, and despite the indifferent anchorages along the coast deep-sea fishing, particularly for herring, was important: but the greater part of the profits from herrings went to trawlermen coming from a distance. The absence of towns, never much of a feature of the Welsh countryside, was more apparent in Merionethshire than elsewhere, and Speed noted how even the county's three market towns of Bala, Dolgellau and Harlech had no 'stately buildings' and little more than local goods available. Of the three market towns, Harlech was the most important, being the county town, but as can be seen from the town plan it consisted of no more than the Edwardian castle commanding the coastline, a scatter of modest-sized houses and a chapel neglected 'and without use'. The unhappy observation in regard to the church at Harlech also applied to well over half the county's thirty-seven parish churches and their dependent chapels of ease. Except for some ironworkings, Merionethshire had no industry. Like other Englishmen who had visited the county earlier, Speed was depressed by what he saw.

Not everything was uniformly bad, however. By the accession of James I, Merionethshire did not suffer much from the thieving and banditry that was endemic to Wales, but this had not always been the case. At the Union the hundred of Mawddwy, which abutted on Montgomeryshire in the south-west, was terrorized by a gang called the red-haired brigands of Mawddwy. Such was their lawlessness that the Council in the Marches singled out Merionethshire for special attention, but nothing was achieved until the early 1550s when two local magistrates, Lewis ab Owen of Plas-yn-dre and John Wynn

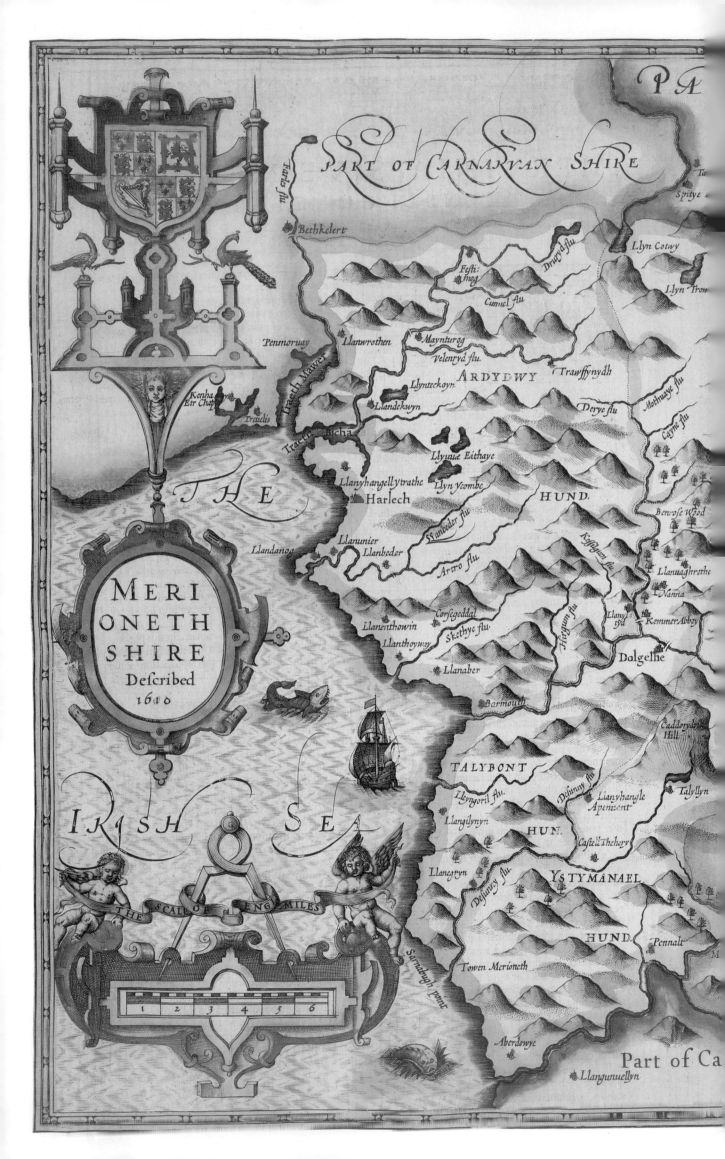

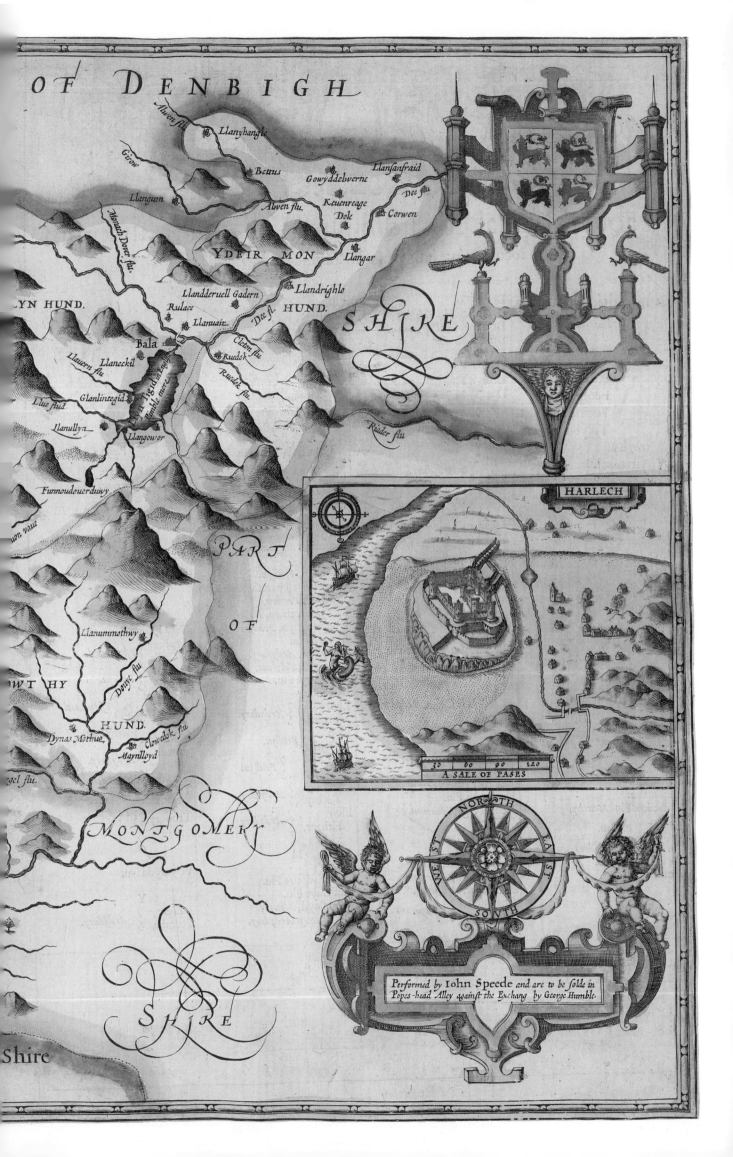

OF DENBIGH

Alwen flu.
Llanyhangle
Bettus
Gowyddelwerne
Llansanfraid
Girow
Llangunn
Alwen flu.
Keuenreage
Dole
Dee flu
Corwen
YDEIR MON
Llangar
Monach Dover flu.
LYN HUND.
Llandderuell Gadern
Llandrighlo
Rulace
HUND.
Dee fl.
Llanuair
Bala
Cleten flu
Ruedok
Llauern flu
Llaneckil
Ruedok flu.
Glanlintegid
Llyn Tegid in englis humble mere
Llue flud
Llanullyn
Llangowor
Funnoudouerduvy

SHIRE

Rieder flu

PART

OF

Llanununothwy

OWTHY
Douye flu
HUND.
Dynas Mothue
Clowedok flu
Maynlloyd

MONTGOMERY

SHIRE

Shire

HARLECH

A SALE OF PASES
30   60   90   120

NORTH
WEST   EAST
SOUTH

Performed by Iohn Speede and are to be solde in
Popes-head Alley against the Exchang by George Humble.

ap Meredydd of Dolwyddelan, set themselves to put down the gang and succeeded in executing about eighty of them. The survivors vowed revenge on Owen, and late in 1555 they ambushed and murdered him while returning from business in Montgomeryshire, the spot being shown to the herald Lewis Dwnn on his visitation to Merionethshire nearly fifty years later. This appalling incident only served to strengthen the resolve to re-establish order in Mawddwy to the long-term benefit of the whole region.

Merionethshire was one of the earliest counties to be created in Wales, dating from 1284, and together with neighbouring Caernarfonshire and the Island of Anglesey it formed part of the Principality of North Wales, administered from Caernarfon.

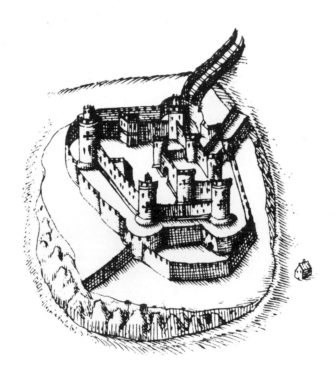

Montgomeryshire

Like other marcher counties, Montgomeryshire had been created a county only as recently as 1536, its boundaries being more or less co-terminous with the ancient Welsh kingdom of Powys or the medieval lordship of Montgomery which had succeeded it, and which belonged to the Crown as part of the Duchy of York. The Crown had long since lost whatever personal interest it had once had in the region, granting away its offices and lands to the interrelated families of Somerset and Herbert, and in 1605 it established the earldom of Montgomery in favour of Philip Herbert, a younger son of the Earl of Pembroke.

If Philip Herbert was something of an outsider, the same could not be said of his kinsfolk with castles at Powys and Montgomery. The fate of these two medieval fortresses was symptomatic of the adaptability, prosperity and vigour of the region in the sixteenth century. Both castles passed through a period of neglect, then in the 1590s Sir Edward Herbert built within the keep of Powys an open-air loggia with a long gallery above finished by painted wainscoting, plaster friezes and patterned ceilings. Meanwhile at Montgomery, deserted for a time in favour of a house at Blackhall, a namesake created Lord Herbert of Chirbury in 1610 built the aptly called New Buildings during the 1620s in the most up-to-date style. Lord Herbert was the personification of the renaissance courtier, being a philosopher, historian and diplomat, accomplished fencer, musician and horseman; he was also one of the earliest in this country to write an autobiography, but his modern fame probably rests on his image as a melancholy knight seeking the solace of the greenwood tree close to a trickling stream in Isaac Oliver's celebrated miniature painted not long after the issue of Speed's *Theatre*.

Montgomeryshire was a predominantly pastoral county with the Shropshire plain extending as a fertile promontory up the Severn valley among its outlying hills on the east, and with mountainous hills in the west (the chief being Plynlimon) which are the source of the Severn and other rivers. With its ancient forests, still thick with oak, its good pasture for cattle, horses and sheep, and its lush grasslands, the county justified its description as the Paradise of Wales: it was agriculturally prosperous, as the wealth of buildings of stone in the countryside and of timber in the towns testifies. However, the picture was changing, and in the course of the sixteenth century Montgomeryshire witnessed much enclosure and encroachment of wood and forest, of moorland waste and mountain pasture, by Welshmen anxious to increase their turnover:

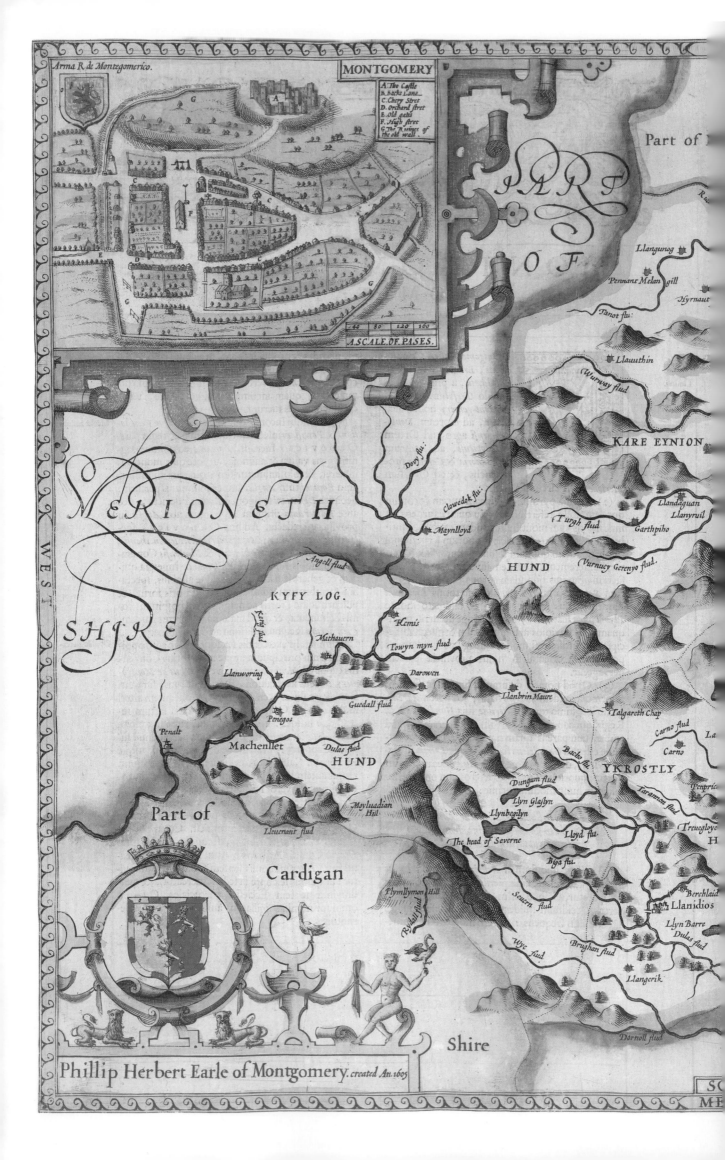

MONTGOMERY

Arma R. de Montegomerico.

A. The Castle
B. backe Lane
C. Chery Stret
D. Orchard stret
E. Old gats
F. High stret
G. The Ruines of the old wall

A SCALE OF PASES.

40 80 120 160

PART OF

Part of

O F

Llangunog

Pennant Melan gill

Hyrnaut

Tanot flu:

Llauuthin

Wurway flud

KARE EYNION

Llandaguan

Llanyruil

Clowedok flu:

Turgh flud

Garthpiho

Maynlloyd

HUND

Vurnuey Gerenyo flud.

Angell flud

KYFY LOG.

Kemis

Mathauern

Towyn myn flud

Llanworing

Darowen

Llanbrin Maure

Talgareth Chap

Guedall flud

Carno flud

Penegos

Bacho flu

Carno

Penalt

Dulas flud

YKROSTLY

Machenllet

HUND

Dungum flud

Taramon flud

Penpric

Llyn Glaslyn

Moyluadian Hill

Llynbeglyn

Lloyd flu

Treucgloye

Part of

Lleuenant flud

The head of Severne

H

Biga flu

Cardigan

Plynllymon Hill

Seuern flud

Berehlaid

Llanidios

Rydall flud

Llyn Barre

Dulas flud

Wye flud

Brughan flud

Llangerik

Dornoll flud

Shire

Phillip Herbert Earle of Montgomery. created An. 1605

SO

ME

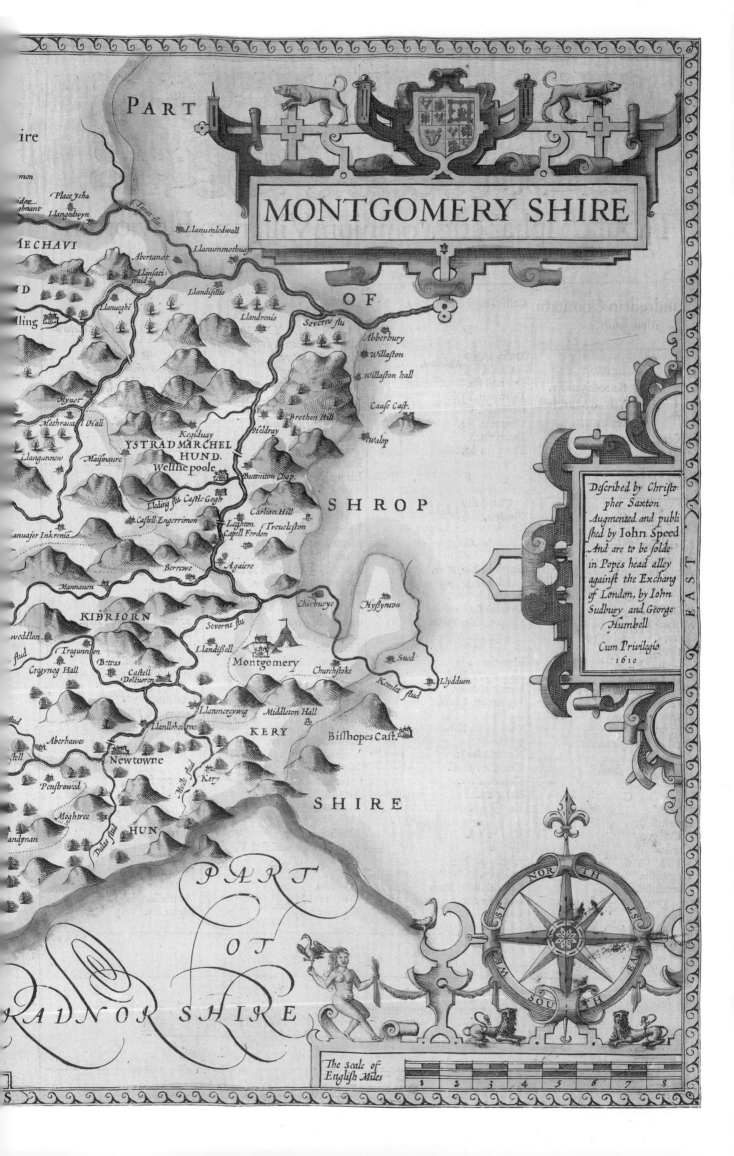

MONTGOMERY SHIRE

PART

OF

SHROP

SHIRE

PART

OF

RADNORSHIRE

Described by Christo-
pher Saxton
Augmented and publi-
shed by Iohn Speed
And are to be folde
in Popes head alley
against the Exchang
of London, by Iohn
Sudbury and George
Humbell

Cum Privilegio
1610

EAST

NORTH
WEST
SOUTH
EAST

The scale of
English Miles

1 2 3 4 5 6 7 8

The scale of English Miles

wealth was unevenly distributed, and set against the castles of the Herberts should be seen the single-hearth hall-houses which remained common there long after they had fallen out of fashion elsewhere.

The county had deposits of iron in which were mined; the ore was purified in forges using charcoal. Of its six market towns the most important was Montgomery, which—although not large—Speed found 'very wholesome for air, and pleasant for situation'.

Apart from its bedevilment by roaming thieves, Montgomeryshire was probably best known in folk lore during Speed's life for Henry of Richmond's march through it during August 1485 before defeating Richard III at the battle of Bosworth.

Pembrokeshire

Speed's map for Pembrokeshire is one of the most successful in the way it conveys a sense of the county's landscape with its hilly uplands and less dramatic southern parts, and the variety of its coastline with its offshore islands and rocks, headlands and havens. It was a county of open pasture with some arable on the lower ground, of isolated settlements and small townships with their common fields still intact, and of extensive woodlands. Most of the wool produced there was shipped either to North Wales or up the Bristol Channel for spinning, but some was kept for the manufacture of the coarse cloth called 'cotton' that Pembrokeshire, Cardiganshire and Carmarthenshire weavers specialized in. There were outcrops of coal in the southern parts, which were used for heating and for cooking: in the poorer uplands, turves continued to be burnt. Slate was quarried in the north of the county, and Pembrokeshire slates had been used in roofing Sir Thomas Gresham's Stock Exchange in London. Despite its sparse population and few products, Pembrokeshire at the south-west tip of Wales with its good harbours and safe anchorages was not only important in the local trade plying the coast but it also had trading links stretching from Anglesey and Ireland to Cornwall and Brittany. With the single exception of Haverfordwest which, strangely, Speed overlooked in his commentary, no Pembrokeshire towns or ports benefited much from this far-flung trade: Speed commented on the number of empty houses at Pembroke and the indifferent state of repair of all its buildings, and of St David's he said: 'A city with few inhabitants, and no more houses than inserted in the draught [drawing]; yet hath it a fair cathedral church.'

Henry VII had been born at Pembroke, and it was at Milford Haven that he landed during August 1485 in his bid to wrest the crown from Richard III. These two facts were never forgotten by the Tudor dynasty, and its recollection of them had had contrary results. Pembrokeshire had benefited from a series of royal acts of singular favour, such as the town of Pembroke's being the first to be incorporated in Wales in 1485, and as the shire being chosen for Anne Boleyn's marquessate before her marriage to Henry VIII. But it was more a source of anxiety 'with one of the fairest and capablest harbours of the realm', blockhouses and forts being erected there by Henry VIII, and repaired and modified by his successors. As it transpired, the greatest danger to Pembrokeshire under the Tudors and Stuarts was not from invasion, but from piracy, in which to the distress of the Crown Pembrokeshire families were deeply

PENBROKE

S.t Annes Chapel
The Grene
Monton Priory
S.ct Maryes
S. Michaels

40 80 120 160
The Scale of Pases.

THE

IRYSHE

Dynas heade
Langlas heade
The Cowe
and y Calfe rockes
Strumble heade
Llanunda
Dynas
Capel Llanyhangle
Manernowen Fiscard
S.t Nicholas
Llanllawyn Llann
Llanachaier Pont
Llanastynan
S.t Katterns
Llanuaier
Merther DEWYSLAVE
Treuenyth Letterstowne Castle Male
Llanryan
Llanrithon Casth
Llandcryn Newcastle
S. Davids heade Gorid Chapell Llanhowel S. Lawrance S.t Dugwele
Whitchurch Llandeloy Revelston
Whitsand Bay S.t Davides Rieston Hayes Castle Travegare
The Bishop and his Clarkes S.t Steuans S.t Nones HUND Spittle
Dshath hauen Brodye DUNGLED
Shirlac Rocke S.t Ayluew Plunston Rocke Redbaxton
Portolais Roche Camrose
Ramsey The Horse R. Castle S.t Leonards Chapell
Island Rihye Rocke Roche castle HU
hill Prende rgest
SEA Knowleton Lamston
The lyttle Haven ROWSE Haverford West
Harreston Harroldston
Goltop Rode West Walton Osnay
S.t Margrets chap. Fresthorp
R.C. Strongbow E. Wil. Marshall E. 2. Talbennye HUND. Bolton Hill
Walwin cast: Johnston
S.t Brides Island Haseard Robertston Llangum
Yardlanston Sandy Neffeton Stanton Rosemar
S. Brides Hubberston The priorye Kings
Marlas Gelliswick rode.
Will. Valence E. 3 Lawrence Hastings 4 S.t Ifinels Harbarston Lanstadwell
Pylles Pylles Newton
Sealine Island Sandy Haven
Midlan Island Penur Mouth
Gateholme Island Dale The Stack Rocke West Popton w. Peter
Hristone Dale Rock West Popton Crosford Potcrachon
Stokeholme Island The Blook house Popton Estngton Hentland
John D. of Bedford E.5. Wil. de la Poole Marque. 6 Rat Island Laure chap Eastn Poteracon
S.t Ane Chap Nangh Estngton
The Blook-house Newton MAR
Kilpaston
Milford Haven Uggarston mill HU
Shepe Island Freshwate Castle Merton
Gupton Waren
Merian
Lynnycrew Levaston
Performed by Iohn Speede. And are to be solde South Carew
in Popes head alley by Iohn Sudbury and George Flynston
Humbell, at London. 1610. Cum Privilegio. Kerikm

Iaspor Hatfeld E. 9. Will. Hameld E. 8. H.t Prince of Wales. 9 Anne Bolleyne Marchionesse Wil. Herbert Erl. 11

The Scale

involved, the worst culprit in this respect probably being Queen Elizabeth's irascible 'cousin' Sir John Perrot of Haroldston: for his repeated disregard of the trust placed in him and on account of a series of abuses and crimes culminating in treason he was arrested, tried, sentenced and executed in 1592. Perrot had been an overbearing subject, presuming on his kinship with the Queen, and while he lived he had divided Pembrokeshire into factions either for or against him, the Wogans of Wiston with their friends and relatives supporting him while the Phillipses of Picton and their connections opposed him. Fortunately Perrot's death did much to heal the rift, and the antiquarian George Owen of Henllys was able—before his own death in 1613—to observe that Pembrokeshire was one of the more orderly and peaceful counties in Wales.

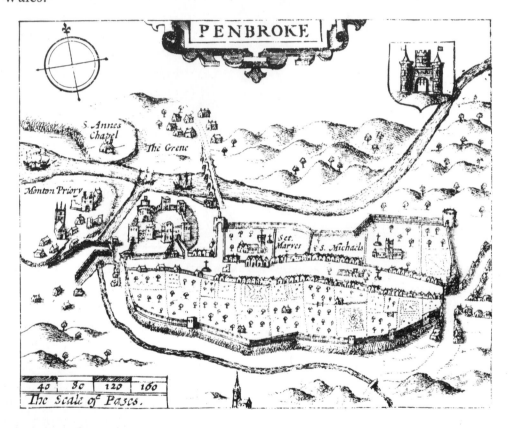

Unfortunately George Owen did not live to complete more than the first book of his 'Description of Pembrokeshire', a detailed history of the county parish by parish conceived in emulation of William Lambarde's work on Kent and Richard Carew's on Cornwall. His hospitality at Henllys was enjoyed by men as diverse as the herald Lewis Dwnn and local Welsh bards, and presumably by Speed—if only as a friend of William Camden—on the visit to the county when he personally surveyed both Pembroke and St David's for the plans included in the Pembrokeshire map. Although Speed does not acknowledge any debt to Owen, the sharpness and accuracy of the commentary would seem to reflect more than Speed's usual standard of observation.

Radnorshire

John Leland noted the fertility of the Radnorshire valleys bordering on England and the quality of the wool produced in the east of the county, but neither William Camden nor John Speed could find much to praise. Speed complained of the 'inaccessible mountains whereof this shire is overpressed and burdened, that many times I feared to look down from the hanging rocks, whereunder I passed into those deep and dark dales, seeming to me an entrance into Limbo'. Save in the valleys the soil was poor, and even the three forests of Knucklas, Bleddfa and Radnor consisted of little more than wasteland and heath with some shrubs and trees. As the ground was so infertile and unproductive, it was largely given over to pasturing livestock, ranging from the sheep noted by Leland and the cattle praised by Speed to goats which, since they could survive unattended, were the mainstay of the county's smallholders. Speed ended his description of the Radnorshire countryside: 'Fatal was this place . . . to Llewelyn, the last prince of the British race, who being betrayed by the men of Builth fled into those vast meadows . . . where by Adam Frankton he was slain and his head (crowned with ivy) set upon the Tower of London.'

Coming upon the county's few towns after passing through the mountains, Speed was pleased by them: Radnor was 'pleasantly seated under a hill, whereon standeth mounted a strong castle'; Presteigne 'for beauteous building' was 'the best in this shire, a town of commerce, wonderfully frequented', and Knighton 'a market town likewise'. But the plan of Radnor with which he adorned the top left-hand corner of the Radnorshire map was in its depiction of vacant burgage plots slightly nearer to the truth. The towns created by the English in the Middle Ages had never proved a success, and Radnorshire remained largely a county of scattered farmsteads and small villages and parish churches. Its poverty, clerical non-residence, religious conservatism and large parishes were matters of concern, for which no solution had been found by the early seventeenth century. Outsiders to the area, like Speed, were simply shocked: at Rhayadr he saw 'the market upon the Sabbath', and as a good churchman he was still upset by the disregard of the Rhayadr traders when he wrote the county commentary.

A stony region without a supply of good building stone, domestic building in Radnorshire was timber-framed, but not of the quality of adjoining Shropshire and Herefordshire. Stone was reserved for use in its six castles and fifty-two churches. Although lawlessness and banditry (thriving mainly on

RADNOR

Arma Donanorum de Radnor

The Ruines of the old wall

The Scale of Pace

PART OF

Llanydlos

Severn flud

Wye flud

Darnal flud

Eland flud

sanit Harmon

Combehire

Hansanfraid

Rayader Gowy

Dulas flud

RAYADERGOWY HUN DRED

Clarwen flud

Clorthy flud

Clarwen flud

Glyngwyn

Llanuthell

PART

OF

PARTOF

CARDIGAN

SHIRE

Dulas flud

Wivery flud

BREKNOKE

THE COUNTIE OF RADNOR DESCRIBED
AND THE SHYRETOWNES
SITTUATIONE
Anno 1608.

Described by Christopher Saxon, Augm...
Iohn Speede servant to his Majesty. And...
head alley by Iohn Sudbury & George Hu...

MONTGOMERYE

PART OF SHROPSHIRE

Whitz hall
Teme flud
Bettus

Begildye
Llanbadernuenythe   KNIGHTON HUND
Llanuarewaterden
Castell Dyubord   The Forest of   Knukles
Llannauo   Knukles   Hiop   Standish   Branton Bryan
Lug flud   Kinghton
Llambister   Llangunllo   Monaghree
Tkon flud   Weston Hall   Pillethe   Llyngan   Lug flud
    KEVENLLICE   Whitton   Norton
Llanddwye   Fuldibrok   PART
    Blethuagh   Cascop   OF HERE   Lug flud
    The Fo rest of   FORD S.
    Blethuagh   PART   Discoyde   Prestayne
    Llanyhangle   Ednall
    Redithon   Newcastle
HUND.   Kinerton   Knyll
Llanbadern   Augop   Somegill flud
Llandeglay   The Forest
Cast. Geuenlles   of Radnor   New Radnor   Old Radnor   Kyneton
nyhargal   Harton
    Llanihangle   RADNOR HUND   Gwithel flud
    Nantmelan
rindod   Vthor Au   Glosfre
Bettus   Chapell   Arro flud   Huntington east
re flud   Glascombt
Llansanfraid   Colwey Chap.
OWINI   Colwin east   Cregrena   Newchurch
    Rulen   Llanihangle:
HUND   Bryngwyn   Arro
Llanelway   Llanbadern   PAINSCASTLE
Llanuareth
Abredway   Castell payne   Bettus   Wye flud
    Llynhoghlen   Machaway flud   Clyfford east
        Llanheddee
        Llandewye Chap.   Clero
    Landilo   HUNDRED   Hay
HIRE   Llanstephan   Llowas
    Glasefhury
    Boughrud
    Pipton

Jodocus Hondius Cælavit
ished by
in popes
ilegio.

PART OF HEREFORDSHIRE

NORTH
WEST   EAST
SOUTH
Miles flud

THE SCALE OF MILES.

1 2 3 4 5 6 7 8 9 10

depredations to livestock) dissuaded owners from forsaking their castles and other generally defensible homes in favour of more commodious dwellings, domestic comforts were not unknown in Radnorshire, as can be seen from the houses built during the Tudor and early Stuart periods still surviving today.

Radnorshire had been created a county only as late as the Union of 1536, and it was more or less co-terminous with the old Welsh tribal kingdom of Rhwng Gwy a Hafren. Notwithstanding its recent creation, it incorporated an outlier of Herefordshire near Presteigne.

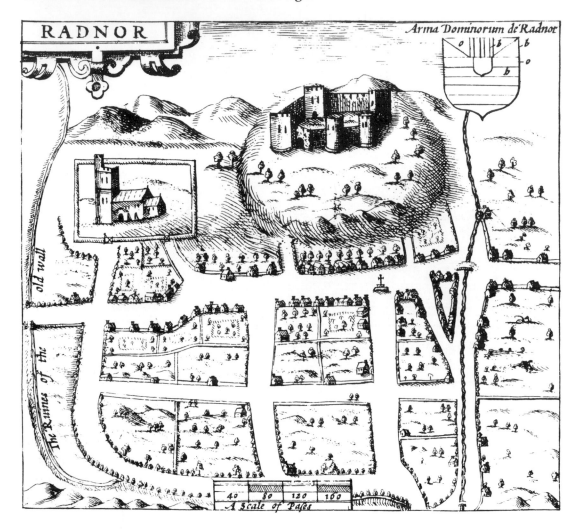

Scotland

Unlike England, Wales and Ireland, there is only one map for Scotland in Speed's *Theatre*. The reason for this is twofold. Firstly, the project seems originally to have been conceived in the early 1590s when the separate kingdom of Scotland was to have been excluded. But delays in production, partly on account of the decision to link the *Theatre* directly with the *History of Great Britain* (which despite its title only covered England), and the Union of the Crowns in 1603 meant that Speed had to modify his original plan. As with the *History*, the modifications to the *Theatre* were kept to a minimum, rather than further delaying publication. Secondly, Speed knew of the Scotsman Timothy Pont's work in surveying Scotland. To have extended the *Theatre* to include maps for Scotland similar to those for England, Wales and Ireland would have been to duplicate Pont's effort, even if cartographic aspects were differently emphasized by the two men. Unfortunately Pont died not long after the publication of the *Theatre* leaving the Scottish atlas unfinished, and his work was not issued until 1654, in a revised form by Willem and Johannes Blaeu.

The map of Scotland is based on Gerardus Mercator's earlier map of the kingdom dated 1595, and not surprisingly it reflects slightly different cartographic criteria from the majority of maps in the *Theatre*. For example, the regions shown are not counties, as Scotland was only in the process of being divided into shires along English lines, but the territories of the principal clans and families, which until the reign of James VI (James I of England) had been accepted by the Scottish crown as the basis for local management. Speed knew of these administrative changes, and some of the changes to Mercator's original reflect this knowledge, albeit imperfectly. The consequent result is a somewhat confusing distillation of information, which does not show Scotland with absolute accuracy at any moment during Speed's life.

Speed's commentary is equally circumscribed. On account of the small amount of space available on the back of the map, it is sometimes brief to the point of being almost worthless, in contrast to the compendium of information accompanying the county maps for the rest of Great Britain. Describing the kingdom of Scotland as 'fair and spacious' and so well provided with 'fish, fowl, and cattle, and corn so plenteous that it supplieth other countries in their want', with curious details (such as that Loch Ness never froze, and that horsemen in some places hunted salmon with spears) could not have been of much help to the users of the *Theatre*. Correctly he observed the division of

265

THE KINGDOME OF SCOTLAND

James King of Great Britain, Fraunce & Ireland.

Henry Prince of Wales & Ireland.

THE DEUCALIDON SEA

C. Wrath or Faro head

Rona Iland
S. Rona

Durnes?

Ilen Handa

Nary
Noys
S. Columban
Bailm traid
LEWYS
Radamach
S. Columbanus
Stornuwaye cast
Stoy cast
L. Stornwaye

Gellisgung
Bailnoheglis
(The Stoir of Assin
Alleroit
Kikail

Skyra
L. As

Barra mayor
Barna minor
Bailnes aleg
Durna
L. Nofallo
Ilen Schent

Rowra
Hilles. of As
Aru

Slew
Loch Brune
ofill
Esbrew

S. Kilder
L. Nealg
Trusk
L. Neala
S. Clement
Ilen Querr
Evern
Scalpa
Boyne

Tranta
Fladda
Trantnes

S. Nicolas
Thanternesca
Allavik
Flodda

Mera
Claight
Zutr
Fewris
Brew

L. Gar Skoire
Assin Shire
L. Hew
Culke
L. Refaire
Dunra
Toir
Brins
allan
Strom cast.
L. Drum.
L. Lange

Freford
Ellan Ronan

SKYB
Dunbegan
Allar towne
Ronaza
scalpa

S. Patricius Eskin.
Euft
Eslir

Valter nes
S. John

Inis Kyntaile
The high moun taynes of Ardmanoth

Stig

Bragdail
Knot fea
Glenela

L. Orte

S. Maria Gilwall

S. Columbanus

The Yles of Hebrides
Caled of Pliny
Hæbudes, of
Beda Meuaniae

Cannay
Rum

L. En ort
L. Eni ea
Touroan
Dunska
Kiltin

L. Orte
L. Newis
L. Errgerd
Sell
L. Owin
Arisk
Dyron

Ha
Sell
L. Zell
Loquhaber

S. Petrus

Egge

Sell flu

Barray
Brog

Muk
Meer
Bailnraid
Quhabyr
L. Aber

Erth
Collen

Ardermouth head
Ilean
Arroit ca
Ardins
Cantuill
Masad
L. Olybe

Soayl
Terrey

L. Ayyryn
Mu
Bailnor
Lismoir
Dovart ca
Caruerei

Bergonum
Dunshrast
et

Cardeburg Cast.
Ulvay

Lac Lephan
Ha
Cowyll
L. Nawell
Esll Torsa
L. Leaue

S. Eugenius
Knapdail

Colmkil or Iona Ile
Skar
huy
Tarbat
Erl
Thorlanca

Oronza
Colonza

Colmekil
Sura
Sodore

Erll
Argi
Naday
L. Skriuer

S. Macha ro
O. L. Weel
Swin ca

Lofauterled
Braig
Ofsir

Dunlin

L. Girvard
L. Arun

Kylmany
Ha

L. Tarban
Satpynche
Karray
Sandell ca

Gegay

Arren
Glenkill
Kyrk
imorich

Wysta
Dunwog ca

Killain

Eyr
Gillcaren
Gallowaren
Pradda
Ar
Sandci

Reumfay
Brydyk

Canty

Dun
oyrt
The Mule of Cantyr

Dunbritain
Air alle

Malin
Coldagh haven

Ship Iland
Harkton bay

Tor bay
Tor Ile

Glenhope

Portrush
Skirries
Dunluce
Whiteland
Dunseoke

Fair Forland

Toc
IRISH

Cafsilt
Kephill

Cast. Corano
Part of Ireland
Loughfoyle
Lough Swilly

The Mul of Galloway or the Miles nuke
SEA
Maides

THE SCALE OF SCOTISH MILES

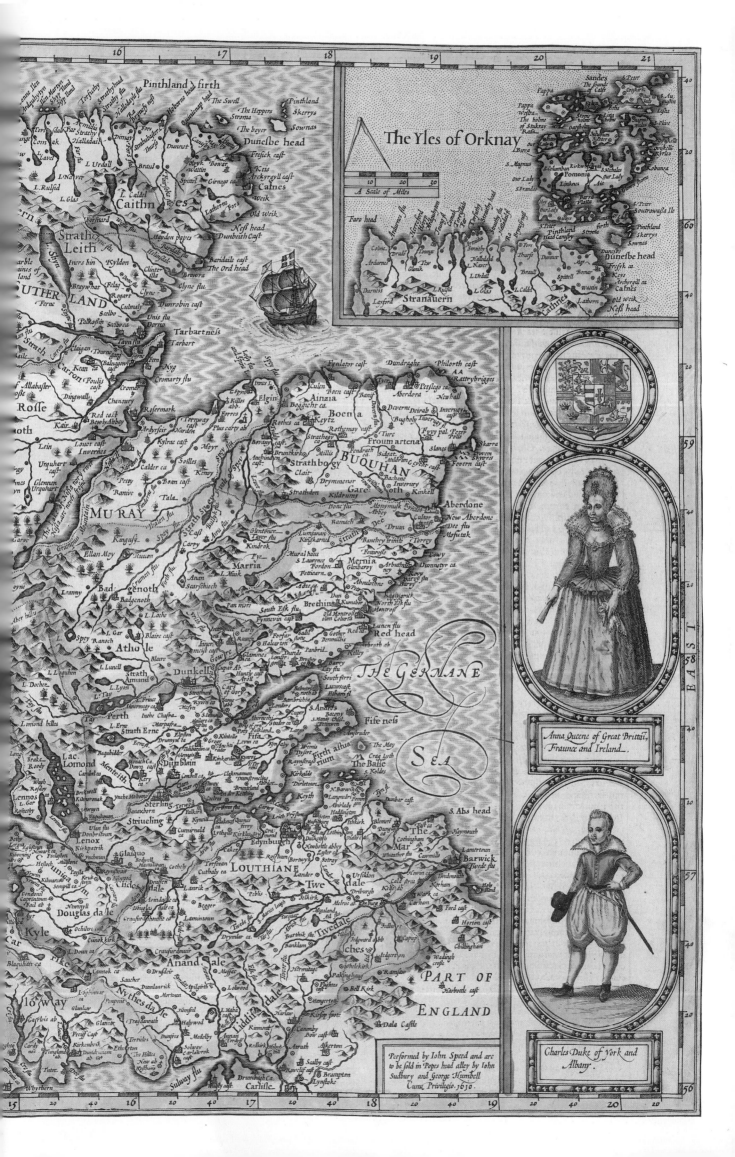

Scotland into two parts by the great river Tay, the populous, richer and more couth Lowlands, and the poorer and 'more rude' Highlands 'retaining the customs of the wild Irish', but in writing this material up Speed must have known that he was making the best of a bad job. What is informative to the discerning modern reader is the light that his commentary throws on the Union of the Crowns, and how he sidestepped or avoided the issues raised by it. Speed described the Scots as 'people . . . of good feature, strong of body, and of courageous mind, and in wars so venturous, that scarce any service of note hath been performed, but they were the first and last in the field: their nobility and gentry are very studious of learning, and all civil knowledge'. Yet he and his readers knew what animosity the Scottish followers of James I had provoked, and were familiar with London and Westminster 'streets swarm[ing] night and day with bloody quarrels' between Englishmen and Scots; meanwhile in Scotland there were already signs of discontent with their legacy of absentee government, and fears that complete union would be an unequal settlement. Presumably Speed was anxious to please the king who was the dedicatee of the *History* and the *Theatre*, but he was also familiar with the arguments being put forward in the defence of the Union of the Crowns, evidently in particular with the tract 'Of the Union of Britain' written by Pont's father Robert in 1606.

The embellishments to the Scottish map deserve attention, as they include full-length portraits of King James and his wife, Anne of Denmark, with their two surviving sons, the heir-apparent Prince Henry (who was to die in 1612), and the Duke of York (who succeeded to the throne in 1625 as Charles I), as well as the arms of James and Anne as King and Queen of Great Britain.

Ireland

The map of Ireland is based on an earlier map published in 1595 by the Flemish cartographer Gerardus Mercator, but it also draws upon the surveys done in the 1570s by Robert Lythe and in the 1590s by Francis Jobson. Lythe and Jobson were only two from a host of cartographers, including Richard Bartlett, Baptista Boazio and John Browne, engaged to remedy the lack of good maps for Ireland which had hampered the English crown's efforts to maintain law and order there from the Kildare Rebellion of 1534–5 until the collapse of Gaelic power at the accession of James I. Surveying Ireland was a dangerous task, at least two surveyors, Bartlett and Browne, being killed by the Irish whose lands they had been recording. In view of dangers such as these—and the persistent political unrest—Speed is unlikely to have travelled the whole of Ireland in person as he evidently tried to do while preparing his commentaries for the English and Welsh counties, and thus, not surprisingly, his Irish observations often do not possess the sharpness of his remarks elsewhere.

Like the map for the kingdom of England, that for Ireland is embellished with a set of three pairs of people, a man and a woman in each, showing how gentle families, town-dwellers and country folk dressed in Ireland. In his general commentary Speed mentions the unhealthiness of the place to strangers, the absence of snakes, and an *aqua vitae* called whiskey.

269

THE KINGDOME OF IRLAND

Devided into severall Provinces, and thē
againe devided into Counties.
Newly described.

The Gentleman of Ireland   The Gentlewoman of Ireland

The Civill Irish Woman   The Civill Irish man

The Wilde Irish man   The Wilde Irish Woman

Iodocus Hondius cælavit

Connaught

'The air is not altogether so pure and clear as in the other provinces of Ireland, by reason of certain moist places (covered with grass) which of their softness are usually termed bogs, both dangerous and full of vaporous and foggy mists,' observed Speed. But Connaught with its complex coastline of offshore islands, bays and inlets, consisted inland of more than bogs and loughs, having some woodland and extensive uplands in Counties Sligo and Leitrim against Ulster, along the coast of Galway, and in Clare. With such a diversity of terrain, farming varied accordingly with livestock predominating, but cereals were also produced in Clare, Galway and Roscommon. Somewhat unusually for Ireland, deer were numerous in County Mayo. However, bitter feuding between the native Irish, aggravated by their employment of gallowglasses—mercenary soldiers from Scotland—to settle their disputes, as well as recurrent rebellions, prevented the inhabitants of Connaught from realizing the province's potential, and large areas of it had been wasted in the closing years of the sixteenth century: in 1598 County Galway was 'in a manner unpeopled by reason of the spoils committed in the last rebellion, partly by rebel and partly by soldier, and the great famine that followed thereupon, which hath so wasted this country that scarce the hundredth men or houses is to be found now that was several years ago.'

Connaught, despite settlements by the Anglo-Normans, had remained a preserve of Gaeldom throughout the Middle Ages, and alone of the Irish provinces it kept its predominantly Gaelic character under the Tudors and early Stuarts, with its Irish inhabitants secure in the tenure of their ancestral lands. Over a span of twenty-five years early in Elizabeth's reign the area had been systematically divided into shires on the English model for reasons of local administration, and in recognition of its distinctive character the province had been allocated a Council with a president of its own. When the Crown's desire to establish law and order by these means had been thwarted by the activities of Scottish mercenaries, these changes were imposed through a military subjugation led by Sir Richard Bingham between 1580 and 1585, and by a streamlining of local dues and taxes to provide an annual revenue for the Crown. Although central authority was to break down in 1598, the removal of gallowglasses with their demands for tribute and the successful superimposition of an orthodox system of provincial government meant that Queen Elizabeth never considered Connaught as suitable for plantation; in 1608,

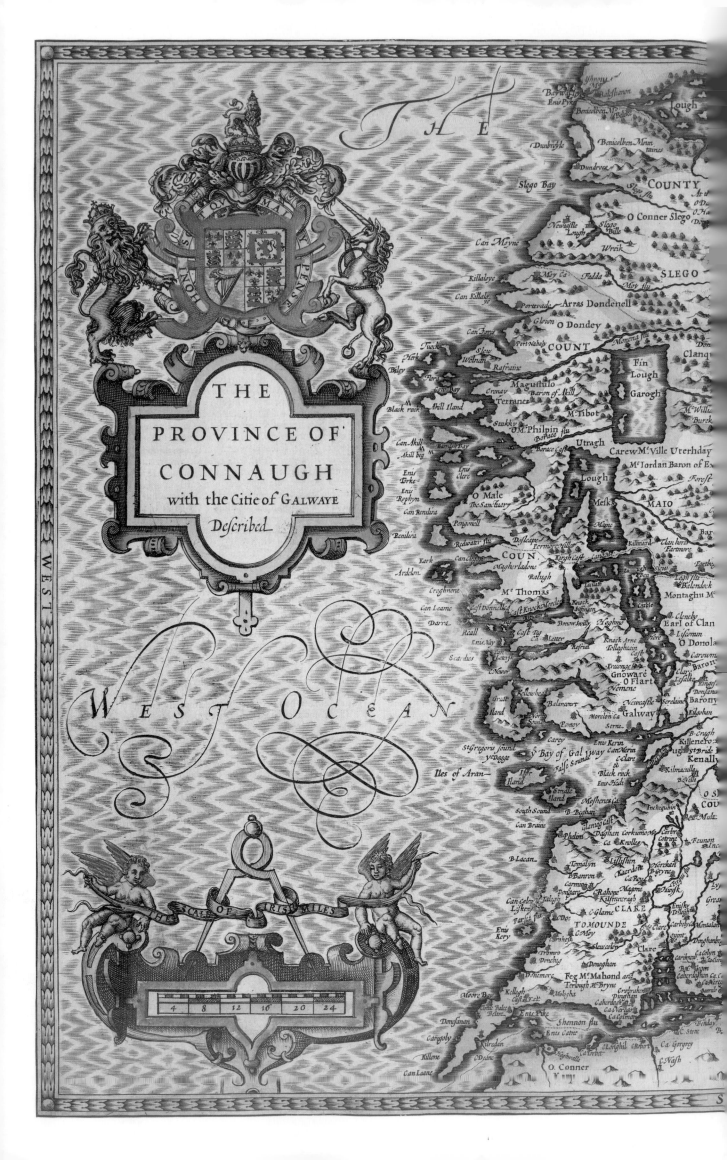

THE

PROVINCE OF
CONNAUGH
with the Citie of GALWAYE
Described

THE

WEST OCEAN

WEST

SCALE OF IRISH MILES

4   8   12   16   20   24

HONI SOYT QVI MAL Y PENSE

Place names (map labels):

Baywalley
Enis Pyke
Benicolben M.
Beloks
Lough
Dunbriyle
Benicolben Moun taines
Dundrose
Slego Bay
COUNTY
At th
O Du
Sleg. fta
O Ha
O Conner Slego
Dong
Newcastle Lough
Slego Bille
Can Moyne
Wreik
Killaloye
Moy Ca
Fadda
SLEGO
Can Killalo
Moy flu
Portevade
Arras Dondenell
Clown
O Dondey
Port Nahaly
Mcmena flu
Don
COUNT
Clang
Twock
Flerk
Slew Welnan
Biley
Rafratine
Fin Lough
Flery
Crenay
Maguhulo
Garogh
Con Bay
Terrance
Baron of Akill
Akill Iland
Stakky
Mc Tibot
McWilliu
Black rock
O Mc Philpin
Burek
flu
Can Akill
Borace
Akill big
Borace Cast.
Utragh
Carew McVille Uterhday
Barnelli Bay
McIordan Baron of E.
Enis Clere
Enis Iorke
Enis Rophyn
O Male
Lough
Forest
Can Renilira
The Sanctuary
MAIO
Mesks
Renilira
Pengonell
Magne
Bar
Redwater flu
Kilhinard
Dosscape
Clan hora
Fartmore
Kark
Fermoure Villes
Cuny Me.
Ardelon.
Can Clafon
Kirgh Cast.
Lough ben
Slew
Magherladone
Lo
Lough flta
Croghnone
Ralugh
Lacuath
Balendock
Mc Thomas
Montaghu Mc
Can Leame
Cast Donnell
Carble
Cloneby
Darra
Cast Knock Mordet
Earl of Clan
Reall
Bonowswilly
Hoghno
Liscorum
Enis Nay
Cast Tog
Letter
Knock Arne
Core
O Donola
Caroum
Ch.
Tellogheam
Enterfu
Rofriat
Cast
Baron
ENeuor
Ercaonge
Clare
Lefalke
Scaidies
Gnoware
Rinagy
Gratt land
Kellowhead
O Flart
Bonfara
Balancomr
Nemene
Barony
North Sound
Newcastle
Serelanie
Kilsohan
Morclon Ca
Galway
Pontoy
Serne.
B. crugh
Carey
Killenero
St Gregoris sound
Enis Kerin
Lugh
St Bride
ye Dogge
Ye Bay of Galyway
Can Merin
Kenally
Iles of Aran
Oclare
Black rock
Kilmacullo
Ifor Iland
Enis Hedst
B Vells
False Sound
Smale Iland
South Sound
Can Braine
Meshenes Ca
Inchequin
Cou
B Beghan
New Mulz
B Lacan
Glanog cast.
Cartbre
Phelim
Dighan
Corkumo
Cotrine
Ca Knolles
Feunon
Tomalyn
Lisslishen
Ince
B Banron
Kaerdom
Ca Roye
Oterckan
Carming
Rahone
Magone
B Gryne
Ponigary
Kilfenveragh
Kuysk
Can Caleg
Valegan
Eglame
CLARE
Lyskeny
Enisky
Tarfet flu
ODe
TOMOUNDE
Telloghe
Enis Kery
CMoy
Carbely
Montala
Corohesse
quint
Tromro
Slew colpn
Ca Colyn
Donchg
Clare
Dinghanby
Dnemore
Feg McMahond ard
Ca.co
Terlogh McBryne
Moore Bay
Crohraken
Ca C
Kellegh
Molygha
Pinghan
CaMerg
Cast Keal.
Caherdoysh
B.C. Sten
Done sinan
Ente Pike
Shennon flu
Caregoly
Ents Catne
Ca.Colmon
Bridas
Killone
Kilredan
ODeane
Laghmilts
Ca.torbet
Can Leane
O. Conner
C. Nash
Ca Gorgrey

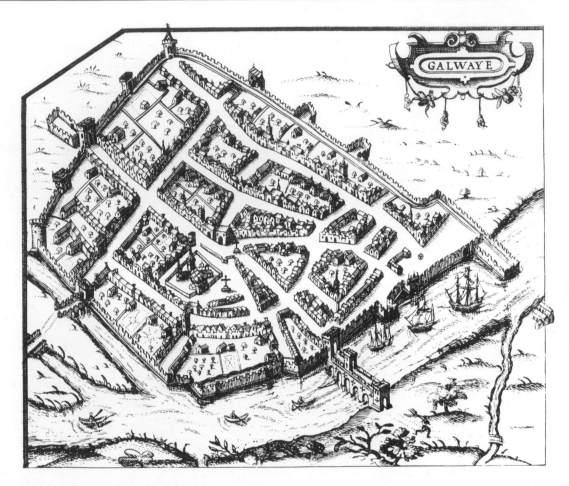

shortly before the publication of the *Theatre*, James I briefly entertained a project for plantation similar to the Ulster settlement, but nothing came of this.

Given its inaccessibility from Dublin, the even greater distance from London, and the poverty and religious conservatism of the inhabitants, many religious houses in Connaught survived the Dissolution of the Monasteries under Henry VIII, and a number still existed at the accession of James I. These had received some succour in the intervening years from churches in Spain and Portugal, using the area's ancient trading links with the Iberian Peninsula, but they did not win the approval of the seminary priests visiting Connaught from the 1590s, or of the Jesuits later. Social disorder and a series of ineffectual archbishops of Tuam meant that the Protestant Reformation had made little impact on the province's bishoprics and parishes by the time of James I's accession. Despite Connaught's links with Spain, the presence of Spanish agents or troops supporting its inhabitants against the English was not welcomed, and the survivors from ships from the Spanish Armada wrecked on its coast were, almost to a man, killed on coming ashore either by the native Irish or else by English soldiers. The unusual conditions prevailing in Connaught also meant that its only town of importance, Galway, singular in its extent and prosperity enjoyed a regional and municipal autonomy otherwise unknown in the British Isles, virtually untrammelled by the Crown's control.

Leinster

Of Ireland's four ancient provinces, Leinster was the most English in the early seventeenth century. Its marcher lordships had been divided into shires in the Anglo-Norman conquest, but its Gaelic lordships not then thus organized had survived until the sixteenth century when Westmeath was created in 1542, King's and Queen's Counties in 1557, and Longford in 1571: the process of shiring Wicklow and Ferns was put in hand in 1560, but it was not brought to completion until 1606, their boundaries not being shown on the map for Leinster which was thus significantly out of date when published in 1612. The English Pale, or March of Dublin, extended to Dundalk in the north through Ardee, Kells, Athboy, Kilcullen Bridge, and Ballymore Eustace to Fansare in the south, but this strip was no less subject to raiding and intermittent warfare than the rest of Leinster or the other provinces: the O'Byrnes and O'Tooles burned and spoiled the Pale from their mountainous uplands in the south, while the O'Mores and O'Connors of Leix and Offaly extorted a 'black-rent' upon it for not pillaging the area. In the north County Louth was subject to raiding from 'the barbarous country of the Fews, part of the country of Armagh to the north, and the country of Feony'. With these and other neighbours 'given over to spoils and robberies' peace and order were fragile commodities even in the most settled and civilized part of Ireland, and in a determined attempt to achieve these two laudable objects the English Crown under Queen Mary and King Philip had promoted the first of a modern series of settlements or plantations, a panacea which had previously been applied in Wales, before attempting similar colonization further afield.

Partly because Leinster was so predominantly English, it was the province which Englishmen and other travellers found the most sympathetic, and Speed was no exception in this. He found the air 'clear and gentle, mixed with a temperate disposition, yielding neither extremity of heat or cold'. Counties Louth, Meath and Dublin were the granary of Ireland, and the less fertile areas supported a type of horse called a hobby, cattle, and other livestock in abundance. Milk, butter and cheese of good quality were produced. As can be seen from the map, Leinster had more woodlands than other provinces except in the county of Dublin 'which complains much of that want'; Dubliners had to use peat or coal for fuel. More important than the woods or bogs to the province's economy were its fish and fowl, both land and sea. Yet even 'this most populous and plentiful country' had been recently devastated by

DUBLINE

A Scale of Pases

50 100 150 200

THE IRISH SEA

North groundes

Middle groundes

The South groundes

The Rushe
The Rannie

EAST

County Dublyn

Boyne flu
Garr
Iulian
Corbell
stamdon
Balrothery
Holywood Ardalla
Agard
Fyngall Guenare
Gralough Lusk Rogers
B.Baghill Forns
Gracedew Lenalton
Donebat Lafenton
Cabliston Corbely
swery Malcheal
Loghren Falrono
Glasfurphin B.Griffith
Dromeco Relbol
Kilhester nstaft
C.Knok
Dublin Dublin hauen
Camoch
Grymo Artion
Cronilion Moncloy
Donecarne Roch
Karaldorgo B.Wugha Bromore
Knukyn Grandon
Igbor kin
Iefferay Shenkin
Kilderman Anna hill Kildernan
B.Sherney Conagh Paaarow
Poures court Bray
blackmorres Malyn
Thre caslelts Dolknew
L.Bray C.Rydon

S.Patriks land Carichufe
Cavan
Kilmorya Stonegrag
Crasbally

Wicklo

O.Brenne
Kileomyn
Ralvayne
C.Henorelay

E.of Ormond
Toghcolycony
Togh: Gheragh Areklo
colin ogh Carikbmk
Newtoune
Mc.Vadok

Mc Damore
Clone dognekely
Shopland
Loughmessyn Ket:
Balanere terion

Clone Kilhobok
B.Bomey

Tenaghill
Graceorchard O Moerough
C.Browne Synnot
Kilpatrik
shiphold
Arcanan
Beg Iland Ihoorde

Wexford hauen

Wexford
Newbarn
Browne

Earyk new
Bay of Greenhorde
Tiscord

Black Rack Barrets
Can Karne al. Karone
Rock William

the Desmond Rebellion and by the Nine Years' War, and when the *Theatre* was published it was still in the early stages of recovery.

Dublin was exceptional in a number of ways: its castle was the seat of government in Ireland with a chancery, exchequer and lawcourts; its cathedral boasted an archbishop with a metropolitan area overlapping the province; it was populous, with thriving crafts and industries, and from 1592 when Trinity College was incorporated it had a university. Also it was a port with safe marine approaches on a coast notorious for its flats and shallows, Dublin being an important line of communication not only with England but with the rest of Ireland, where—in the absence of many roads or bridges—some areas had no adequate link with the capital other than by sea. On seeing Dublin, Speed was deeply moved: 'This is the royal seat of Ireland, strong in her munitions, beautiful in her buildings, and for the quantity matchable to many other cities frequent for traffic and intercourse of merchants.' He found things to praise in Kildare, Kilkenny and Wexford, but his judiciously turned phrases suggest that he did not achieve these without difficulty.

Protestants also found Leinster more acceptable than elsewhere in Ireland. Although civil disorders and rebellions had effectively prevented the imposition of the Anglican Settlement there, all its monastic houses had been dissolved by the late 1540s, and many Catholic practices had been successfully banned. With the establishment of peace in 1603, James I had hopes of Protestantism following in the wake of order, but in this he was to be sadly disappointed. Whatever their English affiliations, the inhabitants of Leinster were, as far as religion was concerned, conservative, and as elsewhere in Ireland they had welcomed the arrival of seminary priests sent with papal approval.

Munster

The province of Munster had long been one of the more Anglicized areas of Ireland, with a Council and president of its own, and it had been divided into shires on the English pattern before the sixteenth century. Although ancient marcherland, Gaelic lordships had survived in the Shannon valley and in the south-west until the failure of the Desmond Rebellion of 1579–83, when the Crown availed itself of some half a million acres declared forfeit by the Earl's treason to colonize Munster. The initial plantation involving over 8,000 people was the largest scheme of its kind undertaken to date by the English, and was far in excess of the hundred or so landed in 1585 on Roanoke Island, the first English settlement in North America: both the Roanoke and Munster schemes were promoted by Sir Walter Ralegh and Sir Richard Grenville, and included many poor Englishmen from Devon and Cornwall. One of the new settlers was Edmund Spenser, deputy clerk to the Council of Munster, who leased some 3,000 acres; unfortunately Spenser's enthusiasm and commitment soon soured, and he came to consider his Munster post and possessions an obstacle in writing what was his poetic masterpiece, *The Faerie Queene*, representing 'all the virtues, assigning to every virtue a knight to be the patron and defender of the same'. Although disillusionment set in early, the plantations survived, and the Munster map shows the newer English countries (such as Sir Peter Carew's in Bantry Bay) which had displaced the previous Gaelic ones. Fear as to the danger if survivors from the Spanish Armada joined the Irish in 1588 had led the English settlers and soldiers to shoot those Spaniards not already massacred by the natives. The landing of Spanish troops at Kinsale in 1598 in support of the O'Neill Rebellion did seriously threaten the future of these precarious settlements, Spenser himself dying from shock and privation following his flight from Kilcolman. For the New English, divided from the Old English and the Irish by mutual distrust and antipathy, Spenser's *View of the Present State of Ireland*, published two years before his death in 1599, was a persuasive rationalization of the dilemma in which they found themselves, and became a handbook for their needs in the years following the peace established shortly before James I's accession in 1603.

Spenser left a heart-rending account of the tribulations and long-term consequences in Munster of intermittent uprisings, of foreign invasions and of personal feuds: 'Like as I never saw in a more pleasant country in all my life, so never saw I a more waste and desolate land, . . . and there heard I such

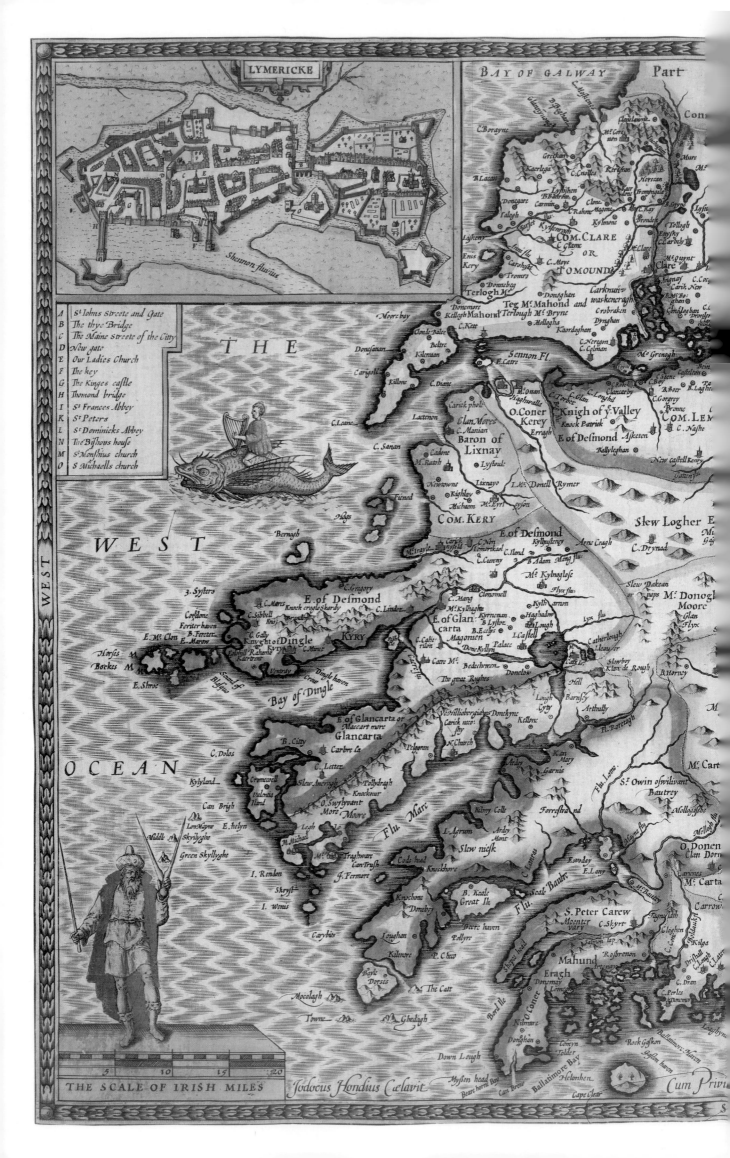

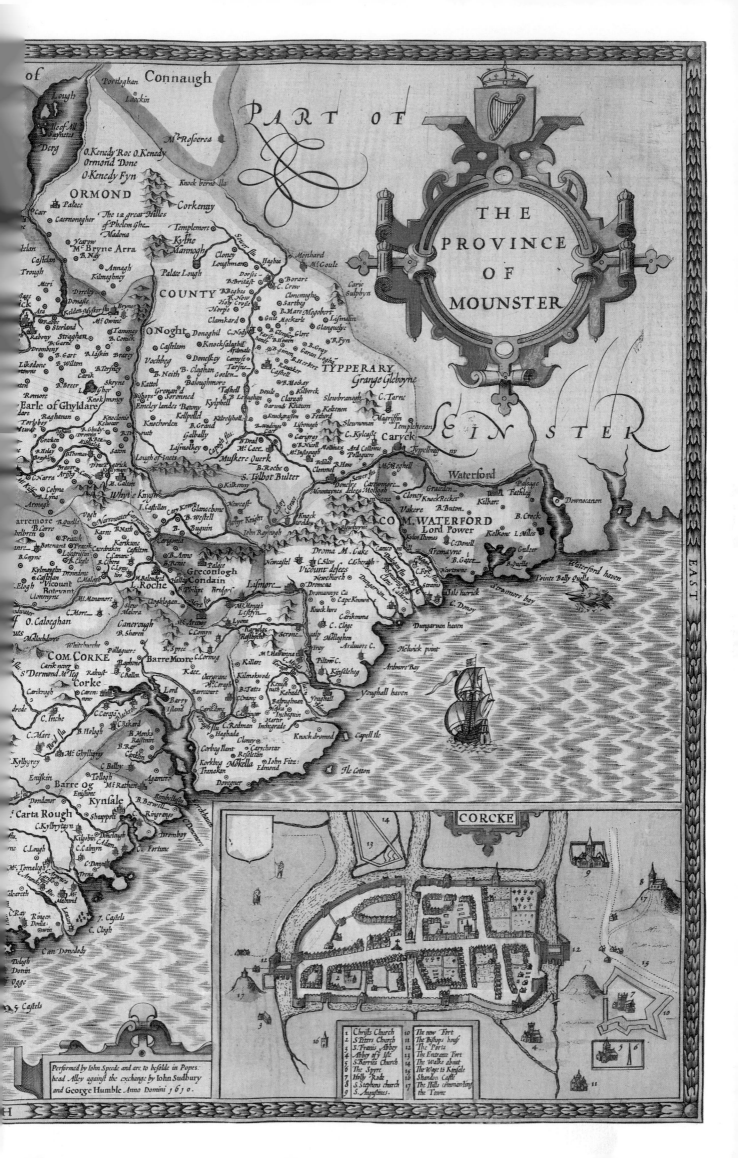

lamentable cries and doleful complaints made by such small remains of poor people who are left. Who, hardly escaping the fury of the sword and fire of their outrageous neighbours, of famine with the same, which their extortious lords hath driven them unto, either by taking their goods from them, or by spending the same by their taking of coign and livery, make demonstration of the miserable estate of that country. Besides this, such horrible and lamentable spectacles there are to behold as the burning of villages, the ruin of churches, the wasting of such as have been good towns and castles: yea, the view of the bones and skulls of the dead subjects, who, partly by murder, partly by famine, have died in the fields; as, in truth, any Christian with dry eyes could behold.' Yet despite these harrowing circumstances both traditional Irish culture and traditional Irish Catholicism had survived, the second as much a source of concern to Protestant reformers as to the post-Tridentine papacy.

Agriculturally Munster depended not upon growing oats and barley in the lowlands nor upon its extensive woodlands, but upon the grazing of horses, cattle, sheep and pigs, which were herded seasonally between different pastures. Fisheries were important, and Munster's many ports and harbours were havens for a flourishing coastal trade bringing goods from England and Wales, and to fishermen from France, Spain and Portugal. Unfortunately, repeated military interference by Spain in Irish affairs and the arrival of seminary priests in the 1590s made the Crown suspicious of such foreign contacts, whatever their commercial and economic advantages. Despite this mistrust, places such as Waterford and Cork flourished, and Waterford was rated by Speed as 'the second city in Ireland'. Unlike their English or Welsh counterparts, Munster towns had up-to-date fortifications kept in good repair with elaborate provision for their defence.

The province of Munster was more or less co-terminous with the arch-bishopric of Cashel, which also included County Clare. Until the 1560s when the district of Thomond was shired as County Clare, Thomond had formed part of Munster, and it is presumably for this reason that Clare is shown as part of Munster on the Munster map, although by 1612 it had long been integrated in Connaught.

Ulster

Speed's description of Ulster was eulogistic: 'The country seldom feeleth any unseasonable extremities, the quick and flexible winds cooling the heat of summer, and soft and gentle showers mollify the hardness of the winter. It was a region of bleak mountains and uplands and of lush loughsides and valleys, with extensive grazing, and an apparent abundance of woodland. Its rivers, saltwater loughs and offshore waters were full of fish. Many of its rivers were navigable, and its coast—although hazardous—well supplied with harbours. But Speed admitted, 'Nature is there so little beholden to Art or Industry.'

With the exception of an enclave around Carrickfergus and a coastal strip extending southwards from the Ards down to the adjoining province of Leinster, Ulster had remained part of Gaeldom throughout the sixteenth century, resistant to change or development, and divided by local feuds. This unhappy situation had been exacerbated by the presence of marauding gallowglasses from the Outer and Inner Isles and from the Highlands of Scotland, with which Ulster had closer cultural and political ties than with the rest of Ireland, and since they were subjects of a foreign power (Scotland) until the Union of the Crowns in 1603 there had been no satisfactory way of controlling them. Over a period of twenty years beginning in 1560 Ulster had been divided into shires and some settlement based on earlier experience in Wales had been promoted in Antrim, the Ards and Monaghan, but law and order had eluded Queen Elizabeth and her successive Lord-Lieutenants. What little had been achieved was virtually lost when in 1593 Hugh O'Neill and Rory O'Donnell rebelled and almost succeeded in their aim of ending English domination in Ireland, before Lord Mountjoy became deputy in 1600 and devised a strategy for the systematic reduction of Ulster. The submission of O'Donnell in 1602 and O'Neill in 1603 inaugurated the first period of sustained peace experienced in the region for a century. Although pardoned and confirmed in their estates, the pair fled abroad in 1607, so forfeiting their lands to James I who in the next three years devised a plan for the plantation of Ulster, which not only was to make Speed's map quickly out of date but was to change the face of the province. Speed's map with its inset showing the fort at Enniskillen seized by the Irish in 1593 and its marking of the cluster of fortifications throughout Monaghan, Armagh and Tyrone, together with such physical features as passes, testify amply to the protracted warfare recently suffered by Ulster.

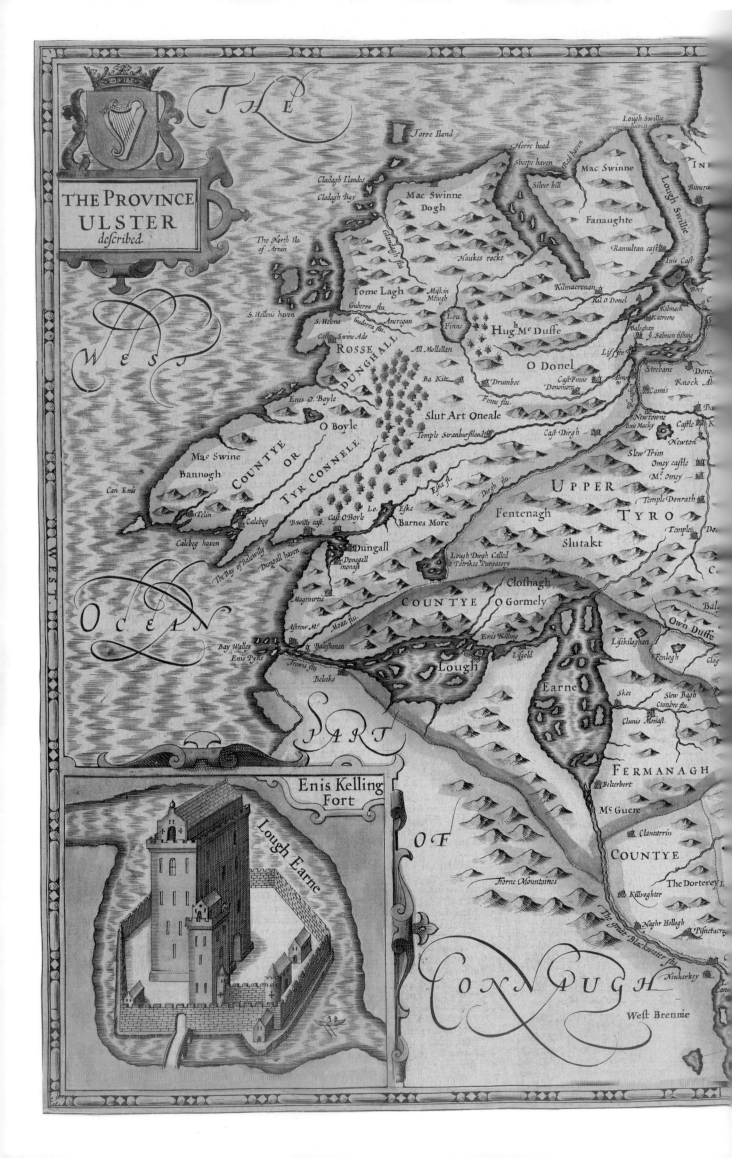

PART OF Dunauert cast

Coldagh haven
Lough Foylle haven
Greene cast
Skerres Porrugh Sand haven
Dunluce Ca.
Lambs Iland
The Raghlins
Donaveny Cast
Whithead ca
Whitehead Bay
Markinton
Bay
Fayre forland Promontory
Knock Caty
Tor Iland
Bay Toraine

ough' Foylle
O Cane
Knock Donoshery
Colrane cast
Mc Neg osarahan
Slu
Tgore
COUNTYE
Enis forsed Logart
Lenuvady cast
Slu Donogh
COLRANE
Kilrough
B. Reagh
Aghren
Colrane mon
Glaslagne
Salmon leape
Mount Sendal
Balenony
THE
Boyshfu
ROWTE
Dunseeke
Donaverony
Whiteland
Sok le Boy
Knock Glad
Cast Balan
Lough Gell
Lo. Hardwarnes
THE Glinnes
Lo Dunuare
Bonatiarga
C. Balteen Bonedrinny

L. Ryan
Coswell SCOT LAND

ough
on
Roe owen
Mc Dogcuene
Banchor
Sawell pit a Mew Allyne ella
Bryan
Lo Rush
Skinne flu
THE
Killetra
Carnantogher
Glankankyne
Mahara Terkin
COUNTYE
Carrogh
Knock
Mullagh
Aparly Hill
Brian Carrogh
Grange
Lo Beg
Mc Guilly
Donmaly
Glanrauen flu
Glanharky
Skirris
Donhaliceug
Slew meset
Kelles Mc
ANTRYM
The Nether
Clan de Boy
Ilanay
Crog Castle
Coraine
Tchever
Olderfleete
Red Bay Cast
Acndone
Red Bay
Dromemark
Owindirgh
Glanarme
Glanarme Bay
Stone ocor
The Maydnes
Olderfleete haven
Kno Iland
Pertnuck
Mages Ile
L. Kow
Black head
Laune
Croffe Ile
Copland Iles
Helflayne Harrons

Iland Fongren
Tormon
Moilogh gora
The forte
Skrine
Slew Gallon
An old forte
Lisham
Tallwen flu
Lo. Difart Ceygh
Donuglas inragh
Desert
Maharleshall
Lo. Lusk
Tallon
Ardtra
Stone where Oniale is Chosen
NE
Killetroe
Lough Neaugh
Enis Garde
L. Der
Knockcerubollegh
Carmacan
Mahonggall
South Glan de Boy
Mc Macomer
Mc Masarnah
cattles
Doh Arubery
Benooll
Benmadi gargh
Mahaline
Knockfergus
White Abb
Donroe
Kilrout
Mc Camber
Scaterick
THE
KELLES
Mc Banger
Hollywoodс Abb
Collumkill
Knock seraboh
Hanuch abb Dony
Greg Abb
Black Abb
Eusfer
Talbot
Newtown Abb
Skyr Martin
North rock
South rock
THE
ARDES

Mailogh gora
THER
Knock Crosse
Terim flu
Donomurk
Douglas
Dunyannon
Fort o Donat
Lo. O Donat
The Largy
TYRONE
magh
ne Trough
Mouterburne
Clanagher
Stokan
Fort Montjoy
Tollaghmny
Clon
Bundorlin
Mc Cane
Terlogh
Brassilogh
ONEALAND
COUNT.
Lo. Coran
Fort Charles
Lo. Carutel
Blackwater
Beneborch
Clandawell
Drumboe
Sidney Iland
Killullagh
Dalyan flu
Baubal
Aghugh Ileu
C. lan Braisil
Lysnafa
Durrey
Slut Mc THE
ONeale KELLES
DUFFRE s Brides
Mc Carten
Kilwarlin
Maharla
L. Ryle
Lo. Aghre
COUNTYE
Donochelon
Dromo re
L. Begna
Whits Cast
Killeagh
Reagh Conner
Welsh at Audley
Pyrne ferry
New castle Savage
Slayne
Mc Argum
Ca. Boy
Mc S. Patriks Rock
Arkue c.
B. Philip

ne
nchtro
enan
YE
land
Dony
Riner
Owen Maugh the ancient seat of the Kinges of Ulster
Tenan
Armagh
Sergeants Towne
Mc Killoran
Doneregs
Maharles
L. Kurkan
Plenam
Custer flu
Ide
Ban flu
Agnaderre
Ca. Lough Breeklin
Knock Euath
Donohnore
Tullash
Mahamly
Patrik
The Fort
Lecale
Legan flu
L. Knock Iorny
L. Shanahan
Mhaterry
Kille cony
Downe
Anaghelome
Dondrom
DOWNE
Ragh Iland
Downeman
Donomawe
Hanloe flu
Dendrom Bay Cow and Calfe
S. Johns poynt
Inch
Ca. Cleghbally
Raynold
Arglas
Arglas haven
M. Sull Kill
Mc Downe cliff
Strangford haven
Anguis rock
Sternah
Arglas haven
IRISH

Otranie
Henry Ogge
L. Kasin
Dornous
Toughaghe
ARMAGH
Monaghan
Wall
Cremourne
Tollagh Corbet
Lo Muckne
Muekte
Slew Gore
Leysennes
Cast Rosse
MONAGHAN
aghne nullen
B. Egges
Lo. Egges
Kilmore
Cast Maing
Lo.
Rosse
Mount Norris
6. Mile bridge
Kilcor way
L. Karic Clyffe
Newry
The Tafa
Narrowater
Ca. Narrowater
Polly Clanall
Mourne
Dromebaly
The Mauntaynes of Mourne
The Passe
The Bishops seat
Grene cast
Relly
Shanan
Carlingford
Grange
Newcastle
Lough
Forway
Mere
Dunmore Toune
Donnegalk
Haygardes
Sarare
Shelton
Dundalke
COUNTYE
Toune
Louth
Ca. Mylle
Warren flu
Carlingford haven
Madarge point
Sheap flu.
Leisfton flu
Melogh flu.
Tragh flu.
Cramfeeld point
Dundalke Haven
SEA

van
Aurelye
Kolmologerogh
Kilmore
Cauan
Lo.
Ranmore
allagh
Enishoen
Carick
Lisharahan
Lismuck
Oxlogh
Ardragh
Almiash
Julian
PART OF LEINSTER
Garland
Cooke
Richard
Dronean
Clyton
Tollaghoasten
Lumnart
Bealintoune
LOUTH
Droghdagh
C. Warren
Dromshallen
Bernoth
Garsboune
Beauith
Glasspith
Droghdagh haven
Gart
Doneriany point
Clogher point

THE Scale of English miles
5   10   15   20
4   8   12   16
The Scale of Irish miles

Performed by John Speede and are to be solde by John Sudbury and George Humble in Popeshead alley at London. Cum Privilegio. An. 1610.

Visitors remarked on the small number of its settlements in contrast with the number of castles kept in repair from the Middle Ages. They were also distressed by the number of religious foundations that had avoided suppression at the Dissolution of the Monasteries and by Ulster's religious conservatism. Ties with Catholic Spain had been fostered by Philip II who had had hopes of Ulstermen breaking the English lordship of Ireland as far back as the 1560s and the warm reception to seminary priests in the 1590s were a measure of his success. The evangelization of Ulster had been contemplated by the Archbishop of Armagh during Queen Elizabeth's reign, but inadequate revenues, an unsympathetic priesthood and the intractable opposition of Irish chiefs and their clans had doomed any effort in that direction almost from the start. In religion, as in other spheres, the accession of James I was to be crucial in Ulster.

FURTHER READING

S. T. Bindoff

Tudor England. 1950.

I. M. Evans and H. Lawrence

Christopher Saxton: Elizabethan Map-Maker. 1979.

S. G. Ellis

Tudor Ireland. 1985.

E. Lynam

British Maps and Mapmakers. 1944.

D. M. Palliser

The Age of Elizabeth: England under the late Tudors, 1547–1603. 1983.

R. A. Skelton

The County Atlases of the British Isles, 1579–1703. 1970.
'Tudor Town Plans in John Speed's Theatre', *The Archaeological Journal.* cviii (1952), pp. 109–20.

Picture Acknowledgements

The publishers would like to thank the following organizations and agencies for supplying illustrations:
The British Library, p14; The Bodleian Library, p11; Mary Evans Picture Library, p19, 20; The Trustees of the National Maritime Museum, Greenwich, p17.